D1293014

THE
SIGNIFICANCE OF NEOPLATONISM

STUDIES IN NEOPLATONISM: ANCIENT AND MODERN
VOLUME I

R. Baine Harris, General editor

THE
SIGNIFICANCE OF NEOPLATONISM

edited by
R. Baine Harris

Professor of Philosophy
Old Dominion University

INTERNATIONAL SOCIETY FOR NEOPLATONIC STUDIES
OLD DOMINION UNIVERSITY
NORFOLK, VIRGINIA 23508

First published in 1976
by the International Society for Neoplatonic Studies
Department of Philosophy
Old Dominion University
Norfolk, Virginia 23508

Distributed by State University of New York Press
Albany, New York 12246

Library of Congress Cataloging in Publication Data

Main entry under title:

The Significance of Neoplatonism.

(Studies in Neoplatonism; v. 1)
Includes bibliographical references.
1. Neoplatonism—Addresses, essays, lectures.
I. Harris, R. Baine, 1927–   II. Series.
B517.S53   141   76-21254
ISBN 0-87395-800-4

CONTENTS

Page

v

PART THREE:
THE INFLUENCE OF NEOPLATONISM

Preface

The essays of this volume provide a sampling of the significance of Neoplatonism in Western philosophy and culture. Some deal with its sources; some with its interpretation, and some with its historical influence.

In his introduction, R. B. Harris defines Neoplatonism, indicates its main documents, and provides a brief introduction to the major Neoplatonists. The remaining papers are divided into three parts:

In Part I. *The Sources of Neoplatonism*, J. N. Findlay's paper concentrates on the close doctrinal affinities between Plato and Plotinus and offers a strong defense of the thesis that Plotinus' philosophical position is an extension and completion of Plato's metaphysics. H. J. Blumenthal's paper then draws attention to certain major Aristotelian ideas in the construction of Plotinus' psychology in order to explore the paradoxical aspect whereby his conception of the soul is akin to Plato's, but his view of its function is closer to Aristotle's—despite the criticism Plotinus advanced against his definition. Michael Dunn then discusses the two reading orders of the Platonic dialogues drawn up by Thrasyllus and the Neoplatonist Iamblichus and shows that the canon of Iamblichus was based on an arbitrary distinction between "physical" and "theological," forcing thus an order that suited "the dogmatic and theological Plato of Neoplatonism."

Part II, *The Interpretation of Neoplatonism,* opens with J. P. Anton's paper in which he assesses Plotinus' understanding of the value and relevance of Aristotle's categorical theory for the comprehension of the sensible world to ascertain whether Plotinus gave a viable analysis of the theory in its original setting, and concludes with the observation that Plotinus' radically different ontology of the sensible object led him to re-cast Aristotle's categories before criticizing them. J. H. Fielder next undertakes an analysis of the problem of *chorismos* in Plotinus in the special context of how the sensible reality is brought about as an image emanating from a higher level, and after narrowing his inquiry to a single pattern of Plotinus' views on this issue, he exhibits the implications they have for *chorismos* as a conception of imaging. R. T. Wallis' basic theme in his paper is the nature of *experience* on which Plotinus' account of the intelligible world rests, and he pursues it by seeking precedents in classical sources and tracing parallel analogues in modern thinkers. He then takes the position that Plotinus' Three Hypostases are from one point of view elevations of psychological experience.

Continuing in the interpretation of Neoplatonism J. Whittaker shows that the ancestry of the Neoplatonic doctrine of the infinity, as stated by Plotinus, is still far from clarified, but that one may, with the aid of philological tools, acquire a better understanding not only of the historical background of the doctrine but also of the doctrine itself. J. P. Atherton explores the difficulties which the Christian defenders of the trinitarian *arche* sought to overcome through their criticisms of the Neoplatonic One, and concludes with an analysis of the relation this issue bears to the identity of the absolute in Schelling and Hegel. A. H. Armstrong opens his paper with an attempt to elucidate the expression "apprehension of divinity in self and cosmos" in order to show how it obtains in the case of Plotinus' philosophy. He then defends the view that the mode of apprehending divinity is actually one, and that when properly understood, the Neoplatonic way of thinking is not without significance and meaning.

In the next paper P. S. Mamo, in opposition to interpreters who find Plotinus' mysticism to be of the theistic type, defends a monistic interpretation which in its proper philosophical context offers a fuller understanding and appreciation of Plotinus' mystical thought. J. M. Rist, taking his cue from certain basic difficulties that confront recent discussions on the concept of moral obligation, then proceeds to explain Plotinus' views and points out that although he has no formal discussion of moral obligation, it can be shown that the issue is carefully examined in the light of the broader concept of the good life and the theory of virtue as a state of the soul. Continuing, Evanghelos Moutsopoulos shows in his paper how enriched the Plotinian theory of the imaginary becomes when interpretation of the pertinent texts makes its starting point not from imagination as a noetic function but from the image, considered as a first datum, irreducible to a product of the imaginative activity and as that which fertilizes the latter. He then takes a view that places the emphasis on the dynamism of the image but without compromising the dynamism of consciousness. Finally, in this section, John Dillon explores the problem of the rules of Neoplatonic allegory through an examination of the possible differences between the two basic and related terms *eikon* and *symbolon,* and shows through a fair sampling of the relevant sources what applications and problems attended the Neoplatonic allegorical exegesis.

Part III, *The Influence of Neoplatonism*, opens with M. T. Clark's paper in which she takes issue with the thesis that Victorinus' views derived directly from Plotinus and adduces evidence to indicate that the differences between their respective metaphysics are traceable in Victorinus' acceptance of the consubstantiality of the Christian Trinity and that Victorinus depends more upon Porphyry than Plotinus. She concludes that Victorinus' own metaphysics was a new departure and influenced medieval metaphysics. M. G. Vater next shows how in the background of Schelling's own eclectic and original thinking there lurks an affinity and preoccupation with Neoplatonic themes. He suggests that evidence for this is found in a number of his writings and is especially reflected in the dialogue *Bruno* written in the year 1802. In the following essay, D. F. T. Rodier shows how the study of Neoplatonism can help elucidate important problems in process philosophy. After focusing on Whitehead's accounts of creativity and non-statistical judgments of probability, he proposes that these areas of philosophic concern have their counterparts in Plotinus' account of matter and *sympatheia* to such an extent that they may be regarded as reinterpretations of a Neoplatonic theme in terms of process metaphysics. Next, J. N. Deck juxtaposes the thought of Plotinus and Sartre in connection with the ontological investigation of "being-other-than," and after disclaiming traceable influences he arrives at the conclusion that there are striking similarities between the two thinkers, especially with reference to Plotinus' *Nous* and Sartre's *For-Itself.* Finally, K. W. Harrington examines the movement of the New Humanists of the 1920's and 1930's and Paul Elmer More in particular, and shows that although More was critical of some aspects of the metaphysics and mysticism of Plotinus his Christianizing Platonism led him to conflate the ethics of Plato and Plotinus, despite their differences, and thus erred in attributing to Plato certain ethical and psychological doctrines which are in fact more Neoplatonic than he was able to realize.

John P. Anton
Emory University

THE
SIGNIFICANCE OF NEOPLATONISM

A Brief Description of Neoplatonism

R. Baine Harris

Old Dominion University

There are essentially three ways in which Neoplatonism may be considered to be significant. It may be seen as the last flowering of Hellenistic philosophy—as the last major attempt to bring into one complete system the same themes debated by the philosophers for the eight centuries preceeding it, an effort that involved not only the attempt to resolve the conflict between Plato and Aristotle, but also between the philosophic and religious elements in Graeco-Roman culture. It may also be seen as one of the basic intellectual forces, sometimes open, sometimes hidden, in the evolution of philosophy and theology in the Western world, a force that usually occurred in combination with some other interest. In addition, it may still be seen in its own worth as a general philosophy with some relevance to some of the issues in contemporary philosophy and in modern life.

In this introduction, which is intended mainly for the non-Neoplatonic expert, I will present a general overview of the school of thought by indicating the meaning of the term, identifying the major Neoplatonists, and describing its primary documents. I will not treat the origin of the movement or its impact upon other movements and thinkers, except in a most cursory way, even though these form a vital part of its actual significance.[1]

I. *What is Neoplatonism?*

Neoplatonism was established as a school of thought by the Egyptian Plotinus (205-270) and his teacher Ammonius Saccas (185-250). Plotinus was the student of

Ammonius in Alexandria for eleven years until he joined the expeditionary force of Emperor Gordianus III in his march against Persia in the year 244. When Gordianus was slain the same year, Plotinus fled to Antioch and then went on to Rome where he set up a school and taught for the next twenty-six years.

The chief document of Neoplatonism is the *Enneads* of Plotinus, a series of fifty-four essays arranged into six divisions of nine each, each division being called an "Ennead." The *Enneads* were composed between the years 254 and 267 and were later arranged according to subjects by *Porphyry* (c. 232-304), Plotinus' most famous student, who also wrote a biography of his master. Although extremely profound and provocative, the *Enneads* probably deserves to be called the world's worst written book since Plotinus seems to presume that the reader already has a complete knowledge of his system when he discusses any topic. The First Ennead presents his moral philosophy; the Second his physics; the Third his cosmology; the Fourth his psychology; the Fifth his philosophy of mind; and the Sixth his doctrine of reality. The direct influence of the book upon the history of philosophy has been minimal, since it was not widely circulated, but its indirect influence through other widely circulated Neoplatonic works inspired by it has been tremendous. Since it was written in Greek, it was not directly available to the Latin West until Ficino made a Latin translation of it in 1492.

Plotinus and Ammonius did not know that they were Neoplatonists. The term "Neoplatonism" has been used only since the mid-nineteenth century when it was invented by German scholars to distinguish the thought of Plotinus and his successors from the more complete form of Platonism that emerges from all of Plato's writings. Ammonius and Plotinus thought of themselves primarily as reformers and not innovators of Platonism; but as a matter of fact they were both. They sought to reestablish the thought of Plato in its original purity, but as reformers six centuries removed from that to which they would return, they did not succeed in freeing themselves from a certain bias in their conception of the fundamentals of Platonism. More than they realized, they were themselves products of the general tendency toward eclecticism in Second Century thought and they may not be regarded as *pure* Platonists.

Taken as a whole, the *Enneads* affirm the same themes common to the Platonic tradition, namely, (1) belief in the immateriality of reality, (2) the conviction that the visible and sensible refer to a still higher level of being than the level on which they occur, (3) preference for intuition over empirical forms of knowing, (4) the affirmation of the immortality of the soul, (5) belief that the universe in its most real state is good, and can be known as good, and (6) the tendency to identify the beautiful, the good, and the true as one and the same.

Plotinus' main thrust in the *Enneads* is a defense of Plato against Aristotle's criticism, but in defending his ancient idol he makes major concessions to Aristotle. Although he mentions Aristotle by name only four times, he shows great familiarity with his writings and borrows a number of his fundamental notions from him, notably those of power ($\delta \acute{\upsilon} \nu a \mu \iota \varsigma$) and energy ($\dot{\epsilon} \nu \acute{\epsilon} \rho \gamma \epsilon \iota a$). The Platonism of the *Enneads* is actually a hybrid resulting from the blending of Platonism and Aristotelianism, and at times it is difficult to determine which one is dominant. Dean Inge suggested that it could be said that Plotinus knew and understood Aristotle better than he did Plato,[2] and Ernst Hoffman thought that Neoplatonism would better be called "Neo-Aristotelianism," especially in view of the fact that the majority of the Neoplatonic systems after Plotinus have been nearer to the dialectic of Aristotle than to Plato's dialectic.[3] Most of Plotinus' immediate successors believed that he had achieved the unification of Platonism and Aristotelianism.

Plotinus was not satisfied with either Plato's or Aristotle's final conception of the Ultimate and he was bothered by Plato's dichotomies. He accepted Aristotle's criticism of Plato as essentially valid and he accepted Aristotle's dialectical method as superior to that of Plato and basically followed it even though he did specifically reject Aristotle's categories (V.I.1-30) and substituted those of his own, namely, Thought ($\nu o \hat{\upsilon} \varsigma$) and Thing ($\ddot{o} \nu$);   Difference ($\dot{\epsilon} \tau \epsilon \rho \acute{o} \tau \eta \varsigma$) and Sameness (ταυτότης); and Permanence (στάσις) and Change (κίνησις) (V.2.1–V.3.27). (See also V.1.4; VI.2.15,19; and VI.2.8) He rejected Aristotle's logic, and specifically his formal logic (I.3.4) and he developed a Platonic-type logic of his own to devise an Aristotelian-type dialectic of his own. He uses logic the way Aristotle does to set up a dialectical system, but his logic is more akin in type to Plato's logic than it is to Aristotle's.[4] Practically all the Neoplatonists who followed him, however, followed the example of his disciple Porphyry in ignoring his logic and substituting the logic of Aristotle for it, so that for all practical purposes Neoplatonic logic is not Plotinian logic.

Plotinus remained a Platonist in his conception of what the nature of the philosophic enterprise is, but he is a post-Aristotelian Platonist. Basically, what he rejected in Aristotle was his world view, his conception of the range of philosophy, and the adequacy of his logic as a basis for dialectics. He objected to Aristotle with the same high level of precision and the same degree of understanding that Aristotle shows for Plato. Whereas Aristotle did not so much challenge the meaning of the root concepts of Plato as he did the basis upon which he established them, Plotinus does not really challenge the basis of Aristotle's thought as much as he questions the adequacy of his system. He conquers him by absorbing him and retaining him almost intact as the middle section of his own highly refurbished and enlarged Platonic system.

Plotinus' own contribution is, however, much greater than that of a harmonizer of Plato and Aristotle. By his identity of the Pythagorean One with the transcendent Good of Plato, but minus Plato's ὄν, his own Ultimate is greater than the Ultimates of either Plato or Aristotle. The Plotinian One should not be conceived of as "sheer unity" in the Parmenidean sense and neither as "barrenness of being," or even "absolute nothingness." τὸ ἕν should rather be understood in the Pythagorean sense of the base unity of all multiplicities. It is nothing because it is everything. It is no-one-thing, non-existent, and non-being, because any sense of thingness, or existence, or its being would be a prostitution of its genuine nature. It is even much more than "the ground of being." It is the point where all themes merge, the one "principle" that contains the fundamentals of all principles, the one line into which all lines merge. It is responsible for being in the only level that being can occur, namely in the level in which the One can be differentiated in Aristotle's νοῦς. At this second and lower ontic, epistimic, and value level, being is determinate, very much as Aristotle suggests, and it is progressively less determinate and "less principled" in all of the myriads of inner sequential levels within the range of νοῦς and on down into the many levels within the level of ψυχή, which is in reality νοῦς in motion. The *One*, of course, is not material, and neither is Mind or Soul, since the purely material cannot exist.

That which is taken to be material is in actuality Soul. It is an extension of Soul down below the normal level of Soul, or better, it is Soul in its lowest possible level of being. Just as all of the level of Soul is an extension of Mind down below its normal level, or Mind in its lowest possible level, so Mind is the One in an extension down below its normal level, or the One in its lowest possible level. Thus Plotinus's Ultimate is transcendent in its level as the One from all determinate being, but it is immanent in it as νοῦς, namely, as νοῦς forms the basis for the various orders and levels of the events of souls. In this way Plotinus sought to establish the spiritual nature of reality, showing the immaterial ground of both spiritual and material things in contrast to the Stoics who sought to establish the material base of spiritual reality.

In his doctrine of emanation, or the procession of all things from the One, Plotinus appears to have taken that which Plato presented as myth and turned it into straight doctrine, namely Plato's analogy of the ἀγαθόν with the radiation from the Sun in the *Republic* (509). The Stoics had already used the idea of emanation or irradiation, and he quite likely borrowed the notion from them, but they used it to illustrate a *material* diffusion and depletion, the one that most naturally comes to the Twentieth Century mind when radiation is mentioned. It is important to note that Plotinus is *not* describing a material structure. Instead, he is trying to convey the idea of the permanent structure of *spiritual* essences. The procession is not a procession in time. He is describing the logical, and not the chronological order of being and is being very Greek in doing so, since he is assuming that the permanent and fixed is more genuine, i.e., more real, than that which is in motion. He is suggesting that that which is in motion, namely, souls, has its reality in its fixed elements, namely, its structure as $\nu o\tilde{\upsilon}\varsigma$. Since he regarded light as an immaterial substance (II. 1.7; IV.5.6-7; I.6.3), his use of it as an illustration of radiation should not be taken to mean radiation in the modern sense.

Plotinus is sometimes labeled a mystic, and this label is correct with certain qualifications. He might be described as a rational mystic or perhaps a "metaphysical mystic," since he believed in the necessity of logic and metaphysical understanding as a means to mystical experience. To him it would be scandalous to think of enlightenment without the prior practice of morality and philosophy. As Erwin Edman puts it, "For Plotinus mysticism is not the evasion but the climax of thought,"[5] Salvation, as Plotinus sees it, is essentially a technique involving three processes: (1) catharsis, or the purification of the soul through morality, (2) dialectics, or the practice of the discipline of philosophy; and (3) illumination, or enlightenment ($\nu\acute{o}\eta\sigma\iota\varsigma$) – a state of ecstasy wherein the soul finally comes into direct communion with that part of the One that is already within it. The way of salvation is a journey from soul to mind to the One during which the soul progressively sees itself as an element of the Ultimate. Salvation is not from above, it is from within; and it is not free – it is very expensive and rarely achieved. By most men it is only relatively achieved, depending upon which level they succeed in attaining.

Plotinus actually placed a higher premium on philosophical activity than did Plato, since he made the practice of dialectics one of the necessary steps of salvation. Salvation begins with self-purification and the practice of ordinary moral life, namely, meeting one's civic responsibilities and the practicing of the Platonic virtues of wisdom, courage, temperance, and justice (1.2.2). The first stage is self-purification, namely, the purification of one's motives and actions. But morality is more than not doing evil, it is doing good in a positive way – it is an expression of the purity of the soul (I.2.7). This leads to the third level, the freeing of the soul from all bodily desires. Only then may the practice of dialectics begin. Essentially it involves the soul's turning away from itself as an object of concern and fixing its attention upon the νοῦς. Dialectics for Plotinus is a science, a form of philosophical analysis in which logic is used as a tool for the analysis of reality, i.e., for the determination of the evidences of νοῦς in everything that there is. It is by means of this form of analysis that the soul eventually turns introspectively into itself and sees itself as essentially νοῦς (VI.7.34; VI.9.11). In this stage, which might be called the highest level of dialectics, the soul sees itself as mind — it has a *soul to Mind* identity, but this is not yet illumination. This occurs only when the soul passes beyond dialectics into a direct grasping of reality that transcends logic and analysis — when the soul passes beyond seeing itself as mind and sees itself as the One in a *soul to One* identity. In this state the soul ceases to know itself as soul or mind and knows itself only as the One (VI.9.9-10).

In some respects Plotinus' way of salvation is reminiscent of Plato's theory of knowledge, since Plato places intuition higher than discursive reason. Plotinus's theory of knowledge, however, goes considerably farther than the limits of Plato's epistemology. Although Plato believes that all universal concepts have objective reference, he did not state very clearly the exact relation between the particular and the universal, a weakness for which he was severely criticized by Aristotle, and a weakness which both Aristotle and Plotinus seek to overcome in very different ways. In Plotinus, as we have just seen, true knowledge passes on beyond general knowledge to a direct knowing of the Ultimate. Although this view is not inconsistent with Plato's epistemology, it is a rather radical development of it in view of the more cautious limits that Plato imposed upon knowing.

Plotinus' view is even more radical than Plato's, since he does not set the knower off from his objects, as do Plato and Aristotle, but rather makes the intelligible universe within the subject as the object for knowledge. Like Aristotle, he makes knowing a form of abstraction, but it is more than the abstraction of common forms out of common sensibles. It is an identity of like kinds when the non-essential elements that confuse the issue have been taken away. It is like perceiving like.

Seen in its boldest profile, then, Neoplatonism is an effort to reconcile Aristotelianism with Platonism through an appeal to a still higher unifying principle than is found in either of the two, namely, an Ultimate First Principle that is *both* transcendent and immanent in all nature, indefinable *and* knowable, self-sufficient *and* creative throughout the universe without an act of will. It is an effort to subsume the major elements of Aristotle's system within a revised but fundamentally *Platonic* framework of thought; an effort that Aristotle himself would have vigorously protested, as most pure Aristotelians down through the centuries have done.[6]

II. *The Early Neoplatonists*

The first authentic Neoplatonist was probably *Ammonius Saccas* (175-250 A.D.), the porter who taught in Alexandria during the last part of the first quarter of the third century. Since he left no writings, his claim to fame rests upon the success of his famous pupils: Plotinus, the two Origens, the philologist Longinus, and Herennius. Although some of them refer to his thought occasionally, it is impossible to determine which of their views were inspired by him. In any case Plotinus (205-270), just discussed, was the first notable Neoplatonist.

Amelius Gentilianus (c. 275), a senior professor in the school that Plotinus founded in Rome, also began his studies in Alexandria. He was responsible for the conversion of Porphyry to Neoplatonism, but he made no written contribution to the school of thought. His principle literary activity was his effort to show the differences in the thought of Plotinus and Numenius of Apamea, whom he also greatly admired. He did alter Plotinus' views slightly by distinguishing three hypotheses within the νοῦς and by holding that all souls find their unity within the World-Soul instead of in the One. In contrast to Plotinus he practiced public religion, praying to the gods and observing the feasts and sacrifices, a practice for which he received no censure from his colleague.

Porphyry (232-c.304). Like Plato, Plotinus also suffered the fate of having his philosophy altered by his disciples. However, if it had not been for Porphyry, who was able to express his rather abstruse ideas in a more palatable form, his philosophy may not have survived at all. As an expositor of the thought of Plotinus, his writings were very widely distributed both in his own time and in later centuries. He wrote one book in defense of vegetarianism, one extolling "abstemiousness," and another entitled *Against the Christians.* The latter had fifteen chapters in which he opposed the divinity of Christ, set forth contradictions in the Christian scriptures, and denied the divine inspiration of the Old Testament, a line of thought that was continued in the Syrian, Pergamumian, and Athenian schools of Neoplatonism. The book, however, was condemned by Emperor Theodosius in 435 and all existing copies were destroyed. He also wrote a book on the *Categories* of Aristotle that was translated into Latin by Boethius and became one of the most widely read philosophical texts of the Middle Ages. In his writings he gave a certain slant in the interpretation of Neoplatonism that was continued by his followers on down until the Ninth Century. He replaced the logic and categories of Plotinus with those of Aristotle and made the aim of philosophy the salvation of the soul. Claiming that evil came from the nature of the soul and not the body, he sought to purify the soul through various forms of asceticism as well as through knowledge of God. He also had a much higher interest than Plotinus in *daemons,* which Plotinus had defined as spirit-beings without bodies (III. 5.6), not born of souls nor produced by the World-Soul and with bodies of fire (II.1.6) that do not participate in bodily matter (III.5.6). Whereas Plotinus put all of nature within the action of souls and hence related it to *νοῦς* and the Ultimate and thus free from the actions of *daemons*, Porphyry and some of his followers allowed nature to be affected by the capricious actions of *daemons.* He also began, but did not develop, the tendency to express the Plotinian system in a series of triads within triads and his system is generally more monistic than that of Plotinus. He also put more emphasis on practical ethical issues.

Iamblichus, (c.250-326) a native of Chalcis in Coele-Syria, studied with Porphyry for some time and then returned to his native country to found the Syrian School of Neoplatonism, which especially emphasized theurgy as a means of salvation.

Although Porphyry retained an interest in theurgic practices after his conversion to Plotinism, he limited it to the very lowest levels of the journey for salvation, while Iamblichus and his followers saw it as a higher way. Iamblichus posited a One above the One of Plotinus, namely, an absolutely ineffable One entirely without attributes. Below this One is the Plotinian One which in turn produces the intelligible world, which has three parts, and which in turn produces the intellectual world, which also has three parts, the latter being the Demiurge, which has seven divisions. Below the level of the intellectual world is the world of souls, which are also divided into a series of triads. Salvation is not ἔκστασις, but union with the gods through rites and ceremonies. A student of Iamblichus, Aedesius, founded a school of Neoplatonism at Pergamum. One of its leaders, Maximus of Smyrna was a Neoplatonic priest to the Emperor Julian the Apostate (331-363), a nephew of Constantine the Great who succeeded Constantius as emperor in 361. Another of Iamblichus' students, Plutarch of Athens (c.350-433) was the first Neoplatonist to become the head of the Platonic Academy in Athens in about the year 400. He was succeeded by Syrianus in about 432 and Proclus in 438, both of whom were Neoplatonists.

Proclus (c. 409-c. 487), the next major Neoplatonist after Prophyry, was a Greek native of Constantinople who had studied with Olympiodorus in Alexandria before coming to Athens at the age of nineteen to study with Plutarch and Syrianus. Being both scholarly and "scholastic," he developed the Iamblichean brand of Neoplatonism to its logical extremes, projecting triads within triads seemingly at every opportunity. A man of great energy and enthusiasm, he lectured five times a day, wrote a great deal, and still found time to give his evenings to his students and to take an active part in municipal government. In addition, he was quite zealous in his religious activities, worshipping the sun three times a day, observing all the Egyptian holy days, and spending part of the night in prayer, praise, and the making of sacrifices. Dean Inge says that his religion was an amalgamation of various cults and might be compared to Comte's "Religion of Humanity."[7]

Metaphysically, Proclus reduced Plotinus' rather loose and organic system to an absolutely complete and rigid one by developing many more triads within triads for Plotinus' three emanations. It was his thesis that all things emanate by triads, and also emanate horizontally by triads as well as vertically. He believed that all things evolve by triads and also need to return, by triads, to the Ultimate. Whereas for Plotinus the procession of the lower stages out of the higher was continuous and equal in degree of emanation, Proclus specified that the lower remains in the higher in its first aspect, leaves it in its second aspect, and returns to it in a third aspect.

Like Plotinus, he taught that man's ultimate goal is union with the Ultimate, but added that theurgy can be an aid higher than the practice of dialectics. He was highly influenced by Plato's *Timaeus*, and once stated that if it were in his power to do so he would withdraw all books from human knowledge except the *Timaeus* and the *Chaldaean Oracles.*

In two of his works, *Elements of Theology* and *Plato's Theology,* he provided elaborate explanations of Neoplatonism. Both were fairly well circulated and had no small influence upon Byzantine, Arabic, and early medieval Latin Christian thought. Indirectly he was the source of many elements of medieval scholastic Christian thought, since the very widely circulated Christian documents, *Divine Names* and *Mystical Theology*, purportedly written by Dionysius the Areopagite, a disciple of St. Paul, but actually written by some unknown monk in the late fifth century, were in actuality adaptations of Proclus' thought.

Proclus' successor was Marinus, a Palestinian Jew. It is possible that he was the source of the Neoplatonism that got into the medieval Jewish tradition, if not of the mysticism of "the Book of Creation," the *Sefer Yezirah.* Athenian Neoplatonism, i.e., the Academy, lasted for about forty years after Proclus, until it was shut down by decree of Justinian I in 529. The last διάδοχος was Damasius (b. 458) whose main innovation was to make not only the Ultimate but all products of it as ineffable, thus carrying Iamblichean Neoplatonism on out to the extreme of severing the connection God and Nature that Plotinus was so concerned to establish.

Neoplatonism continued to flourish in Rome and Alexandria during the time of the late Academy in Athens, but no notable ideolological changes occured in it in either location. It continued in Rome until the latter part of the sixth century. Among its products was the Neoplatonic Christian Marius Victorinus (c. 350), whose Latin translations of Neoplatonic literature were read by Augustine and Boethius (c. 470-525). Boethius' *The Consolation of Philosophy* and his translations and commentaries on Aristotle were widely read and both influenced medieval theology.

The Alexandrian School of Neoplatonism began in the middle of the fourth century and appears to have maintained strong connections with Athenian Neoplatonism at this time, including exchanging professors. Generally, the Alexandrian Neoplatonic professors remained closer to the thought of Plato and the Middle Platonists and did not enter into metaphysical speculations, theology, and theurgy, as did the Athenians, and they displayed a more conciliatory attitude toward Christianity. One of the heads of the school was a female mathematician-philosopher named Hypatia, who in 415 was taken from her carriage by a mob of fanatical Christians and lynched inside a Christian church. The school was shut down with the capture of the city by the Arabs in 642. The last known Alexandrian Neoplatonist was Stephanus (c.600), who later as a Christian went to Constantinople to be the director of the Imperial Academy of Byzantium and was partly responsible for the transmission of Neoplatonism into Byzantine culture.

III. *Later Variations of Neoplatonism*

It could probably be said that there has not been a single pure Neoplatonist since the Fifth Century, since most of those who might be labeled as Neoplatonists have actually held Neoplatonic views in combination with other commitments. Even Eriugena, who would surely be the nearest candidate, held tenaciously to certain points of Christian dogma that would prevent him from being a complete Neoplatonist. In the case of all the Neoplatonists after 500 A. D., it can be debated whether or not they are *actually* Neoplatonists, depending upon which criterion is finally appealed to, whether to the origin of their thought, to the actual percentage of Neoplatonic notions found in their writings, or some dogmatic definition of a Neoplatonist.

A. *Byzantine Neoplatonism*

When Justinian ordered the closing of the Athenian School of Neoplatonism in 529, seven of its professors, including Damascius and Simplicius went into Persia to the court of Chosroes I to continue their profession, but by 533 they had returned to Byzantium where they continued their studies. Although little more has been said about them, there is evidence that Neoplatonism did not die out in Byzantine culture. Apart from the actual influence of these seven and their disciples, we must consider the impact of both the Arabic and Christian Neoplatonists upon Byzantine civilization. Greek Christianity has always been more Neoplatonic than Latin Christianity, likely due to the initial impact made upon it by *Origen of Alexandria* (185-254), the early Greek church father who, like Plotinus, was also a student of Ammonius Saccas. Although he could not officially be labeled a Neoplatonist, he had quite similar views which also got into the thought of other important Greek church fathers such as the Cappadocians, Basil, and the two Gregories—all of whom where taken seriously in Byzantine Christianity.

A certain revival of a purer form of Neoplatonism occurred with the advent of *Michael Psellus* (1018-79), who with the help of Constantine IX re-established the teaching of Neoplatonic philosophy in the University of Byzantium. Psellus chose to go back to Proclus for his main source of inspiration and the Proclean brand of Neoplatonism was carried on by his disciples who produced numerous commentaries on the thought of Aristotle. Psellus was also an intellectual influence on the thought of *George Gemistus Pletho* (c.1360-c.1450) who established a school of Neoplatonism at Mistra in the Pelponnese and was also instrumental in the establishment of the Neoplatonic Academy in Florence.

B. *Islamic Neoplatonism*

One of the most important sources of Neoplatonism for early Islamic scholars was an anonymous Neoplatonic work called *Theologia Aristotelis,* which was in fact a paraphrase of the Fourth, Fifth, and Sixth *Enneads* of Plotinus. *al-Kindi* (c.866 d.) one of the first Muslim philosophical theologians, wrote a commentary on it. *al-Farabi* (c.870-950) also revived the study of Neoplatonism through his *Opinions of the Inhabitants of the Virtuous City,* in which he presented his own essentially Neoplatonic philosophical system. He was especially interested in the thought of Porphyry, having written a commentary of his *Isagoge* and essentially having followed his interpretation of Aristotle. In his *Reconciliation of Plato and Aristotle* he exhibits the same aim of Plotinus in his *Enneads*, an aim shared by Porphyry, Syrianus, Simplicius, and Damascius as well. Generally speaking, it can be said that most of the Arabian Neoplatonists were in the Porphyrian tradition.

A later Neoplatonic Muslim theologian *Avicenna* (980-1037) was influenced by *al-Farabi's* views, but appears to lean more toward Plotinus than Porphyry. His interest in Neoplatonism was mainly in it's use as a device in understanding Islam. The most ideal intellectual outlook, according to him, would be the interpretation of Islam in Plotinian concepts. His position was strongly attacked by *al-Ghazzali*. The views of *al-Farabi* were also echoed in the writings of *Averroes,* (1126-1198) a Spanish Arabic philosopher who was very much interested in Aristotle and in Porphyryian Neoplatonism.

C. *Jewish Neoplatonism*

Jewish Neoplatonism appears to have originated primarily with *Isaac ben Solomon Israeli* (850-950), a court physician at Kairwan who had read the writings of *al-Kindi* and also the *Theology of Aristotle*. His pupil Dunash ibn Tamim wrote a Neoplatonic work entitled the Commentary on *Sefer Yesirah* and his views are also seen in the *Olam Katan* of *Joseph ibn Saddik* (d.1149), a later Jewish Neoplatonist.

The Spanish Jewish philosopher *Solomon ibn Gabirol* (1020-1070), also known as Avencebron, indicated a heavy Neoplatonic influence on his cosmology as expressed in his chief work *The Fountain of Life (Fons vitae)*. His works were well known by the Scholastics. The *Sefer Hobot ha-Lebabot* by Bahya ibn Paquda, written in the eleventh century also contains elements of Neoplatonic mysticism as does the *Hegyon ha-Nefesh (Meditiation of the Soul)* by *Abraham bar Hiyya* of Barcelona (c.1130). A pantheistic variety of Jewish Neoplatonism was developed by *Abraham ibn Ezra* (c.1092-1167). Generally speaking, it may be said that the whole Jewish Neoplatonic tradition had a major share in the development of the *Kabbalah.*

D. *Medieval Christian Neoplatonism*

Two men, *Augustine* (354-430) and *Boethius* (470-525) were mainly responsible for the transference of Neoplatonic ideas from the early Neoplatonists into Latin Christianity. Although neither made any significant contribution to Neoplatonic thought itself, their influence upon the thought of the Christian world in the ten centuries following them was phenomenal.

Augustine's Neoplatonism came from his reading of Victorinus' translation of certain Neoplatonic writings apparently just before and just after his conversion to Christianity in 386. Although he appears to have known quite well the difference between the Gospels and the *Enneads,* the fact remains that his writings are permeated with Neoplatonic notions. Even though he differs with the Neoplatonists in his view of the nature of God and his relation to the world, he essentially agrees with them in his ontology, in his general theory of value, and in his description of the nature of the life of man on earth. Even though their modes of salvation differ, their meaning of salvation is fairly similar—union with the One is very similar to the beatific vision of God. It is a somewhat academic issue whether Augustine can correctly be labeled a Neoplatonist, but due to the very large number of people who have read his writings down through the centuries it is likely that he has introduced more people to some elements of Neoplatonism than has anyone else in history.

Boethius' Neoplatonism came from his reading of the writings of some of the later Alexandrian Neoplatonists, but he was also familiar with Porphyry's *Isagoge.* He wrote a commentary on it. His influence was particularly strong in the court and cloister schools in the period from the sixth through the twelfth centuries through his translation and interpretations of Porphyry's *Isagoge,* a text on elementary logic, his translations and commentaries of the logical treatises of Aristotle, and through his own *The Consolation of Philosophy*. Written in prison while awaiting his execution for treason by the Gothic king Theodoric, the *Consolation* may be described as an exercise in Christian Neoplatonic religious philosophy, with major emphasis being upon the latter element. Although he conceived of himself as a follower of Cicero, the work actually represents the Neoplatonism of the late Alexandrian School (Origen, Hierocles, Syrianus, Hermias). It was widely read throughout the Middle Ages and its influence was most extensive. Alfred the Great translated it into Anglo-Saxon. Chaucer and others translated it into English, and it also appeared in German, French, Italian, Spanish and Greek during the Renaissance. Boethius himself has been variously described as the last Roman philosopher and the first Scholastic.

The next important Christian Neoplatonic philosopher in the West was John the Scot, sometimes known by his Latin name *Eriugena* (c.820-870). An Irish Christian monk, he was brought to the court school of John the Bald in Paris about 847 because he knew Greek and was needed to translate a manuscript of pseudo-Dionysius, *The Divine Names*, kept in the nearby monastery of St. Denis. *The Divine Names* dates back to the late fifth century and is a somewhat Christian adaptation of the thought of Proclus. During his long stay in Paris, until his death in 870, he translated three other Neoplatonic works in the Proclean tradition and wrote at least five books, the most famous being *On the Division of Nature*, a work of a half million words in which he presents his own highly speculative Neoplatonic system. Although this book is ostensively about the nature of nature, he uses the term in the broadest possible sense to mean everything that there is including God. God, the highest reality, he defines as "the nature which creates and is not created." Man fits into the second level of nature, namely, "nature which creates and is created." The chemical elements would illustrate the third level, namely, "nature which does not create and is created."

Eriugena saw clearly that it is necessary to talk about nature in order to talk seriously about God and that it is necessary to talk about God in order to say anything metaphysically significant about nature, a position not well appreciated by his contemporaries. He was generally regarded as a pantheist, which, indeed, he was not. His works exercised no major influence upon the thought of the later Middle Ages, partly because his writings were condemned as heretical by Pope Honorius III in 1225 and again in 1585 by Pope Gregory XIII, and partly because of the Church's general rejection of of Neoplatonic philosophy, and to a lesser degree of all Greek thinkers. They fared somewhat better in later centuries, however, since he is known to have had some influence on the thought of Berengar of Tours, Avicebron, Gilbert de la Porre, Simon of Tournai, the Albigenses and Catharists, Amalric, David of Dinant, Nicholas of Cusa, Giordano Bruno, Eckhart, Tauler, Ruysbroeck, the Kabbalists, and even Hegel. Albert the Great, the teacher of St. Thomas, was quite familiar with the thought of David of Dinant.[8]

Most of the major Christian writers of the late Middle Ages appear to have some knowledge of Neoplatonism. Even St. Thomas Aquinas (1225-1274) has a certain Neoplatonic element in his thought. He wrote a commentary on *The Divine Names* and he was influenced by the Neoplatonic elements in St. Augustine and Boethius. Dean Inge even asserts: "to me, at least, it is clear that St. Thomas is nearer to Plotinus than to the *real* Aristotle." Dante's *Divine Comedy* is highly Neoplatonic in parts, and *Meister Eckhart* (1260-1327) and his pupils *Tauler* (1300-1361) and *Suso* (c. 1295-1366) show evidence of the thought of Dionysius and Eriugena in their writings. Cardinal *Nicholas of Cusa* (1401-1464) arranged for a translation of Proclus' *Platonic Theology* and his own thought may be seen as a bridge between Medieval and Renaissance Neoplatonism.

E. *Renaissance Neoplatonism*

Renaissance Neoplatonism formally began with the founding of the Florentine Academy in 1462 by Cosimo di' Medici, an action inspired by George Gemistus Pletho in 1438 when he was a delegate to the Council of Florence for the reunion of Eastern and Western Christianity. The affairs of the academy mainly revolved around the work of *Marsilio Ficino* (1433-1499) and his pupil *Giovanni Pico della Mirandola*

(1463-1494). Ficino produced an edition of the works of Plato, with commentary, and the first Latin translation (in 1492) of the *Enneads*. His own major work, the *Platonic Theology on the Immortality of the Soul* (1474) and his commentary on the *Symposium* (1469) were also widely read, especially in later centuries. Pico's *Oration on the Dignity of Man* was a basic document of Renaissance humanism. Although the academy dissolved at the death of Ficino, its tradition was carried on at the universities of Florence and Pisa until the seventeenth century.

F. *The Cambridge Platonists*

Some elements of Florentine Neoplatonism were imported into England in the late fourteen nineties by *John Colet* (1466-1519), who was then Dean of St. Paul's Cathedral. Colet carried on correspondence with Ficino, wrote a commentary on the writings of pseudo-Dionysius, and paved the way for the seventeenth century Neoplatonists known as the Cambridge Platonists, namely, *Benjamin Whichcote* (1609-1683); *John Smith* (1616-1652); *Ralph Cudworth* (1617-1685); *Nathaniel Culverwel* (1618?-1651); *Henry More* (1614-1687); and *Peter Sterry* (d. 1672). The main objective of their writings was to work out a blending of English Protestant Christianity and Neoplatonic thought, or more specifically, Plotinian thought. Their views were continued in the Broad Church tradition in the Church of England, represented by such men as F. D. Maurice, (1805-1872), B. F. Westcott (1825-1901), and W. R. Inge, (1860-1954).

G. *German Neoplatonism*

German Neoplatonism stems mainly from *Meister Eckhart* (1260-1327), already mentioned. A monk of the Dominican order, he turned to the writings of Eriugena and pseudo-Dionysius for inspiration and reinforcement in his own reaction to Aristotelianism, a policy continued by Tauler and Suso, and a century later by Nicholas of Cusa, Bishop of Brixen. Although there were no major German Neoplatonists, there is a strong undercurrent of Neoplatonic ideas in the whole German Idealistic tradition. It is seen in Leibniz's monadism, in Schelling's *Naturphilosophie*, and in Hegel's doctrine of the Absolute.

H. *Recent Neoplatonism*

Neoplatonism has had considerably less direct influence on contemporary French and British thought than it has on recent German philosophy. In England its main influence has been in the field of literature, with the possible exception of Berkeley's *Siris*, which has strong affinities with Plotinian mysticism. Neoplatonic notions are found in Spencer, in Wordsworth, in Shelly, in William Blake, in Coleridge, and in Yeats. In France, the influence of Plotinus upon Henri Bergson's thought is quite obvious. For two years (1897-98) Bergson lectured at the College de France on the fourth Ennead of Plotinus (Concerning the Soul) and some of his views on memory very likely came from Plotinus' theory of consciousness.

Even though American Philosophy shows little Neoplatonic influence, it would be possible to note an affinity between certain views of Charles S. Peirce and those of Plotinus, as William James once noted. James' own attempt to ground religious meaning on religious experience had already been accomplished by Plotinus. Whitehead, at least in the mind of this writer, gives certain intimations of a knowledge of Neoplatonism and it would be possible to regard the system that he suggests in *Process and Reality*, as a modern example of the *type* of system produced by Plotinus within the level of νοῦς.

Interest in Neoplatonism has steadily increased over the past seventy five years. Not only has there been a greater recognition of its role in the formation of Western, and especially European thought, but the writings of the major Neoplatonists, and especially Plotinus, have been seriously read for their own worth. Numerous doctoral dissertations have been written on the divergencies of the views of the various Neoplatonists and also on Plotinus' analyses of psychological and theological concepts.

Although we can expect little modern interest in Plotinus' essentially Ptolemaic scientific views, his teachings on the relation of dialectics, art, science, and religious experience may still be seen to be viable in our scientific age; and they may again serve as a humanizing agent in culture, as they have upon various occasions in the past.

NOTES

1. An international conference on the sources of Neoplatonism was held near Geneva in August of 1957. Its papers were published in *Les Sources de Plotin* (Tome V, *Entretienes sur L'Antiquité Classique*) (Geneva: Fondation Hardt, 1960) Another congress on Neoplatonism was held in Rome in 1970. Its papers were published as *Atti del Convegno Internazionale sul tema 'Plotino e il Neo-Platonismo'.*
2. William R. Inge, "Neoplatonism," *Encyclopedia of Religion and Ethics.* IX (New York: Charles Scribner's Sons, 1913), p. 309.
3. Ernst Hoffman, *Platonism und Christliche Philosophie* (Zurich and Stutgart: Artemis-Verlag, 1960) p. 306 ff; 163 & 436.
4. For an extensive treatment of Plotinus' logic see A. C. Lloyd's "Neoplatonic and Aristotelian Logic," *Phronesis* I (1955-56): 58-72, 146-59.
5. Erwin Edman, "The Logic of Mysticism in Plotinus," *Studies in the History of Ideas* (New York: Columbia University, 1918-35), II p. 49.
6. The best brief definition of Neoplatonism is found in Philip Merlan's *From Platonism to Neoplatonism* (The Hague: Martinus Nijhoff, 1960), p.1, n. 1.
7. William R. Inge, *op. cit.*, p. 317.
8. For more complete studies see Henry Bett, *Johannes Scotus Erigena* (New York: Russel and Russell, Inc., 1964).

PART ONE

The Sources of Neoplatonism

The Neoplatonism of Plato

J. N. Findlay
Boston University

I shall begin my somewhat controversial paper with a quotation from Plotinus, Ennead V, Tractate I, Paragraph 8. Plotinus says: "And for this reason Plato established a triplicity. All the prime things stand about the King of All, and secondary things are embraced by a Second Principle and third things by a Third Principle. And he says there is a Father of the Cause, meaning by the Cause the Nous or Mind, for the Mind is his Demiurge who manufactures the Soul in that famous cup. By the Father of the Cause, i.e., of the Mind, he means the Good, which is beyond Mind and beyond Being. And often he uses the term 'Idea' to cover Being and Mind. So that what *we* say represents no novelty, and was said not now, but long ago, though in inexplicit fashion. Our present exposition is merely an exegesis of what was then said, and relies for its proof of antiquity on the writing of Plato himself. Parmenides also took up a like doctrine in his identification of Being and Mind, and in his refusal to locate Being in the sensible world. . . . But the *Parmenides* of Plato achieves greater accuracy in separating from one another the Primal One, which is more preeminently one, a second One which is a One-Many, and third One which is both One and Many. He therefore also agrees with our three natures."

In this passage Plotinus dispersedly quotes and interprets the Second and Sixth Platonic Epistle, the *Timaeus,* the *Republic,* the Dialogues *passim* and the Platonic dialogue *Parmenides,* together with the original poem to which this last distantly harks back. All these, Plotinus says, teach the doctrine of the Three Original Hypostases which are the theme of

Ennead V.1, and which are the foundation of the Plotinian ontology. It will be the argument of this paper that Plotinus is justified in these arguments, and that the basic Neoplatonic doctrines are in fact what can and must be collected from a careful and understanding reading of the main Platonic writings, with some necessary help from Aristotle, who after all heard Plato actually talking in the Academy (though some picture Plato as permanently dumb), and from the statements of the Aristotelian commentators and a few other similar sources. I am not saying that the first Neoplatonists did not carry Plato's doctrine somewhat further at a number of points, and that they did not tinge it with a richer mysticism than is even to be found in Plato. I am also not saying that there are not sides to Plato's thought of which they made practically no sense or use: Plato's interest, e.g., in ingenious and often sophistical argument carried on for its own sake, his deep belief that everything admitted of a mathematical analysis, and his search for Principles of Things which were also Principles of Number, and so on. I am, however, saying that they were right in their interpretation of most of what should be regarded as deeply original and basic in Plato, and that, if many of the Platonic Dialogues do not give us Plato, but Socrates made young and beautiful, so the central Plotinian treatises do not give us Plotinus or Saccas, but rather Plato brought out from hinting incompleteness to expository fullness and coherence, and freed from many of the tiresome stylistic and argumentative reflexes due to a too long impersonation of Socrates.

In my view, then, a very important happening took place in Alexandria at the beginning of the Third Century A.D. when Ammonius Saccas began his exegeses of Plato, basing himself on the important assumption, much more true than false, of a profound *Homodoxy* or agreement in opinion between Plato and Aristotle. His work involved an attempt to see Plato as something more than a brilliant virtuoso of inconclusive, often fallacious, argument—a role only admirable or tolerable in Socrates on account of his existentially revealed conviction as to the impossibility of defining the virtues in any clear-cut manner, or apart from one another, or apart from the critical activity which redefines them unendingly—and as something more than an ancestor of the Neo-Pythagorean mystagogues who dispense a "way of life" to those doomed to live it under the Roman Empire, and as something more, lastly, than one of those philosophical littérateurs who charm us all the more since there is only an appearance of what is clear and compelling in what they say. It represented an attempt to make serious philosophical sense of Plato, as a thinker desirous of determining what primarily is, and what only is in some secondary or derivative manner, and how the various senses and grades of what is may be accommodated to one another and to the human soul and mind with its profound need to understand and love. Obviously it would be in such Dialogues as the *Phaedo* and the *Phaedrus* and the *Symposium* and the *Republic* and the *Timaeus*, and a suitably interpreted *Parmenides,* and also in the Platonic *Letters,* that the materials for such interpretation would be found, and not at all in such brilliant exercises in self-refutation as the latter part of the *Theaetetus* or some of the earlier Dialogues. And it incorporated strands from the pre-Socratics and from Aristotle and the Stoa because these could be regarded either as leading up to or continuing, the serious Platonic effort, which most of the moralizers and argumentative skeptics and mystical Platonizers of the half-millennium between the time of Plato and Plotinus arguably could not. It was not, as some have thought, by borrowings from these transitional people, but by a deep immersion in the writings of Plato and also of Aristotle that Saccas and Plotinus came to create their Neoplatonic philosophy.

I myself am inclined to ascribe the new wave of Platonic *approfondissement* to Saccas rather than Plotinus, basing myself on the fact that it was only when Erennius and Origen, the fellow-pupils of Plotinus, started publishing what they had learnt from Saccas, that Plotinus felt himself freed from any arcane discipline, and began publishing what he must in large measure have derived from Saccas, since he had hesitated to publish it previously. And I also base myself on the fact that I see comparative little development in the treatises of Plotinus. They are the varying expositions of an already established body of doctrine, to which Plotinus may have made some brilliant additions, but whose basic pattern had been previously laid down.

I may say here at the beginning of my paper that no claim for the Neoplatonism of Plato can be sustained if one's conception of what Plato taught and thought is to rest on the assumption that this will be fully explicit in the Dialogues, and that one should not do the least dotting of *i*'s or crossing of *t*'s for which a warrant in the Dialogues is not available. Plato, says Sir David Ross, is nothing if not explicit: to this axiom we may oppose the axiom: "Plato is nothing if not inexplicit". At every point in the Dialogues we meet with assertions regarding which it is far from clear what they mean, or whether Plato agrees with them, or has any clear opinion about them. This is of course the case in the earlier Dialogues where Plato's obvious aim was to recreate the content and atmosphere of the inspired sophistries of his master Socrates. But the Middle Period Dialogues, such as the *Republic*, the *Symposium* and the *Phaedrus*, are likewise the most hinting of documents: they repeatedly suggest that something is being treated in an extremely cursory manner, that it would have to be dealt with elsewhere in much greater depth, e.g. the nature of the Good in *Republic* 506, or of the objects of various mental faculties in *Republic* 534. Plato repeatedly takes refuge in myth, he is whimsically evasive and so on. And in the later Dialogues the difficulty of interpretation is so profound, that it has not been agreed whether their tendency is to undermine or to buttress Plato's characteristic Middle Period doctrines, and in the case of one of the greatest, the *Parmenides,* opinions range from those of Hegel and Proclus, who see in it the supreme expression of Platonic metaphysic and dialectic, to those who would see in it no more than a somewhat frivolous polemical or logical exercise.

All this is very regrettable when we really know from the testimony of Aristotle, despite all his immense misunderstandings, the basic outlines of what Plato taught in the Academy, doctrines that must have been current when Aristotle first joined the Academy in 367, and not, as has been supposed by those who defer too much to the Dialogues, at a much later date, and which impressed Aristotle so deeply that they became for him the very pattern of Platonism, to whose criticism he devoted two complete treatises, one *On the Ideas* and one *On the Good,* the remnants of which are to be found in the *Metaphysics* and in the comments of Alexander and other commentators. From this material we know that Plato, as far back probably as the time of the *Republic,* had replaced the moralisms of Socrates with a thoroughgoing mathematicization of all the Forms, and had come to see in them complex, many-dimensional patterns of numbers and numerical ratios, and believed in some sort of logical procession of all of them all from a supreme Principle of Unity which was also a Principle of Goodness. This Principle of Unity exercised mastery over another Principle of indefiniteness, continuity and badness, and gave rise to the Forms, and it then operated on a second version of the same indefiniteness, continuity and badness, thus giving rise—by way of the soul or souls, which were themselves pure exemplifications of ratio—to the numberless instances of ideal natures that confront us in the world of change and becoming. How Plato expounded these doctrines, whether by formal lecture or informal seminar or tutorial conversation, we do not know, but that they were the important part of Platonism, to whose understanding and refutation Aristotle devoted great pains, we do indeed know. And nothing that Cherniss has written to suggest how the Dialogues may have been misinterpreted to yield the materials for Aristotle's two tomes of criticism, can hold water against the solid uniformity of the Aristotelian testimony as to basic Platonic doctrine. It is not, however, my task this evening to expound the Inexplicit Doctrines of Plato: that I hope to do in a book that will be published before long. It is not my task, because much of what Aristotle said Plato taught was as unclear to the Neoplatonists as it has been to many among ourselves. They arrived at their view of Plato's teaching by painstakingly dotting the *i*'s and crossing the *t*'s of the Dialogues and Letters, and connecting Plato's doctrines with what were undoubtedly Aristotle's modifications of them, e.g. the Aristotelian notion of Matter. If we are sure, as we should be sure, that Plato *had* an inexplicit doctrine or rather programme of investigation, we can come to be sure that Saccas and Plotinus were not deceived as to much of its main outline.

I shall now go through the several characteristic doctrines of Plotinian Neoplatonism and try to show that they repre-

sented no important deviation from the doctrine of Plato. As
you well know, the first of the Divine Hypostases in Neoplatonism is a Principle which is indifferently called the One or the
Good. In calling it the One, we are not, however, saying that it
has Unity as other entities, e.g. an army, an organized body,
even a soul, have Unity, a Unity which entails that they hold
together as entities, and do not wholly disintegrate and cease to
be: it does not even mean that it has Unity as the various
features which make up an *Eidos* have Unity, or as the mind
which envisages *Eide* and their interrelations has Unity. The
Supreme Hypostasis of the system does not *have* Unity, but *is*
the Unity which all other things that are, have in varying
degree: it is therefore of a wholly different order from the
things which merely have Unity. And since having Unity is
tantamount to being, the supreme Unity cannot properly be
said to be: it is what confers being on its participants but
cannot for that reason be one of them or among them (see
e.g. VI.1.3). And since it has no definite form or definable
nature, Unity itself cannot properly be said to be an object of
knowledge, and can neither be written of or spoken of: we can
at best gesture in its direction, and by simplifying ourselves and
abandoning what is specific or individualizing in us, achieve a
presence, coincidence or contact with such Unity (VI. 9. 4.
11). The One is, however, also called the Beautiful (I.1.9). but
obviously this is an extrinsic denomination, applicable because,
through the forms to which it gives unity and being, it also gives
beauty to their instances, and so in the realm of Forms
themselves throws beauty before itself like a garment (I.1.9).
Plotinus indeed says (V.8.11) that the best way to be in
beauty is, not to see it, but to *be* it, but plainly such a being
beauty, is supraaesthetic rather than aesthetic. Even the title
'Good' is arguably an extrinsic denomination; the Good is so
called because it throws a glow on all it produces and awakens
desire in those that see this, and because it is the ultimate object
of desire for all beings (VI.7.22,23,27). The Good is not,
however, a Good to itself, an object of desire or love to itself,
though it may be useful for certain purposes to talk as if it were
(VI.8.12,13). Plotinus is further clear that the One involves in
itself the *power* of everything (V.4.2), and that it can confer

unity and being on all of which it represents the power, and that it has in fact exercised and is always exercising that power. It is further the case for Plotinus, that, being the Good, it logically *must* confer unity and being on inferior things. It will not be what it is if there is not something which enjoys a secondary life which derives from it (II.9.3). This logical necessity does not, however, involve anything like desire or need (V.5.12), and is of course reconcilable with perfect freedom in the sense of an absence of all compulsion.

How now does all this accord with the assertions of Plotinus's master, Plato? Plato, the pupil of Socrates, obviously had to put the Good at the head of the eidetic and the cosmic order, but at even an early phase it was fast assuming the character of an ontological, cosmological and mathematical principle rather than an ethical one. Perhaps one should rather say that its ethical properties were being absorbed in its mathematical ones. And it was fast taking on the hues of transcendent mystery and ineffability that hung round the Good of the Megarians, with whom Plato we know had close relations, and for whom the Good was an Eleatic Unity, capable of carrying many names (Diogenes Laertius, II.106), without thereby involving any inner plurality. Plato's relation with Parmenides was always, we may say, a relation mediated through his Megarian friend Eucleides. Even in *Phaedo* 98ff. the Good is a mysterious principle of cosmic explanation rather than an ethical one, and is more hopefully approached through the assumed being of its shadows, the Forms, regarding which some specifically arithmetical problems are raised, and which, it is suggested, will lead us up to the self-sufficient Good itself. The Good is not to be used to explain things in the naively teleological manner that Socrates tried in Xenophon's *Memorabilia*, though Plato cunningly insinuates that it might, and so has led many commentators up the garden path. The mysterious character of the Good in the *Republic* need hardly be documented in detail. Banal ethical approaches in terms of pleasure and knowledge are repelled, the Good is made responsible for the truth and being of the Forms but transcends this being in dignity and power. If it is called a Form, it is only so called by courtesy, and if we are said to have knowledge of it, the close connection of knowledge with being is such as to prove that this must be more than an ordinary case of knowledge. And that the whole educational ascent to the dialectic which is to lead on to the Good is through a series of purely mathematical studies, provides plain proof that dialectic is basically a philosophy of mathematics, and that the Good in which it culminates can be nothing but Absolute Unity itself. It is quite inconceivable that Plato's Guardians, having reached the ripe age of fifty, and having studied all the intricacies of mathematics, should be subjected to the ethical argy-pargy practised by Socrates on young men and boys. What Plato *says* may lend itself to such interpretation, but what he *does* with his concept shows that it has quite a different content: if the Good is an ethical concept, it is so in a sense that no mere moralist could comprehend. The Absolute Beauty of *Symposium* 211a,b is in no different case, being "neither words, nor knowledge, nor anything pertaining to anything else," but subsisting itself by itself in eternal unity, no matter how its scattered participants wax and wane. When one remembers Plato's close association of beauty with regular mathematical measure and proportion, it is plain that the Beauty here dealt with is simply Unity itself. There is no harm in finding this aesthetically moving.

If we now demand an actual carrying out of the dialectical programme, arguably we have a somewhat joking execution of it in the second part of the dialogue *Parmenides*, where the transcendental character of Unity itself is shown by the fact that, as in the case of the Megarian Good, it has a being-in-itself in which nothing except itself can be said of it, and that it yet also has a being in and for others in which everything can be said of it, and it said of everything, and which is so necessary to all such others that without it they would resolve themselves into sheer formlessness or into nothing at all. I am not, however, so foolish as to think I can pack a good interpretation of the *Parmenides* into a single sentence. In the *Philebus* finally the Good hides itself in a forest of transcendentals among which notions like Measure, Symmetry, and Proportion are prominent: beneath these the Forms are ranged as specific cases of such transcendentals, and far beneath them such human values as knowledge and pleasure. I think it arguable that Plato's thought moved towards the same unification of transcendentals as the Megarians, and that in this unification a transformed mathematical principle quite absorbed the principles of ethics and aesthetics. This also is the doctrine of Plotinus. The references to the Father of the Cause in Epistle VI may also be regarded as authentic, and so may the adjuration of Dionysius in Epistle II not to ask too many questions regarding the supreme Unity.

From the Father of the Cause I turn to the Cause, otherwise, in Plotinus, to the Divine Mind or Intelligence, the Second Hypostasis, surrounded by secondary things. As you all know, Plotinus makes the Divine Mind a double-barrelled affair, whose two sides are welded into inseparable unity. It is a subject-object unity consisting on the one side of the *Noeta,* the *Eide,* on the other side of the *Noeses,* and also the *Noes* or *Noi,* the thoughts and the minds directed upon the *Eide.* The Nous, Plotinus tells us, is a necessary *Perilampsis* or irradiation of Unity: it in fact *is* Absolute Unity separated from itself only by Difference, and returning to itself from Difference (V.1.6). The power of the One is seen by the Nous as strung out into different forms: this is how the Nous must necessarily see the One. The One in a sense feels all the things that lie in its power, and these the Nous distinguishes, defines, and stabilizes, and will not allow to float about in indefiniteness (V.1.7). Mind in fact is a necessary outflow of Absolute Unity: Unity requires Mind logically, and is incomplete without its discerptive diligence, though it does not *need* Mind in the desiderative sense, as Mind needs it. Mind and the *Noeta* it contemplates are held to be inseparable: there is in Mind no reaching out to objects beyond itself that is so characteristic of Soul, with its need, also, for the pricks of external sensuous realities. Aristotle, Parmenides and Heraclitus are invoked to attest the close marriage of Nous and *Noeta,* but strangely enough not Plato himself. Mind is entirely coeval with the forms it knows (V.9.7), which does not, however, prevent Plotinus from constructing temporalized accounts in one of which would otherwise be indefinite and random, and according to the other of which (VI.7.15) the multiplicity of the *Noeta* is due to the

Mind's inability to envisage the supreme Unity, and to its consequent need to split this up into a number of distinct unities of *Eide*. In the Nous, further, all the *Noeta* are together, but can, when needed (for purposes of the Soul) be held apart from one another (V.9.6). This unity in which each is all, and all is all, and the glory infinite, is given lyrical acclaim in the well-known treatise on Intelligible Beauty, the Western equivalent of the Buddhist *Avatamsaka Sutra*. But the supreme Mind also includes minds (in the plural) in its perfect unity (VI.8.17); these are perhaps the eidetic originals of particular minds. It is in fact clear that since the Nous has no principle of individuation, and since it is out of time, it is not really *a* Mind at all, but rather the unique, eternal *Eidos* of Mind as Such, in which particular minds, including the mind of the World Soul, merely participate. Some doubt might be cast on this interpretation because Plotinus in V.9.13 seems to question whether there can be *Eide* of Soul and Mind. What the passage really says, however, is that particular souls and minds are less definitely distinct from their eidetic originals than sensible instances are.

How does the Plotinian doctrine of the Second Hypostasis fit in with the teaching of Plato? Does Plato believe in a timeless eidetic Mind which embraces the *Eide* and is one actuality with them, or is this doctrine derived from Aristotle's Active Intelligence, always one with the immaterial *Eide* that it thinks, and perhaps identical with the thinking on thinking we meet with in God, who thinks all things in thinking only Himself? Is the intrusion of an essentially Aristotelian view into Platonism part of the syncretistic homodoxy which Saccas erroneously introduced? Even such a deep modern interpreter of Plato as Kramer thinks that the *Geistesmetaphysik* starts with Plato's successors. I, however, am of the opinion that the *Geistesmetaphysik* was propounded orally by Plato himself and is documented clearly in his writings, the only reason why Plato did not proclaim it from the housetops being that he did not wish his doctrine to be confused with the doctrines which Aristotle was even then excogitating, according to which the supreme Mind is a high-grade *instance* of mentality and not mentality itself, the doctrine of course which gave comfort to all those in the Middle Ages who believed that the *Eide* could find safe harbourage in the mind of God. For Plato, however, I should hold, the Mind correlated with the *Eide* was a Thinkingness rather than a Thinker, and provided no anchor for those who demand an ultimate concrete, whether mental or anything else.

What reason have we to hold that Plato believed in an enternal Thinkingness and Livingness which were higher than the thought and life present in souls? If we read the *Phaedo* carefully, we shall see how the soul is never fully *identified* with the Form of Life, which it none the less imparts to its instances. If souls impart life to bodies, Life Itself imparts life to souls. If we now turn to the first Sun-passage in the *Republic*, we find it said that, as the Sun is responsible both for sight and the seen, so the Good is responsible both for Mind and what it minds, both for knowledge and for truth. It is of course plain that Plato is here explicitly speaking of instantial minds that know the true being of the *Eide,* but can it be doubted, if the parallelism is to be meaningful, and Plato not idiotic, that there must be an *Eidos* of knowledge or Intelligence correlated with the ideal unities, just as there is an instantial organ of vision correlated with instantial colour, and that souls only come to knowledge of the *Eide* through participation in this Absolute Idea of Knowledge? And if we turn to the Line, this conjecture is amply confirmed, for here there are mental powers correlated with all the objects we can know, and Plato cannot have been so blind or so silly as not to perceive that there must be Forms of characteristic mental exercises and powers as well as of their objects. Plato in fact provides us with forms of the mental faculties inferior to knowledge as well as of pure intellection, just as he for similar reasons, in Books VIII and IX of the *Republic*, provides us with Forms of deviant and pathological states. But that Knowledge at least had eidetic representation is plain from the passage in *Phaedrus* 247d,e where the souls in their upper-world journey are said to behold the form of Knowledge Itself, and it is even clearer in the passage in *Parmenides* 134 where Knowledge Itself and Mastery Itself are correlated with other eternal *Eide,* which are argued to be inaccessible to instantial knowers and masters, whereas, God, the *non*-instantial Knower and Master par excellence, can have no relation to sensible, instantial things. A careful reading of the *Philebus* will likewise show that while it acknowledges the presence of Mind in the cosmos, responsible for all its regularity, and present in the royal soul of Zeus, there is yet said, in carefully chosen language, to be a "Power of the Cause" which has conferred mind and soul on Zeus and the other divinities, a power, therefore, which though of the nature of Mind, is not an instance of Mind, and can obviously be none other than Mind Itself, in association with Life Itself, the eternal Living-Thinkingness which lies way back of all minds and souls and what they envisage. The *Timaeus* in its carefully managed mythology tells the same story: the Demiurge is not the mind or soul which moves the heavens and thinks all the forms and their actual and possible instances in endless cyclical enjoyment. He is an elder, timeless being, hard to know or declare, the essential cognizer of the Forms of life and all other Forms these may involve, and responsible for the being of the soul and for bodies that the soul moves in time. This Demiurge again is our old friend, Thinkingness as such, eternally trained on all thinkables, and welding them all into one vision. And if one questions whether Plotinus is not borrowing from Aristotle when he makes Nous and *Noeta* sides of a single reality, let us remember the possibility that Aristotle may have been plagia- rizing from Plato when he taught a similar doctrine. Philoponus at least, a Christian commentator on the *De Anima*, says that the Aristotelian reference to someone who called the Mind the place of Forms was to none other than Plato. Only for Plato this Mind cannot have been *a* mind, but only Mind Itself.

If we now turn to the third Plotinian Hypostasis, Soul, there is much less discrepancy to adjust between what Plotinus and his master Plato say. The generation of Soul coincides, for Plotinus as for Plato, with the generation of Time. Just as the eternal Mind arises out of the supreme Unity by the holding apart of the *Eide* of which it is the power, so Soul and Time arise for Plotinus out of the eternal Mind by a departure from the *completeness* of the ideal sphere, which permits of neither addition nor subtraction. This departure from completeness is identical with the life of Soul, an essentially unquiet faculty, like Martha busy over many things ($\pi o\lambda v\pi\rho\acute{a}\gamma\mu\omega\nu$, III.7.11) and forced to decode the total message of the *Eide* into a long string of separate messages, each of which it laboriously fits into a growing whole. Plotinus does not, however, regard this declension into temporality as an unfortunate accident: plainly it is as logically necessary for the ultimate Unity to give rise to the mobile, questioning Soul, as excellent in its rule-governed everlastingness as anything temporal can be, as it was necessary for it, at a higher stage, to differentiate itself in the Eide and in the Mind which is the thought of them all. Soul, further, involves a less transparent pluralization than exists at the level of Mind and the *Eide:* our souls do not interpenetrate as do the eidetic minds above them, and have something of the separateness of the bodily masses in which they are active (IV.1.11). There is also somewhat of a gulf between them and their Great Sister, the All-Soul. But, though thus separated in their lower being, souls remain linked together at their highest points, much as light divides itself among separate dwellings, while remaining undivided and truly one (IV.3.4), a beautiful image reminiscent of a passage in the Platonic *Parmenides*. And the All-Soul is of course responsible for the unending turning on itself of the heavens, and for the accompanying thought-circuit through the realm of Forms.

If we turn to Plato, most things stay the same, except that some questions are left unexplored, and mathematical exactnesses are added which are foreign to the genius of Plotinus. The Soul is the mediatrix between the eternal, undirempted Forms and the changeable dirempted sensibles: it has appropriate ways of knowing both spheres, and it is also the vehicle through which the Forms, the ultimate true causes of generation and becoming, become sources of motion in the instantial world. All movements which are externally initiated stem from movements that are self-initiated, and these are the movements characteristic of Soul, which is therefore the source, under the Forms, of all movements in the instantial world. And Soul is equally involved in the perpetual inner circlings of thought and perception about their objects. The great distinction of Plato is, however, as I have said, the belief that the proportions and rhythms and numerical relations which the Soul cognizes in things, and imposes on them, are all mirrored in Soul-structure.

The Soul is a complex structure of numbers, like the things it cognizes and manipulates. This, the doctrine of the *Timaeus* and also referred to in well-known passages in the *De Anima*, comes strange to modern thought, as it also doubtless came strange to the less mathematical Neoplatonists. But it is entirely defensible. Cognition and action may not be exhaustively analysable in terms of numbers and ratios, but they are certainly not intelligible without these. Everything that is objective or subjective is a matter of style, whether existence-style or life-style or thought-style, and style is without doubt a matter of proportion and number.

Beneath Soul, for Plotinus, lies Matter (ὕλη) into which Soul pours the *Logoi,* the ratios, which form the essences of the various species of natural being. Regarding Matter Plotinus has a long, interesting treatise (II.4) in which the Aristotelian accounts of *Hyle* are subtly combined with the accounts of the Receptacle in the *Timaeus,* and with the Aristotelian accounts of the Platonic Great and Small. This is a field in which there is genuinely a profound homodoxy between Plato and Aristotle, the Prime *Hyle* of Aristotle being only in name more substantial than the empty receptacle of Plato. Plotinus follows Plato, as also Aristotle, in recognizing an ideal as well as an instantial matter: the indefinite substrate, which is what is common to all the *Eide,* reappears, at another level, in the basic indefiniteness which underlies sensible instances. Sensible matter, we are told (II.4.6), is required to give bulk to the being of sensible things, which cannot consist in pure form, and to explain the continuous transformation of sensible things into one another. To this omnirecipient Prime Matter Plotinus denies not only every sensible quality, but even bulk (ὄγκος) and size, thereby going beyond Plato's treatment of *Chora* in the *Timaeus.* But Prime Matter, though not intrinsically bulky, has none the less an intrinsic *aptitude* for size and distance. How is such matter apprehended? Like the nothingness of space, not so much by a spurious act of thinking, as by the complete failure of such an act, that is by an indefinite unthinkingness *anoia* in which no clear content comes to light (II.4.10).

Why do souls descend from the intensive parcelling involved in temporal process into the extensive parcelling involved in bodily extension and existence? The Plotinian answer is simply because they are souls, and because, stemming from Absolute Unity, and having in themselves an image of the Unity which abides through flux, they necessarily desire to preside over and impose unity upon a disunity which is further from Absolute Unity than themselves. Necessarily this descent of Soul into the otherness of bodily being entails endless possibilities of defect, miscarriage and corruption—which do not, however, touch our august sister, the World-Soul—and necessarily the Soul must seek to raise itself to the patterns yonder, and to the Unity from which they radiate. But it is only by descending from the supreme Unity that it is possible to return to it, and the descent is in consequence not something misjudged or wanton, even though it may metaphorically be said to involve *Tolma* or audacity. Plotinus, as is well known, magnificently defended the natural world against all those who, like certain Christain Gnostics, would regard it as the evil product of a fallen power. Being an instance, it necessarily falls short of its original, but, *for* an instance, nothing can exceed its beauty and accuracy (II.9.4). All this is said with less fullness in Plato. It is plain that the Divine lack of *Phthonos* or envy in the *Timaeus* is merely a pictorial way of expressing a logical and ontological relation. The timeless perfection present to eternal Thinkingness must, being what it is, seek to carry itself out in the changeable, dispersed, randomized medium of the instance. Being, as the *Sophist* teaches, entails the possession of power. Instantiation is therefore nothing that can or ought to be dispensed with, but it carries with it mutability, externality and chance interferences of all sorts: all that can be done is to resist these disintegrating forces, to make them as little disruptive as possible. This our cosmos, with its everlasting background regularities, and its recurrent restoration of order whenever things get too bad, magnificently achieves, both for Plato and Plotinus. I myself humbly share their logical optimism.

I shall end this paper by dwelling on a few respects in which I think that Plato was a richer and greater philosopher than his Neoplatonic interpreters, and also a few respects in which I think that they were better philosophers than he was. It was, I consider, a great misfortune that the Neoplatonists made the eidetic realm a realm of unmixed perfection, thereby according with a drift in the Academy according to which there were not Forms of everything, but only of certain special, privileged things. Quite plainly this Academic restriction does not accord with the *practice* of Plato who speaks of forms of impiety, injustice and other negatives, and who also devotes two whole books of the *Republic* to studying the deviant forms of the state, deviations not due to chance, but to numerical cycles rooted in the nature of things. Plato in the person of *Parmenides* likewise reproves the doctrinaire Socrates, his former self or some right-wing contemporary, for refusing to admit forms of hair, mud, and filth. There is, however, a line of evidence stemming from a long passage of Sextus Empiricus dealing with Pythagorean and Academic doctrine, and from references in the Aristotelian commentators to one Hermodorus, who wrote a contemporary study of Plato's doctrine, which goes some way towards resolving the discrepancy between the Dialogues and the Aristotelian reports on these points. Plato, it would appear, had come to admit *three* categories of forms: one of self-existent, standard types which obviously occupied a prime place in the ideal order, one of opposites or negations having obviously only a secondary place, and one, lastly, of "relatives", by which it is plain that Plato intended deviations from standard types by way of excess or defect. This doctrine, if we are interpreting it rightly, perfectly explains Plato's practice in the Dialogues, and what Aristotle says of his doctrine in the *Metaphysics*. For it would seem that, while Plato only gave prime status in the world of Forms to models of perfection, he gave secondary and tertiary status to partial or total deviations from such models: these were, after a fashion, involved in the sense of the models from which they deviated, and enjoyed a charter of liberty in the realm of instantiation. (For the material see Sextus Empiricus *Adversus Mathematicos* 248-283, and Simplicius on Aristotle *Physics* 192a). Had the Neoplatonists known of these doctrines, they would have spared us some of the overecstatic accounts of life in the intelligible world, where there is not even a breath of what Hegel called "the seriousness, the suffering, the patience and the labour of the negative". In Plato's later writing

transcendentals fade into the background where their illumina-
tive role plainly lies: while there is no evidence whatever that
Plato ever lost his faith in his supreme Unity, his attitude
towards it became less appallingly light-headed. Lightheaded-
ness, however, is a characteristic of Neoplatonism, and like St.
Teresa one has, in studying them, to fight against unwanted
levitation. It is also a defect of the Neoplatonists that they
failed to make much sense of Plato's attempt to "mathemat-
icize" the forms, to reduce them to numbers, proportions and
patterns of the same, an attempt in which Platonism went far
towards anticipating the temper of modern science. In the
Tractate on Numbers which occurs in the Sixth Plotinian
Ennead, there is much treatment of plurality, but hardly
anything that concerns numbers as such.

On the other hand we may regard it as a great merit of the
Neoplatonists that they systematically side-stepped the rigid use
of the concepts of negation and diversity which is characteristic
of what we may call "logic-chopping", which Plato inherited
from Socrates, and from which he may never wholly be able to
free himself. The soul, e.g., must have three parts because it
does three disparate sorts of things, and there must likewise be
three sorts of entity in the world, Forms, Sensibles and Space,
trichotomies which delight those who like to deduce pluralism
from some such principle as that "Everything is what it is and
not another thing". Plotinus, however, is clear that his
Hypostases are not rigorously distinct, but can slide into, and be
transformed into one another, and that everything that is
yonder is also here, and vice versa. Difference is for him
something like the Hegelian "alienation" which can never be
carried to a limit. Everything is indeed what it is and not
another thing, i.e. everything is the one and only true Unity.

To sum up. The Neoplatonism of Plotinus was not a
distortion of Platonism but a liberation of the main structures
in the Platonic ontology from its Socratic carapace, and from
the necessary limitations of the literary dialogue. Plotinus
offered posterity the essence of Platonism, and as such it
became an infinitely precious strand in Christian theology
which, even when verbally critical of Plato, remained profoundly indebted to him. This essence has, however, largely

been lost by the modern refusal to go beyond the letter of the Dialogues, or to do so only when the results accord with what we may call the "Here we go round the mulberry bush" of modern analysis. Plato and Plotinus should be studied together: the second provides an essential commentary on the first.

Plotinus' Adaptation of Aristotle's Psychology: Sensation, Imagination and Memory[1]

by Henry J. Blumenthal

University of Liverpool

That the *Enneads* contain a great deal of Aristotelian doctrine must be obvious to a fairly casual reader even without the explicit testimony of Porphyry.[2] Nevertheless it is not equally obvious in all parts of Plotinus' thought — sometimes, of course, he is in clear disagreement with Aristotle. For various reasons which we shall have to consider the use of Aristotle's ideas in the construction of Plotinus' doctrines of the human soul is pervasive, but does not present us with a simple case of absorption. That, in the nature of the case, would have been impossible, even if we forget Plotinus' capacity for subtle alteration of views, he might at first sight appear to be taking over as they stood, a process which Professor Armstrong has aptly called 'rethinking',[3] but which might well appear as perverse interpretation. Plotinus, as is well known, claimed to be doing no more than expounding views whose antiquity could be vouched for by Plato's own writings (V.1.8.10-14). Many have referred to this claim in connection with Plotinus' relation to Plato. It is perhaps not equally well understood that a man who could think himself so good a Platonist would have been quite capable of thinking that those parts of his psychology which were Aristotelian were roughly the same as those of his source, or more importantly perhaps, that Aristotle's views were the same as his own. His attitude is not unlike that of those Aristotelian commentators who were later to claim that Aristotle's views were like Plato's if only one understood them aright.[4]

I have made these points at this stage because the basis of Plotinus' psychology is a paradox which, I suggest, can only be understood if one thinks in such terms. The paradox lies in the fact that Plotinus' soul was, like Plato's, separate from and, ideally, opposed to the body, but worked like Aristotle's which was by definition the body's essence. And yet Plotinus was well aware of the crucial difference: he did not fail to criticize Aristotle's entelechy theory, and of course attacked both his definition of the soul and its implications (IV.7.8[5]).

That the body: soul relation was Platonic and dualist is stated nowhere more clearly and emphatically than in the first lines of IV. 3.22: 'Should one say then that when soul is present to body it is present as fire is to air? For that too when it is present is not present, and when it is present all through a thing is mixed with none of it: it remains unmoved while the other flows by'.[5] The independence of soul which this text asserts is not always preserved in practice. One might think of Plotinus' warnings about the consequences of the affections ($\pi\acute{\alpha}\vartheta\eta$), and, in general, the way he regards the lowest phases of the soul as quite closely linked with the body, and always liable to suffer from the association, an association which is even capable of having undesirable effects on the soul's higher ranges (cf. e.g. IV.8.2.26-30, VI.4.15.18ff.)[6]. This is so in spite of the careful way in which Plotinus will, for example, talk of the desiring faculty as having the basis of its action in a certain part of the body, namely the liver (IV.3.23.35-40) — a point, incidentally, on which Plotinus is in a sense more Platonic than Plato, who puts the equivalent 'part' of the soul in the abdomen as if it were a lump of matter.[7] Here it would seem that Plotinus was more scientific, and thus more in sympathy with Aristotle's approach, than his professedly Platonic position should have allowed.

The fact that Plotinus used Aristotle's account of the soul's operations, and, of course, his general view of the way the soul should be divided, while differing with him over the whole basis of psychology, namely what the soul was and how it related to the body, accounts for a large measure, though certainly not all, of the differences between their views about its functions. There are, of course, others. One is Plotinus' view of the soul as a reflection of higher being, itself as a whole dependent on what lies above, and with each phase or section depending on that above and less valuable than it. Here ethics and metaphysics invade psychology. Thus soul for Plotinus is viewed from the top downwards, and lower sections are sometimes regarded as dispensable. When soul is functioning as it should and so looking upwards, the lower section is absorbed in the higher: one might think of a kind of hanging collapsible cup.[8] In Aristotle the situation is reversed: the soul is like a pyramid, where each layer, or series of faculties, cannot exist without that below. As a result Plotinus tends to consider any function of the soul at least partly against the background of its possible contribution to man's upward progress, and perhaps to evaluate it in this light.

Aristotle on several occasions records that there is a progress through the lower to the higher forms of cognition and knowledge, not thereby implying that the 'lower' forms are 'worse' than the 'higher'.[9] His aim is to analyze how one acquires knowledge and he makes it clear on numerous occasions that sense-perception is the indispensable foundation of the process. This no Platonist could admit, though Aristotle's own Platonism does re-assert itself in the view that at the end of the process we have knowledge of things inherently more knowable than the sense-data from which it starts. Here we see one example of Aristotle's different approach, which also shows itself in his more scientific attitude to psychology. Put quite simply, he wants to analyze the functions of soul wherever in the world it might operate, and is particularly interested in the demarcations between various forms of life. Plotinus, unlike Plato, does see, and has perhaps learned from Aristotle, that soul extends to all forms of life (cf.I.4.1.18ff.) — and even finds it in things that Aristotle properly regards as inanimate (IV.4.27) — but he is not really interested in those other than man. It should not be forgotten that, whatever others made of it later, the *de Anima* is a biological treatise.

The differences we have outlined are perhaps most interestingly studied in the middle section of the human soul, at the levels of perception, imagination and memory. The top and bottom are less instructive, for the following reasons. At the top, at the level of *nous*, Aristotle's soul, or at least the active *nous*, is also detached from the body. I shall avoid for now the problems that would be presented if the passive *nous*, whose nature is defined as pure potentiality, were the highest manifestation of the body's actuality, and the no less troublesome matter of the exact level where Plotinus' human *nous* is to be situated. Whether the answer be the hypostasis *Nous* or the hypostasis Soul makes little difference for the present purpose.[10] But in any case this is another area where Aristotle is closer to Plotinus' intentions as well as his practice by virtue of a Platonic feature of his thought. If Aristotle's active *nous* were after all one of the 'intelligences', then Aristotle and Plotinus are here very close.

At the bottom of the scale the two thinkers are again fairly close, but whereas at the upper end of the scale this is explicable in terms of Aristotle's Platonism, at the lower end it is to be seen as a result of Plotinus' apparent Aristotelianism—unintentional though it may have been. Especially at the level of the vegetative soul, which both Aristotle and Plotinus call by a variety of names, what is done by soul in Aristotle is the work of body alone in Plato. Moreover, as soul descends, or reflects itself, further downwards, it becomes more and more closely bound up with body until its function becomes the information of previously formless matter (VI.7.7.8ff.). Here in producing body, the soul is functioning as world-soul: sometimes it is also seen as a manifestation of world-soul at the next level, that of the vegetative soul.[11] Here the gap between body and soul, whether regarded as world-soul or individual soul, is small enough for Aristotle's ideas not to be far removed from Plato's, though of course their professed positions were no less different than elsewhere.

The way both may make the same kind of statements for different reasons is well illustrated when Plotinus, discussing the impassibility of soul when involved with the affections, says that if we say the soul changes in the emotions we are liable to be doing the same sort of thing as if we were to say the soul goes pale or blushes, without taking into account that these things happen through the soul but in some other structure, that is, the body (III.6.3.7-11).[12] Aristotle had compared the notion that the soul is angry with the view that it builds or weaves, and thought it would be better to say not that the soul feels pity, learns or thinks, but that it is the man with his soul that does these things (408b 11-15).[13] Aristotle is concerned to make it clear that the soul does not act independently of the body whose form it is. Plotinus, on the contrary, wants to show that the soul is independent of the body with which it is merely associated.

This requirement is still operative at the level of sense-perception. It is perhaps what made it possible for Plotinus to arrive at the fairly clear distinction he makes between sensation and perception, equipped as he was with no better linguistic tools than his predecessors.[14] Of these none, as far as we know, made the distinction with any clarity. Plotinus did it simply, though perhaps crudely, by separating sense-perception into an affection (πάθος) of the body, and a judgement or act of cognition on the part of the soul. So, for example, at the start of III.6: 'We say that perceptions are not affections, but activities and judgements concerning affections: the affections take place elsewhere, let us say in the body so qualified, but the judgement is in the soul, and the judgement is not an affection – otherwise there would have to be another judgement, regressing to infinity – but we still have a problem here, whether the judgement *qua* judgement takes on anything from its object. If it has a mark from it, then it has undergone an affection.'[15] There are, of course, other places where Plotinus points out that the faculty of sensation is not affected by what happens to its organs, or to the body in general. So at IV.6.2. 16-18 he says that in the case of taste and smell there are affections and also perceptions and jugements of these which are a cognition of the affections, but not identical with them.[16] Perception in general is the soul's judgement of the body's affections (IV.4.22.30-32). But the introduction to III.6 is particularly significant when considered in its context. The whole purpose of the first part of this treatise is to show that the soul is not changed by the emotions (cf. esp. III.6.1.12-14): these being functions of the soul below the sensitive faculty are of course more likely then sense-perception to have some effect on the soul itself. What happens in perception is used as a paradigm of the soul's freedom from the affections of the body and its separation from it. Later in the treatise vision is used to illustrate another point, this time to show how the lower parts of the soul may listen to reason without actually being changed: vision, he says, is simply the actualization of a potency. The act and potency are in essence the same, and so vision entails no essential change: the sense cognizes its objects without undergoing any affection (III.6.2.32ff.). Here we can see clearly what Plotinus is in fact doing: he is discussing sense-perception for the light it can throw on other matters. The two points he wishes to make here are that there may be temporary changes involving parts of the soul either in relation to others, or to the body, and that changes in the body need not, and generally do not, affect the soul. In the area of the affections he does not quite succeed.[17] Elsewhere he will use his basically Aristotelian view of vision as a pattern for the relation of various levels of reality.[18] Its usefulness here, rather than just the normal Greek feeling that vision was the most important sense – stated explicitly by Aristotle at *de Anima* 429a 2f. – is the most likely reason for Plotinus' interest in vision. If this explanation is correct it becomes less surprising that for Plotinus sensation is almost synonymous with vision: he says very little more about taste and smell than the remark we have referred to, virtually nothing about touch and gives a short account of hearing, again primarily illustrative.[19] A sound fills the air for anyone who is there to be able to hear it, and the whole sound is in any one part of the air: that is how we are to understand the presence of soul (VI.4.12). This kind of paradigmatic purpose is at least part of the reason why the distribution of Plotinus' discussions of perception is so different from Aristotle's. There is of course more to be said. In his treatise *Problems about the Soul* (IV.3-5), as well as in one or two specialised smaller treatises, like that on why large objects perceived at a distance appear small (II.8), Plotinus does seem to be interested in the workings of the human soul for their own sake. This is perhaps also true of I.1, but only to an extent, for there Plotinus is primarily concerned with making a distinction between those human activities which involve both body and soul and those which are the work of soul alone.

Such then are the reasons for Plotinus' uneven coverage of the questions that present themselves. What of the details? As far as their general notions of what happens in sense-perception go, Aristotle and Plotinus are not very far apart. Aristotle says that each sense is 'that which is able to receive the sensible forms (i.e. of sense-objects) without their matter',[20] and compares the way wax may receive the imprint of a signet-ring without its material, the metal (424a 17-21). Plotinus' definition is similar, but its intention may be subtly different. For him sense-perception is 'the perception of the soul or the 'living being' (ζῷον) of sensible objects, the soul grasping the quality attached to bodies and receiving an imprint of their forms' (IV.4.23.1-3).[21] By inserting 'quality attached to bodies' Plotinus causes one to wonder just what he means by the word which is translated 'forms' but can equally well mean appearances. Are 'forms' no more than appearances? That would be in order for a Platonist, but perhaps not in harmony with Plotinus' fairly positive attitude to the sensible world in this treatise, and the distinction may be over-subtle. Nevertheless the impression that Plotinus does mean to indicate the illusoriness of sensible qualities is strengthened by the fact that the word he uses for receiving an imprint (ἀπομάττειν) occurs in that part of the *Timaeus* where Plato describes the production of sensible objects in the Receptacle.[22] In any case Plotinus is perhaps closer to Aristotle in another passage, III.6.18.24ff., where he talks of soul not being prepared to accept the forms of sensible objects with multiplicity but seeing them *when they have put off their mass*,[23] if by this he means something like Aristotle's 'without matter'.

Where Plotinus certainly differs from Aristotle is in his view that the soul's power of perception is not properly exercised on the sense-objects themselves, but on the impressions which sensation has produced in the 'living being': these have by then become intelligible (I.1.7.9-12). Here we do have a sensation: perception distinction. For Aristotle there was of course no question of a distinction between what is done by body and soul, and so his account was much simpler: the body and soul unit perceived sensible objects by means of the appropriate faculty, the sensitive, acting through, or in, the appropriate organ. In fact, faculty and organ are the same, except in definition (424a 24-6).

The role of the sense organs was in line with the general requirements of the two thinkers' approaches. In Aristotle's psychology it was possible, not to say desirable, for the organs to be independently active. Vision is, after all, inherent in the eye. It is its form and essence: an eye that cannot see is simply not an eye (412b 18-22). For Plotinus, on the other hand, an eye *qua* part of a body can only see when activated by the relevant faculty of its detached soul, and its function, like that of all the sense organs, is to act as an intermediary, a kind of transformation point, between the sensible objects outside and the immaterial soul 'inside' which is only able to perceive what is presented to it in an intelligible form (IV.4.23). In fact the senses are different only because different sense organs perform this role (IV.3.3.12ff.). By itself soul can only think ($\nu o\varepsilon \tilde{\iota}\nu$) the objects which it already possesses (IV.4.23.5f.). Through the sense organs it can be assimilated to the sensible objects (*ibid*.21ff.), just as in Aristotle's theory the organs, or senses, become like the objects from which they were originally different, though potentially the same (cf. 417a 18-21, 422a 6f.). It should not, however, be forgotten, that for Plotinus the organ must already, if there is to be perception, have a degree of similarity to the object, whether this is described in terms of sympathy as in IV.4.23, or, rarely, more Platonically in terms of being light-like, as at I.6.9.30f. Plotinus' concept of an inward transmission from the organs to the soul as such was of course greatly helped by the post-Aristotelian discovery of the nerves.[24]

A further and immediately obvious difference comes over the question of a medium between object and organ. Quite simply Aristotle thought that one was required while Plotinus did not. This is one of the more technical questions which Plotinus discussed at some length, in IV.5, which is an appendix to the treatise on the soul. Here again he disagrees quite openly with Aristotle, though he does not mention him by name. Plotinus wished to explain the contact between subject and object in perception by means of the sympathy ($\sigma \nu\mu\pi\dot{\alpha}\vartheta\epsilon\iota\alpha$) that existed between all parts of the world in virtue of its status as a living being, a notion he had taken over from certain later Stoics — dare one say Posidonius? This sympathy operated equally between the parts of the world and the parts of each ensouled individual in it, which allowed Plotinus to explain both internal and external perception in the same way. That had the advantage of greater economy and simplicity than a theory which required a medium for external perception when there could be none in the case of internal perception. That was a problem which would not have been serious for Aristotle, since he did not, in general, consider what role perception might have in respect of the percipient subject himself. There is, of course, one exception, the attribution in the *de Anima* to the several sense themselves of awareness than they are perceiving. But Aristotle merely says that they, rather than some other sense, see or hear that they are seeing or hearing (425b 12ff.). His main reason is a fear of regress, and he is not much concerned with how the process works. By his own theory there should be a medium, and that could have been a serious difficulty even in the *de Sensu* version where the senses acting together, as the common sense, are responsible for this kind of perception (*de Sensu* 455a 12 ff.). Here then we have one manifestation of Plotinus' interest in various kinds of self-awareness and self-consciousness. This was an area in which Aristotle had taken little interest and where Plotinus was in advance of his predecessors and sometimes foreshadowed modern developments in psychology — as also in his brief reference to the importance of unconscious memories (IV.4.4.7-13).

To return to mediums. Plotinus arraigned two classes of offenders, one whose own theories required a medium, and another for whom it was unnecessary to the concept of perception with which they worked. Aristotle falls into the latter and worse class. Plotinus discusses the question mainly, but not exclusively, in terms of vision. His general view is that there is no need for anything between object and eye to be affected so long as the eye itself is (IV.5.1.15ff.). He here ignores Aristotle's argument from the impossibility of seeing objects placed directly on the eye (419a 12f.), an argument he is quite prepared to use elsewhere for another purpose.[25] Against the idea that air must be changed before we can see, he argues that we should then be seeing the adjacent air, and not the object itself, just as if we were being warmed by air rather

than by a fire (IV.5.2 50-55). This is not the best of arguments.
A better one is that if vision depended on the air being lit, that
would make nonsense of the fact that we can and do see lights
in the dark: this means that the darkness is still there when we
see. Plotinus rejects any attempt to salvage mediums by arguing
that their absence would break the sympathy between subject
and object: he does so by anticipating his final conclusion that
sense-perception depends on the sympathy which arises from
common membership of one living organism (IV.5.3.1ff.).
Before he reaches that he stops to consider the view that air
might be necessary if one thinks that light can only exist in air.
He points out that the air would then be incidental to the
process of vision (IV.5.4.2-7). It is interesting to note that
Plotinus has here arrived at a correct position for a dubious
reason: we do now know that light can be propagated through a
vacuum. Unfortunately for Plotinus the same is not true of
sound, whose medium Plotinus wishes to abolish by the same
argument. One might wonder, incidentally, whether Plotinus'
unwillingness to accept any kind of medium, against which he
argues mainly in terms of vision, had anything to do with his
views on the exalted status of light. Was light too good to be
involved so basically in sense-perception?

One further question must be considered. How did
Aristotle and Plotinus deal with the assessment of sense-data by
the soul, and what did they think about their objective validity?
The first half of the question is perhaps badly framed in the
case of Aristotle, given his answers to the second. For in the
case of at least one kind of perception, that of the relevant
quality by the appropriate sense, such as colour by vision, there
was no scope, or very little, for error. Error could arise in the
perception of something as an attribute, or, more often, in the
apprehension of the common sensibles, such as size or shape
(428b 17-25). The latter Plotinus attributed to a combination
of perception and opinion (VI.9.3.27-32).[26] Aristotle omits to
tell us how error is detected, but it would seem that it must be
done by reason working with the images which the sensations
produce. This is certainly what Plotinus thought. Incoming
sense-data were compared with a pre-existing pattern derived
from above (VI.7.6.2-7). Reason dealt with images produced by

perception (V.3.2.2ff.): the percept of a man will set off a chain of inference, and reason by using memory can pronounce that it is Socrates (V.3.3.1-5). But here reason performs a function which in Aristotle was a matter of perception: the sense of sight perceives a white object incidentally *as* the son of Diares (418a 20f.). As a result of this difference Plotinus does not need reason to confirm what is its own conclusion. What was in Aristotle a case of perception has become for Plotinus a matter of inference. Some form of verification will, for him, have been necessary even at the level of Aristotle's usually infallible perceptions: as far as Plotinus was concerned, sense-perception produced opinion, not truth (V.5.1.62-5). Here Plotinus' Platonism is clearly responsible for his view.

For Plotinus the faculty of imagination is the terminus for perceptions as such (cf. IV.3.29.24f.). They may be passed on to reason for processing, or retained as memories. Imagination is also responsible for other forms of transmission between parts of the soul, or between soul and body. Its duties in connection with memory are particularly complex. It is probably because of this wide variety of functions that Plotinus tended to see imagination as a faculty – or rather two – in its own right. Aristotle, on the other hand, tended to think of it as a subdivision of the sensitive faculty, different by definition rather than in essence (*de Insomn.* 459a 15ff.). He defined it as a 'movement caused by the activity of perception' (428b 13f.).[27] Nevertheless he will sometimes speak of imagination acting independently of sensation, and in particular producing sense-like images, as in dreams, when no sensation is present. This is one of the differences between imagination and perception that he mentions in the course of framing the definition: others are that all animals have sensation but not imagination, and that perceptions are true whereas imaginings (φαντάσιαι) – for want of a better English word – are usually false (428a 5ff.). We may note in passing that whereas Plotinus regarded perception as unreliable and was less suspicious of imagination, which usually acted as an agent of some other power, Aristotle held perception to be reliable and thought that imagination was usually wrong: he was still influenced by its connection with the verb meaning 'to appear' with its strong connotation of appearing other than is the case (428b 2ff.).

Notwithstanding such differences one can see that Plotinus is working with the same concept as Aristotle, though he adapts it, exploiting a certain vagueness in some of Aristotle's statements, and extends the sphere of its operation. Both clearly and primarily associate imagination with the sense, both use it as a means of presenting material acquired by the senses to the reason, both hold that it is the basis of memory.

In its connection with sense-perception imagination presents the fewest problems. It is the power of soul by which we have available for consideration, or for subsequent use through memory, the information provided by the senses. We have seen that in Plotinus sense-percepts, as processed by imagination, were presented to the reason. Similarly in Aristotle reason deals with images which it has before it in the manner of perceptions (413a 14f.). The contexts are different, but since for both images derive from sensation, and are considered by reason, we may take it that the underlying doctrine is the same. There is, however, an important difference in the use of images. For Aristotle they are probably necessary for thought of any kind (413a 16f.), while for Plotinus the thinking of the true *nous*, the intuitive thinking which is superior to mere reasoning, can and does proceed without them, since *nous* is simply present among its objects. In fact the reason is informed of intuitive thought by means of images, and imagination makes the results of both kinds of thinking known to the rest of the soul (IV.3.30.5-11). When the imaginative faculty is disturbed then thinking proceeds without images (I.4.10.17-19).[28]

At the other end of Plotinus' scale, imagination makes the condition of the lower faculties, and that part of the body for which they are responsible, known to the higher soul (cf.IV.4.17.11ff., 20.17f.). In the case of desire the sensitive faculty perceives an image which conveys to it the condition of the lower soul (IV.4.20.12ff.). Thus we have a kind of sub-sensitive imagination in addition to that which operates between sensation and reason, and on one occasion Plotinus goes so far as to say that the former is imagination in the strict sense (VI.8.3. 10 ff.). Transmission of information about the body was of course a problem for Plotinus in a way that it was not for Aristotle, but it is possible that he constructed this downward extension of the activities of the imaginative faculty on the basis of Aristotle's remarks in the *de Anima* and elsewhere about the role of imagination in desire — and other emotions — and movement: an animal can move in so far as it is equipped with appetition, and appetition does not exist without imagination (433b 27-30). So appetition and imagination are both involved in the causation of movement (433a 20): at *de Motu Animalium* 702a 17-19 Aristotle says that imagination prepares appetition. Further, Aristotle does, at *de Anima* 433b 31ff., raise the question of how the imperfect animals, that is those which have only the sense of touch, can have imagination, which normally presupposes all five senses, a question presented by the fact that these animals appear to have pleasure and pain. If so, they must have desire, which should imply imagination. Aristotle suggests that they perhaps have it in an indeterminate way (ἀορίστως). This last suggestion in particular could be a starting point for Plotinus' lower imagination, which he describes as 'unexamined' (ἀνεπίκριτος), in a context where the term may well imply that vagueness makes this kind of imagination unverifiable (III.6.4.18-23).[29]

Plotinus' most radical alteration of Aristotle's scheme of faculties comes when he considers the role of imagination as the basis of memory. Aristotle had little difficulty in coming to the conclusion that memory and imagination belong to the same faculty since all memories, even those of intelligible objects, require mental pictures *(de Mem.* 450a 11-14). Plotinus comes to the conclusion by a more difficult route, by way of considering from various points of view the possibility that each faculty could have those memories relevant to its peculiar activities. His difficulties arise mainly from two requirements, first the need to clarify the relation of memory and its faculty to the 'living being', the compound of body and the lower faculties, and then the apparent impossibility of having the activities of the higher part of the soul remembered by the lower, and *vice-versa*. Here the role of imagination as a transmitter and mediator between the different sections of the soul provides the solution.

But of course there are further difficulties, which I have discussed in detail elsewhere.[30] Before we consider them briefly for their relevance to the present question, something should be said about the actual functioning of memory. Basically, in both Plotinus and Aristotle, the faculty retains images presented to it either from sensations below or reasonings above. But Plotinus, whose discussion in the treatise *On Sensation and Memory* (IV.6) is clearly based on Aristotle's account in the *de Memoria*, as Bréhier showed,[31] does not simply accept it as it stands.[32] He makes several alterations of detail, mainly with a view to removing materialistic, or at least apparently materialistic, features of Aristotle's account. In the first place he objects to Aristotle's talk of memory being the retention of some sort of imprint (τύπος) produced by perception or learning (*de Mem.* 450a 30-32). As Plotinus says at the start of his discussion (IV.6.1.1-5) it would make no sense to talk in these terms if one holds that perception does not involve any imprint, and the rest of the chapter argues once again that it does not. Plotinus was certainly not the first to be worried about the implications of the impression concept: Alexander had already expressed concern and said that the word was used only for lack of an appropriate one.[33] Plotinus says we must think rather of some sort of translation of the impression which affects the body: in an earlier treatise he speaks of 'something like indivisible thoughts' (IV.7.6.23).[34] For similar reasons Plotinus rejects Aristotle's explanation of the decline in old people's memory. Aristotle had accounted for it in terms of bodily changes, which he also took to be the cause of poor memory in the very young (*de Mem.* 450b 5-7). Plotinus substituted the suggestion that the psychic power involved declined, which enabled him to offer the same explanation for the fall-off in both memory and sense-perception (IV.6.3.51-5). As to the young, Plotinus argues, surely rightly, that they in fact remember better because they have as yet less material to remember (*ibid.* 21-4).

Let us return now to the problem of faculties. Here Plotinus innovates by splitting the faculty of imagination. This is the only way he feels able to explain how the higher soul which survives this life can, as it does, retain memories from it without being affected during life by the less elevated forms of memory which a person must have in the ordinary life of this world (IV.3.31-2). He thus requires a lower imaginative faculty to deal with such lower memories and protect the higher memory, a need arising from his basic position that the soul, and particularly the upper soul, remains unaffected by its administration of the body with which it is, in theory, merely associated. Since, however, the soul as a whole must in this life have certain information available to it, the information stored by the lower soul is available to the higher. Moreover the break may, at least partly, be obscured if we think in terms of Plotinus' view of the lower soul as a product of the upper soul's attention to what lies below. Similarly the lower soul can become reassimilated to the higher—though if this were to happen happen definitively the activities of the lower would disappear. That would remove the very reason for the lower imaginative faculty's existence.

This radical innovation is by far the clearest case of the changes in Aristotelian psychology that arose from the needs of Plotinus' brand of Platonism, and in particular from the need to defend the soul's autonomy. Yet even this change may have been suggested by Aristotle's references, both in the *de Anima* and the *de Motu Animalium*, to two types of imagination, one rational and the other perceptual,[35] and also the hint in the *de Anima* of a lower kind of imagination which we have already mentioned.[36] For the purposes of this paper too much attention may have been focused on the similarities between Aristotle's views and Plotinus'. Perhaps as a corrective it would be as well to remember that there were a number of questions in which Aristotle was interested and to which Plotinus simply paid no attention. Such are the nature of sense objects and the sense organs, and the forms of sense-perception which had little relevance to Plotinus' higher interests. In the workings of the soul at the level of plants and animals Plotinus shows very little interest. At the risk of speaking in cliches one might suggest that the differences are to a large measure due to the fact that Aristotle was a scientist as well as a metaphysician, and simply wanted to know. If one wonders why Plotinus adopted and adapted Aristotle's psychology the answer would seem to be that — apart from certain historical factors — he wished to remain a good Platonist and yet felt obliged to give a more

satisfactory account of the soul's workings than Plato himself
had found either possible or desirable.

NOTES

1. For the purposes of this paper I have deliberately left aside
   the history of psychology between Aristotle and Plotinus.
   Much of this is still inadequately treated, and some will
   remain so for sheer lack of evidence. But it is of interest in
   considering Plotinus' psychology to see what he chose to
   use. Note: all unspecified references to Aristotle are to the
   de Anima.
2. *Vita Plotini* 14.4-7.
3. 'The Background of the Doctrine "That the Intelligibles
   are not Outside the Intellect" ' *Les Sources de Plotin.*
   Entretiens sur l'Antiqité Classique V. Fondation Hardt
   (Geneva 1960) 402.
4. Cf. e.g. Simplicius, *de Caelo* 640-27-30. See further my
   paper 'Some Observations on the Greek Commentaries on
   Aristotle' in Actes du XIVe Congrès International des
   Études Byzantines.
5. Ἆρ᾽ οὖν οὕτω φατέον, ὅταν ψυχὴ σώματι παρῇ, παρεῖναι
   αὐτὴν ὡς τὸ πῦρ πάρεστι τῷ ἀέρι; καὶ γὰρ αὖ καὶ τοῦτο
   παρὸν οὐ πάρεστι καὶ δι᾽ ὅλου παρὸν οὐδενὶ μίγνυται καὶ
   ἔστηκε μὲν αὐτό, τὸ δὲ παραρρεῖ. It is clear from the
   context here, and also from what he says later when he
   refines the analogy from light to heat (IV.4.29 *init.*), that
   Plotinus is here thinking of fire primarily as light. One
   might wonder if even this Platonist statement is not itself
   suggested by Aristotle's description of light being the
   presence of fire in the transparent (418b 13-16).
6. On this see further my *Plotinus' Psychology. His doctrines
   of the embodied* soul (The Hague, 1971) 64-66.
7. Plotinus may well be deliberately improving on Plato since
   he offers this statement in IV.3 as an explanation of why
   the desiring part had been put in the liver.

8. Sometimes Plotinus thinks of these lower phases as belonging to the world-soul in its capacity of informing matter, rather than to the individual soul, cf. e.g. IV.9.3.11ff. and *Plotinus' Psychology 27-30*.

9. Cf. *Anal. Post* 99b 26ff., *Met.* A 980a 21ff.

10. For discussion of this problem cf. *Plotinus' Psychology* 115ff., and also my paper "*Nous* and Soul in Plotinus. Some Problems of Demarcation" in *Atti del Convegno Internazionale* sul tema *Plotino e il Neoplatonismo*. Roma 5-9.10-1970 Problemi attuali di Scienza e di Cultura. Accademia Nazionale dei Lincei (Rome 1974) 203-219.

11. Cf.n.6. above.

12. κινδυνεύομεν γὰρ περὶ ψυχὴν ταῦτα λέγοντες ὅμοιόν τι ὑπολαμβάνειν, ὡς εἰ τὴν ψυχὴν λέγομεν ἐρυθριᾶν ἢ αὖ ἐν ὠχριάσει γίγνεσθαι, μὴ λογιζόμενοι, ὡς διὰ ψυχὴν μὲν ταῦτα τὰ πάθη, περὶ δὲ τὴν ἄλλην σύστασίν ἐστι γιγνόμενα.

13. τὸ δὴ λέγειν ὀργίζεσθαι τὴν ψυχὴν ὅμοιον κἂν εἴ τις λέγοι τὴν ψυχὴν ὑφαίνειν ἢ οἰκοδομεῖν· βέλτιον γὰρ ἴσως μὴ λέγειν τὴν ψυχὴν ἐλεεῖν ἢ μανθάνειν ἢ διανοεῖσθαι, ἀλλὰ τὸν ἄνθρωπον τῇ ψυχῇ.

14. See further *Plotinus' Psychology* 67f.

15. τὰς αἰσθήσεις οὐ πάθη λέγοντες εἶναι, ἐνεργείας δὲ περὶ παθήματα καὶ κρίσεις, τῶν μὲν παθῶν περὶ ἄλλο γινομένων, οἷον τὸ σῶμα φέρε τὸ τοιόνδε, τῆς δὲ κρίσεως περὶ τὴν ψυχήν, οὐ τῆς κρίσεως πάθος οὔσης – ἔδει γὰρ αὖ ἄλλην κρίσιν γίνεσθαι καὶ ἐπαναβαίνειν ἀεὶ εἰς ἄπειρον – εἴχομεν οὐδὲν ἧττον καὶ ἐνταῦθα ἀπορίαν, εἰ ἡ κρίσις ἧ κρίσις οὐδὲν ἔχει τοῦ κρινομένου. ἤ, εἰ τύπον ἔχοι, πέπονθεν (III. 6.1.1-8).

16. γεύσεως δὲ καὶ ὀσφρήσεως τὰ μὲν πάθη, τὰ δ᾿ ὅσα αἰσθήσεις αὐτῶν καὶ κρίσεις, τῶν παθῶν εἰσι γνώσεις ἄλλαι τῶν παθῶν οὖσαι.

17. See above p. 42.

18. E.g. *Nous* formed by the One .... like vision in act: οἷον ὄψις ἡ κατ᾿ ἐνέργειαν (V.1.5.17f.).

19. All five senses are mentioned together in connection with the provision of appropriate powers to the various organs

by an undivided soul at IV.3.23.1ff.
20. τὸ δεκτικὸν τῶν αἰσθητῶν εἰδῶν ἄνευ τῆς ὕλης.
21. τὸ αἰσθάνεσθαι τῶν αἰσθητῶν ἐστι τῇ ψυχῇ ἢ τῷ ζῴῳ ἀντιλῆψις τὴν προσοῦσαν τοῖς σώμασι ποιότητα συνιείσης καί τὰ εἴδη αὐτῶν ἀποματτομένης.
22. *Tim.* 50E.
23. . . . .ὀρῶσα οὐκ ἀνέχεται μετὰ πλήθους δέχεσθαι, ἀλλ᾿ ἀποθέμενα τὸν ὄγκον ὁρᾷ.
24. By Herophilus and Erasistratus in the third century B. C.: their work was later advanced and refined by Galen.
25. To argue against the impression theory of perception (IV.6.1.32-5).
26. αἰσθήσεως καὶ δόξης ἐπομένης αἰσθήσει.
27. κίνησις ὑπὸ τῆς ἐνεργείας τῆς αἰσθήσεως.
28. That this is what Plotinus means can be seen by comparing this chapter with IV.3.30.
29. On the relation of the different kinds of imagination cf. *Plotinus' Psychology* 92f.
30. Ibid. 83ff.
31. In the Notice to IV.6 in the Budé edition of the *Enneads.*
32. The parallel emerges more clearly in IV.6 than in IV.3-4 because, unlike the latter, the former is not concerned with eschatology.
33. *de Anima* 72.11-13.
34. οἷον ἀμερῆ νοήματα.
35. All imagination is rational or perceptual: φαντασία δὲ πᾶσα ἢ λογιστικὴ ἢ αἰσθητική (433b 29); the imagination is due to thought or perception: ἡ φαντασία. . . .γίνεται ἢ διὰ νοήσεως ἢ δι᾿ αἰσθήσεως (*de Mot. Animal.*7021 19).
36. See above p. 54.

Iamblichus, Thrasyllus, and the Reading Order of the Platonic Dialogues

Michael Dunn

The University of Texas at Austin

The details of the well-known selection of twelve Platonic dialogues originally made by Iamblichus and later described by Proclus[1] and by the anonymous sixth-century *Prolegomena to Platonic Philosophy*[2] need not be expounded to modern Platonic scholars. Iamblichus' 'canon' codified certain preferences among the dialogues which were already apparent in Plotinus,[3] and after Iamblichus it became the standard format for the study of the Platonic dialogues in the Neoplatonic schools.[4] It was not, however, merely a random selection of what Iamblichus regarded as the most important Platonic dialogues: it also constituted a systematic and coherent course of reading in Plato. The student was to begin with the *First Alcibiades,* "because in it we come to know ourselves," and then was to ascend gradually through the different levels of virtues—'political' (the *Gorgias*), 'cathartic' (the *Phaedo*), and 'contemplative' (the *Cratylus, Theaetetus, Sophist, Statesman,*[5] *Phaedrus,* and *Symposium*)—ending at the *Philebus,* "because in it he [Plato] discusses the Good." Finally, the student was to approach the "perfect" dialogues, the *Timaeus* and the *Parmenides,* which summed up all the preceding ten.[6]

I will return to the implications of this reading course a little later in this paper. I would like to remind you first, however, that Iamblichus was by no means the first or even the last Platonist to propose a systematic reading order for the

Platonic dialogues. Proclus, for example, appears to have proposed a more comprehensive grouping which contained 32 dialogues;[7] but well before Iamblichus formed his canon, if we may rely on the evidence from the handbooks of Diogenes Laertius and the so-called Middle Platonists, the question of the order in which the dialogues should be read was often discussed. There is not enough time for me today even to mention all the proposals for a reading course that were made in the first and second centuries; but I would like to draw your attention in this paper to the most important of them all, both historically and as an interpretation of the Platonic dialogues, which has been strangely neglected and misunderstood by modern scholars. This is the division of the Platonic dialogues into nine 'tetralogies' which is associated in our ancient sources particularly[8] with the name of Thrasyllus, a Platonist, mathematician, and astrologer in the service of Tiberius, who died a few months before that emperor in A.D. 36.[9]

The tetralogies had a long history in Platonic studies: in the second century they were known and perhaps adopted by Theon of Smyrna,[10] while at approximately the same time they were being criticized and rejected by Albinus;[11] Diogenes Laertius devotes a lengthy discussion to them.[12] Among the Neoplatonists the tetralogies were superseded by Iamblichus' canon, but it is probable that they contributed to the formation of that canon,[13] and they were still thought worthy of refutation by the author of the sixth-century anonymous *Prolegomena*.[14] As the principle by which the manuscripts of Plato were organized, the tetralogies passed down to the Arabs, to the Renaissance, and to us; and we still find them used for the same purpose in modern editions of Plato.

In the time available today I intend to suggest three theses about the tetralogies:

I. That they constitute a coherent reading course in the Platonic dialogues, and were so regarded by the ancient Platonists.

II. That the main outlines of this reading course can be discovered.

III. That the tetralogies as a reading course are superior in important respects to the Iamblichan canon.

I. Modern scholarship has tended to emphasize the role of the nine tetralogies in the history of the transmission of the Platonic corpus: whether they are held to have originated in the early Academy or in the first century B.C.,[15] their chief significance has been taken to be that they were the framework of a great edition of Plato, and that they remained through the centuries "the great constant in the transmission of Plato."[16] This aspect of the tetralogies is certainly important, but is an historical accident, and one or two citations will, I hope, be sufficient to show that when ancient Platonists referred to the tetralogies they were not thinking of them primarily as editorial tools.

The clearest statement of the function of the tetralogies is made by Albinus in chapter IV of his *Introduction to the Dialogues of Plato:*

Since we have looked at the natural differentiation of the dialogues, and at their "characters", let us say next with what kind of dialogues we should begin reading Plato's philosophy. There have been different opinions. Some begin with the *Letters,* some with the *Theages*; and there are those who divide up the dialogues according to the principle of the tetralogy, and arrange the first tetralogy to contain the *Euthyphro, Apology, Crito,* and *Phaedo* ... Of this opinion are Dercyllides and Thrasyllus.[17]

Albinus goes on to criticize the tetralogies and substitutes for them two proposals of his own, but in any case his meaning is plain: there were different opinions as to which dialogues should be read first by the beginning student, and Dercyllides and Thrasyllus were of the opinion that he should begin with the *Euthyphro, Apology, Crito,* and *Phaedo.* While it does not necessarily follow from Albinus' words that the rest of the tetralogies were also meant to be read in sequence, nothing in the passage excludes this possibility.

A second piece of evidence that the tetralogies were regarded as a reading order is a remark from Theon of Smyrna, a Platonist of the second century, preserved by the tenth-century Arab encyclopedist Ibn al-Nadim:

Theon said: "Plato arranged his writings for reading.

Each group consisting of four books, he called a tetralogy."[18]

Al-Nadim's epitome of Theon is abbreviated and sometimes confused, but if this passage is sound, Theon not only thought of the tetralogies as a reading order, but also believed that the tetralogical principle had the authority of Plato behind it; and since this claim was also made by Thrasyllus himself,[19] it provides some grounds for believing this citation from Theon to be authentic.

II. We must now examine the tetralogies themselves, and the ancient evidence about their contents, to see whether we can discover the principles behind this arrangement of the dialogues.

It will be helpful first to examine comparable organizational schemes which were applied to the works of two other ancient philosophers.

(1) Thrasyllus himself arranged the works of Democritus in tetralogies, probably on the model of the Platonic tetralogies.[20] An interesting thing about these Democritean tetralogies, however, is that Thrasyllus organized them into six larger groupings, under the headings 'ethical' (2 tetralogies), 'physical' (4 tetralogies), 'mathematical' (3 tetralogies), and so forth; in all, four of these six larger groupings are made up of two tetralogies each. In this case, therefore, Thrasyllus did not intend for the single tetralogies to stand by themselves, but that they should combine to form larger groups. We will see in a moment that he or someone else applied the same principle to the Platonic dialogues. It should be added, however, that the Democritean tetralogies do not seem to constitute a reading course.

(2) When Porphyry prepared his edition of the treatises of Plotinus, he selected as his basic group the ennead, or group of nine. Here again, we find the individual enneads combined to form larger groups, of which "the first contains three enneads; the second contains two; and the third contains one."[21] Furthermore, Porphyry's arrangement is clearly intended to be a reading order, beginning with the "lighter"[22] problems of moral behavior on earth (*Enn.* I), and ascending through Nature (*Enn.* II-III) to Soul (*Enn.* IV), Nous (*Enn.* V), and finally to the categories at the summit of Being, and to the One (*Enn.* VI).

Using the principles which we see to be at work in these other organizational schemes, I would like to suggest for your consideration the following analysis of the nine tetralogies.[23]

(1)   There is an introductory group, consisting of the first tetralogy only and containing the four dialogues which deal with Socrates' trial and execution:

> I. *Euthyphro*, or On the Holy, peirastic
> *Apology of Socrates*, ethical
> *Crito,* or What Must Be Done, ethical
> *Phaedo,* or On the Soul, ethical

Our   sources,[24]   which   tell   us   little   more   about   the tetralogies than their contents, do agree in singling out the first tetralogy from the others. Diogenes Laertius, moreover, preserves a valuable fact about Thrasyllus' attitude toward it:

> He [sc. Thrasyllus] establishes a first tetralogy containing the common theme: for he wishes to give a paradigm of what the life of the philosopher would be like.[25]

Diogenes words, unfortunately, leave it doubtful whether Thrasyllus meant that the theme of the life of the philosopher was confined solely to the first tetralogy, or whether this first tetralogy   contained   within   it   the   common   theme   of   the whole.[26]   I am inclined to think that Thrasyllus meant the latter, and that the common theme of the whole reading course was the life of the philosopher in its different aspects, but I do not wish to affirm it as a fact, in the absence of more explicit evidence.[27]   I   believe   we   can   say,   however,   that   the   first tetralogy stands apart from the rest as an introduction to the whole sequence.

(2)   In   defining   the   remaining   groups   of   dialogues   we cannot   rely   on   specific   evidence   from   the   ancient   sources; however, I believe we may make certain plausible conjectures on the basis of the contents of the dialogues themselves, and what   is   known   of   the   interpretation   of   them   by   ancient Platonists.

I suggest, then, that we may see a second main grouping in the second and third tetralogies:

> II. *Cratylus,* or On the Correctness of Names, logical
> *Theaeteus,* or On Knowledge, peirastic
> *Sophist,* or On Being, logical

Statesman, or On Kingship, logical
Parmenides, or On the Ideas, logical
Philebus, or On Pleasure, ethical
Symposium, or On the Good, ethical
Phaedrus, or On Love, ethical

It will be observed, first of all, that all of the dialogues which had been characterized by the Platonic tradition as "logical" are contained within this group. Just as later Platonists would preface the study of Plato with Aristotle's logic, so in Thrasyllus' reading course the student who is fresh from reading about the trial and death of Socrates will begin his study of philosophy with a group of dialogues which deal with knowledge and the dialectical means of arriving at it. He begins with the consideration of language, in the *Cratylus,* then proceeds to the inquiry into knowledge, the *Theaetetus.* Plato himself could then be taken to indicate, by the repetition of characters and by many cross-references, that the *Sophist* and the *Statesman* should follow the *Theaetetus.*

The precise function of the next four dialogues is a little difficult to determine, and the *Parmenides* provides a good illustration of the problem we face. We may fairly safely assume that it was not yet given the characteristically 'theological' interpretation familiar to us from Plotinus and his successors. Yet Proclus knew of at least two other interpretations of the *Parmenides* which were current among the earlier commentators: one along the lines of its secondary title, *On the Ideas,* and one which treated it as a "logical exercise".[28] The latter interpretation may be reflected in the writings of Albinus, who refers to the *Parmenides* as a place where one may find numerous examples of the hypothetical syllogism,[29] or an outline of the ten Aristotelian categories.[30] Galen, similarly, speaks of the "exercise" (*gymnasia*) of the method of diaeresis in the *Sophist* and *Statesman,* and finds it "most clearly and most perfectly" demonstrated in the *Philebus* and *Phaedrus.*[31] It is certainly possible that, at the very beginning of a reading course in Plato, the beginner might be encouraged to look for this "gymnastic" element in the dialogues, in order to learn logical or dialectical methods.

On the other hand, this severely pragmatic interpretation of these dialogues as mere exercises in method is not what we would expect from the Pythagorean and astrologer Thrasyllus. Should we not also see in this group of dialogues a gradual ascent from the subject of language in the *Cratylus* to a culminating vision of the Good in the *Symposium* and *Phaedrus*—a vision, of course, only attainable through dialectic? In this case, the last four dialogues would not only be exercises in logic but also descriptions of the higher kinds of knowledge.

If the dialogues of this group *were* understood as an ascending order culminating in a vision of the Good, then we probably need look no further for the origins of Iamblichus' canon. A glance at the two lists will show how strikingly similar they are:

Thrasyllus' tetralogies	*Iamblichus' canon*[32]
Euthyphro	Alcibiades I
Apology	Gorgias
Crito	Phaedo
Phaedo	1. Cratylus
1. Cratylus	2. Theaetetus
2. Theaetetus	3. Sophist
3. Sophist	4. Politicus
4. Politicus	8. Phaedrus
5. Parmenides	7. Symposium
6. Philebus	6. Philebus
7. Symposium	Timaeus
8. Phaedrus	5. Parmenides

(3) The third group of dialogues, like the second, contains two tetralogies:

    III. *Alcibiades I*, or On the Nature of Man, maieutic
        Alcibiades II, or On Prayer, maieutic
        Hipparchus, or Lover of Profit, ethical
        Anterastae, or On Philosophy, ethical
        Theages, or On Philosophy, maieutic
        Charmides, or On Temperance, peirastic
        Laches, or On Courage, maieutic
        Lysis, or On Friendship, maieutic

In the same way that the "logical" dialogues were all contained in the second group, Thrasyllus or the inventor of the tetralogies included all the "maieutic" dialogues within this third group. The term "maieutic", which we might render clumsily as "obstetric", derives from the well-known passage in the *Theaetetus* (149a-151e) in which Socrates compares himself to a midwife, and his characteristic activity to midwifery. In the traditional characterizations of the dialogues,[33] therefore, "maieutic" was the term applied to dialogues in which Socrates is seen in this activity, and it is this "midwifery", rather than any formal philosophical theme, which forms the connecting link between the dialogues of the third group. Another theme, closely related to it, is that of love.[34] Often Socrates pretends to be in love himself, as in the *First Alcibiades*, and the *Charmides*; at other times he converses with lovers, as in the *Anterastae* and *Lysis*; in the *Hipparchus*, in addition to playing on the word "lover of gain", Socrates tells the story of the famous lovers Harmodius and Aristogeiton. The themes of midwifery and love, finally, are seldom separated in these dialogues from the question "who is the best educator of the young?", which is discussed on its own in the *Theages* and *Laches*.

(4)   A fourth group is easily recognized in the next two tetralogies:

IV. *Euthydemus,* or the Lover of Contest, anatreptic
Protagoras, or On Rhetoric, anatreptic
Meno, or On Virtue, peirastic
Hippias I, or On the Beautiful, anatreptic
Hippias II, or On Falsehood, anatreptic
Ion, or On the Iliad, peirastic
Menexenus, or Funeral Oration, ethical

This fourth group, like the preceding two, contains a concentration of dialogues to which tradition had assigned the same philosophical 'character'. That is, in this group are found all of the 'anatreptic' dialogues (dialogues in which the opponent is "overthrown"), together with the single 'endeictic' or 'exhibitory' dialogue; and according to Diogenes Laertius III.49 these two groups together form the class of 'agonistic' dialogues, or dialogues of contest.

Wilamowitz observed how useful the *Euthydemus* is as a means of transition from the third sequence to this one:[35] the question it raises, again, is "who is to educate the youth in virtue?" In this fourth sequence of dialogues, however, particular attention is paid to the philosopher's rivals as educators, the sophists. Ion is not technically a sophist, of course, but is included in this group as a false teacher. And finally, the *Menexenus* seems to have been placed at the end of this group for two reasons: first, Thrasyllus or the author of the tetralogies in all likelihood took the funeral oration seriously, as an example of sound oratory which could be contrasted to the false oratory of the sophists; secondly, the political theme of the oration would have seemed an excellent transition or introduction to the political dialogues of the last two tetralogies.

Before proceeding, however, I would like to point out briefly that, if I have described the third and fourth groups of dialogues correctly, then *concepts* and *doctrines* would seem to have played less important a part in Thrasyllus' reading of these sixteen dialogues than did the *personae*, their relationships, and what they do or experience. It may also be recalled that Albinus rejected at least the first of Dercyllides' and Thrasyllus' tetralogies on the grounds that they intended to apply an ordering to "personae and the circumstances of their lives."[36] A modern reader, however, might well approve of this emphasis on the personae in the dialogues of the third and fourth groups. The characters of the *Laches*, for example, learn nothing positive about the abstract concept of courage, but they do find in the person of Socrates an answer to their original question, "who is to educate the young in virtue?" In the *Charmides*, again, every abstract definition of temperance is called into doubt, but the dialogue ends with the young interlocutor placing himself under the tutelage of Socrates, because Charmides has come to realize that he does not know if he is temperate or not. In both cases the modern reader might be inclined to emphasize the confusion or "aporia" of the interlocutor, while Thrasyllus, perhaps, more accustomed to emphasize Socrates' midwifery, would point rather to the saving presence of the philosopher; but both alike would locate the significance of these dialogues in what happens to the characters.

That I am not merely reading modern preoccupations into these dialogues can be shown from a passage in Albinus' *Eisagoge*, in which he declares that dialogues of an "expository" character aim at *things* or *topics*, while those of an "inquiring" type aim at *personae*.[37] Now, of the sixteen dialogues contained in the third and fourth groups, thirteen are characterized as maieutic, peirastic, endeictic, or anatreptic, which are the four lowest divisions, according to Diogenes Laertius III, 49, of the "inquiring" type of dialogue.

(5) The political theme of the fifth group of dialogues, which is made up of the last two tetralogies, is so evident that it hardly needs comment:

> V.   *Cleitophon,* or Protrepticus, ethical
> *Republic*, or On the Just, political
> *Timaeus*, or On Nature, physical
> *Critias*, or Atlanticus, ethical
> *Minos*, or On Law, political
> *Laws*, or On Legislation, political
> *Epinomis,* or Nocturnal Assembly, or Philosopher,
>   political
> *Epistles*, ethical

The *Timaeus*, a 'physical' dialogue, is only apparently an anomaly among the political dialogues, since of course Plato himself in the prologue to the *Timaeus* makes it a continuation of the *Republic* and the cosmological background to the history contained in the *Critias*. The *Cleitophon* must have seemed the natural preface to the *Republic*, since Cleitophon represents himself as a pupil both of Socrates and of Thrasymachus, discusses justice with Socrates, and appears briefly as an interlocutor in the *Republic* (I. 328b and 340a-b). The inclusion of the *Minos, Laws, Epinomis* and *Epistles* among the 'political' dialogues hardly needs any explanation.

From Diogenes Laertius we already know that the "common theme" of the first tetralogy was the life of the philosopher. From the survey we have just made I think we can now take the common theme of the second group of dialogues to be knowledge and dialectic; that of the third to be midwifery, love, and education; that of the fourth, sophistry; and that of the fifth, politics. In emphasizing these aspects of the Platonic dialogues the author of the tetralogies was certainly suggesting no categories that would not occur to any modern reader: they really are primary elements in Plato's dialogues, perhaps *the* primary elements.

There is a coincidence, however, to which I would like to draw your attention, because it suggests that Thrasyllus or whoever invented the tetralogies may have had a definite model before him for these divisions of the reading sequence. The coincidence is in the apparent correspondence of the four dialogues of the second tetralogy with the last four sequences of the reading order. The correspondence can be illustrated most clearly with a diagram:

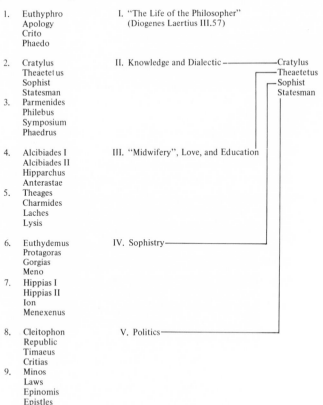

1.	Euthyphro Apology Crito Phaedo	I. "The Life of the Philosopher" (Diogenes Laertius III.57)
2.	Cratylus Theaetetus Sophist Statesman	II. Knowledge and Dialectic ——————Cratylus ┌——Theaetetus ┌—Sophist Statesman
3.	Parmenides Philebus Symposium Phaedrus	
4.	Alcibiades I Alcibiades II Hipparchus Anterastae	III. "Midwifery", Love, and Education
5.	Theages Charmides Laches Lysis	
6.	Euthydemus Protagoras Gorgias Meno	IV. Sophistry———————
7.	Hippias I Hippias II Ion Menexenus	
8.	Cleitophon Republic Timaeus Critias	V. Politics———————
9.	Minos Laws Epinomis Epistles	

In other words, the *Cratylus* ("On the Rightness of Names", "Logical"), might be compared to the whole group of dialogues in which knowledge and dialectic are the main themes. The *Theaetetus,* which follows it, contains Socrates' comparison of his conversations with the young to midwifery, or *maieutike,* the comparison which gave the name "maieutic" to more than half of the dialogues of the second main group. The third dialogue of the second tetralogy, the *Sophist,* defines the character to which the philosopher is opposed in the dialogues of the fourth main group. Finally, the definition of the noble statesman in the *Statesman* corresponds to the concern with the philosopher and politics in the last main group. It may well be that, after establishing the first tetralogy as the introduction to Plato's philosophy, Thrasyllus or the inventor of the tetralogies then deliberately employed the second tetralogy as the Platonic model and authority for the four main divisions of the reading order.

III. I said at the beginning of this paper that I would suggest the thesis that the nine tetralogies are in several respects superior to Iamblichus' canon as a reading course in Plato's dialogues. I hope that the reasons for this claim have become a little clearer as I have tried to bring to light what I believe to be the principle themes around which the tetralogies are organized.

I acknowledge at the outset that the tetralogies fail in several fundamental ways as a tool for the understanding of Plato. These failures derive from an important error, which is the impulse to synthesize the different dialogues without also keeping in mind their specific differences. Plato never intended that all the dialogues should form a coherent sequence, much less a complete philosophical education; consequently, any attempt to establish such a sequence necessarily has something fraudulent about it, and is obtained at the cost of emphasizing similarities between dialogues while sacrificing what is unique and different in every dialogue: the *Symposium,* for example, becomes a few paragraphs of Diotima's speech, in order to be the culmination of the "dialectical" dialogues.

This impulse to synthesize, however, was the very spirit of the age, and no commentator on Plato living at the time could expect to escape it. Once we grant Thrasyllus, or the inventor of the tetralogies, this impulse, it becomes possible to argue that he produced a relatively successful reading course, one certainly superior to Iamblichus' canon. In Iamblichus the synthesizing went too far: not only did he "reduce"[38] all the Platonic dialogues to his twelve selected ones, but he also "reduced" these twelve to the *Timaeus* and *Parmenides*. When Professor Hathaway says of the Neoplatonists that "we cannot suppress the suspicion that they believed that every dialogue was about the same thing,"[39] he is pointing out a very real tendency in their exegesis. A continuous movement in this direction can be traced in the history of the philosophical "characters" or "types" of the dialogues. There were originally eight of them; in Thrasyllus' tetralogies only four are significant, the logical, maieutic, agonistic (combining the anatreptic and endeictic), and political; eventually Iamblichus had only two, the physical and the theological.[40]

The difference between Thrasyllus' four dialogue-types and those of Iamblichus, however, goes beyond the difference in number. Thrasyllus' groups of dialogues express what really are pervasive themes in Plato's dialogues: knowledge and dialectic; midwifery, love, and education; sophistry; and politics. In other words, Thrasyllus' categories come out of the dialogues themselves. Iamblichus' categories of "physical" and "theological", on the contrary, and his association of the dialogues with different levels of virtues, are arbitrary categories forced on the dialogues to make them conform to the dogmatic and theological Plato of Neoplatonism.

If I am right that the dialogues of Thrasyllus' second group describe an ascent to the Good, then Thrasyllus' Plato, too, is theological, but unlike Iamblichus' Plato, he is not only that. In Thrasyllus' tetralogies the ascent to the Good occurs early in the reading course, and it is not the culminating event it seems to be for Iamblichus, who borrowed this part of the tetralogies and threw away the rest. The reader of the tetralogies, after ascending out of the Cave with Plato the theologian in the *Symposium* and the *Phaedrus*, descends back into the Cave again immediately with Socrates the midwife. Prof. Hathaway has summed up Iamblichus' interpretation of the Platonic dialogues by saying it leaves out both Socrates himself and the characteristically Socratic sense of aporia.[41] Thrasyllus' tetralogies do at least give us Socrates—not, I think, a genuinely aporetic one, wise only in the knowledge that he knows nothing, but a Socrates nevertheless, one who has already achieved wisdom, but who will be midwife, lover, and teacher to other human beings.

Finally, it can be said that the tetralogies leave us with a truer picture of the importance of political virtue in Plato's thought. In Iamblichus' canon political virtue is the least of the virtues to be learned from the study of Plato. The reader concerns himself with it just after reading the introductory *Alcibiades I,* and then moves on to higher virtues. In the tetralogies, on the contrary, the political dialogues have equal standing with the logical or maieutic or agonistic groups; they are in no way subordinated to the ascent to the Good contained within the logical group. In fact, the reader comes to Plato's political treatises last of all, after much experience of Plato; far from being simply an intermediate stage, the political dialogues in Thrasyllus' reading order actually conclude and perfect the reader's philosophical education.[42]

NOTES

1.   Proclus, *Commentary on Alcibiades I,* ed. Westerink, 11, 11-17.

2.   *Anonymous Prolegomena to Platonic Philosophy,* ed. Westerink, 29, 12-34.

3.   R. F. Hathaway, "The Neoplatonic Interpretation of Plato: Remarks on its Decisive Characteristics", *Journal of the History of Philosophy* 7 (1969) 20-22.

4.   *Anon. Prol.* 26, 17-18. τούτων [sc. τῶν διαλόγων] δὲ ἄξιον ἐστιν τὴν τάξιν ζητῆσαι, διότι καὶ τούτου ἠξίωσαν πάντες πράττεσθαι.

5.   The text of the anonymous *Prolegomena* appears to have a gap at 26, 31-32, εἶτα ἐρχόμεθα μετὰ τούτους εἰς τὸν ⟨. . .⟩ περὶ φυσικῶν διδάσκοντα and mentions only ten dialogues in all, including the *Timaeus* and *Parmenides.* Proclus,

however, definitely states that there were twelve in the canon (*Comm on Alec. 1*, 11, 15-17). Westerink, xxxvii-xxxix, suggest excellent reasons for inserting the *Sophist* and *Statesman* in the supposed gap, and this has been accepted by A. J. Festugière, "L'ordre de lecture des dialogues de Platon aux Ve/VIe siècles", *Mus. Helv.* 26 (1969) 284-85; but Hathaway, p. 23, n. 23, still expresses doubt.

6. *Anon. Prol.* 26, 14-16 and 18-34. The anonymous goes on to add that "some think that one should 'do' the *Laws* and the *Republic* also, καὶ τοὺς Νόμους καὶ τὰς πολιτείας πράττειν ἀξιοῦσί τινες."

7. *Anon. Prol.* 26, 5-13 mentions this grouping, but passes it over as for brevity's sake and because it was "not particularly useful" (μὴ πάνυ τι χρησιμεύουσαν).

8. Only Thrasyllus is mentioned by Diogenes Laertius (III. 56-62), who cites him directly. But Albinus (*Eisagoge* IV, 12-13, ed. Hermann) also speaks of Dercyllides (ταύτης τῆς δόξης εἰσὶ Δερκυλλίδης καὶ θράβυλλος.) Dercyllides is otherwise known from a few citations in Theon, Proclus, and Simplicius, but nothing in these citations adds to our knowledge of his use of the tetralogies, or even enables us to declare with any confidence when he lived. The common assertion that he preceded Thrasyllus in framing the tetralogies depends for evidence, apart from the inconclusive order of the names as Albinus gives them, upon a sentence in Varro's *De Lingua Latina* (VII.37), in which Varro apparently refers to the myth of the *Phaedo* with the words, "Plato in IIII", which seems to mean "in the fourth (dialogue)". Between 47-45 B.C., then, Varro may have known of some listing or edition of the dialogues in which the *Phaedo* was fourth, as it is in the tetralogies; but Thrasyllus lived until A.D. 36, and cannot have been Varro's authority. Since Dercyllides is the only other name to which we can definitely attach such an arrangement in this period, it is plausible to think that Varro was referring to the tetralogies of Dercyllides.

9. *Schol. Vet. in Juvenalem Sat.* VI. 576: "Thrasylus [sic] multarum artium scientiam professus postremo se dedit

Platonicae sectae ac deinde mathesi, in qua praecipue viguit apud Tiberium, cum quo sub honore eiusdem artis (in) familiaritate vixit. . ." By the time of Tacitus there were legends about his skill in predicting the future (*Ann.* VI. 21); according to Dio Cassius (*Hist. Rom.* LVIII. 27.1) Thrasyllus accurately foretold the day and hour of his own death. But he seems also to have had a reputation for less arcane knowledge: in the third century Longinus mentions his interpretations of the "Pythagorean and Platonist first principles" together with those of Moderatus, Cronius, and Numenius (Longinus *apud* Porphyry, *Life of Plotinus*, 20, 71-76).

Friedrich Nietzche conceived a remarkable fascination with "die düstre faustische Persönlichkeit Thrasylls" (Friedrich Nietzsche, *Werke*, 3. Band, ed. H. J. Mette and K. Schlechta, München 1935, p. 349). Inquiring how the practitioner of so feeble a science as astrology could escape the suspicions of a Tiberius, Nietzsche concluded: "Es müssen da persönliche Eigenschaften gewesen sein, etwa eine strenge asketische Haltung, ein Auge voller Trauer, eine würdevolle Gestalt, tiefe Stimme und dergl. was Tiberius in dem Glauben bestärkte, er habe es mit einem ungewöhnlichen überlegen(en) Menschenkind zu thun" (*Werke*, 3. Band, p. 366).

10. Theon's work has perished in the original, but was known to the Arabs. The tenth-century encyclopedist Ibn al-Nadîm says under the heading "Theon": "He was a zealous partisan of Plato. Among his books there was *Sequence of Reading Plato's Books and the Titles of his Compositions*" (Ibn al-Nadîm, *The Fihrist*, tr. Bayard Dodge, N. Y. 1970, p. 614). Al-Nadîm ascribes brief and unfortuanately confused statements to Theon which probably derive from this work (in which we may recognize a standard introduction to the Platonic dialogues, comparable to Albinus' *Eisagoge*, Diogenes Laertius III. 48-51 and 56-66, and the *Anon. Prol.* 13-27). One such statement shows that Theon discussed the tetralogies: "Theon said: 'Plato arranged his writings for reading. Each group, consisting of four books, he [Plato] called a tetralogy'" (*Fihrist*, pp. 593-4, Dodge).

Al-Nadim also gives a list of dialogues on the authority of Theon which do not reproduce the tetralogies, and which I believe to be based on the traditional philosophical characters, or 'types' of the Platonic dialogues; but J. Lippert and K. von Fritz are probably correct to assume that Theon did not intend this second order as a substitution for the tetralogies (see von Fritz, "Theon" *RE* A10, col 2069). Another Arab author, Ibn Abi Usaybiyah, reproduces a recognizable version of the tetralogical ordering which may also derive from Theon; however, he does not mention Theon by name (*'Uyun al-Anba*, ed. A. Müller, Königsberg 1884, pp. 53-54). Miss Tamar Frank of Yale University has very kindly supplied me with English translations of the relevant Arabic texts.

11. Albinus, *Eisagoge* IV (p. 149, 1-17 Hermann).
12. Diogenes Laertius III. 56-61.
13. See below, p. 65.
14. *Anon. Prol.* 24, 20; 25, 29. Since so much of the material treated by the anonymous author under this rubric had also been dealt with by Proclus (Westerink, xxxii-xxxiii), and since the anonymous introduces certain objections made by Proclus into his discussion of the tetralogies, it is likely that Proclus, too, discussed the tetralogical ordering. It is entirely possible, in fact, that the grouping of 32 dialogues which the anonymous ascribes to Proclus may simply have been the traditional nine tetralogies, less the four dialogues which Proclus omitted for reasons of his own.
15. Two theories are held about the date of origin of the tetralogies: (1) that they were drawn up by Plato's successors in the Academy at a very early date, or at least the earliest date consistent with the presence of the spurious dialogues in the corpus. The supporters of this theory have included Wilamowitz, *Platon* II (Berlin 1920), p. 324; Bickel, *Rhein. Mus.* 92 (1943-44), pp. 94-96 and 97-159; Erbse, *Geschichte der Textüberlieferung* I (Zürich 1961), pp. 219-221; and recently Pfeiffer, *History of Classical Scholarship* (Oxford 1968), pp. 196-197.

(2) that they were drawn up in the first century B.C., either by Dercyllides or by some near contemporary of his and of Varro's (see note 8, above). This view was first proposed by K. F. Hermann, *De Thrasyllo grammatico et mathematico* (Göttingen 1853, p. 13, who believed, however, that Dercyllides was responsible only for the first tetralogy, Thrasyllus for the rest. The case for the date in the first century was stated in its most cogent form by Usener, *Gött. Nachr.* 1892, Nr. 2, pp. 25-50; Nr. 6, pp. 181-215 (=*Kleine Schriften* III, pp. 104-162). See also Alline, *Histoire du texte de Platon* (Paris, 1915), p. 113; Susemihl, *Philologus* 54 (1895), p. 573; and Chroust *Hermes* 93 (1965), pp. 34-46.

　　For reasons too complicated to discuss here, I think (2) the more likely explanation.

16. "Die grosse Konstante der Platonüberlieferung," E. Bickel, *Rhein. Mus.* 92 (1943-44), pp. 100-101.

17. Albinus, *Eisagoge* IV (P. 149, 1-13 Hermann): ἐπεὶ οὖν τεθεωρήκαμεν τὴν διαφορὰν αὐτῶν ὡς πέφυκε γίγνεσθαι καὶ τοὺς χαρακτῆρας, ἐπὶ τούτοις λέγωμεν, ἀπὸ ποίων διαλόγων δεῖ ἀρχομένους ἐντυγχάνειν τῷ Πλάτωνος λόγῳ. διάφοροι γὰρ δόξαι γεγόνασιν· οἱ μὲν ἀπὸ τῶν Ἐπιστολῶν ἄρχονται, οἱ δὲ ἀπὸ τοῦ Θεάγους· εἰσὶ δὲ οἱ κατὰ τετραλογίαν διελόντες αὐτοὺς καὶ τάττουσι πρώτην τετραλογίαν περιέχουσαν τὸν Εὐθύφρονα καὶ τὴν Ἀπολογίαν καὶ τὸν Κρίτωνα καὶ τὸν Φαίδωνα . . . . ταύτης τῆς δόξης εἰσὶ Δερκυλλίδης καὶ Θράσυλλος.

18. Al-Nadim, *The Fihrist*, pp. 593-594 Dodge. Ibn al-Qifti (A.D. 1172-1248) reproduces the same statement, but appears simply to be copying Nadim Ta'rikh al-Hukama', ed. J. Lippert, Leipzig 1903, pp. 17-18).

19. Diogenes Laertius III.36, 20-25: Θράσυλλος δέ φησι καὶ κατὰ τὴν τραγικὴν τετραλογίαν ἐκδοῦναι αὐτὸν [sc. Plato] τοὺς διαλόγους (cf. *Anon. Prol.* 24, 20). This statement does not necessarily mean that Thrasyllus thought his *own* tetralogies were anything more than an approximation of the original ones.

　　Theon's extant work *Mathematics Useful for the Reading of Plato* cites Thrasyllus frequently, which suggests the possibility that Theon's lost work on the dialogues, called by Nadim *The Sequence of Reading Plato's Books and the Titles of his Compositions,* may also go back to Thrasyllus.

20. Diogenes Laertius IX. 45-49.
21. Porphyry, *Life of Plotinus,* 26.
22. Porphyry, *Life of Plotinus,* 24: ἑκάστῃ δὲ ἐννεάδι τὰ οἰκεῖα φέρων συναφόρησα δοὺς καὶ τάξιν πρώτην τοῖς ἐλαφροτέροις προβλήμασιν.
23. Although modern scholars have not noticed the significance of the tetralogies as a reading course, the attempt to find an explanation for the order of the dialogues within the tetralogies is by no means a new one: see H. Alline, *Histoire du texte de Platon* (Paris 1915), pp. 115-117; and U. von Wilamowitz, *Platon* II (Berlin 1920), pp. 324-325. Both of these discussions, which are too long to summarize here, contain many valuable observations; but both men were concerned primarily with the mechanical process of getting from Plato's own "trilogies" to the tetralogies, and so tend to explain the placing of individual dialogues in terms of filling "gaps". I wish to claim, on the contrary, that the dialogues were deliberately arranged to form a systematic and coherent progression from beginning to end.
24. Primarily Diogenes Laertius III. 56-61; Albinus *Eisagoge* IV, 1-14; and the *Anonymous Prolegomena* 24.20-25.24.
25. Diogenes Laertius III. 57, 5-6: πρώτην μὲν οὖν τετραλογίαν τίθησι τὴν κοινὴν ὑπόθεσιν ἔχουσαν· παραδεῖξαι γὰρ βούλεται ὁποῖος ἄν εἴη ὁ τοῦ φιλοσόφου βίος.
26. There are at least two ways of construing the word τήν in the first sentence:
(1) τὴν goes with ἔχουσαν, both referring back to τετραλογίαν. It might be inferred from this, however, that the first tetralogy is the only one which has a common subject, and that the rest do not, while in fact Thrasyllus and the inventor of the tetralogies must certainly have ascribed common subjects to at least the second and the eighth tetralogies, which are at least partially suggested by Plato himself.

(2) τὴν goes with κοινὴν ὑπόθεσιν, i.e., "he establishes a
first tetralogy having the common subject; for he wishes to
give a paradigm of what the philosopher's life is like." To
speak of the first tetralogy containing *the* common subject
would appear to refer this common subject not
only to the first tetralogy, but to the entire series, so that
we might paraphrase it, "Thrasyllus establishes a first
tetralogy having (within itself) the common subject (of the
whole reading sequence)". This would be a very significant
addition to our knowledge of the tetralogies if it is what
Diogenes meant. It should be noted that this way of taking
the sentence derives some support from a similar turn of
phrase in Albinus' description of the same tetralogy (*Eis.*
IV, p. 149, 6-7 Hermann): τάττουσι πρώτην
τετραλογίαν περιέχουσαν τὸν Εὐθύφρονα κτλ. If τὴν went
with ἔχουσαν in Diogenes, we might expect a similar τὴν
before περιέχουσαν in Albinus; instead, we find τὸν
Εὐθύφρονα used in the same way as τήν κοινὴν ὑπόθεσιν.

27. Albinus' account of the first tetralogy is no help, since
although it roughly corresponds to that found in Diogenes,
it diverges in a significant detail. After mentioning that the
first tetralogy contains the *Euthyphro, Apology, Crito,*
and *Phaedo,* Albinus goes on to give the reasons for their
inclusion together:

> . . . the *Euthyphro,* since in it the trial is an-
> nounced to Socrates; the *Apology,* since it was neces-
> sary for him to give a defence; next the *Crito,* because
> of the homily in the prison; then the *Phaedo*, since in it
> Socrates reaches the end of his life. Of this opinion are
> Dercyllides and Thrasyllus; but they seem to me to have
> intended to apply an order to personae and to circum-
> stances of lives, which is perhaps useful for other
> purposes, but not for what we want now. . . .

Albinus refers the first tetralogy to *specific* personae and
what happen to them, that is, to Socrates and his trial.
Diogenes, on the other hand, speaks of these personae and
events as paradigmatic, referring not to Socrates but to
"the philosopher" in general. Since Albinus clearly states

his interpretation of the first tetralogy as a personal opinion (δοκοῦσι μοι) "they seem to me . . ." it is likely that if either of these two sources preserves Thrasyllus' own explanation, it is Diogenes rather than Albinus.

28. Proclus, *Commentary on the Parmenides*, p. 630, 37ff. Cousin: εἰσὶ δέ τινες καὶ γεγόνασι τῶν ἔμπροσθεν, οἳ τὸν τοῦ διαλόγου τοῦδε σκοπὸν εἰς λογικὴν ἀνέπεμψαν γυμνασίαν, τὴν μὲν ἐπιγραφὴν καίτοι παμπάλαιον οὖσαν τὴν Περὶ τῶν ἰδεῶν ἀτιμάντες . . .

29. Albinus, *Didaskalikos* VI. (p. 159, 4-7): τοὺς δὲ ὑποθετικοὺς ἐν πολλοῖς βιβλίοις εὑρήσομεν ἐρωτωμένους ὑπ' αὐτοῦ, μάλιστα δ' ἐν τῷ Παρμενίδῃ τοιούτους εὕροιμεν ἄν λόγους.

30. *Did.* VI. (p. 159, 34-35): καὶ μὴν τὰς δέκα κατηγορίας ἔν τε τῷ Παρμενίδῃ καὶ ἐν ἄλλοις ὑπέδειξε . . . .
Galen, *De Placitis Hippocratis et Platonis*, p. 767, 10ff. Müller speaking of ἡ διαιρετικὴ μέθοδος: ἧς τὴν μὲν γυμνασίαν ὁ Πλάτων ἐν Σοφιστῇ καὶ Πολιτικῷ πεποίηται, τὴν δὲ ἐξ αὐτῆς χρείαν ἐπέδειξεν οὐκ ἐν τούτοις μόνον, ἀλλὰ σαφέστατα μὲν ἅμα καὶ τελεώτατα κατά τε Φίληβον καὶ Φαῖδρον.

31. Galen, *De Placitis Hippocratis et Platonis*, p. 767, 10ff. Müller speaking of ἡ διαιρετικὴ μέθοδος: ἧς τὴν μὲν γυμνασίαν ὁ πλάτων ἐν Σοφιστῇ καὶ πολιτικῷ πεποίηται, τὴν δὲ ἐξ αὐτῆς χρείαν ἐπέδειξεν οὐκ ἐν τούτοις μόνον, ἀλλὰ σαφέστατα μεν ἅμα καὶ τελεώτατα κατά τε Φίληβον καὶ φαῖδροη.

32. As reconstructed by Westerink, xl. – It is interesting to compare the recent study by E. Wyller, *Der späte Platon* (Hamburg 1970), in which it is argued that Plato describes an ascent from the Cave in the *Cratylus* and the *Theaetetus;* then describes the synthesis achieved once outside the Cave, in the *Sophist, Statesman,* and *Parmenides;* and finally describes the descent back, in the *Philebus, Phaedrus, Timaeus, Laws, Epinomis.*

33. See Diogenes Laertius III.49.

34. H. Alline, *Histoire du texte de Platon,* p. 116, emphasizes the theme of love in these dialogues. Counting the *Symposium* and *Phaedrus* among them (mistakenly, I

believe), he speaks of them as "un groupe de dix dialogues érotiques où Socrate converse avec des jeunes gens ou à propos de jeunes gens que généralement il est censé d'aimer."

35. Wilamowitz, *Platon* II, p. 325: "Von der Sechsten [Tetralogie], die die grossen Kämpfe mit den Sophisten enthält, wies der Euthydem durch dem Protreptikos des Kleinias auf die Fünfte zurück. — Both Alline and Wilamowitz recognized a grouping of dialogues on the sophists, but Wilamowitz excluded the *Menexenus* from it, and Alline the *Ion* and the *Menexenus*.

36. Albinus, *Eisagoge* IV (p. 149, 12-14 Hermann): ταύτης τῆς δόξης εἰσὶ Δερκυλλίδης καὶ Θράσυλλος, δοκοῦσι δέ μοι προσώποις καὶ βίων περιστάσεσιν ἠθεληκέναι τάξιν ἐπιθεῖναι.

37. Albinus, *Eisagoge* III (p. 148, 28-29 Hermann): ... ὁ μὲν ὑφηγητικὸς τῶν πραγμάτων στοχάζεται, ὁ δέ ζητητικός τῶν προσώπων.

38. *Anon.* Prol. 26, 12-16: λέγομεν δὲ ὃ ὁ θεῖος Ἰάμβλιχος ἐποίησεν. αὐτὸς τοίνυν πάντας εἰς ιβ΄ διήρει διαλόγους, καὶ τούτων τοὺς μὲν φυσικοὺς ἔλεγεν, τοὺς δὲ Θεολογικούς· πάλιν δὲ τοὺς δώδεκα συνήρει εἰς δύο, εἴς τε τὸν Τίμαιον καὶ τὸν Παρμενίδην, ὧν τὸν μὲν Τίμαιον ἐπὶ πᾶσι τοῖς φυσικοῖς, τὸν δὲ ταρμενίδην τοῖς Θεολογικοῖς. Westerink translates διήρει and συνήρει as "reduced". Hathaway, p. 23 n. 24, suggests "abridged".

39. Hathaway, p. 25.

40. *Anon. Prol.* 26,14.

41. Hathaway, p. 26.

42. This paper, written in 1973, was based upon an unfinished chapter of my doctoral dissertation, and the argument of the first two sections of this paper was subsequently enlarged and improved by a number of revisions. The changes, however, have been changes of detail, and my interpretation of the tetralogies remains essentially the same as that proposed here. The final version may now be seen in Ch. 3 of "The Organization of the Platonic Corpus Between the First Century B.C. and the Second Century A.D.", unpublished dissertation (on microfilm), Yale University 1974.

PART TWO

The Interpretation of Neoplatonism

Plotinus' Approach to Categorical Theory

Emory University

I

Contemporary writers on Plotinus and his Neoplatonism have found it difficult to agree on his definitive position concerning the value and relevance of Aristotle's categories for understanding the nature of the sensible world. W. R. Inge, a generation ago, stated that "the long discussion of the categories in the Sixth Ennead seems to me . . . the least interesting part of the whole book."[1] On the other hand, we have such interpreters as P. V. Pistorius who find this part of Plotinus' philosophy not only theoretically significant but also a definite advancement in the history of the subject. Pistorius has gone as far as to say that "the categories of Plotinus are the expression of his superiority over Greek thinkers before his time."[2] The evaluative aspect of this view need not concern us for the moment. The issue which deserves close examination as being directly related to our theme is whether Plotinus retained the Aristotelian categories in their original meaning as giving a fundamentally correct analysis of the most general properties of sensible objects. Opinion is divided on this crucial issue between (a) those who say that Plotinus subordinated the Aristotelian categories of the sensible to the Platonic Forms of the intelligible world, and (b) those who take the position that Plotinus accepted Aristotle's categories as proposed but limited their usefulness exclusively to the domain of the sensible.

The position I take in this paper is closer to (a) but for a number of reasons I have found it necessary to go beyond its mild claims. Thus I wish to argue here that certain profound differences in the world-views of Plotinus and the philosophers of the Hellenic period, Plato and Aristotle in particular, led Plotinus to a radical transformation of the metaphysical concepts he borrowed from both Plato and Aristotle. On the theoretical side, it should be noted that whenever Plotinus discusses categorical concepts, he is always viewing Aristotle as an enemy of Platonism;[3] again, it is he, not Plato, who is regarding the highest genera of the *Sophist* as rival categorical principles. On the cultural side, Plotinus' Oriental and strong religious concerns, important as these are to his conception of the One and Good, union with which is the goal of life, as beyond Being, necessarily molded his theoretical orientation and called for a reworking of the significance of (i) the five highest genera of the intelligible world and (ii) the highest types of predication of the sensible world. Hence, when discussing Plotinus' indebtedness to the terminology of his predecessors it is misleading to assume that he puts their conceptual apparatus to the same use. It is the purpose of this paper to exhibit in general outline the basic considerations that define the Plotinian approach to categorical theory and also expose the grounds on which he builds his case for recasting the meanings of categorical concepts.

Two basic considerations appear fundamental to Plotinus' critique and recasting of the classical categorical theories but only one of these pertains to his approach to Plato's highest genera, whereas both are needed in the case of Aristotle's concepts.

1. The One is the source of the Intellectual Principle and hence above predication.[4] Being ultimate, it is beyond the predicative relevance of the highest genera. Furthermore, since the realm to which Plato's highest genera pertain is not ultimate but derivative, their ontological significance cannot possibly be that which Plato assigned to them when he understood them as having ontological primacy.

2. The sensible world for Plotinus is neither ultimate in the Aristotelian sense, nor the work of the Demiurge as depicted in Plato's *Timaeus.* Hence the Aristotelian categories are not the appropriate concepts the sensible realm requires for its intelligibility precisely because its ontological structure and

significance are to be understood in ways that cannot be fully illumined even on Platonic grounds. If so, the referential adequacy of Aristotle's categories must be adjudicated at the level of the Intellectual Principle and only after the logical and ontological significations of the Platonic highest genera have been properly worked out on exclusively Plotinian criteria.

Thus, by way of ordering these tasks we have: (a) the recasting of Plato's highest genera in the light of Plotinus' own view of *Nous* as the first emanation from the One; (b) the recasting of the Aristotelian categorical concepts in the light of the redefined functions of the highest genera designed now to refer to and explore conceptually the Intelligible Realm; (c) the recasting of the Aristotelian categories in the light of (a) and (b) to refer correctly to Plotinus' own view of the nature of the sensible object. Given this program, it should not be too difficult to understand why Plotinus insists on saying that if the same predicates are said of both sensibles and intelligibles, the particular sensibles admit such predicates only equivocally. Thus no problem in the methodology of categorical significa-tion can be solved apart from the fundamentals of Plotinus' ontology.

II

Philip Merlan adopted the view that Plotinus accepted the Aristotelian categories but limited them to the sensible world:

> Plotinus refused to accept any doctrine of categories which would apply the same concepts to the world of the intelligence and that of the sensible. When he developed his own doctrine of categories . . . he applied Aristotelian categories only to the realm of the sensible. As categories of the world of the intellect, he applied the five genera of the *Sophist*. Prophyry did not follow Plotinus; nor did other Platonists.[5]

Professor John M. Rist defended the position of the subordination of Aristotelian (and Stoic) categories to "thor-oughly Platonic principles":

> Although no one can deny the difficulty and sometimes the tedium of this section of the *Enneads* it has consider-able philosophical value. It appears to be the opinion of certain polemical interpreters that Plotinus' whole discus-

sion is misguided—and so it is if looked at solely from an
Aristotelian point of view. For the fact is that Plotinus'
critique of both the Aristotelian and Stoic categories
depends upon certain of his own thoroughly Platonic
principles. And these principles need clarification not
merely to show the presuppositions with which Plotinus
approaches the Aristotelian categories but for their own
sake, since in the section of the *Enneads* devoted to the
categories we find almost the only passages where Plotinus
deals with the metaphysical status of the sensible object.[6]

It would not be necessary to treat these two positions
separately since any remarks on the claims of the "subordination" position pertain *a forteriori* to the other. One must
readily concede that the immediate impression the reader has
from a first reading of *Ennead* VI is that Plotinus, reacting
strongly against the Aristotelian principles needed to render
intelligible the particularized sensible *ousia*, proceeded to
establish a modified version of Plato's highest genera to replace
Aristotle's categories. It is a correct impression but it does not
take us very far.

Professor Rist is correct in suggesting that we concentrate
on understanding the Plotinian position on the status of the
sensible object, but to say that the principles upon which
Plotinus depends for his critique are "throughly Platonic" is
misleading. As we hope to show, the context of Plotinus' theory
of categories is defined by considerations that are far more
Hellenistic than they are Hellenic, and this applies equally to
the so-called Platonism of Plotinus. The consequence of the
position I take in this paper is that Plotinus may emerge as more
original than he is usually taken to be, but also that he departs
so far from the classical outlook of Plato and Aristotle as to
raise doubts about calling him "the last of the Greeks." In fact,
he is closer to the Middle Ages and Renaissance thought, and in
a great many cases to modern philosophy than many a historian
of philosophy has been prepared to recognize. To this topic we
will return later in the paper.

The basic question that awaits an answer is: if we assume
that Plotinus has a theory of categories comparable in interest,
say, to that of Aristotle and the Stoics, to what entities does his

set of categorical principles pertain and what is their status? In this connection we need to understand what Plotinus had in mind when he discussed the sensible object. Three things must be remembered here: (a) Aristotle and Plotinus differ significantly in their approaches to the sensible realm and hold profoundly diverging interpretations on the nature of the sensible object. (b) Plotinus places the sensible object in a light very different from the way Aristotle does, to the point that his way of understanding the Aristotelian categories of sensible *ousia* is controlled by his determination to relegate the sensible *ousia* to the status of pseudo-substance. Thus, according to Plotinus, the Aristotelian *tode ti*, the *ousia prote* of the *Categories*, is not really *ousia* in the highest meaning of the word; this being the case, the Aristotelian way of understanding the relationship between *ousia* and quality in the sensible object must be rejected. (c) Plotinus deliberately alters the meanings of Aristotle's concepts for the analysis of *ousia* through his own position on the nature of the sensible, to wit, that the sensible is something analysable into a finite number of immanent qualities each of which is dependent on its corresponding form. If I am correct in these observations, it would follow that Plotinus' critique of Aristotle is more devastating in intent than has hitherto been suspected. For it would appear that the Aristotelian categories are not simply inapplicable to the realm of the intelligible; they are inadequate even for the task of understanding the nature and properties of the sensible object. Recognition of this radical aspect of Plotinus' criticism makes him the theoretical forerunner of all modern thinkers who rejected Aristotle's conception of physical substance and the categories as the ultimate types of attribution and property analysis.

III

Let us assume that Plotinus' uttermost purpose was to delineate the role of reason as paving the path for the soul's union with the One—there is good ground for this position since Plotinus' concern extends beyond that of the knower. In *Ennead* IV. 8. 1, Plotinus speaks unmistakably about his *union with the One:*

Many times it has happened; lifted out of the body into myself; becoming external to all other things and self-encentered; beholding a marvellous beauty; then, more than ever, assured of community with the loftiest order; enacting the noblest life, acquiring identity with the divine; stationing within It by having attained that activity; poised above whatsoever within the Intellectual is less than the Supreme: yet, there comes the moment of descent from intellection to reasoning, and after that sojourn in the divine, I ask myself how it happens that I can now be descending, and how did the Soul ever enter into my body, the Soul which, even within the body, is the high thing it has shown itself to be.[7]

It is this ontological union with the source of *being* that determines the place to be assigned to categorical theory and how the highest genera as concepts must be employed for the attainment of the goals of knowledge.[8] It would seem then that if categorical thinking in Aristotle's sense has a role to play in the return or *nostos* of the soul, this is limited to understanding the sensible world, and hence it is only propaedeutic to the higher dialectic employed in the exploration of the intelligible realm. Small wonder, then, that the application of the Aristotelian categories to the ethical, above and beyond the sensible, is abhorrent to Plotinus. To talk of *being* as having many meanings (*pollachōs legomenon*) in the realm of the sensible is one thing, but to do the same in the intelligible realm is quite another.

Be that as it may, Plotinus is unable to accept Aristotle's views on the relevance of categorical theory even to the sensible realm unless the categories are decidedly recast in the light of the Neoplatonic views on ontology so that they may be assigned new functions deriving from a higher authority. It appears, then that Plotinus' position is not just a case of outright or uncritical rejection of Aristotelianism in the field of categorical thought; the issue is further complicated by the complex case of his half-hearted Platonism. If we may speak of his goal in this connection, it seems to involve more than the restoring of the highest genera at the heart of the conceptual analysis of the intelligible realm. More fundamentally, he is concerned with assigning to these genera new axiological functions above and beyond anything suggested in Plato's *Sophist.*

We must ask: what sort of Platonist is Plotinus? One thing shines clearly thoroughout the *Enneads:* Plotinus is bent on including into Plato's universe a kind of world which was hardly familiar or even of immediate interest to Plato, but it was a universe Plotinus could not do philosophy without. That Plato's Dialogues lend themselves to a broadening of their conceptual and mythological boundaries is a most relevant fact, but too vast to be treated in this paper. Suffice it to say that Plotinus was neither the first nor the last to inflate and expand the dramatic universe found in Plato's works. The Neoplatonism Plotinus ushered in was one he found in the making and to which he gave a most powerful and decisive direction by intensifying the concern for the intelligible, to be more precise, the *superlunary* or, if one prefers, the trans-physical universe. The outlook was sustained by a religious fervor that found in Plotinus a willing and dedicated advocate. By seeking to complete and round off this outlook, Plotinus shifted also the center of gravity of the ancient world from the naturalistic ethic of the Greeks with its emphasis on the excellences of the *politēs* to the trans-physical quest of philosophical salvation with its unrequited desire for the flight or rather the return to, and union of the soul with, the source of all *Being.* The sensible world, its processes, its principles, kinds of being, its conditions and ends, the environment it provides for human beings, natural and political, the excellences it demands for the understanding and the completion of human happiness, all these and more became secondary concerns and only preliminaries to the new Platonists. They created the trend of reading the *Timaeus* with religious zeal but hardly any concern for Plato's humor, irony, least of all his authentic Athenian passion for the fate and fortune of the Greek *polis.*

What the Neoplatonists on the whole ushered in during the critical times of the late Hellenistic period was a kind of intense awareness of a realm of cosmic existence that could make life worth living and the soul worth having. They cultivated this realm with the dedication of a single-minded lover, bent on inventing even the form of the beloved if he had to do it. It was the probing into the imaginatively expanded superlunary region of the universe and the tracing of its origins back to the source, its goodness, so to speak, that fired their intellectual imaginations. In the process, they found in this region things Plato never dreamt of, things far beyond the limits of Aristotle's ontology, and in general, things no Hellenic thinker was prepared to acknowledge without serious reservations. Yet it was a realm, in principle at least, familiar to the Greeks, the understanding of which some of the best minds had made it their highest goal. But Plato was not a Neoplatonist; nor was Aristotle. That both had contributed to the logical exploration of a universe far exceeding the boundaries of the sensible domain does not make them Plotinus' intended forefathers, for the Neoplatonic universe, in its ethical and metaphysical aspects, had in a serious way turned its back on the classical outlook.

The Hellenistic mode of philosophizing found in Neoplatonism an effective medium to transpose the levels of value familiar to classical Platonism as levels of supersensible reality. To this spiritual world the Aristotelian categories of being were their sensuous design. Although Plotinus assigned new functions and tasks to the revitalized highest genera of Plato's *Sophist,* he recognized that even the recharging of these principles could not carry the philosopher beyond the level of *Nous.* Even the higher dialectic fell short of what was needed for "the flight of the alone to the alone." This last step toward the final ecstacy Plotinus must take alone. Here he is no longer Plato's disciple. Being neither master nor disciple, he is all by himself, except for Porphyry's witness. In hope of losing the self, he concludes a *nostos* of the soul to the realm where the categories do not obtain and even above that which the higher dialectic illumines. It is a *nostos* that makes Plotinus the first of the non-Greeks.[9]

IV

The Neoplatonic conception of the intelligible world to which Plotinus subscribes involves more than a difference in content from what Plato believed it to be. It called for a new approach to the intelligible beings (*noēta onta*), and hence a categorical theory appropriate to them. The human act of intellection or *noesis* must be suitable to the object of intellection. To meet his task he needed two things in order to develop an adequate set of categorical concepts: (1) examine the possibilities the Aristotelian concepts have for being redefined so as to serve the Neoplatonic intelligible beings; (2) return to Plato's highest genera of the *Sophist*. Thus, in *Ennead* V. 1. 4, where he discusses "The Three Initial Hypostases," he states:

> ... the Intellectual Principle is all and therefore its entire content is simultaneously present in that identity: this is pure being in eternal actuality; ... and everything, in that entire content, is Intellectual-Principle and Authentic-Existence; and the total of all in Intellectual-Principle active and Being entire. (MacKenna)

Further in the same chapter he adds the following statement:

> Thus the Primals (the first 'Categories,' *ta prōta*) are seen to be: Intellectual-Principle (*nous*); Existence (*on*); Difference (*heterotēs*); Identity (*tautotēs*): we must include also Motion (*kinēsis*) and Rest (*stasis*): Motion provides for the intellectual act, Rest preserves identity as Difference gives at once a knower and a known, for, failing this, all is one, and silent. (MacKenna)

The chapter concludes: "The Intellectual Cosmos thus a manifold, number and Quantity arise: Quality is the specific character of Ideas which stand as the principles for which all else derives" (MacKenna). The variations of this list of *noēta* which we find in VI, 2, 15 and VI, 2, 8 need not concern us here since they do not raise relevant fundamental problems. What is important, however, is to note that Plotinus (a) is not strictly adopting Plato's highest genera, and (b) is using them in novel ways to develop a theory of his own and to criticize Aristotle. Plotinus' understanding of the meaning of the Aristotelian categories, and why they do not apply to his supersensible reality, is clearly stated in *Ennead* VI, 2, 4:

> If we had to ascertain the nature of body (*sōmatos physin*) and the place it holds in the universe, surely we should take some sample of body, say stone, and examine into what constituents it may be divided. There would be what

we think of as the substrate of stone; its quantity—in this case, a magnitude; its quality—for example, the colour of stone. As with stone, so with every other body: we should see that in this thing, body, there are three distinguishable characteristics—the pseudo-substance (*hoion ousia*), the quantity (*poson*), the quality (*poion*)—though they all make one and are only logically trisected, the three being found to constitute the unit thing, body. If motion were equally inherent in its constitution, we should include this as well, and the four would form a unity, the single body depending upon them all for its unity and characteristic nature.

The same method must be applied in examining the Intellectual Substance (*ousia noētē*) and the genera and first principles of the Intellectual sphere. (MacKenna)

The important thing to remember here is that what Plotinus is looking for is nothing less than a set of concepts that are neither abstractions nor generic properties of sensible things. All characteristics of sensible reality must be dropped when thought proceeds to comprehend the nature of the Intellectual Principle. Thus, whenever he seems to employ Aristotelian concepts originally designed to apply to the sensible world, he is actually stripping such concepts of all their sensible referential efficacy in order to have them take on a radically new meaning applicable exclusively to the intelligibles; and when they pertain to the sensible entities they do so only homonymously. That is why he says at VI, 2, 4: "It is an Intellectual Being we have to consider, an Authentic Existent, possessed of a unity surpassing that of any sensible thing" (MacKenna). Now this topic brings us to Plotinus' similarities with Plato and his use of the highest genera.

1.   Plotinus postulates (when all passages are taken together) the following categories: *Being, Motion, Rest, Identity, Difference* and *Nous* or *Thought,* the last one as correlative to *Being;* Plato's highest genera are: *Being, Non-Being, Identity, Difference, Motion* and *Rest.*[10]

2.   With Plotinus, the Ultimate One is beyond all plurality but includes the One-in-Many (*plethos hen*) of the Intellectual Principle. There is no such principle in Plato, and it

would take quite a bit of straining to interpret the Form of the Good as being the equivalent of the One.

3.   The world of the Platonic Forms is a plural world and there is no definitive doctrine in the Dialogues in favor of a unifying principle comparable to that found in Plotinus' system.

4.   There is no movement in Plato's world of the Forms. Plotinus interprets motion to be real but supersensible. *Nous* is also movement; its *dynamis* is the efficient cause.

The detailed treatment of any single one of the Plotinian intelligibles and how each differs from its original Platonic correspondent, will require the length of a monograph. Our purpose is not to undertake to demonstrate the actual differences between Plato and Plotinus on any particular doctrinal point, but to indicate the deeper issues that underlie Plotinus' recasting of the metaphysical significance of each of the highest genera. Hence the Plotinian innovations in ontological theory, for instance, the placing of the intelligibles in the Divine *Nous* or the attribution of infinity to Nous, and other related doctrines, are sufficient to suggest some of the grounds for Plotinus' transformation of the meaning of certain Platonic concepts which his brand of Neoplatonism mistakenly associated with categorical principles. Be that as it may, without this revision of the Platonism he inherited it is next to the impossible to capture the full effect of his approach to Aristotle's categories.

V

What remains to be explored in general outline is Plotinus' criticism of the Aristotelian theory of categories. What is relevant to our theme is not the details of the argument or the subtle points in Plotinus' refutations, but rather the broader vision of the Neoplatonic tradition on which he bases his effort to identify and evaluate the usefulness of the Aristotelian view.

Plotinus, because of the fact that he bases his critique on an idealistic, superlunary expansion of the cosmos, a view developing out of a radical shifting from the classical orientation of metaphysical concerns, next to the Stoics, is the first major critic of Aristotle's *ousia*. In other words, he sets the pattern of criticism the purpose of which is to expose the inadequacy of Aristotle's ultimate types of predicates of beings for a complete account of reality. The basic idea here is that Plotinus shows how a conceptualization of *ousia* and *on,* different from that of classical Aristotelianism, requires a critique and reconstruction of categorical theory. In this sense, Plotinus is more than the leading Neoplatonist who comes to grips with the problem of the categories of being in the late Hellenistic period. He is in a definite sense the precursor of the medieval Arabic, Jewish, and Christian efforts to replace Aristotle's categories with more "adequate" theories; also he sets the tradition for the Renaissance and modern developments in continental philosophy, from Spinoza, Leibniz and Kant to Hegel and the German, British and American neo-Hegelians, that sought to reveal the categories of ultimate reality as process and dialectical movement.

However, the crucial problem in understanding Plotinus' attack rests with the correctness of his interpretation of Aristotle. A careful reading of the text will convince even the most sympathetic of his readers that Plotinus utilizes Plato in order to criticize Aristotle, often with such severity as to cause Porphyry's systematic protestation.[11] The fact remains that Plotinus appears unwilling to accept the full range of Aristotle's meaning of sensible *ousia*. He is equally if not more reluctant to appreciate the relevance of Aristotle's categorical theory to the dialectical clarification of the various theories of soul or the aid it offers toward solving problems of definition as well as fact in the study of living beings. In any event, the Aristotelian model of categorical analysis remains on the whole outside the Plotinian philosophy of method. With Plotinus, the primacy of the sensible object, which characterized much of the classical ontology, steadily vanishes. Thus the categories associated with this sort of ontology recede into the background as concepts of lesser significance. It is no accident that the only place where Plotinus deals extensively with the sensible object is the section where he discusses and criticizes the Aristotelian and Stoic categories. His own view of the sensible objects appears quite close to Plato's but with a heavier accent on the low place it assigns to them in the scale of ontic levels. The sensibles belong to the world of becoming; they are subjects of meaningful statements, either true or false; they are analyzable into a finite number of qualities—immanent, to be sure—each of which is dependent on its corresponding Form; they admit the same predicates as the Forms but only equivocally; even if called "wholes" they are not true substances but imitations of reality; their essences are not part of their being but to be found only by looking at the Intellectual Principle.

Given this "ontology" of the sensible objects it is small wonder that Plotinus assigns to the categorical theories dealing with their nature a low place in the hierarchy of intellectual tools and rational order. At best, such theories can be regarded as propaedeutic only to yield to the higher dialectic. Equally limited is their usefulness to ethics, for if man is a dweller in two realms, the sensible and the intelligible, it is only the latter which gives knowledge and value. Given the division of realms, categorical thinking about the sensible object receives the significance of its quest from a higher authority. This applies more so to the signification of its constituent concepts. To illustrate this important point, one need only recall here *Ennead* II, Tractate 6, which deals with "quality." It affords a clear-cut case of the recasting of a key concept used by both Plato, Aristotle, and also the Stoics, with reference to understanding certain properties of the sensible object.

Plotinus' way of handling the signification of quality is quite ingenious; it makes the reader suspect that Plotinus is most eager to isolate this concept for special treatment since its troublesome character could prove a source of embarrassment for his system. In addition, Plotinus comes to grips with the category of quality because he is anxious to settle the difficulties he has with explaining the presence of qualities in the sensible objects. The result is that he offers his solution with the aid of subtle distinctions not required by Plato's or Aristotle's ontologies. In other words, we have in this case a clear example of his recasting of a classical concept to suit the demands of a radically different metaphysical outlook.

In effect, Plotinus' position leads to the condemnation of Aristotle's emphasis on inquiry into sensible or natural subject-matters and also a return to an alleged Platonic view which more than heralds the recession of sensible *ousiai* to the background of ontological investigations. It quite strongly advocates the demise of the Aristotelian model and its replacement by the dialectic of intercategorical concepts in the form of reconstituted highest genera. With Plotinus, these concepts were elevated to a higher ontological and axiological place than either Plato or Aristotle were prepared to grant. This is one of the major legacies of Neoplatonism to modern metaphysics. It contributed in no small measure toward giving *Logos* its supremacy over *Being*.

VI

Plotinus' views in the area of categorical thought came at a time when the transition from the ancient world to another period was gaining momentum and the transformation of concepts and ideas had become indispensable to the needs for intellectual adjustments. What Plotinus did for categorical theory far exceeded his designs for a critique and reconstruction of basic views in metaphysical analysis. He provided a model and a direction which proved influential for many centuries to come. Every extant commentary of the late and post-Hellenistic periods on Aristotle's *Categories* was written by Neoplatonists who interestingly enough in their tone and style followed Porphyry's conciliatory approach rather than Plotinus. Somehow, the realm to which metaphysical reflection turned to satisfy its quest had been substantially delineated by the Neoplatonic vision of the intelligible universe. In the light of these considerations, the present paper was so designed as to consider Plotinus' views on the question of the categories for the purpose of (a) understanding the intent and scope of his theory and (b) placing in proper perspective the critical side of Plotinus' approach to Plato's genera and Aristotle's categories.

The familiar Plotinian commonplace that the ideal world is the archetype of the sensible world is as correct as it is misleading. The difficulty with it is that if taken literally it tends to obscure Plotinus' significant differences with Plato's cardinal doctrines just as it exaggerates those between Plato and Aristotle. Part of the thesis of this paper is the claim that Plotinus is no closer to Plato than he is to Aristotle. His alleged affinity to Plato owes more to the cliches perpetuated by the phraseology of the

Neoplatonic tradition than to the innovations the Neoplatonists introduced in ontology and cosmology in the name of Plato. It is these new winds of doctrine that should count heavily in the comparative analyses of the theoretical affinities between Plotinus, Plato and Aristotle. With Plotinus, we have the appearance of a radically different ontology of the sensible object. If anything, it is non-Hellenic in character. To be more precise, it lies at the heart of an effort to hellenize an already conceptualized Oriental heritage and render it intelligible with the aid of established philosophical concepts to which new meanings had been assigned in order to perform novel cultural tasks. Plotinus proved to be a major force in the transformation of the classical heritage to intellectualize the emerging demands of a new religious ethos. Seen in this light Plotinus should be regarded not as "the last of the Greeks" but the first of the post-classical metaphysicians.[12] In any event, he appears to be the key transitional figure between the ancient and the post-classical modes of ontological thinking.

NOTES

1. W. R. Inge. *The Philosophy of Plotinus* (London, 1929, 3rd edition) I, p. 58.
2. P. V. Pistorius. *Plotinus and Neoplatonism* (Cambridge, 1952), p. 39.
3. E. Brehier, in his "notice" to the *Enneads* VI, Part 1 (Paris, 1936), p. 8.
4. He states in *Ennead* VI. 9. 3: "Strictly speaking, we ought not to apply any terms at all to It; but we should, so to speak, run around the outside of It trying to interpret our own feelings about It, sometimes drawing near and sometimes falling away in our perplexities about It." Translation by H. Armstrong, in the Preface to the Loeb edition of Plotinus' *Enneads,* I, p. xv.
5. See Merlan's essay, "Greek Philosophy from Plato to Plotinus," Part I in *The Cambridge History of Later Greek and Early Medieval Philosophy*, edited by A. H. Armstrong

(Cambridge University Press, 1967), pp. 37-38. Even the return to the five highest genera of the *Sophist* may be questioned on technical grounds, but this is a separate issue and deserves special analysis. Comp. P. V. Pistorius, *Plotinus and Neoplatonism* (Cambridge, 1952) pp. 35 ff.

6. J. M. Rist. *Plotinus: The Road to Reality* (Cambridge, 1967), p. 103.

7. MacKenna's translation ... ζωήν τε ἀρίστην ἐνεργήσες καὶ τῷ θείῳ εἰς ταὐτὸν γεγενημένος καὶ ἐν αὐτῷ ἰδρυθεὶς εἰς ἐνέργειαν ἐλθ ὼν ἐκείνην ὑπὲρ πᾶν τε ἄλλο νοητὸν ἐμαυτὸν δρύσας...

8. I find it difficult to accept John H. Randall Jr's interpretation of Plotinus. In his article, "The Intelligible Universe of Plotinus," in the *Journal of the History of Ideas* III (1965), 3-16, he states: "In his analysis of the intelligible universe in which we find ourselves, Plotinus starts from the cardinal fact of Greek experience: man is a dweller in two realms, that of the senses and that of thought; and the latter is the 'real' realm in which we alone find genuine knowledge. Plotinus proceeds to elaborate the necessary distinctions within the realm of thought" (9). Randall's position makes Plotinus a "knower," and plays down those aspects that enable Plotinus to seek and claim union with the One. It is the latter side of Plotinus that explains his "Neoplatonism," namely, his radical departure from the classical view of ethics and ontology, and also throws the needed light on his criticism of Aristotle's categories.

9. Plotinus speaks of the return of the soul to the source of all as an "odyssey," a going back to the fatherland: I. 6. 8. 16; VI. 9. 7. 3 and 9. 9.

10. Dean Inge adopts the peculiar position that the Platonic categories tend to supercede the Forms in the later Dialogues (II, p. 58). This is questionable doctrine not only because of the problems involved in the comparison between the Forms and the highest genera but also because of the misleading identification of the latter with categorical concepts. There is no evidence in the Platonic Dialogues that Plato meant the highest genera to have this use.

11. See Elias, *In Isagogen,* 39. 6 ff. Simplicius refers explicitly to Porphyry's defence of Aristotle's categories against his teacher's criticisms (*In Categ.* 2. 5 ff); in so doing Porphyry prepared the way for the softer interpretations of this doctrine by later Neoplatonist commentators.

12. Compare, for instance, the view of Clifford H. Moore: "It is evident that Neoplatonism, the last stage of Greek philosophy, is no isolated or strange phenomenon. On its metaphysical side it is the consummation and final synthesis of the whole course of Greek thought from the sixth century to its own day; likewise in ethics it combined the views of its chief predecessors as its leaders understood them; and finally in the doctrine of the soul's union with God it only carried the mystical tendencies of previous centuries to their natural conclusion." *The Religious Thought of the Greeks: From Homer to the Triumph of Christianity* (Cambridge: Harvard University Press, 1916), p. 220.

Chorismos and Emanation
in the Philosophy of Plotinus

by John H. Fielder

Villanova University

I.   Introduction

For Plotinus, and for Platonists generally, the sensible world is not the only reality. A philosophical examination of this world reveals higher realities of which this world is said to be an 'image'. Thus the problem of *chorismos* is not simply that the higher realities are ontologically 'separate' from the sensible world, but that this separation must be consistent with a very close connection between them. Whatever unity, structure, and value sensibles have is provided by the higher realities despite their ontological separation. The philosophical account of this relationship must, as it were, bring the higher realities into the world without sacrificing their ontologically distinct status. Too sharp a separation tends to preclude any influence, while too close an association tends to eliminate the separation.

One major difficulty is already present in the presentation of the problem, and that is the metaphorical language in which it is stated. To say that the sensible world is an image of a higher reality is to pose the first problem of giving some philosophical meaning to this metaphysical claim.

In Plotinus' metaphysics both of these issues are complicated by another ingredient in his account of the relationship between the sensible world and the higher realities, the doctrine of emanation. Although this doctrine has several functions in Plotinus' philosophy, one of them is to contribute to the account of the relationship between sensible reality and the higher reality of which it is an image. The problem of *chorismos* cannot be fully understood in Plotinus' metaphysics apart from some view of how sensible reality is brought about as an image emanated from a higher level of existence. We can say that the problems posed by the world as an image must be seen as problems concerning the world as *imaged*.

It is this understanding of the sensible world as something imaged by higher reality that I propose to investigate in this paper. Since this is a very large topic, I have narrowed my inquiry to a single pattern of Plotinus' thought on this issue. Rather than exhibiting all of the many facets of Plotinus' thinking on emanation and *chorismos*, I have chosen to single out one line of his thought and follow up some of its implications.

In order to bring out this pattern of thought with some clarity and in a short space, I have had to ignore many other important issues that are related to this problem as well as overlook many complications and confusions in Plotinus' views. Although the issues I discuss are, in Plotinus' writings, more complex than they are presented here, this approach seems well suited to Plotinus' philosophy. His thought embraces many different philosophical conceptions from diverse sources that are brought together in a frequently uneasy coexistence. Understanding Plotinus' philosophy will in part be achieved by sorting out how particular conceptions and patterns of thought are applied to particular problems. Having clarified particular lines of thinking we will be in a position to more accurately determine where and why Plotinus deviates from it or adopts others. Then we will be able to see more clearly how those patterns of thought work - or fail to work - together. My contribution to this task will be to exhibit one of Plotinus' responses to the problem of *chorismos*, a conception of imaging.

II.   Levels of Reality

For Plotinus the sensible world is incomplete, pointing beyond itself to higher realities. His writings are full of philosophical analyses of sensible phenomena which lead to the conclusion that such phenomena can only be understood in terms of their relationships to non-sensible realities. An examination of beauty reveals the existence of the Form of Beauty and of the soul that grasps it.[1] Knowledge is possible because of our use of the objects of knowledge, the Forms in Nous.[2] Pain, and sentience in general, requires a non-physical soul to account for the pain in my finger being my pain and not the finger's pain.[3] Natural science points to the role of Nous in the sensible world.[4]

It is not germane to this inquiry to respond to the difficulties involved in determining how many and what kinds of higher realities Plotinus acknowledges as a result of these analyses. What is important here is that these realities form a hierarchy in which each lower reality points beyond itself to something higher. Thus Nous is said to be the image of the One;[5] Soul is likewise the image of Nous;[6] and in general each lower level is the image of its higher, generating reality.[7] The organization of these Platonic entities into a hierarchy is effected by regarding them as a series of images of something higher. Hence the problem of *chorismos* occurs at every junction of higher and lower realities, for at each of these there is ontological separation and the relationship of archetype and image.

The force of this notion of image can be expressed in four characteristics. First, being an image entails being distinguished from that which is the archetype or original. An image is an image *of* something, so that the two are in some sense different things. This alone does not commit one to a view of how that distinction of archetype and image is to be understood, for that requires a further inquiry into what Plotinus understood this distinction to mean in his metaphysical system. At this point only the necessity for the distinction is claimed. Plotinus' view that a lower level of reality is an image of a higher entails that some kind of metaphysical distinction must be drawn between the two or the meaning of "image" is lost.

Second, the notion of image contains the important idea of likeness or similarity. To say that this is an image of that means that some kind of likeness is being claimed. It would not make sense to speak of something as an image unless we can point out that it is an image of *this* rather than something else. Of course, an image - say a painting - can be mistakenly thought to be an image of something or someone other than what it does represent. The portrait of the father may be mistaken for the son. But it could hardly be mistaken for the family dog, except perhaps in unusual families or circumstances, but even there we could find other things of which it would be impossible for one to think that the portrait was an image of them. Without some kind of likeness we cannot associate the image with that of which it is an image or contrast it with other things of which it is not an image.

Plotinus has this feature of "image" in mind when he speaks of the sensible world as an image of an eternal archetype[8] or eternal model.[9] Plotinus emphasizes that this universe is "a representation carrying down the features of the Intellectual Realm."[10] Plotinus frequently speaks of Nous as containing in archetype all of the kinds of things found here.[11] Nous is also described as being brought to likeness of the One-Good.[12] Again, this is not to specify the content of this idea of likeness. We cannot assume, for example, that this talk of likeness commits Plotinus to univocal self-predication of Forms, but only that some non-metaphorical account of the similitude of image and archetype must be given if the notion of "image" is used to describe the relationship between levels of reality.

Third, the image is in some way inferior to the archetype. The Platonic use of "image" includes a judgment of the deficiency of the image in comparison to the archetype. This, too, is clear from Plotinus' writings, but the sense of the deficiency is not. Thus Plotinus, in a discussion of emanation, states that "the engendered offspring is always minor".[13] And in V.1.1 the beauty in a statue is said to be "derivative and a minor" in comparison to the Form of Beauty.

In arguing against the Gnostics Plotinus points out that although this world is imperfect in comparison to its archetype, it is the best sensible world possible. "No doubt it [the sensible world] is a copy, not original ... but to say that it is an inadequate copy is false: nothing has been left out which a beautiful representation within the physical order could include."[14] This world is an image, and therefore deficient, but it is the best image that could be obtained.

When Plotinus speaks of Matter in the sensible world he emphasizes the inferiority of sensibles compared to Soul or

Nous,[15] whereas in combating the Gnostics he points out the similarity of image to archetype. There is no inconsistency here, for both likeness and deficiency are contained in the notion of image. It is the relative perfection of the archetype in comparison to its diminished image that results in Plotinus' hierarchy having at its extremes the perfection of the One-Good and the absolute deficiency of Matter. As one proceeds from the One the levels of reality are more and more deficient as a result of the process of each being less than its predecessor, so that the end of the process, Matter, is characterized solely by its deficiency. It is the last, and therefore "pure lack" and "privation."[17] Thus the process of emanation of increasingly deficient realities is used as a proof that there must be a last product of emanation which is the principle of evil.[18]

Fourth, the image is dependent on its archetype. The existence of the image requires the existence of the archetype. Without the archetype the image could not exist. This is clear from the idea of emanation, in which the image must be generated in order to exist. Thus "the offspring is attached [to the generator] by a bond of sheer necessity."[19] Plotinus also speaks of the image as "continuously attached"[20] to the generating reality, meaning that the generating hypostasis sustains the image in its existence, just as the mirror image lasts as long as the object remains in front of the mirror. Just as the idea of image presupposes that of which it is an image, so for Plotinus the existing image is ontologically dependent upon its archetype for its existence.

There is an important complication here that needs to be mentioned. Plotinus sees this dependence as operating in one direction only, so that the lower depends upon the higher but not the other way around. "Not that God the One has any need of His derivatives: He ignores all that produced realm, never necessary to him . . ."[21] But there is a kind of dependence of the higher on the lower in that the creation of an image is a necessary process. The higher hypostasis must create its image as part of its nature. We can extend Plotinus' metaphor and say that one cannot walk away from the mirror.

Given these four characteristics of "image" it is necessary to further specify their philosophical meaning. We need to explicate each of these aspects of the notion of image. How are the image and its archetype different from each other? In what sense are they similar? What kind of likeness is appropriate here? What does it mean to say that one level of reality is inferior to another? How, exactly, is the image dependent upon the archetype? In general, we need to know how these four characteristics are metaphysical characteristics of Plotinus' system of reality.

One way of putting philosophical content into these four terms - the image as different, inferior, dependent and similar to its archetype - is to determine how they are used in another context where their metaphysical meaning is clearer. The process by which images are generated reveals a philosophical conception of imaging that will provide us with an interpretation of these four characteristics of being an image.

III.   Emanation

As we move from the idea of image to that of imaging, we find that Plotinus employs a variety of metaphorical terms to describe this doctrine. The most common are the sun and its light, heat, cold, perfumes, the growth of a seed, a spring and its waters, a mirror.[22] Each of these metaphors suggests a different sense of generation. The mature plant comes to be only through the destruction of the seed, whereas the sun continues to exist despite its production of light. A spring does not create its waters in the way that an image is created in a mirror, for it makes no sense to ask if the image were existent before the object was in front of the mirror, whereas the water was already in the ground. In a similar way the light does not preexist in the sun before its radiation.

These differences in the logic of the generation metaphors result in differences in the meanings of the four criteria for being an image. Thus the dependence of the mirror image is unlike that of the dependence of the mature plant on the seed. Once the plant is grown its existence does not require the existence of the seed, a situation that it reversed in the case of the image and the mirror. Another obvious example is the senses in which we speak of the image being diminished. Perfumes are weakened or diluted by the air as they are diffused, but the mature plant, the mirror image, a portrait, are not diminished copies in this way. The spring waters spread out but are not thereby weakened in the sense that heat or odors are weakened by diffusion and dilution.

Obviously we have to settle on one of these metaphors and then determine how it gives meaning to the four characteristics of image that are central to the problem of *chorismos*. Fortunately there is a discussion in the *Enneads* that enables us to do this. In VI.4 Plotinus analyzes the metaphor of light and its source, indicating how that metaphor is to be explicated. The metaphor of light emanating from the sun was especially in need of clarification because of its materialistic origins in Stoicism. Plotinus is always on guard against a materialist conception of reality, and this metaphor had to be carefully dematerialized.

There is a great deal that can be said concerning Plotinus' understanding of light and about the history of that concept in Neoplatonism. But our concern here is only with the philosophical use that Plotinus made of that metaphor in explicating his concept of image and emanation. The passage in which Plotinus is most explicit in such an explication is a famous one and worth quoting at length.

> Or imagine a small luminous mass serving as center to a transparent sphere, so that the light from within shows upon the entire outer surface, otherwise unlit: we can surely agree that the inner core of light, intact and immobile, reaches over the entire outer extension; the single light of that small center illuminates the whole field. The diffused light is not due to any bodily magnitude of that central point which illuminates not as body but as body lit, that is by another kind of power than corporeal quality: let us then abstract the corporeal mass, retaining the light as power: we can no longer speak of the light in any particular spot; it is equally diffused within and throughout the whole sphere. We can no longer even name the spot it occupied so as to say whence it came or how it is present; we can but seek, and wonder as the search shows us the light simultaneously present at each and every point of the sphere. So with the sunlight: looking to

the corporeal mass you are able to name the source of the
light shining through all of the air, but what you see is one
identical light in integral omnipresence. (VI.4.7) (Mac-
Kenna translation)

In this passage Plotinus indicates how we are to give a more
philosophically precise meaning to the way we speak of
emanation and image. In the corrected metaphor the light no
longer springs from a center but is simply present throughout
the sphere. The material source is eliminated and only the
power to illuminate is left to light the sphere. Armstrong[2][3]
claims that this analysis destroys the idea of emanation, but this
would be true only if we continued to understand radiation in a
spatial sense. The notion of light radiating from one spatial
location to a different set of spatial locations is replaced by the
conception of one kind of reality giving its power to another,
different kind of reality. The reference to a power different
from corporeal quality indicates that this incorporeal power is
now the source of the sphere's illumination. Instead of A being
spatially separate from B and radiating its influence to B,
Plotinus proposes that A influences B by its immaterial presence
through B. The light in the sphere comes from ('radiates' from)
a source but the source is not concentrated in one spatial
location. Its 'concentration' is its being a different kind of
reality, a principle of illuminating power that is omnipresent in
the sphere.

A similar analogy is used at VI.4.12 with regard to sound.
The one sound is present to each listener from its source. If we
remove the physical source of the sound and leave the power of
sound to permeate space, then the analogy with light is the
same. Plotinus' shift from the corporeal source to the power of
light or sound is a shift from one kind of reality to another. The
power to illuminate is ontologically different from a corporeal
mass, for the illuminating power can be identically present to
many different spatial locations without suffering any kind of
partitioning. The discussion recalls Socrates' conversation with
the Platonic Parmenides over how sensibles could participate in
Forms. At one point Socrates suggested the analogy of the day,
which is present without division everywhere, unlike the other

example of the sail, which could cover many individuals only on the basis of a part of the sail for each thing covered.

All of the diffusion metaphors suggest this kind of presence. The perfume that we smell is the perfume itself, dispersed through the air from the source. But the difference between the perfume metaphor and the light is crucial for Plotinus. The particles of perfume that I inhale are not the same individual particles that you inhale. They may be identical in the sense of being the same kind of particles, but they are not the same individuals.[24] For Plotinus, light is immaterial[25] so that it could be identically present to many locations. The light illuminating the sphere, in other words, is one and the same power of light present throughout. Light, because of its immateriality, was exempt from the spatial limitations of corporeal beings who can be present in a variety of locations like the sail, by division into parts. Light was also thought to be indestructible as long as the source continued to exist, an obvious parallel to the eternal generation of the levels of reality in emanation.[26]

In his analysis of the light metaphor Plotinus made it clear that he did not introduce a new kind of separation between the source and its power. He specifically argued against a doctrine of 'presence by powers' in which the higher reality is distinct from its powers which go out from it. The power would be present but the source would not. Plotinus held that "where these powers appear, their source must be with them."[27] and further, "thus, once more, that source itself must be omnipresent as an undivided whole."[28] The distinction between source and power is, for Plotinus, a spurious one, for the powers immanent in sensible reality are the Plotinian *logoi*. Soul contains *logoi* as indwelling powers which enter the sensible world and account for the qualities that sensibles exhibit.[30] Thus the omnipresence of the Soul, which is the subject of VI, 4 & 5, is the immanent presence of the powers of Soul in the sensible world, so that there is no distinction between the *logos* and the power to illuminate, for that power *is* the logos present in the sphere.

This conception of immanent omnipresence is found in many places in Plotinus' philosophy, wherever a unity must be found in plurality. In his view of universals he speaks of the white in two bowls of milk being one and the same whiteness.[31] Soul gives the body unity by being numerically one throughout the plurality of bodily parts and locations.[32] The doctrine of 'sympathy' and the governance of the sensible world by the world soul are further examples of Plotinus' use of this conception.[33]

The conception of imaging as the immanent presence of the generating reality in its image is also found in the One's emanation of Nous. The metaphor of light is again used,[34] and Nous is described as holding the One's light within itself.[35] A similar description occurs at V.5.7 where Plotinus speaks of Nous as finding the light from the One within itself. Nous receives power to produce its multiplicity of Forms from the radiation from the One-Good. The One's light is broken into fragments by Nous, resulting in the multiple unities which are the Forms.[35] Rist notes that Plotinus speaks of the One as present with its effects,[36] and this is, for Plotinus, a closer presence in the case of Nous, for Nous is separated from the One only by its being distinct from it.[37]

Plotinus is clearly using the same metaphor of light and of presence associated with it that he explicitly developed in his analysis of the sphere and the light. He has simply transferred the same explanatory terms to the connection between One and Nous that he explained in VI.4 for the relationship of Soul to the sensible world. The plurality of Nous that is filled by the One's power obviously parallels the spatial plurality of the sphere that is illuminated by the omnipresent power of light. And where the One's power is found the One is there also, present in its effects. Hence the One's generation of Nous as its image is quite similar to the Soul's generation of the sensible world for in both instances sees that imaging in terms of the light metaphor and of the immanent presence of the higher reality in the lower.

The relationship between Nous and Soul does not seem to fit this pattern. Although Plotinus does speak of Nous being in Soul, he does not seem to have in mind the kind of immanence characteristic of the light and the sphere. Soul is dependent upon Nous, as its image, and is sometimes described using the vocabulary of light, but the Soul's function requires a different kind of relationship to its generator. Soul is frequently viewed as a being in the realm of Being, Nous, rather than as a separate hypostasis.[38] Again, Soul is sometimes spoken of as having parts, the uppermost being in Nous, the lower in the sensible world.[39] Both of these roles conflict with the conception of a reality that carries Nous immanently within it. In the latter role Nous is only in one part of Soul rather than omnipresent. Soul also is said to be an emissary from Nous,[40] so that Nous is seemingly separate from Soul which is its messenger.

This is an intriguing problem which is unfortunately beyond the scope of this inquiry. However some further elements will be added to our understanding of the anomalous status of Soul from a consideration of the role of matter in the concept of imaging developed from Plotinus' critique of the light metaphor in VI.4.

We can say, then, that this conception of imaging, though it does not apply to the relationship of Nous to Soul, views the higher reality as generating its image by immanent omnipresence within it. Although this is still not entirely clear, we can at least specify more determinate meaning for two of the four requirements for being an image. We now have a better understanding of how dependence is to be understood. For the image to be dependent on its archetype means that the significant characteristics of the image - its unity, structure, value - are dependent upon the existence of a higher reality that is immanently present throughout the plurality of the image. Without the presence of the generator the image would not be in existence: its very being depends upon the inner presence of a higher reality that fills it and makes it what it is.

The characteristic of likeness is also explicated by this conception of imaging. The resemblance of archetype and image is found in the likeness of the higher reality to the same reality present within the conditions of the lower level of reality. Thus the comparison is between the light principle and the light principle as illuminating the sphere. Such a comparison requires that we be able to separate the light principle from its presence in the sphere so that the immanent reality can be related to the illuminated sphere which is its image. For Plotinus this means that we must undertake philosophical dialectic in order to be guided to a direct experience of the higher realities. Thus one of the functions of the *Enneads* is to be a spiritual guide to this transcendence of the physical world. Plotinus wants us, through philosophical reflection, to rise to those higher levels of reality and grasp the principles of this world in their purity, apart from their presence in something else. In his discussion of beauty in V.1.1-2 Plotinus distinguishes the beauty that is above the sensible world of art. It exists "in a far higher state than in the art" where the beauty "does not come over integrally into the work." Hence "In the degree in which the beauty is diffused by entering into Matter, it is so much the weaker than that concentrated in unity . . ." The task is to become men who "in the keenness of their sight, have a clear vision of the splendor above." And, as he states in that same discussion, the clue to this transcendence is the realization that "the beauty perceived on material things is borrowed."[41]

It is difficult to talk about this kind of likeness without invoking vision and visual analogies. Light alone in comparison with the light diffused in air is a better parallel than one might at first realize, for Plotinus believed that the air was dark and that light had to overcome this darkness in its diffusion into space.[42] And in the passage where Plotinus speaks of the splendor of the higher realm, he contrasts it with the 'fog and cloud' of earth, again invoking the visual metaphor of something obscured by the surrounding atmosphere. The task of the philosopher is to pierce through the fog rather than ascend from the cave.

Thus the ontological basis for the likeness of archetype and image has been established, although one must rise above one's physical existence in order to actually grasp the likeness.

Two other criteria for image remain and must be explained by extending the inquiry into another area. The concept of matter is used by Plotinus to explicate the ontological distinction between image and archetype, and the deficiency of the image.

IV. Matter

The conception of image that is derived from Plotinus' analysis of the light metaphor is completed by the concept of

Matter. Matter explains the ontological distinction between archetype and image, and the diminished nature of the image. Thus it completes the philosophical explication of the four characteristics of image.

There are many passages where Plotinus has this function of Matter in mind. Perhaps the clearest are those in which the light metaphors are extended to these situations. The Soul's relation to Matter is described in terms of the Matter darkening the Soul's seeing.[43] In I.8.14 Plotinus says that "the illumination, the light streaming from the Soul, is dulled, is weakened, as it mixes with Matter which offers birth to the Soul, providing the means by which it enters into generation, impossible if no recipient were at hand." Besides the familiar theme of diffusion (mixing), there is also the explicit statement that Matter is providing the principle by which a different level of reality — the sensible world of generation — can exist. This world is Soul present in Matter.

The same point is made in other passages where Plotinus speaks of Matter as the substratum or base for form.[44] And in II.4.12 he states "No doubt there must be a container, as it were, a place and space; the primary necessity in order for the existence of body, is Matter." Obviously the metaphor of the container is continuous with the language of immanence, as the light is contained within the sphere.

The mixing of Soul with Matter is not to be understood materialistically. It is clear that their relationship is conceived in a way similar to the immanent presence of the light-principle in the sphere: "Matter exists; Soul exists; they occupy so to speak, one place . . . the Soul's separation is simply its not being in Matter; that is, its not being united with it . . ."[45] Like the light in the sphere, Soul is not combined with Matter but is immanently present in the Matter. Or, to use another Plotinian metaphor, the light permeates or pervades the Matter but does not combine with it. This is aptly expressed in this passage dealing with the generation of the Sensible world by Soul: the Soul must pervade all things, and make all, but not be the universe it makes."[46]

A similar situation holds with regard to the role of Intelligible Matter in Nous. The Matter of the intelligible world is also a substratum, for the Forms in Nous.[47] Plotinus argues that the existence of Form compels the existence of Matter, for we cannot conceive of form without a substrate in which form is lodged. Division and differentiation of a plurality of Forms is possible only with a material principle, just as the sensible world requires its material principle as a container for the powers of Soul. And just as sensible Matter is filled by the immanent presence of a higher reality, so also Plotinus speaks of Intelligible Matter as the 'dark' element in the Intelligible, taking light from outside itself, i.e. the One.[48] Despite the differences of the two realms, Nous is also described in the same terms of generation as the sensible world, the illumination of (Intelligible) Matter by the One. Both material principles provide the matrix in which a higher level of reality is immanently present.

Thus both material principles function as preconditions for the generation of a different level of reality. In passages describing the generation of Nous and the sensible world[49] Plotinus introduces Matter as necessary for a level of reality different from the One or Soul to be generated. Hence Deck states that if Intelligible Matter were removed Nous would be the One.[50] The case of sensible Matter is more complicated because of the difficulty in locating the proper role for Soul, but if we strip away sensible Matter the remainder is the higher level of reality immanent in it.

We can now bring the anomalous position of Soul into sharper focus. If Soul is an hypostasis between Nous and the sensible world, an image of Nous, then the generation of Soul by this model of reasoning so far developed would require a material principle for Soul. But such a principle is conspicuously absent, Plotinus speaking only of the "two orders of Matter."[51] As we noted before and now see more clearly, Plotinus does not use this pattern of thought in explicating the relation of Soul as the image of Nous.

In connection with this anomaly Deck cites a "line of reasoning" in Plotinus in which the intermediation of Soul between Nous and the sensible world is unnecessary because of the sensible world's direct participation in Nous.[52] Wallis also claims that the distinction between Nous and Soul tends to dissolve, which would leave open the direct participation of the sensible world in Nous.[53] The analysis of this issue is another topic, but whatever explanation we give for Soul's anomalous status must also include an explanation of why Plotinus did not extend this concept of imaging to Soul by providing it with a material principle. It is certainly possible that the tendency of Soul to be assimilated to Nous is the result of the hold that this conception of imaging had on Plotinus' thinking.

Matter also serves to account for the diminution of the lower level of reality that results from the higher level being immanent within it. Again, the light metaphors are adapted to this purpose. The Soul's light being dulled and weakened by the darkness of Matter is an obvious use of the metaphor. We find more explicit passages that make clear that the light metaphor is to be understood in terms of immanence in a principle that differentiates and diminishes: "Forms lodged in Matter are not the same as they would be if they remained in themselves; they are Reason-principles materialized, they are corrupted in Matter, they have absorbed its nature . . . Matter becomes mistress of what is manifested through it . . ."[54] The form in itself is contrasted with the form in Matter, the latter being the cause of the imperfection of the image. The role of Matter in the production of a diminished image is explained a few lines further. "Matter substitutes its own opposite character and kind, not in the sense of opposing, for example, concrete cold to concrete warmth, but by setting its own shaplessness to shape, formlessness to the Form of heat . . ."[55] The reference to heat recalls the diffusion metaphors in which the diffusion of heat through the air results in its being weaker (cooler) than at the source. Similarly Form must bring the formless Matter to form, and in so doing must lose its concentration in permeating Matter. Just as light is weakened through its dispersion in the air so also is form weakened when dispersed into Matter. The principle itself is not so much opposed as diluted. Opposition would require a contrary form – i.e. concrete cold to concrete heat – whereas the kind of process that results in a deficient image is the opposition of formlessness to form, so that the immanent reality generates a diminished image by a kind of dispersal of its energy through Matter.

This conception of Matter appears to identify Matter with a principle of plurality. The unified reality that enters Matter is pluralized by its entry into Matter. The incoming reality is not partitioned by rather dispersed throughout a plurality that results in sensible reality.[56] The higher reality is capable of being identically present throughout that plurality but the resulting immattered reality is thereby diminished, just as the light is diminished through diffusion into space. Hence we can say that plurality is the principle of imperfection for Plotinus, for it is the principle of plurality that results in the generated reality being inferior to its generator. In VI.6.1 Plotinus is quite explicit in identifying this pluralization with diminution. Again using the example of beauty, Plotinus states that "in the degree of the sensible world's extension it was void of beauty and to that degree ugly. Thus extension serves as Matter to Beauty since what calls for its ordering is a multiplicity. The greater the expansion the greater the disorder and ugliness." Beauty, like all form, unifies, and to the extent that multiplicity is present to dilute that unity there will necessarily be imperfection. We can therefore see the truth of Wallis' claim that Plotinus' levels of reality are levels of decreasing unity.[57] The fundamental features of his metaphysical system increasingly seem to be the One as the source of unity and Matter as plurality, with those terms being further identified with Good and Evil.

Intelligible Matter is also a source of plurality. As we saw above, Nous fragments the light from the One with the resulting plurality of unities – Forms – in Nous. The One is present in Intelligible Matter resulting in the first level of multiple reality, Nous. Although Intelligible Matter provides the plurality for the generation of Nous, Plotinus is reluctant to view this as also a principle of diminution. Nous is the image of the One and therefore inferior to it, but Plotinus does not explain that in terms of the plurality provided by Intelligible Matter. Plotinus is always very much concerned to safeguard the Intelligible realm from any kind of disvalue. In the discussion of Intelligible Matter he is careful to point out that, unlike sensible Matter, Intelligible Matter belongs to Being, and has a "life defined and intellectual."[58] But Plotinus seems to be trapped here, for the concept of image requires that the image be inferior to the archetype. And some metaphysical principle is necessary to account for that inferiority.[59] This is especially true for this conception of imaging in which the One is immanent in Nous. If the unity in Nous *is* the One, then whatever else is constituent of Nous must account for its deficiency.

Plotinus', refusal to allow Intelligible Matter to be the source of Nous' deficiency contradicts the identification of plurality with deficiency. Intelligible Matter does provide plurality but that plurality is not acknowledged as the source of Nous' being a diminished image of the One. Here, too, this aspect of imaging is not applied or followed through in order to exclude any principle of disvalue in the Intelligible realm.

This analysis supports the claims by Wallis and Deck that the second and third hypostases might be regarded as defective ways of viewing the One,[60] especially since both of them also assert that the distinction between Soul and Nous tends to disappear. For if Nous is the One viewed through Intelligible Matter — i.e. as pluralized into Forms — then Nous is a way of viewing the One since the fragmented unity we see in Nous *is* the One, grasped through the plurality of Intelligible Matter.[61] Similarly the sensible world can be regarded as a way of viewing Soul (or Nous) through Matter. However, the fact that Soul does not have a material principle means that this explanation will not work for it. If Soul is to be regarded as a defective way of viewing the One, then some other account of how this is to be understood will have to be established.

V. Conclusion

This conception of imaging answers important philosophical questions concerning emanation and *chorismos*. It gives an account of the generation of lower levels of reality as well as an explication of what is meant by the lower level of reality being an image of the higher. It also brings out the anomalous status of Soul and problems concerning the role of Intelligible Matter in accounting for the image-quality of Nous.

There is a final problem for Plotinus that grows out of this concept of imaging, and that is the attempt to account for the existence of Matter through emanation. Can the material principles themselves be generated or must they be independent of that process? It is clear that on the model of imaging developed here that Matter cannot be generated. If generation is the immanent presence of a higher reality in a lower by means of a material principle, then the material principle itself cannot be generated without presupposing another material principle. Hence the attempt to generate the material principle on this conception of imaging always results in the positing of another, ungenerated material principle. This is a more philosophically specific way of expressing a long-standing problem in Plotinus' philosophy, his attempt to generate plurality from the pure unity of the One.

Plotinus attempts to view sensible Matter as the image of Intelligible Matter in II.4.5 but it is clear that this attempt must fail if the conception of imaging remains the same as above. Matter's role places it outside the process of unity.

Since the two roles of Matter are similar in providing the plurality necessary for immanence, and the plurality of Nous is superior to that of sensible existence, it is natural that Plotinus would consider the possibility of relating these two similar principles as archetype and image. However these principles are necessarily independent of the One, generated not by emanation but by the kind of explanation Plotinus gives of emanation and *chorismos*

NOTES

1. V.1.1 f. and V.9.2 f.
2. V.9.7
3. IV.7.7.
4. IV.4.37.
5. Plotinus speaks of the dependent hypostasis as *eikon, mimema,* and *eidolon.* I have taken the references in this and the following two notes from John Deck, *Nature, Contemplation, and The One,* (Toronto, Univ. of Toronto Press, 1967), p. 15. Cf. V.1.7 and V.4.2 for Nous as image.
6. V.8.12: V.1.7.
7. III.8.7.
8. V.9.5.

9.   III.7.1.
10.   II.9.8
11.   VI.7.12.
12.   III.8.11; V.1.7.
13.   V.1.6.
14.   II.9.8.
15.   I.8.8 & 14.
16.   II.4.13
17.   II.4.16.
18.   I.8.7.
19.   V.1.6.
20.   V.1.6.
21.   V.5.12.
22.   V.1.6.
23.   A.H. Armstrong, " 'Emanation' in Plotinus,' " *Mind*, XLVI, N.S., no. 181, p. 62.
24.   The same point is made by Augustine in *On The Freedom of the Will*, (New York, Bobbs Merrill), p. 51. The example of sound is specifically contrasted with odors and tastes.
25.   IV.3.10. Cf. Deck, *op. cit.*, p. 12.
26.   IV.8.4; III.5.2; V.1.6.
27.   VI.4.9.
28.   VI.4.9.
30.   R.E. Witt, "The Plotinian Logos and Its Stoic Basis," *Classical Quarterly*, XXV, (April 1931), p. 106. Cf. IV.7.9.
31.   Cf. A.C. Lloyd, "Neoplatonic Logic and Aristotelian Logic," *Phronesis* I (1955-6), p. 62.
32.   IV.7.7.
33.   II.3.7; IV.4.32 for sympathy; IV.4.11 for the World Soul.
34.   VI.7.16; V.1.6; V.1.7.
35.   VI.7.16.
36.   J.M. Rist, *Eros and Psyche*, (Tornoto, University of Toronto Press, 1964), p.81.
37.   V.1.6
38.   Deck, *op. cit.* p. 31.
39.   II.1.5; IV.3.24; II.9.2.
40.   VI.4.15.
41.   V.9.2.

42. R. E. Witt, "Plotinus and Posidonius", *Classical Quarterly,* XXIV, (July 1930), p. 205. Cf. IV,5,2.
43. I.8.4.
44. II.4.6.
45. I.8.14.
46. III.9.3.
47. II.4.4.
48. II.4.4.
49. II.4.5 and III.9.3-4. respectively.
50. Deck, *op. cit.*, p. 116.
51. II.4.3.
52. Deck, *op. cit.*, p. 73.
53. R. T. Wallis, *Neoplatonism,* (London, Duckworth, 1972) p. 93.
54. I.8.8.
55. I.8.9.
56. Wallis, *op. cit.*, p. 49.
57. *Ibid.,* p. 48.
58. II.4.5.
59. L.J. Eslick, "The Material Substrate in Plato," in *The Concept of Matter in Greek and Medieval Philosophy,* (Notre Dame Press, Notre Dame Indiana, 1965), p. 40-1.
60. Deck, *op. cit.*, p. 115; Wallis, *op. cit.,*p. 92.
61. Cf. Deck, *op. cit.*, p. 116.

ΝΟΥΣ as Experience

by Richard T. Wallis

University of Oklahoma

As its title implies, this paper is an attempt to clarify the nature of the experience on which Plotinus' account of the Intelligible world is based by determining, first, what anticipations of it, complete or partial, can be found in Plotinus' classical sources and, secondly, what parallels exist in more modern writers or in non-Western religious traditions. That this is a bold undertaking needs no stressing; it is also, as I should admit at the outset, one severely limited both by my own knowledge and by the restrictions of space imposed on a paper like the present one. That I have had to confine myself to accounts known to me is obvious; I hope very much that some of the other participants will be able to supply further parallels. Limitations of space, on the other hand, have forced me to confine myself, first, to accounts obviously based on experience and not mere theory and, secondly, to experiences whose relevance to Plotinus is obvious; hence the omission of many fascinating passages from authors both classical and modern. Finally, I had had in most cases to restrict my own interpretative comments to a minimum, especially since much of the paper had to be taken up with quotations from the relevant sources, particularly those unlikely to be familiar to classicists. Where the parallels to Plotinus are clear, as is happily often the case, the resulting harm is comparatively small, but readers will see that in dealing with Plato and Aristotle I have had to state dogmatically views on disputed questions of classical scholarship and textual interpretation which require argument at much greater length than is possible here. I have, however, tried to phrase my account in such a way as to secure maximum assent to what I say, with as little as possible dependent on whether my views on such points are accepted. For all these reasons, therefore, this paper can be only a preliminary clearing of the ground and one whose main aim is to inspire others to seek further.

That the most original feature of Plotinus' doctrine of the Three Hypostases is its elevation of psychological experiences into metaphysical realities is now commonplace.[1] And there is no great difficulty in identifying the experiences corresponding to his First and Third Hypostases. The latter is evidently the sphere of discursive thought (διάνοια), the process familiar in our everyday lives, discursive (at least as far as the human soul is concerned) in the sense of involving both reasoning from premises to conclusion[2] and simple transition from one object of thought to another.[3] For both these reasons it necessarily involves time; hence Plotinus' famous "psychological" definition of the latter presented at III. 7. 43-5.[4] The First Hypostasis, by contrast, corresponds to the mystics' "undifferentiated unity",[5] "a state in which sensuous imagery and conceptual thought are transcended, the mind becomes perfectly unified and individual limitations are felt to be abolished".[6] Whether Plotinus' mysticism is "theistic", "monistic" or something between the two is the subject of another paper;[7] all that matters here is to emphasize that the "undifferentiated unity" occurs in mystics of *both* types and that the distinction between the One and the Second Hypostasis (*Noūs*) cannot therefore correspond in any form to that between theistic and monistic mysticism (or vice versa).[8] Nor can we identify the experience of *Noūs* with what has been called "extrovertive mysticism", that is, with the vision of a unity running through the external world (as opposed to the introvertive mysticism of which union with the One is clearly an example.)[9] This identification, which has misled some excellent students of mysticism, appears to have originated with Rudolf Otto,[10] whose analysis of Enn. I. 8. 2 certainly shows, as do some passages to be considered later, how much Plotinus' account of *Noūs* has in common with mysticism of this type. But whereas extrovertive mysticism, as Otto rightly states, "knows nothing of inwardness",[11] Plotinus, by contrast, as a good Platonist, is emphatic that *Noũs* is attained by turning within and leaving sense-perception behind.[12] But what then *is* the experience on which his Second Hypostasis is based? Or, in order not to beg the question, what evidence is there that Plotinus' *Noũs* is experientially based at all, and not a mere theoretical construction out of Aristotelian and Middle Platonic tradition?

That Plotinus' account indeed incorporates a vast amount from these traditions modern studies have proved.[13] Yet scholars, sometimes the same ones, have equally felt that Plotinus' descriptions of *Noũs* suggested an empirical basis. Professor Dodds thus states that "for Plotinus the world of Platonic Forms is already the object of a kind of mystical experience".[14] And in his admirable account in the "Cambridge History of Later Greek and Early Medieval Philosophy" Professor Armstrong has gone further and quoted some specific passages from the treatise V. 8, "On Intelligible Beauty," and the first part of VI.7, "On the Ideas and the One," that lend strong support to this view. Attention may especially be drawn to two passages from the latter treatise; as we shall later see, their exact formulation is sufficiently important to require quotation in full. The first is VI. 7. 12. 23-30. "All flows, so to speak, from one fount not to be thought of as some one breath or warmth, but rather as one quality englobing and safeguarding all qualities – sweetness with fragrance, wine-quality, and the savours of everything that may be tasted, all colours seen, everything known to touch, all that ear may hear, all melodies, every rhythm".[15]

The other is VI. 7. 15. 24-30: – "It might be likened to a living sphere teeming with variety, to a globe of faces radiant with faces all living, to a unity of souls, all the pure souls, not the faulty but the perfect, with Intellect enthroned over all so that the place entire glows with intellectual splendour".[16]

These passages and others, especially those, like the one just quoted, describing the radiant luminosity of the Intelligible world, are one type of evidence that Plotinus has an actual experience in mind. Another is provided by his exhortations to the reader to attain the experience for himself. Thus the passage just quoted continues – (again, we shall see, the exact wording is important): – "But this would be to see it from without, one

thing seeing another; the true way is to become Intellectual-
principle and be, our very selves, what we are to see".[17] In
similar vein, Plotinus states elsewhere, at the end of a chapter
(V. 8. 10) containing a particularly vivid description of
Intellectual vision and of the radiance of the world "yonder": –
"To those that do not see entire, the immediate impression is
alone taken into account; but those drunken with this wine,
filled with the nectar, all their soul penetrated by this beauty,
cannot remain mere gazers; no longer is there a spectator
outside gazing on an outside spectacle; the clear-eyed hold the
vision within themselves, though, for the most part, they have
no idea that it is within but look towards it as to something
beyond them, and see it as an object of vision caught by a
direction of the will.

All that one sees as a spectacle is still external; one must
bring the vision within and see no longer in that mode of
separation but as we know ourselves; thus a man filled with a
god – possessed by Apollo or by one of the Muses – need no
longer look outside for his vision of the divine beings; it is but
finding the strength to see divinity within".[18]

In these passages, as can be seen, a brief hint is given of the
way to attain the experience described; we must bring the vision
within and no longer see it as a distinct object, but become
wholly identified with it. The process is elaborated at greater
length in the relatively few passages in which scholars have
detected references to the "spiritual exercises" of the Plotinian
school, the best known being V. 8. 9. 1. ff.[19] We must first, we
are told there, visualise a complete and accurate image of the
physical universe; then we must utterly remove from it (and not
merely attenuate) its spatial and material limitations, at the
same time praying God and the gods of the Intelligible world to
enter it. The parallel noted by scholars to the exercises of other
religious traditions suggests that such passages are no mere
poetic imagery, and thus constitutes a third type of evidence
that a definite experience is involved.

If then, we accept this and, leaving such poetically-tinged
passages, seek a more cold-bloodedly analytic account of the
differences between *Noūs* and our everyday consciousness, it is
to such chapters as I. 8. 2 and V. 1. 4 that we must turn. The

main differences, we there learn, are two. First, since *Noûs* contains the totality of True Being and hence has nothing further to seek, its thought is free from change and therefore transcends time; (since Professor Armstrong has cast some doubt on the accuracy of this description, it might be safer to say "transcends time as we know it").[20] Secondly, while discursive thought contemplates its object, as it were, "at a distance," since it cannot attain perfect unity therwith, on the level of *Noûs* there is perfect identity between subject and object and hence complete self-awareness.[21] Some doubt may, however, be felt whether these two points have an empirical basis, since both of them demonstrably derive from reflection on Aristotle's conception of *Noûs*.[22] The former point, *Noûs's* alleged timelessness, has been fully considered, as stated, by Professor Armstrong, and I do not propose to discuss it further here. The latter point, however, that *Noûs* enjoys perfect unity with its objects, was clearly alluded to in the "empirical" passages already quoted, and we may therefore provisionally take it to be part of the experience. Confirmation of this will be provided by the parallel experiences to be examined later though, as we shall also see, Plotinus' account is by no means free from difficulty). We may finally note two corollaries of the latter point. First, the objects of *Noûs* are Pure Forms, whereas discursive thought, contemplating the Forms at a distance, must be content with images of them, which represent them to her consciousness "as in a mirror".[23] In other words *Noûs* transcends mental images and the faculty contemplating them (φαντασία), on which our normal consciousness relies and, for similar reasons, it transcends abstract verbal formulae; the gods' knowledge is not composed of "premisses, axioms or predicates".[24] The secondary corollary of Plotinus' view of *Noûs* is that each member of the Intelligible world, contemplating as it does the whole of that world, is identical with the whole of that world and with each individual member thereof. "The sun, There, is all the stars; and every star, again is all the stars and sun. While some one manner of being is dominant in each, all are mirrored in every other".[25]

Such then is Plotinus' account of Intellectual vision. But what exactly is he talking about and what anticipations or parallels exist either in classical Greek thought or elsewhere? The question, it should be emphasised, is not what are the classical Greek antecedents of *Noũs* as a metaphysical hypostasis; this has been exhaustively treated elsewhere. Our search here is rather for antecedents of and parallels to the *experience* described. And here two difficulties arise. First, as even a little investigation shows, the territory between discursive thought and *unio mystica* is filled not by a single experience, but by a whole family of experiences, often with only the barest "family resemblances" between them. Secondly, as is well known, in Classical writers the term *Noũs* is not confined even to experiences within this already large family, but sometimes applied to reason as a whole, while in Hermetic and Middle Platonic texts it is frequently applied to an entity little, if at all, less transcendent than the Plotinian One.[26] I must therefore stress once again that my concern is with experiences which anticipate or otherwise illuminate the nature of Plotinus' Intellectual vision, whether or not the term *Noũs* is specifically applied to them. It will, however, be useful to begin by considering Von Fritz's far too little known elucidation of the original meaning of the term, as revealed by Homer and the Presocratics.[27]

According to Von Fritz "originally and in Homer, νοῦς never means 'reason' and νοεῖν never 'to reason,' whether deductively or inductively";[28] indeed it is not until Parmenides that logical reasonig is consciously included in the term's meaning.[29] In Homer, by contrast, νοῦς is associated with sensation rather than with intellectual thought, but differs from external perception in constituting "a kind of sixth sense which penetrates deeper into the nature of the objects perceived than the other senses".[30] Hence its fundamental meaning "may be defined as the realisation of a situation";[31] for instance, at *Iliad* III. 30 ff., when Paris sees Menelaus, "it is not the sight of Menelaus as such that strikes him, but the realisation that Menelaus has no more ardent desire than to take revenge by killing him on the battlefield".[32] As we shall see, the relation of such insight to the senses is a major point of controversy among the authors we shall consider; the other features of the Homeric conception, by contrast, are more consistently present among them.

First, insight of this type, though often preceded by logical reasoning, is not experienced as the abstract conclusion of such reasoning, but rather as a sudden and immediate realisation. "The process through which we arrive at this conclusion may require considerable time, but the realisation itself ... usually comes like a flash ... We are then much more conscious of this sudden realisation which has the appearance of a perception than of mental process which has led to it".[33] Secondly, the function of such insight is not usually conceived as being to provide wholly new knowledge. In Homer, we saw it to denote realisation of a situation's true meaning, whereas in Plato we shall find it affording a direct and more complete insight into truths previously grasped only in the abstract. In Plotinus it was seen to provide a vision of the true archetypal Reality of which this world constitutes a partial image, while yet other writers regard it as bringing out fresh and hitherto unrealised aspects of long familiar facts. It is intuition of this last type that has played so important a part in scientific, and especially in mathematical, discovery.

The role of intuition in scientific discovery has been especially popularized in Koestler's "Act of Creation".[34] Here I am not concerned with the merits or demerits of Koestler's theories, but merely with the fact, already well known to mathematicians, that experiences of this type are by no means rare in the history or thought. A comparison of Greek accounts of *νοῦς* with those quoted by Koestler, or in the earlier essay of Hadamard,[35] will prove extremely illuminating. Most striking, perhaps, are the accounts of eminent mathematicians quoted by Hadamard and conveniently summarised on p. 115 of Koestler's book. We there find Poincaré referring to the "appearance of sudden illumination, a manifest sign of long unconscious prior work," Hadamard to "the sudden and immediate appearance of a solution ... without the slightest instant of reflection on my part" and Gauss to solving an enigma "as a sudden flash of light" which comes "not by dint of painful effort, but so to speak by the grace of God." Classical instances quoted by Koestler are Pythagoras' intuition of the world's underlying mathematical harmony and Archimedes' discovery of the principle which bears his name.[36] A parallel from the field of artistic creation is provided by the poet John Masefield.[37] In his words "instantly the poem appeared to me in its complete form, with every detail distinct ... This illumination is an intense experience so wonderful that it cannot be described. While it lasts the momentary problem is merged into a dazzlingly clear perception of the entire work in all its detail. In a moment of mental ecstacy the writer ... perceives what seems to be an unchangeable way of statement." In such cases, it would appear, the data relevant to the problem in hand had been previously amassed, but after a period in which the discursive intellect had considered them without apparent success, had been laid aside until an appropriate stimulus suddenly precipitated their emergence into consciousness in an instantaneous blaze of light. The same schema of four stages — (1) amassing data, (2) logical reasoning, (3) unconscious incubation and (4) sudden vision — would appear to be present in those cases where there is neither problem nor solution, but simply a vivid and direct insight into truths previously known only as abstract propositions. A case of the latter type would appear to be what is described in the Seventh Platonic letter.

I do not propose to consider here, nor have I space to do so, whether the Letter is a work of Plato's old age or one composed by a close disciple shortly after his death — a question on which I personally have an open mind. Nor, more regrettably, have I the space to argue, what I would maintain emphatically, that in either case its philosophy is on all essential points Platonic.[38] Here I must limit myself to the experience of which the Letter's philosophical digression provides an account.

At 341 C in the Letter occurs the famous denial that the science of ultimate truth is expressible in words like other sciences. It arises, we are told, only after long philosophical communion concerning the subject, when a light suddenly springs up in the soul and thereafter nourishes itself.[39] The reason, we subsequently learn, is the inadequacy of "the four," names (ὀνόματα), definitions (λόγοι), sensible images (εἴδωλα) and human knowledge based on these,[40] to express the nature of "the Fifth," i.e. the Pure Form (342 A ff.).[41] It is, of course, fundamental to Platonism that sensible images are only inferior imitations of the Forms. Similarly names are not fixed to objects by nature and nor are definitions, since they are composed of nouns (ὀνόματα) and verbs (ῥήματα). Hence all four are defective in that they express only a thing's quality (τὸ ποῖον τι) instead of its essence (τὸ τί) (342 E - 343 C). But it is only by first grasping these four that one can subsequently attain knowledge of the Fifth.[42] It is by passing through the four, "ascending and descending to each in turn," that true knowledge can be generated with difficulty in the souls of intellectually and morally suitable pupils.[43] After "rubbing them against one another" wisdom can finally be made to shine forth within such disciples.[44]

The Letter's philosophical digression, of which the above was a necessarily short and inadequate summary, thus forms the most detailed description of the psychology of the philosopher's supreme vision to be found in the Platonic Corpus. The echoes of the accounts of intuition quoted earlier are no less evident. As I have stated, I cannot argue here, what I think can be proved, that its teaching is on all major points consistent with that of the dialogues; nor can I discuss the problems posed by the Letter's technical terminology, problems by no means unparalleled in Plato's certainly genuine writings.[45] It is, however, clear that the Letter describes two ways of knowing the Forms, an imperfect way based on words and on the Forms' sensible images, and one that is at least more nearly adequate and which transcends these. Similarly, it will be recalled, one of the two points in which νόησις in the Republic was claimed to be superior to διάνοια was in dealing with the Forms themselves and making no use of their sensible images (εἰκόνες) (the other, of course, being its ability to rise above hypotheses to the unhypothetical First Principle of the Good) (510 B, 511 A ff.). What is unfortunately less clear in the Republic is whether both faculties are concerned with Forms, or at any rate with the same type of Form.[46] It is sufficient for our purposes, however, to observe, first, that no one doubts, and Plato explicitly states, that the objects of νόησις are the Forms themselves (510 B, 511 C) and, secondly, that he further states that the objects of διάνοια become objects of νόησις "in conjunction with a First Principle".[47] We may therefore take it that νόησις affords a more perfect knowledge of the objects initially known through διάνοια and that these include some, if not certainly all, the

Forms.[48] Similarly the *Cratylus,* a dialogue in which the role of words (or more especially of names)[49] as images of Realities is examined at length, refers to the need for a faculty that will grasp Realities by themselves (αὐτὰ δι' αὐτῶν) and independently of names (ἄνευ ὀνομάτων), since only so can we be sure that our application of names is correct (438 D-E). Here again, however, it is far from clear at first sight that the Realities mentioned are the Forms. The view that they are can be supported, first, by the mention of the Forms towards the end of the dialogue[50] and, secondly, by the fact that only so can we suppose the procedures described in the *Cratylus* to have serious philosophical significance.[51] Finally we may compare the terms in which Socrates describes the nature of the faculty in question as too hard for him or Cratylus to determine[52] with *Republic* 506 D-E, where Socrates disclaims ability to give an account of the Good, and 533 A, where he declares that Glaucon will be unable to follow an account of Truth itself as opposed to an image thereof.[53] It is thus natural to infer that the faculty alluded to in the Cratylus is νόησις and that its objects, as in the Republic, are the Forms. In this case the doctrine of the two works, and of the Letter, would, thus far at least, be substantially identical.

Unfortunately, as has been objected, it is hard to see what a form of knowledge entirely independent either of words or of sensible images would be like.[54] That the passages just considered speak of the possibility of such a knowledge is clear enough. But it is certainly possible that Plato has been led to exaggerate in the sense that all he would seriously wish to maintain is that such knowledge is *no longer dependent* on words or images, not that it does without them altogether.[55] This, however, is not necessarily so, since we found Plotinus likewise maintaining that *his* Intellectual vision does without words or images. But of course, to note that the two philosophers agree, at least verbally, on the point mentioned neither makes the nature of such knowledge any clearer nor even establishes that it can exist at all. For the present we need merely note the difficulty; we shall have occasion later to return to it.

In general, moreover, despite the two philosophers' agreement on the above-mentioned point, the Seventh Letter's account of the supreme vision seems decidedly less intense (to use a convenient term), that is to say, less mystically-tinged and closer to the world of our everyday experience than that given by the Enneads. In particular it seems much closer to the mathematical intuition described by us earlier. There is, of course, a more mystical tone to the visions described in the *Symposium* and the *Phaedrus* (not to mention the enigmatic allusion to the Form of the Good in the *Republic*). The *Symposium* vision, however, is concerned solely with the Form of the Beautiful, not with the whole world of Forms. And even in the *Phaedrus,* which of all the dialogues comes closest to the Plotinian vision, it is noteworthy how many features of that vision are lacking. The timelessness of Plotinus' *Noũs* is indeed partially anticipated by the instantaneousness of the visions of the Symposium and the Seventh Letter.[56] But there is no suggestion in Plato of the Soul's identity with the Intelligible world or of the mutual identity existing between that world's members. The union of subject and object in Intellectual vision may be partially anticipated in the metaphors of sexual union applied by Plato to the Soul's contemplation of the Forms, but their significance is greatly lessened when we recall that he applies them no less to the soul's contact with the objects of sense-perception.[57] It seems therefore that we must look elsewhere for the closest parallel to Plotinus' Intellectual vision.

Nor will Aristotle advance our search very far. This statement may seem astounding in the light of the very large Aristotelian component in Plotinus' conception of *Noũs*, which I certainly do not wish to contest.[58] Here, however, we are seeking anticipations of the experiential rather than the metaphysical side of *Noũs*, whereas it would appear from such points as Aristotle's arguments for the self-awareness of *Noũs*,[59] that his position rests on theoretical rather than experiential grounds. It is especially noteworthy that his argument in the *De Anima* is paralleled by, perhaps even based on, his argument for the self-awareness of sense-perception,[60] and that it depends on the "informing" of the soul by a mental image,[61] whereas in Plotinus φαντασία, like sense-perception, precludes the possibility of pure self-awareness.[62] This conclusion might have to be modified if more of Aristotle's early works survived – in particular if it could be proved that in them he had allowed the possibility that the soul may attain a direct vision of her own nature,[63] an idea of which the later passages would then be relics. This, however, must remain speculative. It is clearly true that the fragments of Aristotle's early works show decided echoes of the Platonic view of intuition.[64] But if we turn to the accounts of νοῦς in the Analytics and Ethics,[65] we find that, so far from going beyond Plato, Aristotle significantly restricts the capacity of νοῦς in comparison with his master.

The most obvious difference between the two is that whereas for Plato, at least in some and perhaps in all cases, νοῦς and ἐπιστήμη had been concerned with the same objects, for Aristotle this is no longer true. Or perhaps we should rather say (to keep our account consistent with our earlier observations) that the two faculties deal with different *aspects* of our knowledge, scientific knowledge (ἐπιστήμη) having as its object truth reached by discursive syllogistic reasoning, whereas the function of νοῦς is to apprehend the first principles (ἀρχαί) implicit in all our reasoning and on which that reasoning depends, but which cannot themselves be reached by syllogistic reasoning.[66] Aristotle indeed makes two concessions to the Platonists, first that perfect knowledge is impossible without grasping the first principles on which that knowledge rests (N. E. 1139b 31 ff.), and secondly that intuition is more accurate than knowledge reached by discursive reasoning (Post. An. II. 19. 100b 8-9). But he maintains against Plato that there is no more perfect means than demonstration of knowing demonstrative truth (Post. An. 83b 34 ff.). And the superior accuracy of νοῦς depends on a further difference between the two faculties, that, whereas discursive thought involves the combination of concepts, νοῦς has as its province the apprehension of simple concepts and is therefore infallible.[67] We may further note that the gulf between νοῦς and sense-perception appears less wide in Aristotle than it had been for Plato. Thus Posterior Analytics II. 19 appears to conceive of a continuous process from the intuitive apprehension of the simplest universal concepts out of the data of sense-perception to the apprehension by νοῦς of the

ultimate principles of all such reasoning. And while Nicomachean Ethics VI declares νοῦς and the practical man's common
sense to be opposed in the status and dignity of their objects
(1142 a 25 ff.), Aristotle's subsequent discussion reveals strong
analogies between the operations of the two faculties and thus
associates them in a way with which Plato would have had little
sympathy.[68] A more detailed comparison of the two thinkers'
views both with one another and with modern accounts of
intuition would be a fascinating and illuminating exercise. It
would not, however, bring us any closer to an understanding of
Plotinus, and cannot therefore be pursued further here.

The difficulty posed by writers of the Hellenistic-Roman
period is a different one. It is not that there is any lack in their
writings of experiences going beyond normal consciousness. As
writers such as Dodds and Festugiere have shown,[69] writings
such as the Hermetica and those of Philo, the Gnostics and the
Middle Platonists reveal a profusion of such experiences,
experiences recalling Platonic — Aristotelian intuition,[70] mystical or quasi-mystical experiences foreshadowing Plotinus' Union
with the One,[71] prophetic experiences, experiences of divinisa-
tion, extrovertive mystical experiences,[72] as well as not a few
experiences whose interpretation is throughly ambiguous. What
we do not find, as far as I am aware, is a detailed account
clearly anticipating Plotinus' description of Intellectual contemplation,[73] and, even if we are looking for detailed accounts
bridging the gulf between that experience and those considered
earlier, our harvest will be disappointingly small. The danger, in
short, is that, so far from advancing our understanding of
Plotinus, the Hellenistic-Roman texts will merely complicate
our problem by adding a vast number of further experiences
themselves needing elucidation and classification. At all events,
such an inquiry cannot be undertaken in a paper like the
present one. I shall therefore confine myself to a single account,
which goes some way towards bridging the gulf referred to and
which has significant links both with Plotinus and with some
parallel experiences which we shall consider.

The text in question is Philo's well-known description at
Migr. Abr. 31-35 of his own literary inspiration. Sometimes he

relates, despite having in his mind a clear conception of the subject on which he intends to write, he has been unable to produce any work, whereas at other times, "coming to work empty," he has suddenly ($\dot{\epsilon}\xi\alpha\dot{\iota}\varphi\nu\eta\varsigma$) become full of ideas "invisibly showered upon him"[74] and thereby attained a vivid and direct vision of what to say. In his own words he attain "language, ideas, an enjoyment of light, keenest vision, pellucid distinctness of objects, such as might be received through the eyes as the result of keenest shewing".[75] Under the influence of divine possession he further becomes unconscious of his surroundings, of those present and even of himself and of what he is saying and writing.[76] At such moments of "release," he writes, the mind gives up its own activities and abandons its will to a higher inspiration.[77] Finally we may note Philo's contrast between such inspiration and the laborious processes that normally occupy the mind[78] and his consequent stress on the superior excellence of the products of inspiration.[79]

The resemblances between Philo's account and those considered earlier are obvious, in its stress on the suddenness and clarity of intuitive insight and its contrast between the effortlessness of intuition and the laboriousness of the mind's usual processes, as also between periods of sterility and of inspiration. Only three further features require special comment. The first is the Jewish contemplative's description of his experience in terms of prophetic inspiration and his consequent ascription of it to divine power. The "grace of God," which for Gauss was a mere metaphor,[80] is meant by Philo in real earnest. The second is Philo's reference to surrendering his individual will, a point to which we shall return. Finally there is his statement that the vision bring oblivion of one's surroundings and even of oneself. In this respect it appears somewhat more intense and further from our normal consciousness than those described earlier and to mark an intermediate stage between them and Plotinus' account of the Intelligible world. It may also be regarded as intermediate between the latter and the experiences to which Plotinus appeals in support of his claim that consciousness (of the type familiar to us)[81] has a blunting effect on our activities. When we are absorbed in reading or an act of bravery, he states, we have no awareness that we are performing those actions; such awareness arises in proportion as our absorption in them grows less (I. 4. 10. 21-33). Philo's experience resembles such cases in involving action (in this case writing) in the sensible world, but his references to inspiration give it a deeper, more mystical tone.

An experience which comes even closer to bridging the gulf between Plotinus and the writers so far considered is the aesthetic contemplation described by Schopenhauer, from whom it will therefore be desirable to quote a fairly lengthy passage. A further reason for doing so is furnished by Friedlander's observation that while by "confining the intuitive to the aesthetic," Schopenhauer made his account of the Platonic Idea unduly restrictive," apart from this, however, Schopenhauer had a more profound understanding of the intuitive element in the Idea than anyone else in recent times, no doubt because what he found in reading Plato coincided with his most personal experience".[82] After declaring, like our previous sources, that the vision comes "suddenly," the relevant passage continues as follows:[83]

"If, raised by the power of the mind, a man relinquishes the common way of looking at things, gives up tracing, under the guidance of the forms of the principle of sufficient reason, their relations to each other, the final goal of which is always a relation to his own will; if he thus ceases to consider the where, the when, the why and the whither of things, and looks simply and solely at the what; if, further, he does not allow abstract thought, the concepts of the reason, to take possession of his consciousness, but instead of all this, gives the whole power of his mind to perception, sinks himself entirely in this, and lets his whole consciousness be filled with the quiet contemplation of the natural object actually present, whether a landscape, a tree, a mountain, a building, or whatever it may be; inasmuch as he *loses* himself in this object ... i.e., forgets even his individuality, his will, and only continues to exist as the pure subject, the clear mirror of the object, so that it is as if the object alone were there, without any one to perceive it, and he can no longer separate the perceiver from the perception, but both have become one, because the whole consciousness is filled and occupied with one single sensuous picture, if thus the

object has to such an extent passed out of all relation to
something outside it, and the subject out of all relation to the
will, then that which is so known is no longer the particular
thing as such; but it is the *Idea*, the eternal form, the immediate
objectivity of the will at this grade; and, therefore, he who is
sunk in this perception is no longer individual, for in such
perception the individual has lost himself; but he is *pure*
will-less, painless, timeless *subject of knowledge"*.

The resemblances between the above passage and Plotinus
are clear. Both describe a vision transcending spatio-temporal
restrictions and abolishing the subject-object distinction.[84] The
Schopenhauer passage, furthermore, agrees with Philo that the
vision involves abandonment of one's individual will, just as for
Plotinus it is the "will to belong to oneself" that leads the soul
to leave the Intelligible world and forget her true identity.[85]
Hence return to that world for him as for Plato, involves a
moral as well as an intellectual purification;[86] indeed, since
what we contemplate depends on what interest us, the two are
linked and the soul's return "yonder" abolishes not merely all
interest in the sensible world and one's separate existence
therein, but all consciousness and memory of these.[87] Finally,
Plotinus' account of *Noũs* as the Totality of Being is echoed in
Schopenhauer's vision of the World as Idea, in which individual
limitations are transcended and the whole world is felt to
depend on one's own consciousness. This point Schopenhauer
summarises in the Upanishadic dictum *"hae omnes creaturae in
totum ego sum, et praeter me aliud ens non est"*.[88] Yet, despite
these resemblances, there is the contrast that for Schopenhauer
the way to attain the vision is to lose oneself in an external
object of perception, "a landscape, a tree, a mountain, a
building," etc., so that "the whole consciousness is filled and
occupied with one single sensuous picture." This experience is
therefore clearly of the *extrovertive* type and thus, as we have
seen, to be contrasted with Plotinian contemplation. The closest
parallels to that contemplation must therefore be sought
elsewhere.

There are to be found in Indian mysticism. Both Hindu
and Buddhist mysticism distinguish between contemplation of
the Realm of Pure Form (Buddhist rupa jhana, Hindu savikalpa

samadhi) and contemplation of the Formless realm (Buddhist arupa jhana, Hindu nirvikalpa samadhi), and the traditional accounts leave no doubt that these are both levels of *intro-vertive* contemplation. The obvious reflection that we have here a parallel distinction to that in Plotinus between *Noûs* and the One receives powerful support from a modern description of the Buddhist scheme, that of Lama Anagarika Govinda, which it will therefore be desirable to quote in full. I say "powerful support," however, and not "confirmation," since it is to be feared that the German-born author may have been influenced by Plotinus and by Plotinian-influenced German idealists in writing it. But though caution must obviously be used in evaluating what he says, I have found that most of his substantial points can be verified from other Buddhist writers. Before attempting a detailed analysis, however, it is best to set out what he has to say.[89]

"Between the two extremes, the domain of the sensuously bounded, or of form bound by craving (kāmadhātu) and the domain for [sic.] the formless (arūpadhātu), the unlimited that is free from craving, there comes in intermediately a group of objects which are not perceptible indeed to the lower senses, namely those (of contact, of the non-spatial) of smell, of taste and of touch, but certainly to the higher senses, in so far as these are free from all entanglement with the ego, that is, free from discordance (craving), and therefore able to merge completely into the object, to become one with it, to experience it from within. These objects are designated as pure forms, untarnished by any kind of entanglement with the 'I' or as absolute form (rūpa), since they belong neither to the domain of the formless (they possess shape), nor yet correspond to the sensuous form bound by craving. The realm of Pure Form (rūpadhātu) is thus not a domain of intellectual abstractions but of intuitive (because 'I' − freed) contemplation of form. Corresponding to these three groups of objects, we get three basic planes of consciousness; the consciousness which dwells in the domain of the sensuous, of forms of craving (kāmāvacara-citta); the consciousness which dwells in the domain of Pure Form (rūpāvacara-citta); and the consciousness which dwells in the domain of the Formless, of Non-Form (arūpāvacara-citta).

The Realm of Pure Form is intermediary between the other two realms inasmuch as it has something in common with each of the two – with the sense-domain, the property of form-ness; with the formless domain, the property of abstraction, namely from the egocentricity of the lower domain of the senses filled with desires. That this is no mere artificial, intellectual abstraction, follows from the intuitive character of these two domains. The properties of each domain are not something added to their particular character, but only modifications of the same. Thus the sense-world is designated as partly the domain of sensuous desires, since its objects are bounded, 'I' – conditioned, in their individualness set in contrast with the subject, incapable of union with the subject, and hence beget the state of tension (dualism) which we call craving. The objects belonging to the realm of Non-Form possess no limiting boundaries, are beyond all multiplicity and every kind of isolation or 'I'-entanglement. With this is excluded all possibility of tension, of craving. It is the same with pure forms, for their boundaries are only of an ideal, a formal sort, they are not essential to them and can therefore be filled by the experiencing subject."

For those who know the Enneads the above passage will have a very familiar sound. How close the resemblances really are and how far they are due simply to Neoplatonic reminiscences in the mind of its author may best be ascertained by an analysis of its contexts. Six points may be singled out:–

1.   The World of Pure Form is intermediate between the realm of discursive thought and the purely formless domain, with both of which it has something in common.

2.   It is thus characterised by a purely intuitive contemplation, to be contrasted with discursive thought.

3.   It breaks down the barrier between subject and object found in normal thought and perception.

4.   It involves relinquishment of the ego and of sensual craving.

5.   Its objects are Pure Forms.

6.   These are perceptible only to the higher senses (sight and hearing) in so far as they are able to merge with their object and experience it from within.

The resemblances between the first five of the above points and Plotinus' account of *Noũs* are evident enough; indeed the first three of them are so basic to it that no more need be said. With point four, that intuitive contemplation involves abandonment of sensual craving and one's own will we have dealt sufficiently in connection with Schopenhauer; it is equally fundamental for Buddhist contemplatives that meditative absorption requires relinquishment both of sensual desire and of discursive thought,[90] while the statement that it abolishes the subject-object distinction is also found in sources not open to the suspicion of Neoplatonic influence.[91] Hence when both Plotinus and the Buddhists describe the objects of intuitive contemplation as Pure Forms we may conclude a priori that here too they are likely to be talking about the same thing, despite the obscurities of their accounts. (Thus on the one hand we read that Pure Forms "have shape," on the other that "their boundaries are only of an ideal, a formal sort, they are not essential to them.") The only major divergence between the two accounts concerns point six; for, as we have seen, for Plotinus *Noũs* involves complete abandonment of sense-perception and mental images, whereas for the Buddhists, as for Schopenhauer, it involves merging the senses with their objects. Not only, however, will it be recalled that we found Plato and Plotinus extremely obscure as to what contemplation without mental images would be like; if we refer back to Plotinus' accounts of *Noũs,* with their rich sensuous imagery, and especially to VI. 7. 12. 23-30's comparison of it to "one quality englobing and safeguarding all qualities," we may wonder whether his experience may not in fact be closer to that of the Buddhists than his formal theory allows. Is he not, in fact, attaining it by merging his (inner) senses with their objects? At least we may ask him and Plato how, if the Intelligible world is as removed from sense-experience as they claim, it is legitimate to use sensuous imagery of that world at all. Even so the resemblance to the Buddhist position would still be incomplete, since the Plotinus passage refers to scent, taste and touch, whereas for the Buddhists only sight and hearing have a place in the Form World.[92] And it may also be felt that the nature of the experience in question remains obscure, whichever formulation is correct. But such obscurity is evidently inherent in any experience going beyond our normal consciousness, and the only remedy, as all the authors in question assure us, is to undertake the arduous course of training necessary to attain such experience for ourselves.[93]

Recent years, however, have brought us what in many quarters is regarded as a short cut to such experiences, by means of psychedelic drugs. That I have left dealing with these until now is due once again to the temendous *variety* of experiences involved and the danger, as before, that so far from finding illumination for our problem we shall find ourselves faced with a vast new family of experiences, themselves needing clarification. Nor do I propose to deal with the vexed question whether psychedelic drugs can produce mystical experience and, if so, what kinds of mystical experience. All I propose is to quote two accounts of such experiences which on significant points recall Plotinus' description of *Noũs* and thus provide final confirmation that his description is indeed experientially based. I shall add as little explanatory comment of my own as possible since most of the resemblances, and their implications, should be clear from our previous discussion.

The first passage is the account by a modern American journalist of his experience under mescalin.[94] This experience appears to differ from that of Plotinus in being of the extrovertive type, but, as in other extrovertive experiences, the echoes of Plotinus (in the words italicised), are clear enough. What is unfortunately unclear is how far they result from reminiscences of the Enneads on the author's part; all that can be said is that his references to Plotinus elsewhere do not suggest profound or detailed acquaintance.[95] A second significant difference is that the passage to be quoted is an account of a "bad trip." Thus, while Plotinus stresses the "ease" and "gentleness" of the Intelligible world,[96] the American journalist feels only meaninglessness and horror, Hence, presumably, his insistence that "we were not God." Once again, I refrain from discussing whether this is a correct interpretation of the experience; here it is only the experience and the resemblances to Plotinus that concern us.

"Finally it all fell together, and I remembered who I was. And it was all so simply, really, *I was life. I was being.* I was the *vibrant force* that filled the room, and was the room. *I was the world, the universe. I was everything.* I was that which always was and always would be. *I was Jim, and Jim was me, and we were everybody else; and everybody else was us,* and all of us put together were the same thing, and *that same thing was the only thing there was* and all that there was wasn't God. It was us, alone. And *we were each other*, and nowhere anywhere was there anything else but us and we were always the same, *the one and only truth*" (my underlinings).

The second passage is the account by the modern Buddhist writer John Blofeld of a 'high Yogic' experience also achieved through mescalin.[97]

"Suddenly there dawned full awareness of three great truths which I had long accepted intellectually but never, until that moment, experienced as being fully self-evident. (I quote only the first of these, R. T. W.) Now they had burst upon me, not just as intellectual convictions, but as experiences no less vivid and tangible than are heat and light to a man closely surrounded by a forest fire.

There was awareness of undifferentiated unity[98] embracing the perfect identity of subject and object, of singleness and plurality, of the One and the Many. Thus I found myself (if indeed the words 'I' and 'myself' have any meaning in such a context) at once the audience, the actors and the play. Logically the One can give birth to the many and the Many can merge into the One or be fundamentally but not apparently identical with it; they cannot be in all respects one and many simultaneously. But now logic was transcended. I beheld (and myself was) a whirling mass of brilliant colours and forms which, being several colours and several forms, were different from one another – and yet altogether the *same* at the very moment of being different! I doubt if this statement can be made to seem meaningful at the ordinary level of consciousness. No wonder the mystics of all faiths teach that understanding comes only when logic and intellect are transcended! In any case, this truth, even if at an ordinary level of consciousness it cannot be *understood,* can, in a higher state of consciousness, be directly *experienced* as self-evident. Logic also boggles at trying to explain how I could at once *perceive* and yet *be* those colours and those forms, how the *seer*, the *seeing* and the *seen*, the *feeler,* the *feeling* and the *felt* could all be one; but, to me, all this was so clearly self-evident as to suggest the words "childishly simple."

In quoting this passage a modern psychologist notes significant points on which it recalls the accounts of intuition given by such philosophers as Spinoza and Bergson;[99] the resemblance between the sudden illumination of Blofeld's first paragraph and that described in the Seventh Platonic Letter is equally striking. No less remarkable is the resemblance between the second paragraph and Plotinus' account of the unity-in-diversity of the Intelligible world, the mutual identity of its members and the unity between subject and object on which this depends. This last point, of course, was equally noticeable in the first psychedelic experience we considered, but, since Blofeld makes no reference to a transfiguration of the external world, his account would seem more clearly an experience of the introvertive type and therefore closer to Plotinus. On the other hand his reference to "a whirling mass of brilliant colours and forms" ("forms" here clearly meaning no more than "shapes") suggests an experience which, though paradoxical, is decidedly less intense and less mysterious than Plotinus' intellectual vision, and experience in fact intermediate between Plotinus' φαντασία and his *Noûs,* resembling the latter in involving union of subject and object, but the former in not having passed entirely beyond sensuous imagery. It is true that we saw reason to believe that Plotinus' analysis of Noûs was not wholly in accordance with his experience on the latter point, but even so it is surely hard to accept that his language implies nothing more mysterious than what Blofeld is talking about. What is less clear is where the Buddhists stand on the question, with their enigmatic reference to "Pure Forms." Fortunately the Buddhist scheme itself provides an easy answer for, since that scheme recognizes four (or sometimes five) divisions of the Form World,[100] it is a natural inference that Blofeld is describing one of the lower levels and Plotinus one of the higher ones.

Once again, however, it becomes clear that only by having the experience for ourselves will we achieve full certainty on the point. I hope, however, that the above account has, first of all, demonstrated that Plotinus' Intelligible world is beyond doubt empirically based (at least in part) and, secondly, done something, by assembling a deliberately restricted number of parallel passages, towards clarifying that experience. Once again I must stress that this paper is only a preliminary attempt to illuminate some of the territory lying between our normal consciousness and full mystical experience. If it prompts others to seek further and more fully, it will have achieved its purpose.

NOTES

1. Cf. especially E. Bréhier, *The Philosophy of Plotinus,* pp. 182 ff. and his notices to his Budé edition (especially that to Enn. V. 1); also P. O. Kristeller, *Der Begriff der Seele in der Ethik des Plotin* (Tubingen 1929), H.-R. Schwyzer *Die Zweifache Sicht in der Philosophie Plotins* (Museum Helveticum 1. 1944, pp. 87-99) and the first chapter of my *Neoplatonism* (London 1972). While recent studies have shown that Plotinus' "metaphysical" and "experiential" sides should not be separated too sharply, it is still helpful to distinguish these two aspects of his thought.

2. Termed by Aquinas discursiveness "secundum causalitatem" (Summa Theol. Ia. 14.7). Discursiveness of this type is denied to divine souls in e.g. Enn. IV. 3. 18, IV. 4. 12, etc.

3. Termed by Aquinas (Summa Theol. ibid.) discursiveness "per successionem tantum"; affirmed (apparently) of all souls in III. 7. 11, V. 1. 4. 10-25, denied of divine souls in IV. 4. 15-16.

4. III. 7. 11. 44: ψυχῆς ἐν κινήσει μεταβατικῇ ἐξ ἄλλου εἰς ἄλλον βίον ζωήν.

5. Cf. W. T. Stace *The Teachings of the Mystics* (New York 1960) and *Mysticism and Philosophy* (London 1961) passim.

6. *Neoplatonism* p. 3.

7. For the terms cf. R. C. Zaehner, *Mysticism Sacred and Profane* (Oxford 1957). That only a difference of interpre-

tation, not of actual experience, is involved is argued against Zaehner by Stace, whose view is endorsed by Dodds, *Pagan and Christian in an Age of Anxiety* p. 90. That Plotinus' mysticism is theistic is argued by Rist, *Plotinus, the Road to Reality*, ch. 16, pp. 213-30 and by Armstrong, *Cambridge History of Later Greek and Early Medieval Philosophy* p. 263. On the other side, see the paper of Prof. Mamo in the present volume; also my remarks in *Neoplatonism* pp. 89-90 and the (apparently conflicting) statements of Dodds at *Les Sources de Plotin* (Vandoeuvres - Geneva 1957) p. 22n. 2 and *Pagan and Christian* pp. 88-90.

8. Obvious examples from theistic mystics include Gregory of Nyssa, Pseudo – Dionysius and St. John of the Cross; from non-theistic mysticism cf. e.g. the Buddhist experiences described below pp. 136-37.

9. On extrovertive mysticism cf. Stace, *Teachings of the Mystics* pp. 62 ff. The experience is termed "the Mysticism of Unifying Vision" by Otto, *Mysticism East and West* pp. 38 ff.; Zaehner's term (*Mysticism Sacred and Profane* p. 28) is "panenhenic."

10. *Op. cit.* pp. 41-7, followed by Stace, *Mysticism and Philosophy* p. 77. For the correct view cf. Dodds, *Pagan and Christian* pp. 83-4; Rist, *Plotinus, the Road to Reality* pp. 215-16.

11. *Op. cit.* p. 42.

12. Cf. V. 8. 11. 10-12: δραμὼν δὲ εἰς τὸ εἴσω ἔχει πᾶν, καὶ ἀφεὶς τὴν αἴσθησιν εἰς τοὐπίσω τοῦ ἕτερος εἶναι φόβῳ εἰς ἐστιν ἐκεῖ.

13. The best account is that of Armstrong, *Sources de Plotin* pp. 393-413, with the subsequent discussion; cf. also recently the relevant sections of P. Merlan's account of Plotinus' background in the *Cambridge History of Later Greek and Early Medieval Philosophy* pp. 13-132, with the references given there.

14. *Pagan and Christian* p. 84 n. 1.

15. MacKenna's translation (as is also the case with the following passages). The passage is quoted by Armstrong, *Cambridge History* pp. 245-46.

16. Quoted by Armstrong *ibid*. p. 221.
17. VI. 7. 15. 30-2.
18. V. 8. 10. 31-43.
19. Cf. the discussion at *Sources de Plotin* p. 338 of this passage and VI. 4. 7. 23-40; also Dodds, *Pagan and Christian* pp. 86-7 and my *Neoplatonism* p. 42.
20. Cf. e. g. V. 1. 4. 1-25 and the other passages listed at *Neoplatonism* p. 53n. 2. For the difficulties in *Noûs's* alleged "timelessness" cf. Armstrong, *Le Néoplatonisme* (Paris 1971) pp. 67-76.
21. Cf. e.g. I. 8. 2. 7-21, III. 8. 8. 1-30, V. 3. 1-9, V. 5. 1-2.
22. That the divine Noûs transcends change is argued at Met. Λ. 9. 1074b 26-7; for the interdependence of change and time cf. the definition of time at Phys. IV. 11. 220a 24-5 (Cf. also *ibid*. IV. 12. 221b 3-7 and the puzzling chapter De Caelo I. 9.). On the identity between subject and object in *Noûs* cf. Met. ibid. 1074b 33-1075a 5, De An. III. 4. 429b 22-430a 9.
23. That *Noûs* cannot contemplate mere images is argued in V. 5. 1-2. For the comparison of φαντασία, on which our soul's consciousness rests, to a mirror cf. I. 4. 10. 6 ff., IV. 3. 30. 7 ff. The contrast between the two Hypostases is most concisely summarized at VI. 5. 7. 3-4: νοοῦμεν ἐκεῖνα οὐκ εἴδωλα αὐτῶν οὐδὲ τύπους ἔχοντες. εἰ δὲ μὴ τοῦτο, ὄντες ἐκεῖνα.
24. For verbal formulae as the objects of φαντασία cf. IV. 3. 30. 5 ff. That *Noûs* does not contemplate προτάσεις, ἀξιώματα or λεκτά is argued at V. 5. 1. 38-9.
25. V. 8. 4. 9-11, on which cf. Armstrong, *Cambridge History* p. 245.
26. Cf. especially Festugière's discussion in *La Révélation d'Hermès Trismégiste*, Vol. IV, *Le Dieu Inconnu et la Gnose* pp. 92-140. On the absurdities resulting from this linguistic confusion cf. p. 139 of Festugière's work.
27. "Noûs, νοεῖν and their derivatives in Homer" (*Classical Philology* 38 (1943) pp. 79-83; "Noûs, νοεῖν and their derivatives in Presocratic Philosophy" (ibid. 40(1945) pp. 223-242, 41(1946) pp. 12-34). Cf. also the summary in W. K. C. Guthrie *A History of Greek Philosophy* Vol. II pp. 17-19.

28. C P 1943 p. 90.
29. C P 1945 p. 242.
30. C P 1943 p. 90.
31. *Ibid.* p. 91, quoted by Guthrie *op. cit.* p. 18n. 1.
32. C P 1943 p. 85.
33. *Ibid.* p. 89.
34. London 1964.
35. J. Hadamard, *An Essay on the psychology of invention in the mathematical field* (Princeton 1945).
36. On Pythagoras cf. *op. cit.* pp. 111-12, on Archimedes *ibid.* pp. 105-8.
37. Quoted by Stace, *Mysticism and Philosophy* p. 82.
38. The most serious detailed attack on the Letter's authenticity in recent times is that of L. Edelstein, *Plato's Seventh Letter* (Leiden 1966); cf. also G. Ryle, *Plato's Progress* (Cambridge 1966). That the Letter's philosophy is substantially Platonic is argued by Von Fritz in *Phronesis* XI. 2(1966), pp. 117-153, with whose conclusions I am in substantial agreement, though they need supplementing on certain points. Von Fritz's remarks on pp. 134-5 of the article in question are for me the strongest argument in favour of the view that the Letter is in fact Plato's. On the historical side cf. now Von Fritz's *Platon in Sizilien* (Berlin 1968) ch. 1 (pp. 5-62).
39. ῥητὸν γὰρ οὐδαμῶς ἐστιν ὡς ἄλλα μαθήματα, ἀλλ' ἐκ πολλῆς συνουσίας γιγνομένης περὶ τὸ πρᾶγμα αὐτὸ καὶ τοῦ συζῆν ἐξαίφνης, οἷον ἀπὸ πυρὸς πηδήσαντος ἐξαφθὲν φῶς, ἐν τῇ ψυχῇ γενόμενον αὐτὸ ἑαυτὸ ἤδη τρέφει.
40. More strictly the terminology at 342 D (τούτων δὲ ἐγγύτατα μὲν συγγενείᾳ καὶ ὁμοιότητι τοῦ πέμπτου νοῦς πεπλησίακεν) would suggest that *all* human knowledge is there condemned as inadequate, whereas a distinction is subsequently made between two forms of knowledge, of which the higher (at 344B termed φρόνησις .... καὶ νοῦς) is at least more adequate than the lower. It is also unclear whether the statement of 342 D means (a) that knowledge in general approaches closer to the nature of the Forms than the first "three" or (b) that νοῦς is closer to the Forms than other kinds of knowledge; the latter is the view of Morrow (*Plato: Epistles* p. 73.).

41. The terms εἶδος and ἰδέα are not used in the Letter, but it is clear that this is what is meant by such phrases as ὃ δὴ γνωστόν τε καὶ ἀληθῶς ἐστιν ὄν (342B).

42. 342E: οὐ γὰρ ἂν τούτων μή τις τὰ τέτταρα λάβῃ ἀμῶς γέ πως, οὔποτε τελέως ἐπιστήμης τοῦ πέμπτου μέτοχος ἔσται.

43. 343E: ἡ δὲ διὰ πάντων αὐτῶν διαγωγή, ἄνω καὶ κάτω μεταβαίνουσα ἐφ᾽ ἕκαστον, μόγις ἐπιστήμην ἐνέτεκεν εὖ πεφυκότος εὖ πεφυκότι.

44. 344B: μόγις δὲ τριβόμενα πρὸς ἄλληλα αὐτῶν ἕκαστα, ὀνόματα καὶ λόγοι ὄψεις τε καὶ αἰσθήσεις . . . . .ἐξέλαμψε φρόνησις περὶ ἕκαστον καὶ νοῦς.

45. For the parallel fluctuations in Plato's technical terminology cf. Rep. 533E-534A, where νόησις (which at 511D-E had denoted the higher form of knowledge) becomes the term for knowledge as a whole, while ἐπιστήμη (formerly the more general term) is now applied to what had previously been called νόησις. For 342C's failure to distinguish knowledge and true opinion cf. Phil. 60D and 66B-C.

46. While Adam's view, in his edition of the Republic, that the objects of διάνοια are the intermediate "mathematicals" has not found general acceptance, other scholars have been sufficiently impressed by Rep. 477C-D's claim that different faculties have different objects to incline to see them as concerned with different kinds of Forms; cf. e.g. Ross, *Plato's Theory of Ideas* pp. 64-5. On the other side cf. Cross and Woozley, *Plato's Republic; a Philosophical Commentary* pp. 237-8, with whose conclusions I am in general agreement.

47. 511D: καίτοι νοητῶν ὄντων μετὰ ἀρχῆς.

48. Reference should also be made to 510D's mention of the "square itself" and "the diagonal itself", which strongly suggest that it is the mathematical Forms (and perhaps other Forms as well), rather than the "intermediates", that are the objects of διάνοια.

49. Reference is also made, however, at 431B-C, to the combination of words in propositions (λόγοι) as fulfilling a similar function. For the doctrine of the "verbal image" cf. also Phaedo 99D-100A. Among later Platonists cf. esp.

Plutarch Gen. Socr. 589B, Proclus Th. Pl. I. 10. (p. 46.2-5
Saffrey – Westerink), I. 29 (p. 124. 7-22 ibid.) and many
passages of his *Cratylus* commentary. The doctrine is a
clear anticipation of Wittgenstein's early "picture" theory
of language.

50. 439C ff.; cf. N. Gulley, *Plato's Theory of Knowledge*, pp.
     68-9.

51. This conclusion would not, of course, hold for anyone
     who regards the *Cratylus* as dating either (a) from a time
     before the Forms had achieved full transcendence for Plato
     or (b), with Owen, from a time when he was preparing to
     abandon the theory. Against the former view cf. Hack-
     forth, *Plato's Phaedo* p. 9; against the latter cf. most
     recently N. H. Reed, "Plato on Flux, Perception and
     Language" (*Proc. Cambridge Philol. Soc.* 198 (n.s. 18),
     1972, pp. 65-77).

52. 439B: ὄντωα μὲν τοίνυν τρόπον δεῖ μανθάνειν ἢ εὑρίσκειν
     τὰ ὄντα μεῖζον ἴσως ἐστὶν ἐγνωκέναι ἢ κατ᾽ ἐμὲ καὶ σέ.

53. Cf. especially the language of the latter passage: οὐκέτ᾽ . . .
     οἷος τ᾽ ἔσει ἀκολουθεῖν · ἐπεὶ τό γ᾽ ἐμὸν οὐδὲν ἂν
     προθυμίας ἀπολίποι οὐδ᾽ εἰκόνα ἂν ἔτι οὗ λέγομεν ἴδοις,
     ἀλλ᾽ αὐτὸ τὸ ἀληθές, δ᾽ γε δή μοι φαίνεται – εἰ δ᾽ὄντως ἢ
     μὴ οὐκετ᾽ ἄξιον τοῦτο διϊσχυρίζεσθαι· ἀλλ᾽ ὅτι μὲν δὴ
     τοιοῦτον τι ἰδεῖν ἰσχυριστέον.

54. Cf. Ross, *op. cit.* pp. 54-5, Cross and Woozley, *op. cit.* pp.
     241-2, Gulley, *op. cit.* p. 69.

55. Gulley's view (*op. cit.* p. 69) that the *Cratylus* is merely
     protesting against inadequacies in *existing* language (a view
     which Edelstein actually uses to distinguish its doctrine
     from that of the Letter and thus argue that the latter
     cannot be Plato's – cf. *op. cit.* p. 104 n. 76) ignores the
     fact that for Plato an image can *never* fully reproduce the
     nature of its original and that verbal images must thus
     always remain to some extent inadequate; cf. Crat. 432B:
     τοῦ δὲ ποιοῦ τινος καὶ ξυμπάσης εἰκόνος μὴ οὐχ αὕτη ᾖ ἡ
     ὀρθότης, ἀλλὰ τὸ ἐναντίον οὐδὲ τὸ παράπαν δέῃ πάντα
     ἀποδοῦναι οἷόν ἐστιν ᾧ εἰκάζει, εἰ μέλλει εἰκὼν εἶναι.

56. Symp. 210E, Ep. VII. 341C-D.

57. For the metaphor applied to union with ultimate Truth,

cf. Rep. 490A, Symp. 212A; to sense-perception Theaet.
156A ff., etc., Soph. 248A; Cf. further Cornford, *Plato's
Theory of Knowledge* pp. 239n. 1, 246.

58. Cf. above n. (13).
59. Cf. the passages listed above n. (22).
60. De An. III. 2. 425b 12 ff.
61. On this point cf. esp. the discussion in De An. III. 8.
62. Cf. above p. 125 and the passages quoted in n. (23).
63. Cf. Psellus Schol. in Joh. Clim. (=CMAG. VI. 171. 10-18, a
    continuation of περὶ Φιλ. fr. 15 Ross) and Cicero Tusc. I.
    27. 66 (which inclines, however, to set limits to the soul's
    self-awareness). If these passages are in fact based on
    Aristotle's early teaching, the implications for the origin of
    the νοήσεως νόησις doctrine would be far-reaching; for
    scholars' views on the question cf. the discussion in
    Untersteiner's edition of the περὶ Φιλοσοφίας.
64. This is proved by περὶ Φιλ. fr. 15 Ross and Eud. fr. 10
    Ross (= Plutarch De. Is. 382D-E); cf. especially the claim
    in the former passage that intuition occurs αὐτοῦ παθόντος
    τοῦ νοῦ τὴν ἔλλαμψιν and is thus comparable to
    illumination in the Mysteries; (I therefore dissent from
    Dörrie's interpretation of the passage as abandoning Plato's
    analogy between philosophy and the Mysteries, a view
    presented in *Akad. des Wissensch. und der Liter., Abhandl.
    der Geistes - und sozialwiss. Kl.*, Wiesbaden 1956, 5 pp.
    32-4).
65. Cf. esp. Post. An. II. 19, E. N. VI. 6-11.
66. E. N. VI. 6. 1140b 30 ff., Post. An. II. 19. 100b 5-17. On
    the nature of the ἀρχαί in question cf. Post. An. I. 10,
    Ross, *Aristotle* p. 55, *Prior and Posterior Analytics* pp.
    55-9.
67. De An. III. 6. 430a 26 ff., Met. θ. 10. 1051b 17 ff. We
    may note that, whereas for Koestler scientific discovery
    depends on "bisociative thinking," for Aristotle such
    thinking, involving as it does a combination of concepts, is
    always the work of διάνοια. It seems evident that a
    satisfactory theory of intuition must find some way of
    mediating between the two views.

68. Cf. E. N. VI. 11. 1143a-b, a doctrine which appears in a different light, however, when we recall the Eudemian Ethics' claim that the practical man's success depends on divine inspiration (E. E. VIII. 2. 1248a 29 ff.).

69. For Festugière cf. the discussion referred to above n. (26); for Dodds cf. *Pagan and Christian* chs. 2 and 3.

70. Cf. e.g. Albinus' claim that intuition works περιλήψει τινι καὶ οὐ διεξόδῳ (Epit. IV. 6) From an earlier period we should probably place the claim of Theophrastus' metaphysical fragment (VIII. 25) that the radiance of τὰ ἄκρα καὶ πρῶτα permits them to be apprehended only by an intuitive contact (αὐτῷ τῷ νῷ ... ... θίγοντι καὶ οἷον ἀψαμένῳ) in this class; (on the fragment cf. Merlan, *Cambridge History* p. 108).

71. Cf. esp. C. H. X. 5-6 and (more doubtfully) Numenius fr. 11 (on which cf. Dodds, *Sources de Plotin* pp. 16-17, 22-23, with the earlier discussions mentioned there), *Pagan and Christian* pp. 93-4.

72. For experiences of these types cf. Dodds, *Pagan and Christian* pp. 70-83.

73. We may note, however, from the post-Plotinian period, Marinus' claim that Proclus αὐτόπτης ἐγίνετο τῶν ἐκεῖ μακαρίων ὄντως θεαμάτων, οὐκ ἔτι μὲν διεξοδικῶς καὶ ἀποδεικτικῶς συλλογιζόμενος αὐτῶν τὴν ἐπιστήμην, ὥσπερ δὲ ὄψει, ἁπλαῖς ἐπιβολαῖς τῆς νοερᾶς ἐνεργείας θεώμενος, τὰ ἐν τῷ θείῳ νῷ παραδείγματα (V. Pr. 22).

74. *Op. cit.* 35: ἐπινιφομένων καὶ σπειρομένων ἄνωθεν ἀφανῶς τῶν ἐνθυμημάτων.

75. *Ibid.*: ἑρμηνείαν, εὕρεσιν, φωτὸς ἀπόλαυσιν, ὀξυδερκεστάτην ὄψιν, ἐνάργειαν τῶν πραγμάτων ἀριδηλοτάτην, οἷα γένοιτ᾽ ἂν δι᾽ ὀφθαλμῶν ἐκ σαφεστάτης δείξεως. Text and translation are those of the Loeb edition.

76. *Ibid.*: ὡς ὑπὸ κατοχῆς ἐνθέου κορυβαντιᾶν καὶ πάντα ἀγνοεῖν, τὸν τόπον, τοὺς παρόντας, ἐμαυτόν, τὰ λεγόμενα, τὰ γραφόμενα.

77. *Ibid.* 32: καλεῖται δ᾽ ἡ φορὰ τῶν αὐτοματιζομένων ἀγαθῶν ἄφεσις, ἐπειδήπερ ὁ νοῦς ἀφεῖται τῶν κατὰ τὰς ἰδίας ἐπιβολὰς ἐνεργειῶν καὶ ὥσπερ τῶν ἑκουσίων

ἠλευθέρωται διὰ τὴν πληθὺν τῶν ὑομένων καὶ
ἀδιαστάτως ἐπομβρούντων.

78. *Ibid.* 31: τότε μελέται μὲν καὶ πόνοι καὶ ἀσκήσεις
ἡσυχάζουσιν, ἀναδίδοται δὲ ἄνευ τέχνης φύσεως
προμηθείᾳ πάντα ἀθρόα πᾶσιν ὠφέλιμα.

79. *Ibid.* 33: ἔστι δὲ ταῦτα θαυμασιώτατα φύσει καὶ περικαλ-
λέστατα· ὧν μὲν γὰρ ἂν ὠδίνῃ δι᾽ ἑαυτῆς ἡ ψυχή,
τὰ πολλὰ ἀμβλωθρίδια, ἠλιτόμηνα. ὅσα δὲ ἂν ἐπινίφων ὁ
θεὸς ἄρδῃ, τέλεια καὶ ὁλόκληρα καὶ πάντων ἄριστα
γεννᾶται.

80. Cf. above p. 127.

81. On the passage cf. especially H.-R. Schwyzer, *Sources de
Plotin* pp. 370-1 and my *Neoplatonism* p. 81.

82. *Plato* I. p. 219.

83. *World as Will and Idea* (tr. Haldane and Kemp) I. p. 231.

84. On the latter point cf. especially the passage just quoted
with Enn. IV. 4.2. 3-8. πρὸς δὴ ταῦτά τις ἀναμνησθήτα
ὡς ὅταν καὶ ἐνταῦθα θεωρῇ καὶ μάλιστα ἐναργῶς, οὐκ
ἐπιστρέφει πρὸς ἑαυτὸν τότε τῇ νοήσει, ἀλλ᾽ ἔχει μὲν
ἑαυτόν, ἡ δὲ ἐνέργεια πρὸς ἐκεῖνο, κἀκεῖνο γίνεται οἷον
ὕλην ἑαυτὸν παρασχών, εἰδοποιούμενος δὲ κατὰ τὸ
ὁρώμενον καὶ δυνάμει ὢν τότε αὐτός.

85. III. 7. 11. 15-16, IV. 4. 3. 1-2, V. 1. 1. 1-5.

86. For Plotinus cf. esp. I. 3. 6. 16-17, VI. 7. 36. 6-10; for
Plato Rep. 518-9, Ep. VII. 344A.

87. On the need to abandon memory cf. IV. 3. 32 - IV. 4.2; on
the interdependence of awareness and interest IV. 4.3. 6-8,
25. 1-11.

88. *World as Will and Idea* I. p. 234.

89. *The Psychological Attitude of Early Buddhist Philosophy*
pp. 81-2.

90. More strictly, the Form world is divided into four (or
sometimes five) levels, of which only the upper three have
fully transcended discursive thought; cf. Govinda op. cit.
pp. 84-5.

91. Cf. e.g. Paravahera Vajirañana Mahathera, *Buddhist Meditation in Theory and Practice* (Colombo 1962) p. 46: "In
this stage of Samadhi the mind and its object of
concentration are identical." I have not, unfortunately,

been able to trace the authority for such statements in the original Buddhist texts.

92. There is, of course, an obvious parallel here to Aristotle's early view (περὶ Φιλ. fr. 24) that the celestial gods have only the two higher senses (on which cf. R. Walzer in I. Düring and G. E. L. Owen, *Aristotle and Plato in the Mid-fourth Century,* pp. 105-12). Once again, one would like to know more about Aristotle's views, and their sources, during this period.

93. Another obvious parallel to the Plotinian Hypostases, which, for lack of detailed evidence, I have not pursued further here, is the Mahayana Buddhist doctrine of the Three Bodies of the Buddha; for a preliminary comparison cf. J. Przyluski, *Les Trois Hypostases dans l'Inde et à Alexandrie* (Ann. de l'Inst. de Philol. Orientale (Brussels) 4 (1936) ("Mélanges Cumont") pp. 925-33. Plotinus' account of the Intelligible world has also a strong resemblance, at least superficially, to the doctrine of the Mahayana Buddhist Gandavyuha Sutra, notably in its stress on the radiance of the Ideal world and the mutual interpenetration of its members. How close the resemblance really is, however, can hardly be determined without a complete translation of the Sutra; cf. in the meantime D. T. Suzuki's discussion in his *Essays in Zen Buddhism: Third Series,* reprinted in *On Indian Mahayana Buddhism* ed. E. Conze (London and New York 1968) pp. 147-226. It must also remain undecided, in the light of our present evidence, how far such resemblances are due to similarity of experience and how far to borrowing by one system from another. The former seems to me certainly the explanation of the resemblances noted in the text; but with regard to those mentioned in the present footnote, borrowing by one side or the other seems to me by no means impossible.

94. W. Braden, *The Private Sea: LSD and the Search for God* (Chicago 1967) pp. 238-9.

95. Cf. the reference to Plotinus at op. cit. p. 76.

96. Cf. V. 8.4.1, III. 2.1. 30 ff., II. 9. 13. 8 (the last passage actually referring to the celestial gods) and the passages

quoted by Hadot, *Plotin ou la Simplicité du Regard* pp. 132-5.

97. *Psychedelic Review* 7(1966) pp. 29-30.
98. Clearly not "undifferentiated" in Stace's sense; cf. above p. 122 and no. (5).
99. M. R. Westcott, *Towards a Contemporary Psychology of Intuition* (New York 1968) pp. 76-7.
100. Cf. above n. (90).

Philological Comments on the Neoplatonic Notion of Infinity

JOHN WHITTAKER

MEMORIAL UNIVERSITY OF NEWFOUNDLAND

As E. R. Dodds has shown,[1] Plotinus' conception of the One as ἄπειρον derives, terminologically at least, from the First Hypothesis of Plato's *Parmenides*. But in regard to content Plotinus' claim that the One is ἄπειρον . . . οὐ τῷ ἀδιεξιτήτῳ ἢ τοῦ μεγέθους ἢ τοῦ ἀριθμοῦ, ἀλλὰ τῷ ἀπεριλήπτῳ τῆς δυνάμεως[2] seems to find no support in the *Parmenides* where the conclusion that the One is ἄπειρον is based solely on the claim that, in order to be One, it must have no parts and therefore neither a beginning nor an end: the One is ἄπειρον because it has no πέρατα, i.e. no ἀρχή and no τελευτή (*Parm.* 137 D 4 ff.) In a valuable discussion of the matter H. J. Krämer has attempted[3] to trace the doctrine of the dynamic infinity of the One back to the Old Academy. But although Krämer is able to point to *Republic* 509 B where the "ἀγαθόν = ἕν" is defined as ἐπέκεινα τῆς οὐσίας πρεσβείᾳ καὶ δυνάμει ὑπερέχον,[4] he is forced to conclude with regard to the Old Academic background of the doctrine that "Bei der Dürftigkeit und der mangelhaften Präzision der Belege empfiehlt es sich indessen, die Entscheidung vorläufig offenzuhalten."[5] In spite of much patient research the ancestry of the Neoplatonic doctrine, not merely in its dynamic aspect but in general, is still far from clarified.

One aspect of the problem which has not, I think, been hitherto noticed concerns the meaning of the term ἄπειρος. The usual connotation is that to which Plotinus referred first in the passage quoted at the outset, i.e. that of being ἀδιεξίτητος in one respect or another. There is, however, a further and precisely opposite meaning of the term which finds no mention in Liddel and Scott nor in Lampe's *Patristic Greek Lexicon*, but which is especially relevant to any qualification of the One as ἄπειρον. In the course of a passage fraught with significance for the history of ideas Clement of Alexandria writes (*Strom.* V. 12. 81. 5 f.) πῶς γὰρ ἂν εἴη ῥητὸν [sc. Θεός] ὃ μήτε γένος ἐστὶ μήτε διαφορὰ μήτε εἶδος μήτε ἄτομον μήτε ἀριθμός, ἀλλὰ μηδὲ συμβεβηκός τι μηδὲ ᾧ συμβέβηκέν τι. οὐκ ἂν δὲ ὅλον εἴποι τις αὐτὸν ὀρθῶς· ἐπὶ μεγέθει γὰρ τάττεται τὸ ὅλον καὶ ἔστι τῶν ὅλων πατήρ. οὐδὲ μὴν μέρη τινὰ αὐτοῦ λεκτέον· ἀδιαίρετον γὰρ τὸ ἕν, διὰ τοῦτο δὲ καὶ ἄπειρον, οὐ κατὰ τὸ ἀδιεξίτητον νοούμενον, ἀλλὰ κατὰ τὸ ἀδιάστατον καὶ μὴ ἔχον πέρας, καὶ τοίνυν ἀσχημάτιστον καὶ ἀνωνόμαστον. The term ἄπειρος, says Clement in effect, is applicable not only to that which is infinite in extent (ἀδιεξίτητον), but also to that which is infinitely small (ἀδιάστατον).[6] That this conception of the infinite is not simply a product of Clement's own cogitations and therefore peculiar to himself is evident from a consideration of a passage in Plutarch's *Cons. ad Ap.*, in which, commenting upon the indifference of whether a human life be long or short, Plutarch writes (111 C): τό τε πολὺ δήπουθεν ἢ μικρὸν οὐδὲν διαφέρειν δοκεῖ πρὸς τὸν ἄπειρον ἀφορῶσιν αἰῶνα. τὰ γὰρ χίλια καὶ τὰ μύρια κατὰ Σιμωνίδην (fr. 648 Page) ἔτη στιγμή τίς ἐστιν ἀόριστος, μᾶλλον δὲ μόριόν τι βραχύτατον στιγμῆς.[7] Thus, like ἄπειρος, the term ἀόριστος can be applied not only to that which is too large to admit of definition but also to that which is too small. Once again there is no reference in Liddel and Scott nor in the *Patristic Greek Lexicon* under ἀόριστος or its cognates to this somewhat unusual conception of the indefinite.[8]

But though unusual, there is nothing "non-Greek" about the conception: already Anaxagoras was familiar with the notion of the infinitely small (fr. 1 Diels-Kranz): ὁμοῦ πάντα χρήματα ἦν, ἄπειρα καὶ πλῆθος καὶ σμικρότητα· καὶ γὰρ τὸ σμικρὸν ἄπειρον ἦν. Moreover, Clement's characterization of the One as ἄπειρον seems to coincide precisely with that of the First Hypothesis of the *Parmenides*. According to Plato, as we have seen, the One is ἄπειρον because it has no parts and in consequence no πέρατα. Similarly Clement claims that, since it is indivisible and has no parts, the One is ἄπειρον, not indeed in extent but κατὰ τὸ ἀδιάστατον καὶ μὴ ἔχον πέρας. However, the similarity between Clement's argumentation and that of the First Hypothesis does not end here. Both Clement in the passage quoted above and Plato (*Parm.* 137 C 4 - D 8) argue (1) that the One is not a whole (ὅλον), (2) that the One cannot be spoken of as having parts (μέρη), (3) that the One is infinite (ἄπειρον), and (4) that the One has no form (ἄνευ σχήματος Plato; ἀσχημάτιστον Clement). At this point Plato goes on to list further limitations (the One is neither round nor straight, etc.) which Clement (or perhaps his source) has omitted, presumably because they were not considered theologically relevant. But the next characteristic which Clement assigns to the One - that of being nameless (ἀνωνόμαστον)- appears at the close of the First Hypothesis (142 A 3): Οὐδ᾿ ἄρα ὄνομα ἔστιν αὐτῷ . . . Though this is noted neither in Stählin's *Index fontium* nor in L. Früchtel's *Nachträge*, there can be no question but that Clement's presentation is dependent ultimately upon the First Hypothesis of the *Parmenides*. However, one may go further than this. That Clement's negative theological utilization of the First Hypothesis derives from, or is at least influenced by, a Middle Platonic commentary or adaptation is evident from a consideration of a parallel passage in the *Didaskalikos*, to which Früchtel drew attention, but without noting that both authors were dependent, through an intermediate source, upon the *Parmenides:*[9]

ἄρρητος δ᾿ ἔστι καὶ νῷ
5 μόνῳ ληπτός, ὡς εἴρηται, ἐπεὶ οὔτε γένος ἐστὶν οὔτε εἶδος οὔτε
διαφορά, ἀλλ᾿ οὐδὲ συμβέβηκέ τι αὐτῷ, οὔτε κακόν · οὐ γὰρ
θέμις τοῦτο εἰπεῖν · οὔτε ἀγαθόν · κατὰ μετοχὴν γάρ τινος ἔσται
οὕτως καὶ μάλιστα ἀγαθότητος · οὔτε ἀδιάφορον · οὐδὲ γὰρ τοῦτο
κατὰ τὴν ἔννοιαν αὐτοῦ · οὔτε ποιόν · οὐ γὰρ ποιωθέν ἐστι καὶ
10 ὑπὸ ποιότητος τοιοῦτον ἀποτετελεσμένον · οὔτε ἄποιον · οὐ γὰρ
ἐστέρηταί τινος ἐπιβάλλοντος αὐτῷ ποιοῦ · οὔτε μέρος τινός,
οὔτε ὡς ὅλον ἔχον τινὰ μέρη, οὔτε ὥστε ταὐτόν τινι εἶναι ἢ ἕτε-
ρον · οὐδὲν γὰρ αὐτῷ συμβέβηκε καθ᾿ ὃ δύναται τῶν ἄλλων
χωρισθῆναι · οὔτε κινεῖ οὔτε κινεῖται.

Didask. p. 165.4 ff. Hermann (In line 8 H. οὕτως is my suggestion for the οὗτος of the mss., whilst ἀδιάφορον is Festugière's conjecture in place of the impossible mss. reading διαφορά. The phrase οὔτε διαφορά is omitted at this point, perhaps intentionally, in *Marcianus gr.* 513 and *Laurentianus* 71. 33. In line 12 ταὐτόν τινι is the correct reading not only because it conforms with *Parm.* 139 B 4 ff., but also because it is attested by *Parisinus gr.* 1962, *Vindobonensis phil. gr.* 314 and the mainstream of the mss. tradition. Hermann had been misled by *Parisinus gr.* 1309 into reading ταὐτόν τι (though in fact this latter aberrant reading also occurs in five further mss. which Hermann did not consult). In the final line the phrase οὔτε κινεῖ οὔτε κινεῖται constitutes, since the immobility of the supreme deity was one of the presuppositions of Middle Platonic speculation, a not unimportant revision of the argument of *Parm.* 139 B 3 that οὔτε ἔστηκεν οὔτε κινεῖται. Numenius (fr. 24 Leemans) declares, perhaps with the *Parmenides* in mind, that though the First God is ἑστώς he may be said to have a κίνησις σύμφυτος, namely στάσις. Plotinus does not hesitate to follow the *Parmenides* the whole way in arguing that the One is (*Enn.* VI. 9. 3. 42 f.) οὐδὲ κινούμενον οὐδ᾽ αὖ ἑστώς).

Since the resemblances between the above passage of the *Didaskalikos* and that of Clement extend beyond their mutual dependence upon the *Parmenides* we are forced to conclude either that both are dependent upon the same intermediate source, or that Clement was drawing upon the *Didaskalikos.* This latter possibility is, however, excluded by the fact that Clement's presentation reveals features of the First Hypothesis which are lacking from the *Didaskalikos*: i.e., the introduction of the term τὸ ἕν and the qualification of this first principle as ἄπειρον, ἀσχημάτιστον and ἀνωνόμαστον. We must therefore conclude that independently of each other Clement and the author of the *Didaskalikos* have drawn from a theologically inclined Middle Platonic Commentary upon the *Parmenides*, or at least from a Middle Platonic theologico-metaphysical adaptation of the First Hypothesis. Thus, the Middle Platonists did not, as has been frequently supposed, regard the *Parmenides* solely as a "logical exercise-book"[10] without metaphysical relevance. The above passages from Clement and the *Didask-*

alikos provide incontestable proof of a pre-Plotinian theological interpretation of the First Hypothesis of the *Parmenides,* and they must be taken seriously into account when one weighs the value of Simplicius' report (drawn from Porphyry) of a metaphysical interpretation on Neoplatonic lines of the first three Hypotheses by the Platonist Moderatus in the first century after Christ.[11]

The ambiguity of the term ἄπειρος, which may be employed legitimately not only κατὰ τὸ ἀδιεξίτητον to indicate the interminable but also κατὰ τὸ ἀδιάστατον to indicate the infinitesimal, is well brought out, as we have seen, by Clement. It must be mentioned that such terminological ambivalence is not necessarily a deficiency, and in the case of ἄπειρος can well be turned to account in the service of mystical theology. The Neoplatonic conception of αἰών is a good case in point. Plotinus (*Enn.* III. 7. 11. 2 ff.) speaks of this as τὴν ἀτρεμῆ ἐκείνην καὶ ὁμοῦ πᾶσαν καὶ ἄπειρον ἤδη ζωὴν καὶ ἀκλινῆ πάντη καὶ ἐν ἑνὶ καὶ πρὸς ἓν ἑστῶσαν. Clearly the juxtaposition of ὁμοῦ πᾶσαν (which implies that αἰών is ἀδιάστατος, a *totum simul*)[12] and ἄπειρον is eased by the latent ambivalence of this latter term, in that each of the two meanings of ἄπειρον specified by Clement may be considered relevant to the doctrine in hand. For Plotinus is at pains to point out not only that αἰών is a ζωὴ ὁμοῦ πᾶσα (= ἀδιάστατος)[13] but also, as a long established etymology dictated,[14] that the term αἰών derived ἀπὸ τοῦ ἀεὶ ὄντος (*Enn.* III. 7. 4. 42 f.). We must of course beware in this and similar contexts of understanding ἀεί in a too literally temporal sense,[15] but nonetheless there remains an unavoidable and insoluble contradiction in the paradoxical identification of νῦν and ἀεί which is the essence of the doctrine and a principal source of its fascination. Consider, for example, Plutarch, *De E apud Delphos* 393 A εἰς ὢν ἑνὶ τῷ νῦν τὸ ἀεὶ πεπλήρωκε [sc. ὁ θεός]. Or Porphyry, *Sententiae.* p. 44. 13 ff. Mommert εἰ δὲ μὴ τόδε μετὰ τόδε ἐπ' αὐτοῦ γίνεται, ἅμα πάντα νοεῖ [sc. νοῦς]. ἐπεὶ οὖν πάντα ἅμα καὶ οὐ τὸ μὲν νῦν τὸ δὲ αὖθις, πάντα ἅμα νῦν καὶ ἀεί. εἰ οὖν ἐπ' αὐτοῦ τὸ νῦν, ἀνήρηται δὲ τὸ παρεληλυθὸς καὶ τὸ μέλλον, ἐν ἀδιαστάτῳ τὸ νῦν ⟨καὶ⟩ ἀχρόνῳ παραστήματι. ὥστε τὸ ὁμοῦ κατά τε τὸ πλῆθος κατά τε τὸ χρονικὸν διάστημα ἐπ' αὐτοῦ. διὸ καθ' ἓν πάντα καὶ ⟨ἐν⟩ ἑνὶ καὶ ἀδιαστάτῳ καὶ ἀχρόνῳ.[16]

Particularly instructive with regard to the ambivalence of
the term ἄπειρος is Boethius' account in *Cons.* V. 6 of the
nature of *aeternitas,* since the discussion maintains a rigid
distinction between *interminabilis* (= ἄπειρος/ἀδιάστατος, applicable to the eternal) and *infinitus* (= ἄπειρος/ἀδιεξίτητος,
applicable to the temporally everlasting). Thus, after offering
his familiar definition (Aeternitas igitur est *interminabilis* vitae
tota simul et perfecta possessio) Boethius underlines the
distinction between the eternal and the merely temporally
everlasting as follows:

> Quod igitur temporis patitur condicionem, licet illud, sicuti
> de mundo censuit Aristoteles, nec coeperit umquam esse nec
> desinat vitaque eius cum temporis *infinitate* tendatur, non-
> dum tamen tale est ut aeternum esse iure credatur. Non enim
> totum simul *infinitae* licet vitae spatium comprehendit atque
> complectitur, sed futura nondum transacta iam non habet.
> Quod igitur *interminabilis* vitae plenitudinem totam pariter
> comprehendit ac possidet, cui neque futuri quidquam absit
> nec praeteriti fluxerit, id aeternum esse iure perhibetur, idque
> necesse est et sui compos praesens sibi semper adsistere et
> *infinitatem* mobilis temporis habere praesentem.

Only on one occasion in the course of his discussion and in
order to achieve a special emphasis does Boethius permit
himself to use the one term in both senses (*loc. cit.*): Aliud est
enim per *interminabilem* duci vitam, quod mundo Plato tribuit,
aliud *interminabilis* vitae totam pariter complexum esse
praesentiam, quod divinae mentis proprium esse manifestum
est. The very fact that Boethius has bothered to create and
maintain this distinction between *interminabilis* and *infinitus*
suggests that the ambiguity of the notion of the infinite caused
him some embarrassment. As Proclus puts it (*In Tim.* I. 278. 10
f. Diehl) οὐδὲ γὰρ ἡ αὐτὴ ἀπειρία χρόνου καὶ αἰῶνος· οὐδὲ γὰρ
ταὐτὸν αἰών καὶ χρόνος. But Proclus makes no terminological
distinction between the various types of ἀπειρία.[17]

More direct influence of the argument of the First
Hypothesis that indivisibility into parts implies infinity is
evident in Proclus' claim that unity and infinity must be
regarded as correlates (*El. theol.* prop. 86, p. 78. 29 f. Dodds
καὶ ὅσῳ δὴ μᾶλλον ἕν καὶ μᾶλλον ἀμερές, τοσούτῳ καὶ ἄπειρον

μᾶλλον. Cf. also prop. 95 Πᾶσα δύναμις ἑνικωτέρα οὖσα τῆς πληθυνομένης ἀπειροτέρα.). Proclus is, however, not entirely consistent in the matter of the infinity of the One. *Contra* Dodds[18] he does not argue at *In Parm.* 1124 with regard to αὐτοαπειρία and αὐτόπερας that "τὸ αὐτόπερας is the 'higher' of the pair, as being more akin to the One." In fact in the passage in question Proclus is at pains to explain how τὸ ἄπειρον (since this is the term with which Plato qualifies the One in the First Hypothesis) is superior to τὸ πέρας; cf. *In Parm.* 1123. 30 ff. καὶ γὰρ τῷ πάντων ἀρίστῳ χρὴ προσφέρειν τὸ ἀόριστον, ἀλλ᾽ οὐ τὸ ὁπωσοῦν καταδεέστερον. On this point there is nonetheless an ill-concealed ambivalence in Proclus' thought, in that he finds the terminology of the First Hypothesis in conflict with his natural preference for the finite. Thus at *Theol. Plat.* p. 133 he writes ἀπάσης τῆς ἐν τοῖς θείοις γένεσιν ἀντιθέσεως τὸ μὲν κρεῖττον ἐπὶ τὸ πέρας τὸ δὲ καταδεέστερον ἐπὶ τὴν ἀπειρίαν ἀνοίσομεν. However, already Plotinus (cf. *Enn.* VI. 8. 9. 42) qualifies the One as ἀόριστος. St. Basil (*Adv. Eunomium* I. 7, PG 29, 525) finds it natural to speak of God as τὸν ἀόριστον καὶ ἄπειρον, and both these terms are applied to the supreme divinity by both Gregory Nazianzen and Gregory of Nyssa.[19] Marius Victorinus emphasizes the ἀοριστία of the First Principle at *Adv. Arium* IV. 23. 12 ff. Henry-Hadot: Sed cum in uno omnia vel *unum omnia* aut cum *unum omnia* vel *nec unum nec omnia*, fit infinitum, fit incognitum, indiscernibile, incognoscibile, et quod vere dicitur ἀοριστία, id est infinitas et indeterminatio. And Ps.-Dionysius makes an interesting identification of ἀοριστία and ἑνότης (*De div. nom.* I. 1, PG 3. 588) ὑπέρκειται τῶν οὐσιῶν ἡ ὑπερούσιος ἀοριστία· καὶ τῶν νοῶν, ἡ ὑπὲρ νοῦν ἑνότης.[20]

Nicholas of Cusa took careful note of Proclus' vacillation regarding the priority of the infinite. On the guard-sheets of *Strasbourg, Bibliothèque nationale et universitaire, cod. 84 (lat. 81)* he has copied an excerpt from William of Moerbeke's rendering of Proclus, *In Parm.* corresponding to cols. 1123 f. in Cousin's edition of the Greek text, i.e. the passage to which we have just made reference.[21] To this Nicholas has added *inter alia* the following comment:[22] Arguit, quod deo non conveniat infinitum, quia *finis melior*, sed concludit, quod merito convenit infinitum. Quod nota! On another occasion Nicholas comments as follows in the margin of Moerbeke's version of the *In Parm.*:[23]

> Nota et considera quomodo 'in' dicitur ut 'non' et 'valde'. Illa si simul consideras, ut unum et idem sit 'non' et 'valde', tunc subintrare poteris intellectum huius, scilicet quomodo negatio est plus quam affirmatio, ut cum deus dicitur infinitus, id est non et valde finitus. Nota: 'in' est copulatio sive unio affirmationis et negationis; sicud enim prima elementa de 'ita' et 'non', scilicet i et n in se unit, ita et utriusque significatum, et est equalitas 'non' et 'valde'. Et resolvitur sic: 'non', quod 'valde', ut infinitum dicatur sic non finitum, quod valde finitum. Sed melius sic resolvitur: non solum nōn finitum, sed simul et valde finitum.

Apart from the fanciful etymology of the prefix in-, the version of the *coincidentia oppositorum*[24] which Nicholas here offers conforms with the legitimate meanings of ἄπειρος and is not entirely out of keeping with the argument of Proclus that (*El. Theol.* prop. 93) Πᾶν τὸ ἄπειρον ἐν τοῖς οὖσιν οὔτε τοῖς ὑπερκειμένοις ἄπειρόν ἐστιν οὔτε ἑαυτῷ. Cf. also the interpretation of the ἄπειρον of the First Hypothesis which Proclus quotes with approval at *In Parm.* 1118. 10 ff. Cousin:

> καὶ οἱ μὲν οὕτω φασὶν ἄπειρον προσειρῆσθαι τὸ ἕν, ὡς ἀδιεξίτητον καὶ ὡς πέρας τῶν ὅλων (διχῶς γὰρ λέγεται τὸ ἄπειρον, τὸ μὲν οἷον τὸ ἄληπτον καὶ ἀδιεξίτητον, τὸ δὲ οἷον ὃ πέρας ἐστὶ τὸ μὴ ἔχον ἄλλο πέρας· καὶ τὸ ἓν οὖν ἀμφοτέρως εἶναι ἄπειρον, ὡς ἄληπτόν τε καὶ ἀπεριήγητον πᾶσι τοῖς δευτέροις, καὶ ὡς πέρας τῶν ὅλων καὶ μὴ δεόμενον αὐτὸ πέρατος ἄλλου μηδενός).

The doctrine that the Infinite is infinite not to itself but only to its inferiors lies at the close of a long development. Origen (*De princip.* II 9. 1, PG 11, 225) had argued that one must admit that God's power is limited for the following reason: ἔαν γὰρ ᾖ ἄπειρος ἡ θεία δύναμις, ἀνάγκη αὐτὴν μηδὲ ἑαυτὴν νοεῖν· τῇ γὰρ φύσει τὸ ἄπειρον ἀπερίληπτον. πεποίηκε τοίνυν τοσαῦτα ὧν ἐδύνατο περιδράξασθαι, καὶ ἔχειν αὐτὰ ὑπὸ χεῖρας, καὶ συγκροτεῖν ὑπὸ τὴν αὐτοῦ πρόνοιαν. Whilst Alexander of Aphrodisias (cf. *De fato* 200, 12 ff. Bruns and *In Metaph.* fr. 36 Freudenthal)[25] claimed that since the infinite is essentially incomprehensible, God cannot possess knowledge of the infinite details of the events of this world.[26] St. Augustine (*De civ.Dei* XII. 18, PG 41, col. 367 f.) attacks the views of those who hold that *nec Dei scientia quae infinita sunt posse comprehendi* in the following terms:

Infinitas itaque numeri, quamvis infinitorum numerorum nullus sit numerus, non est tamen incomprehensibilis ei cuius intellegentiae non est numerus. Quapropter si, quidquid scientia comprehenditur, scientis comprehensione finitur; profecto et omnis infinitas quodam ineffabili modo Deo finita est, quia scientiae ipsius incomprehensibilis non est. Quare si infinitas numerorum scientiae Dei, qua comprehenditur, esse non potest infinita; qui tandem nos sumus homunculi, qui eius scientiae limites figere praesumamus, dicentes quod, nisi eisdem circuitibus temporum eadem temporalia repetantur, non potest Deus cuncta quae facit vel praescire ut faciat, vel scire cum fecerit ? Cuius sapientia simpliciter multiplex et uniformiter multiformis, tam incomprehensibili comprehensione omnia incomprehensibilia comprehendit, ut quaecumque nova et dissimilia consequentia praecedentibus si semper facere vellet, inordinata et improvisa habere non posset; nec ea praevideret ex proximo tempore, sed aeterna praescientia contineret.

This theme of the infinite but nonetheless unitary and indivisible nature of divine πρόνοια is pursued in almost identical terms by Proclus at, e.g., *De decem. dub. 5. 30 ff.* Boese: . . .καὶ ἡ τῆς προνοίας ἐνιαία γνῶσις ἐν τῷ αὐτῷ ἀμερεῖ πάντων ἐστὶ τῶν μεριζομένων γνῶσις καὶ τῶν ἀτομωτάτων ἑκάστου καὶ τῶν ὁλικωτατῶν· καὶ ὡς ὑπέστησεν ἕκαστον κατὰ τὸ ἕν, οὕτως καὶ γινώσκει ἕκαστον κατὰ τὸ ἕν. καὶ οὔτε ἡ γνῶσις διῄρε τοῖς γινωσκομένοις, οὔτε τὰ γινωσκόμενα συγκέχυται διὰ τὴν μίαν τῆς γνώσεως ἕνωσιν· μία δὲ οὖσα, πᾶσαν μὲν ἀπειρίαν τῶν γνωστῶν περιέχει, πάσης δὲ τῆς ἐν αὐτοῖς ἑνώσεως ὑπερήνωται. Thus, the quandary that lies behind Origen's claim regarding divine providence and the incomprehensibility of the infinite, finds its solution in Proclus' considered doctrine of the identity of the infinite and the unitary: as Cusanus put it, "infinite" means *non solum non finitum, sed simul et valde finitum.*[27]

It is not surprising that the latent ambiguity of ἄπειρος appears to be utilized also in discussions of the immanence-transcendence antinomy - God is not only πανταχοῦ but also οὐδαμοῦ.[28] Plotinus puts the problem succinctly thus (*Enn.* VI. 4. 1. 11 ff.) Τό τε ἀμερῆ λεγομένην καὶ ἀμεγέθη εἶναι πανταχοῦ εἶναι μέγεθος οὐκ ἔχουσαν πῶς ἄν τις παραδέξαιτο; and goes on to discuss it at considerable length (*Enn.* VI. 4 and 5), emphasizing that the doctrine in question is not simply a philosopher's fancy but conforms to common opinion (*Enn.* VI. 5. 1.1 ff): Τὸ ἕν καὶ ταὐτὸν ἀριθμῷ πανταχοῦ ἅμα ὅλον εἶναι κοινὴ μέν τις ἔννοιά φησιν [εἶναι], ὅταν πάντες κινούμενοι αὐτοφυῶς λέγωσι τὸν ἐν ἑκάστῳ ἡμῶν θεὸν ὡς ἕνα καὶ τὸν αὐτόν.[29] In the course of the discussion Plotinus dwells upon the potential identity of unity and infinity in the following terms (*Enn.* VI. 4. 14. 3 ff.): καὶ γὰρ ἕν ἐστι καὶ ἄπειρον αὖ καὶ πάντα ὁμοῦ καὶ ἕκαστον ἔχει διακεκριμένον καὶ αὖ οὐ διακριθὲν χωρίς· πῶς γὰρ ἄν καὶ ἄπειρον ἤ οὕτω λέγοιτο, ὅτι ὁμοῦ πάντα ἔχει, πᾶσαν ζωὴν καὶ πᾶσαν ψυχὴν καὶ νοῦν ἅπαντα; ἕκαστον δὲ αὐτῶν οὐ πέρασιν ἀφώρισται· διὰ τοῦτο αὖ καὶ ἕν. οὐ γὰρ δὴ μίαν ζωὴν ἔδει αὐτὸ ἔχειν, ἀλλ᾽ ἄπειρον, καὶ αὖ μίαν· καὶ τὴν μίαν οὕτω μίαν, ὅτι πάσας ὁμοῦ οὐ συμφορηθείσας εἰς ἕν, ἀλλ᾽ ἀφ᾽ ἑνὸς ἀρξαμένας καὶ μενούσας ὅθεν ἤρξαντο, μᾶλλον δὲ οὐδὲ ἤρξαντο, ἀλλ᾽ οὕτως εἶχεν ἀεί. Within the same Neoplatonic framework and probably in dependence upon Proclus, Meister Eckhart in a sermon upon the theme *Deus unus est* attempts a solution of the problem of the omnipresence of the transcendent One:[30] Deus simplicitate est infinitus et infinitate sua est simplex. Ideo et ubique est et ubique totus est. Ubique infinitate, sed totus ubique simplicitate. Deus solus illabitur omnibus entibus, ipsorum essentiis. Nihil autem aliorum illabitur alteri. Deus est in intimis cuiuslibet et solum in intimis, et ipse solus *unus est.* Even though the links may be both many and tenuous, Meister Eckhart's explanation builds upon the equation of the infinite and the indivisible which Plato had made in the First Hypothesis, but which in turn possessed (as Plutarch's στιγμὴ ἀόριστος shows)[31] a basis in popular usage. We cannot suppose that Meister Eckhart himself was aware that any such basis in popular usage had ever existed. Indicative of this is the fact that in discussing the problem of God's *ubiquitas* Thomas Aquinas (*Summa.* I a. 8, 2) dwells not upon the ambivalence of the infinite but upon a supposed ambiguity of the term *indivisibile*. To the objection that God who is indivisible cannot be in all places at the same time he makes the following rejoinder:

...dicendum quod indivisibile est duplex. Unum quod est terminus continui ut punctus in permanentibus et momentum in successivis. Et hujsmodi indivisibile in permanentibus, quia habet determinatum situm, non potest esse in pluribus partibus loci vel in pluribus locis; et similiter indivisibile actionis vel motus, quia habet determinatum ordinem in motu vel actione, non potest esse in pluribus partibus temporis. Aliud autem indivisibile est quod est extra totum genus continui, et hoc modo substantiae incorporeae ut Deus et anima et substantiae separatae dicuntur esse indivisibiles. Tale igitur indivisibile non applicatur ad continuum sicut aliquid ejus sed inquantum contingit illud sua virtute. Unde secundum quod virtus sua se potest extendere ad unum vel multa, ad parvum vel magnum, secundum hoc est in uno vel pluribus locis, et in loco parvo vel magno.

Though the infinite has here been supplanted by the indivisible, it may be noted that the second of the two senses which Thomas assigns to *indivisibile* conforms closely to the doctrine of Proclus (to which we have already had occasion to refer)[32] that ὅσῳ δὴ μᾶλλον ἕν καὶ μᾶλλον ἀμερές, τοσούτῳ καὶ ἄπειρον μᾶλλον.

We have noted that the contradictory meanings which ἄπειρος is capable of bearing give to the term, particularly in the instances when it is not apparent that a writer had in mind the one meaning rather than the other, a certain affinity to Cusanus' *coincidentia oppositorum*. The resemblance is hardly more than superficial, for the whole philosophy of the *coincidentia* is foreign to the negative theological tendencies of later antiquity. Thus, Martin Luther, perhaps under the influence of Cusanus, could write as follows:[33]

Nichts ist so klein, Gott ist noch kleiner, Nichts ist so gros, Gott ist noch grösser, Nichts ist so kurtz, Gott ist noch kürtzer, Nichts ist so lang, Gott ist noch lenger, Nichts ist so breit, Gott ist noch breiter, Nichts ist so schmal, Gott ist noch schmeler und so fort an, Ists ein unausprechlich wesen

uber und ausser allem, das man nennen odder dencken kan.
But to Luther's litany the following Middle-Platonic inspired
negative theology from the Gnostic *Apocryphon of John*
presents a remarkable contrast:[34]
It is not perfection or beatitude or deity, but something far
more excellent. It is not boundless nor are limits set to it; it is
something far more excellent. It is neither corporeal nor
incorporeal, not great, not small, not a quantity, not a
creature; no one can think it. It is not anything existent, but
something prior - not as if in itself it were prior, but because
it is its own.

As the *Apocryphon* indicates, the Platonists of later antiquity
were concerned not to assert the applicability to the first
principle of both opposites, but rather to deny the applicability
of both. Consider, for example, Plotinus, *Enn.* V. 3. 14. 3 ff.
Πῶς οὖν λέγομεν περὶ αὐτοῦ, εἰ μὴ αὐτὸ ἔχομεν; "Η, εἰ μὴ
ἔχομεν τῇ γνώσει, καὶ παντελῶς οὐκ ἔχομεν; 'Αλλ' οὕτως
ἔχομεν, ὥστε περὶ αὐτοῦ μὲν λέγειν, αὐτὸ δὲ μὴ λέγειν. Καὶ γὰρ
λέγομεν, ὅ μὴ ἔστιν · ὁ δὲ ἐστιν, οὐ λέγομεν. That Plotinus is
simply echoing a theological commonplace of the period is
evident from, e.g., Clement of Alexandria, *Strom.* V. 11. 71. 3
εἰ τοίνυν, ἀφελόντες πάντα ὅσα πρόσεστι τοῖς σώμασιν καὶ τοῖς
λεγομένοις ἀσωμάτοις, ἐπιρρίψαιμεν ἑαυτοὺς εἰς τὸ μέγεθος
τοῦ Χριστοῦ κἀκεῖθεν εἰς τὸ ἀχανὲς ἁγιότητι προίοιμεν, τῇ
νοήσει τοῦ παντοκράτορος ἀμῇ γέ πῃ προσάγοιμεν ⟨ἄν⟩, οὐχ ὅ
ἐστιν, ὁ δὲ μή ἐστι γνωρίσαντες.[35] But as a purely philological
explanation of the meanings of the term ἄπειρος Cusanus'
postulate (*non solum non finitum, sed simul et valde finitum*)
would have won the approval of Clement of Alexandria.

FOOTNOTES

1. In his "The Parmenides of Plato and the origin of the
Neoplatonic 'One'," *The Classical Quarterly* 22 (1928) 129
ff.
2. *Enn.* VI. 9. 6. 10 ff. Cf. further, e.g., *Enn.* VI. 7. 32. 14 ff.
(πάντα δὲ ποιεῖν δυνάμενον τί ἄν μέγεθος ἔχοι; ἢ ἄπειρον

ἂν εἴη, ἀλλ᾽ εἰ ἄπειρον, μέγεθος ἂν ἔχοι οὐδέν· καὶ γὰρ μέγεθος ἐν τοῖς ὑστάτοις· κτλ.); *Enn.* VI. 6. 17. 13 f.; *Enn.* V. 5. 10. 19 ff.

3. *Der Ursprung der Geistmetaphysik* (Amsterdam 1964) 363 f.

4. More pertinent to the Neoplatonic doctrine is Aristotle, *Phys.* 8. 10, where it is shown that the Unmoved Mover, though neither πεπερασμένον nor ἄπειρον (i.e., in extent) does possess δύναμις ἄπειρος and ἀδιαίρετόν ἐστι καὶ ἀμερὲς καὶ οὐδὲν ἔχον μέγεθος (i.e., immaterial); cf. *Metaph.* 1073 a 5 ff.

5. Cf. R. Mondolfo, *L'infinito nel pensiero dell' antichità classica* (Florence 1956); A. H. Armstrong, "Plotinus's doctrine of the infinite and its significance for Christian thought," *The Downside Review* 73 (1955) 47 ff.; L. Sweeney, "Infinity in Plotinus," *Gregorianum* 38 (1957) 513 ff. and 713 ff.; W.N. Clarke, "Infinity in Plotinus: a reply," *Gregorianum* 40 (1959) 75 ff.; A. H. Armstrong and R. A. Markus, *Christian Faith and Greek Philosophy* (London 1960) Chapter 2: God's transcendence and infinity; E. Mühlenberg, *Die Unendlichkeit Gottes bei Gregor von Nyssa:* Gregors Kritik am Gottesbegrifi der klassischen Metaphysik (Göttingen 1966); W. Theiler, "Das Unbestimmte, Unbegrenzte bei Plotin," *Revue Internationale de Philosophie* 92 (1970) 290 ff. There is a valuable account of the persistence and development in the medieval Cabbala of the Neoplatonic conception of infinity in G. Scholem,"Das Ringen zwischen dem biblischen Gott und dem Gott Plotins in der alten Kabbala," *Eranos-Jahrbuch* 33 (1964) 9 ff. (reprinted in Scholem's *Über einige Grundbegriffe des Judentums* (Frankfurt 1970) 9 ff.). Scholem's essay provides a necessary corrective to the brief account of infinity in the Cabbala given by E. R. Goodenough, *By Light, Light: The Mystic Gospel of Hellenistic Judaism* (New Haven 1935; rp. Amsterdam 1969) 359 ff.

6. Mühlenberg, *op. cit.* 75 ff. rightly criticizes the interpretation of this text of Clement offered by E. F. Osborn, *The Philosophy of Clement of Alexandria* (Cambridge 1957)

42. However, Mühlenberg himself is forced to underestimate the significance of Clement's words (not to mention the importance of Plotinus' contribution) in order to support his own thesis that (*op. cit.* 26): "Die negative Theologie, die Platon begründet hat, hat ein Gottesprädikat niemals aufgenommen: das Unendliche. Bei Gregor von Nyssa findet sich dieses Gottesprädikat zum ersten Male in der Geschichte des philosophischen und christlichen Denkens."

7. The conception of human life as a στιγμὴ χρόνου was a Stoic commonplace; cf. Marcus Aurelius II. 17, and the parallels thereto cited by Farquharson in his edition of the *Meditations* II (Oxford 1944) 537.

8. ἀπέραντος is no doubt similarly ambiguous. Following *Laurentianus* 5. 3 it should be retained in the text of Clement at *Strom.* V. 12. 81. 3 βυθὸν ⟨δ'⟩ αὐτὸν [sc. Θεὸν] κεκλήκασιν ἐντεῦθεν τινὲς ὡς ἂν περιειληφότα καὶ ἐγκολπισάμενον τὰ πάντα ἀνέφικτόν τε καὶ ἀπέραντον. Früchtel (*Nachträge* p. 535) proposes that one should prefer ἀπερινόητον, the reading of the pertinent extract of Clement in *Lavra* B. 113. ἀπέραντον is not only in keeping with ἄπειρον in *Strom.* V. 12. 81. 6, but also appears as a divine epithet in the *Corpus Hermeticum* (IV. 8 [I. 52. 11 f. Nock-Festugière] ἀδιάβατον γὰρ τὸ ἀγαθὸν καὶ ἀπέραντον καὶ ἀτελές), in the Ps.-Clementine *Homilies* (cf. Lampe's *Patristic Greek Lexicon* s.v.), and e.g. in the *Anonymous Gnostic Writing* in the *Codex Brucianus* (cf. the *Index* s.v. in GCS, *Koptisch-gnostische Schriften* I). Irenaeus at *Haer.* I. 17. 2, PG 7, 641 writes of the Marcosians that Πρὸς δὲ τούτοις θελήσαντά φασι τὸν Δημιουργὸν τῆς ἄνω ὀγδοάδος τὸ ἀπέραντον καὶ αἰώνιον καὶ ἀόριστον καὶ ἄχρονον μιμήσασθαι, καὶ μὴ δυνηθέντα τὸ μόνιμον αὐτῆς καὶ ἀίδιον ἐκτυπῶσαι, διὰ τὸ καρπὸν εἶναι ὑστερήματος, εἰς χρόνους καὶ καιροὺς ἀριθμούς τε πολυετεῖς τὸ αἰώνιον αὐτῆς κατατεθεῖσθαι, οἰόμενον ἐν τῷ πλήθει τῶν χρόνων μιμήσασθαι αὐτῆς τὸ ἀπέραντον. This text suggests that the Marcosians, like the Neoplatonists, distinguished between an instantaneous indivisible Eternal Now (characterized as τὸ ἀπέραντον καὶ αἰώνιον καὶ

ἀόριστον καὶ ἄχρονον) and the divided nature of created time. On the Neoplatonic notion of Eternity cf. further below. *Contra* J. Daniélou, *Message évangélique et culture hellénistique* (Tournai 1961) 301, ἀπέραντος is not employed in a transcendent sense by St. Paul at Romans 11. 33 or elsewhere. Except at I Timothy 1. 4 (γενεαλογίαις ἀπεράντοις) the term is entirely absent from the New Testament.

9. Cf. Früchtel's "Clemens Alexandrinus und Albinus," *Philologische Wochenschrift* 57 (1937) 591 f.

10. Cf. R. E. Witt, *Albinus and the History of Middle Platonism* (Cambridge 1937; rp. Amsterdam 1971) 4, and, e.g., R. Klibansky, "Ein Proklos-Fund und seine Bedeutung," *Sitzungsberichte der Heidelberger Akademie der Wissenschaften.* Phil.-hist. Klasse 1928/29 No. 5, p. 7. That the author of the *Didaskalikos* was in the relevant passage influenced by the First Hypothesis has been emphasized by A. H. Armstrong, *The Architecture of the Intelligible Universe in the Philosophy of Plotinus* (Cambridge 1940) 10. Professor Armstrong went on to argue (*op. cit.* 16, n. 3) as follows: "It must be remembered, however, that Albinus regards the *Parmenides* simply as a logical exercise, not as containing any profound metaphysical teaching *(Didaskalikos* 6). He must, therefore, be held to be unconscious of the source of his "negative theology"." I have expressed reservation regarding this latter conclusion in my "ΕΠΕΚΕΙΝΑ ΝΟΥ ΚΑΙ ΟΥΣΙΑΣ," *Vigiliae Christianae* 23 (1969) 99 f. Any assessment ancient or modern of Plato's intentions in the second half of the *Parmenides* must of course take into account that Plato himself had employed the terms γυμνασία (*Parm.* 135 D 7) and πραγματειώδη παιδιὰν παίζειν (*Parm.* 137 B 2) in reference to this portion of the dialogue.

11. Cf. Simplicius, *In Phys.* 230. 34 ff. Diels. On the interpretation of this important passage cf. E. R. Dodds, *op. cit.* 136 ff.; A. H. Armstrong, *op. cit.* 16 ff.; A. J. Festugière, *La révélation d'Hermès-Trismégiste* IV, *Le Dieu inconnu et la Gnose* (Paris 1954) 22 f.; P. Merlan in *The*

Cambridge History of Later Greek and Early Medieval Philosophy, ed. A. H. Armstrong (Cambridge 1967) 90ff.; my *op. cit.* 95 ff., where I have drawn attention to further instances of the pre-Plotinian "Neoplatonic" interpretation of the Hypotheses of the Parmenides; on this topic cf. also my "Neopythagoreanism and the Transcendent Absolute," *Symbolae Osloenses* 48 (1973) 75 ff.

12. Cf. *Enn.* III. 7. 3. 37 f. ζωὴ ὁμοῦ πᾶσα καὶ πλήρης ἀδιάστατος πανταχῇ. On the development of the doctrine of non-durational eternity cf. *Plotin: Über Ewigkeit und Zeit (Enneade III. 7),* übersetzt, eingeleitet und kommentiert von W. Beierwaltes (Frankfurt 1967); my "The 'Eternity' of the Platonic Forms," *Phronesis* 13 (1968) 131 ff.; my "Ammonius on the Delphic E," *Classical Quarterly* 19 (1969) 185 ff.; my *GOD TIME BEING: Two studies in the transcendental tradition in Greek philosophy (Symbolae Osloenses Fasc. supplet.* XXIII, Oslo 1971); A. H. Armstrong, "Eternity, Life and Movement in Plotinus' Account of Noῦς" in *Le Néoplatonisme* (Paris 1971) 67 ff.

13. Cf. *Enn.* III. 7. 3. 19 f. οἷον ἐν σημείῳ ὁμοῦ πάντων ὄντων.

14. Cf. Aristotle, De *caelo* 279 a 28f. For the history of the term αἰών see C. Lackeit, *Aion. Zeit und Ewigkeit in Sprache und Religion der Griechen. I. Teil: Sprache* (Königsberg 1916); and (with useful bibliography) E. Degani, *AIΩN da Omero ad Aristotele* (Padua 1961).

15. Proclus warns, not entirely convincingly, against this at *In Tim.* I. 239. 2 ff. Diehl ἄλλο γὰρ τὸ ἀεὶ τὸ χρονικὸν καὶ ἄλλο τὸ αἰώνιον· τὸ μὲν ἀθρόως πᾶν ὄν, τὸ δὲ τῇ ὅλῃ συνεχείᾳ τοῦ χρόνου συνεκτεινόμενον καὶ ἄπειρον, τὸ μὲν ἐν τῷ νῦν, τὸ δὲ ἐν διαστάσει, τῆς διαστάσεως ἀκαταλήκτου τυγχανούσης καὶ ἀεὶ γιγνομένης. Cf. also Simplicius, *In Phys.* 777. 13 ff. Diels.

16. On the history of the term ἄχρονος cf. my *GOD TIME BEING* (cf. note 12 above) 40 ff.

17. Pointing out the distinction between the two conceptions of ἄπειρος was almost a Neoplatonic commonplace; cf., e.g., Gregory Nazianzen, *Orat.* 38. 8, PG 36, 320.

18. *Proclus: The Elements of Theology* (Oxford 1933; rp. 1963) 247.
19. Cf. Lampe's *Patristic Greek Lexicon* s.vv.
20. Cf. also *De cael. hierarch.* II. 3, PG 3, 141 ἀγνοοῦμεν δὲ τὴν ὑπερούσιον αὐτῆς καὶ ἀνόητον καὶ ἄρρητον ἀοριστίαν.
21. Cf. R. Haubst, "Die Thomas- und Proklos-Exzerpte des 'Nicolaus Treverensis' in Codicillus Strassburg 84," *Mitteilungen und Forschungsbeiträge der Cusanus-Gesellschaft* I (1961) 17 ff., in particular 26 ff.
22. *Op. cit.* 31.
23. Cf. Nicolaus de Cusa, *De principio*, ed. J. Koch (Heidelberg 1948) 102 (Adnotationes); and G. von Bredow, "Die Bedeutung des Minimum in der *Coincidentia oppositorum*," in *Nicolò Cusano agli Inizi del Mondo Moderno* [Atti del Congresso internazionale in occasione del V centenario della morte di Nicolò Cusano: Bressanone, 6 – 10 settembre 1964] (Florence 1970) 364 f.
24. On which see G. von Bredow, *op. cit.* 357 ff., and P. Wilpert, "Das Problem der *Coincidentia oppositorum* in der Philosophie des Nikolaus von Cues," in *Humanismus, Mystik und Kunst in der Welt des Mittelalters*, hrsg. v. J. Koch (Leiden-Cologne 1953) 39 ff.
25. Cf. R. T. Wallis, *Neoplatonism* (London 1972) 29 f.
26. The same view seems to lie behind *Didask.* 179. 2 ff. H. πάντα μέν φησιν [sc. Πλάτων] ἐν εἱμαρμένῃ εἶναι, οὐ μὴν πάντα καθειμάρθαι. ἡ γὰρ εἱμαρμένη νόμου τάξιν ἐπέχουσα οὐχ οἷον λέγει, διότι ὁ μὲν τάδε ποιήσει, ὁ δὲ τάδε πείσεται· εἰς ἄπειρον γὰρ τοῦτο, ἀπείρων μὲν ὄντων τῶν γεννωμένων, ἀπείρων δὲ τῶν περὶ αὐτοὺς συμβαινόντων.
27. Proclus' view that (*El. Theol.* prop. 93) Πᾶν τὸ ἄπειρον ἐν τοῖς οὖσιν οὔτε τοῖς ὑπερκειμένοις ἄπειρόν ἐστιν οὔτε ἑαυτῷ is nonetheless firmly anchored in the Greek theological tradition. Cf., e.g., Tertullian, *Ap.* 17. 2 quod vero immensum est [sc. Deus], soli sibi notum est. And Minucius Felix, *Octav.* 18. 8 sensibus maior est [sc. Deus], infinitus, inmensus et soli sibi tantus, quantus est, notus. For the Hellenistic background of these statements cf. my "A Hellenistic context for John 10. 29," *Vigiliae Christianae* 24 (1970) 241 ff.

28. The doctrine can be traced back in clearly enuntiated form as far as Philo of Alexandria at least. Cf. E. R. Dodds, *op. cit.* 251 ff.

29. Cf. also *Enn.* VI. 5. 4. 2 ff. ἔστι γὰρ ἀξιούμενόν τε παρὰ πᾶσι τοῖς ἔννοιαν ἔχουσι θεῶν οὐ μόνον περὶ ἐκείνου, ἀλλὰ καὶ περὶ πάντων λέγειν θεῶν, ὡς πανταχοῦ πάρεισι, καὶ ὁ λόγος δέ φησι δεῖν οὕτω τίθεσθαι.

30. Meister Eckhart, *Die lateinischen Werke*, Bd. IV *Sermones* edd. Benz/Decker/ Koch (Stuttgart 1956) 263 ff. I owe this reference to Professor Egil A. Wyller.

31. Cf. pp. 156 ff. above.

32. Cf. p. 160 above.

33. *Werke* Bd. 26 (Weimar 1909; rp. Graz 1964) 339 f. On the possible influence of Cusanus cf. F.E. Cranz, "The Transmutation of Platonism in the Development of Nicolaus Cusanus and of Martin Luther," in *Nicolò Cusano agli Inizi del Mondo Moderno* (cf. note 23 above) 73 ff. and in particular 101.

34. Cf. *Gnosticism: An Anthology*, ed. R. M. Grant (London 1961) 71.

35. On the *Via negationis* cf. H.A. Wolfson, "Albinus and Plotinus on divine attributes," *Harvard Theological Review* 45 (1952) 115 ff; Wolfson, "Negative attributes in the Church Fathers and the Gnostic Basilides," *Harvard Theological Review* 50 (1957) 145 ff.; my "Basilides on the ineffability of God," *Harvard Theological Review* 62 (1969) 367 ff.; my "Neopythagoreanism and negative theology," *Symbolae Osloenses* 44 (1969) 109 ff.; my "Neopythagoreanism and the transcendent absolute," *Symbolae Osloenses* 48 (1973) 75 ff.

The Neoplatonic 'One' and the Trinitarian 'ΑΡΧΗ'

the conflict over the unity of the principle and its relation to the 'identity' of the absolute in Schelling and Hegel.

by J. Patrick Atherton

Dalhousie University

In his book, *Pagan and Christian in an Age of Anxiety*, E. R. Dodds, after discussing many of the subordinate aspects of the conflict between the Christian and the Hellenic tradition, turns finally to the intellectual side of the issue and raises the question: "what was the debate about?"[1] If an answer were to be attempted in a language appropriate to the time, it could be said to be "a dispute about the ἀρχή, or more particularly about the precise nature of the 'unity' to be ascribed to the principle." All the secondary conflicts, whether of thought or of practice, - the origin of evil, the status of matter, the authority of the imperial order - can be clarified only so far as they are understood in relation to their source or principle and recognised as consequences of the demands upon men as they moved at all levels towards a re-definition of the ἀρχή.

The recognition of the predicateless unity or pure self-identity of the ἀρχή lay at the root of the entire Neoplatonic tradition: in its utter simplicity, raised above all duality – even the primary differentiation of the intelligence from the intelligible world – the ἀρχή retreated into inaccessibility and unknowability. On this point the later elaborators of the position found the Plotinian doctrine insufficiently precise: Iamblichus and Damascius exhausted the resources of language and intellectual virtuosity to ensure the simplicity and transcendence of the One. Besides the unknowability of the principle – a result of its pure indeterminateness or simplicity – a further consequence of the of the purely self-identical ἀρχή of the Neoplatonists was the ἀπορία encountered in explaining satisfactorily the relation of the principle to its derivatives, that is, of p r i n c i p i u m to p r i n c i p i a t a: if the ἀρχή was complete *in itself*, prior to its diremption into the world of which it was nevertheless the source, how could these two aspects of the principle – as self-sufficient in its abstract unity or *causa sui*, yet also *causa omnium rerum* – be intelligibly related to each other? As M. Trouillard says: Neoplatonism "pose a priori qu'entre le Principe et ses dérivations aucune déduction, aucun processus logique n'est concevable, parce que le Bien n'est plus Idée."[2]

The trinitarian ἀρχή, by contrast, appears as an attempt to reconcile the requirement of unity with that of difference within the principle itself: ἑτερότης is now recognised as a moment within the unity, as belonging to the principle *as unity*. Such a position requires a very different interpretation of the relation between the principle and its derivatives than that found in Neoplatonism: the manifestation of the ἀρχή in the sensible and intelligible orders belongs to its essential nature as principle – the principle is essentially self-revealing. According, the procession of all things from the ἀρχή as their source and their return to it as their end have to be understood as constituting its very identity: the 'process' is one of *self*-determination, that through which the principle attains its unity with itself. The primary opposition, then, between the two positions can be characterised as follows: for the Neoplatonists the unity of the ἀρχή is a *unity of indeterminateness* – just because it is the source of all the differences between things, prior even to the difference between subject and object, the principle excludes distinction from itself and is, in this way, 'one'; on the trinitarian position however, the principle is a *self-determining unity* – determinateness does not fall *outside* the unity of the principle: rather, in the completest differentiation the principle returns upon itself, is one with itself.

It is this distinction – between the ἀρχή as the purely indeterminate and as self-determining unity – that this paper will examine as its primary concern; it is hardly necessary to add that the question on the Christian side is discussed in a language suitable to the religious consciousness, that is, with the admixture of an unavoidable representational element; the inadequacy of the language to the doctrine it expressed became apparent only with the later development of philosophy; in our period it was entirely appropriate to the intellectual culture of the times. Secondarily, however, since in this conference we are concerned with the relation between Neoplatonism and modern culture, it may be permitted to relate the discussion to that moment in the history of modern though when the intellectual content of the ancient dispute was recognised with something like its original profundity: in the conflict between Schelling and Hegel over the nature of the absolute, Hegel was able to find in the trinitarian position a principle which, when developed into its proper philosophical form, would permit him to emancipate himself from Schelling's 'Philosophy of Identity'. In recognising that the absolute had to be conceived not as "substance but as subject", or, in the precise sense of his later philosophy as "Geist", Hegel separated himself decisively from Schelling's principle of "Absolute Indifference".

I

Why does Plotinus regard it as necessary to go beyond the level of *νοῦς* to find the *ἀρχή*? The argument is found in many texts but the expression of it at *Enneads V, 3, 13* will be most suitable for our purposes: there it is claimed that the principle is in truth unspeakable because "if you say anything of it, you make it a particular thing." But that which is beyond all things, beyond even the "most venerable of all things, the intelligence" cannot be regarded as one of them; if we speak of it as knowable and as knowing, we are making it manifold. If we attribute thought to it, we are treating it as in need of thinking. If, indeed, in any way we suppose thinking to be associated with the One, we must regard such thinking as unessential to it. What thought does is to gather many elements to a unity and so become conscious of a whole. This is true even when the mind does not regard the object as external to itself as it does in discursive thinking; even in self-consciousness the attempt to turn upon itself introduces division. When, in the very act of apprehending its own simple nature, it says 'I am in being' (ὄν εἰμί), it fails to grasp either being or itself . . . therefore, if there is something which possesses absolute simplicity, it cannot think itself.

The intent of the argument is perfectly clear: the unity of the intellect with itself in self-consciousness − of νοῦς with νοητόν in νόησις − is imperfectly 'one', therefore the ἀρχή, which must be independent of all 'otherness', be purely self-referred, in order to be a principle, must be sought 'beyond'. If, as is commonly supposed, the Plotinian doctrine on the νοῦς hypostasis incorporates Aristotelian teaching on the point, it is worth while considering briefly the Aristotelian sources and Plotinus' treatment of them. The main sources are doubtless the treatment of the divine thinking in Book Lambda of the *Metaphysics* and the relevant passages on νοῦς in the *De Anima;* the doctrine Plotinus finds there is considerably fuller than that usually allowed by modern interpreters. Nothing in these passages has perplexed modern exegesis more than the question of the relation of the divine thinking to its object.[3] It is in the divine thinking that Aristotle finds the primary substance, pure ἐνέργεια, that in which there is no potentiality: what does this pure thinking think of? Evidently of itself, for if it thought of anything external to itself "there would evidently be something more precious than thought, viz. that which is thought of" (1074b 29-30). The divine thinking must then be a self-thinking: does it follow that the divine thinking has no knowledge of the world? Many in recent times have concluded that it did[4]; however, the tradition of comment in ancient times (Alexander, Themistius, Plotinus) was rather that the divine self-thinking is a knowledge of 'things' in their forms or definitions, their εἴδη, for which its (i.e. pure intelligence) apprehension of the indivisible unity of elements in the object (as ἁπλᾶ), is, at the same time, a grasping of the unity of the object itself. In νόησις there is no piecing together of the elements of the form in the syllogistic manner of 'scientific' knowing or ἐπιστήμη; the mind is not externally related to its objects at all − the objects are either possessed or not possessed, and the only alternatives are knowledge or ignorance; as Aristotle puts it, in νόησις we are either in contact or touch (ϑιγεῖν) with the things or we are not. The mind cannot be mistaken about what constitutes an element in its consciousness of itself; at 1072b 20 Aristotle explicitly asserts that the mind thinks itself by participation in the intelligible object; for, "it becomes an object of thought in coming into contact with and thinking its objects, so that thought and object of thought are the same" (ταὐτὸν νοῦς καὶ νοητόν). The divine life is precisely this actual identity of thinking with its object (1072b 21-25).

What the ancient interpreters found in these texts was a doctrine of νοῦς in its completeness (that is, as divine or completely 'actual') including the world (or more precisely, the εἴδη of things) as its object. How this divine principle is present in nature; how this pure self-consciousness, which in its perfection includes the forms of things as one with itself, is present in human cognition, which only attains its objects gradually by laboriously connecting together the data of the senses (that is, is only 'potentially one with the intelligible object' δυνάμει τὰ νοητά) are questions of the greatest importance for later philosophy; we must leave these aside to look more closely at the unity of the intelligence with its object suggested by these texts, because it is this conception of the unity of the ἀρχή that Plotinus finds inadequate and which moves him to posit a principle beyond νοῦς.

The ἀρχή (according to these Aristotelian texts) is not νοῦς; it is νόησις νοήσεως, the actuality of mind thinking its objects and thinking *itself* in its objects. Therein lies the unity of the principle: subject and object are one in νόησις — a unity which is, in a sense, *prior* to the distinction between them, in that, separated from the unity which is their truth, they are subordinate and incomplete elements in the ἀρχή. The unity of the principle is a unity of these essentially correlative elements: it is not abstract self-consciousness which is the Aristotelian principle but the concreter unity of thought with itself in its object.

The Plotinian doctrine of νοῦς, however, fastens upon the moment of distinction within self-consciousness and regards the unity of the two sides as something secondary, so that the

intelligence and the intelligible world have a certain completeness in their independence of each other – outside their unity
with each other. Since they are not seen as forming a perfect
unity in their inseparable opposition to each other, a principle
that is properly one must be sought beyond them.[5] The
question then arises: what is the character of this unity, and
how, in its isolation, does it generate a world?

The primary unity can, according to this position, have no
character, no determinateness; all the differences between
things, the distinction between mind and its object, presuppose
and point towards it, but none are applicable to it. We can only
indicate its nature negatively – by saying what it is not. The
'negative theology' is not, however, as reliable an approach as
has sometimes been supposed; a negative relation remains a
relation and compromises the utter transcendence of the One; it
seems we cannot attach *any* name to the principle, even the
'One' or the 'Good' without bringing it down into a relation
with something other than itself. It is, nevertheless, this very
dependence of all other things on something beyond themselves
that has necessitated our affirmation of its transcendence: we
are required to think of it in relation to them in order to know
it as absolute or primary. We must accordingly understand the
terms we use as expressing its proper nature: it is really One – if
it is to be the source from which all things derive; it is really the
Good – if it is to be the final cause to which all things move. It
is this consideration that drives (probably) Iamblichus and
(certainly) Damascius to double the first principle or posit a
One beyond the One: Damascius will not even allow 'transcendent' ἐξῃρημένον to be used since that presupposes a relation to
other things; we cannot know it even negatively – we must
simply experience its presence in a prophetic way
(μαντεύεσθαι) –οὐδὲ ἄρα ἀρχήν, οὐδὲ αἴτιον ἐκείνην κλητέον,
οὐδὲ πρῶτον, οὐδέ γε πρὸ πάντουν, οὐδ᾽ ἐπέκεινα πάντων. At
the end of its development Neoplatonism cannot reach the
principle either by affirmation or negation: indeed not even
negation of the negation can avoid positive reference, and the
inadequacy of language presses heavily upon Damascius. This,
doubtless, is why commentators have discerned an 'inclination
to irrationalism'[6] as the tradition drew to its conclusion; the

whole philosophical enterprise is called in question, for, as Professor Wallis has remarked "the consequences [of Damascius' position] were little less than the annihilation of the whole Neoplatonic hierarchy."[7]

Another consequence of the transcendence of the One is the difficulty involved in understand its relation to its derivatives. We ascend the scale of being because each lower level is defective or incomplete and has need of a higher to explain it; but, though the lower has need of the higher, the higher does not in turn seem to require the lower or bear any essential relation to it. When, therefore, we reach the highest, this is regarded as having need of nothing but itself. The One, as complete in itself, has no need to produce a world; the *principium* need not disclose itself in *principiata*; since in fact there are *principiata*, some way of connecting the derivatives with their principle must be found. The connection is made, of course, through 'emanation': the Good can look to nothing but itself, without any activity directed towards them. The process is compared to 'irradiation' or 'overflowing'; Plotinus is quite aware of the deficiency of these metaphorical analogies as he shows in his critique of Gnostic theories of emanation. But even when expressed more adequately as an essential characteristic of perfection that it should generate something other than itself, it hardly elucidates the division between what a thing is and does in relation to itself, and what it is and does in relation to other things: the metaphors merely indicate the difficulty in trying to separate a thing's inner nature from its outward activity – a self-involved activity, which only accidentally discloses itself outwardly, is an incoherent conception. In the case of the One, it would require that the principle should have an external effect which is not necessarily involved in its own nature. The difficulty points in truth to a very different conception of the principle as essentially self-manifesting: to such a principle we now turn.

*

The trinitarian position appears as a different solution to the problem of the relation between the moments within the ἀρχή. No less than the Neoplatonic tradition did it hold to the strictest unity and transcendence of the principle; but it conceived of this transcendent ἀρχή as in some way having 'revealed' itself. The unknown god had made himself known; and this 'making himself known' was not considered an inessential aspect of the divine nature, but a constituent moment of his very identity – the moment of manifestation was god himself, and not some 'intermediate' entity. The effort to hold together in a unity the two essential aspects of the ἀρχή as this tradition understood it – as *causa sui* and *causa omnium rerum* – resulted in the triadic formula agreed upon as orthodox in the fourth century. This defined a principle which was a perfect unity, although differentiated into three 'persons'. In the language of philosophy, the ἀρχή was *both* one *and* many: μόνος ὢν πολὺς ἦν (Hippolytus, Contra Noetum, 10). This came to be regarded as the *sine qua non* of orthodoxy, through which the new religion distinguished its belief from all previous formulations of the ἀρχή, both philosophical and those of its own heretical variants: all the resources of the Greek language were exploited in the attempt to fix the new ἀρχή in an unambiguous definition. The trinitarian formula was understood as reconciling unity with difference in the most satisfactory way. The difficulty facing the framers of the doctrine was to avoid sacrificing the unity of the ἀρχή in the attempt to explain its self-differentiation – and self-differentiation was essential, if it was to be held that the ἀρχή had fully revealed himself and disclosed his real nature. On the other hand, this manifestation of the ἀρχή had to be regarded as a 'substantial' or necessary moment in its identity: the process of self-differentiation constituted the very being of god and was not merely a camouflage behind which the true deity subsisted as an abstract unity. To insist upon the two aspects with equal firmness was a more difficult and ambitious position than that of the opponents of the orthodox formula: at bottom, all the rival positions were variations of the more easily comprehensible doctrine that the divine unity necessarily excluded multiplicity; on such a view the full trinitarian formula was merely a cover for tritheism.

It is impossible to trace here the process by which the new ἀρχή acquired an adequate terminology and formulation; it is sufficient to indicate it was accomplished through a re-shaping of the Logos doctrine. The intellectual effort of the earlier centuries was to overcome all suggestion of inferiority in the status of the Logos or the Son — an effort which went against the grain of all emanation theories of derivation from the principle: this expressed the insight that the object of pure or divine knowing was not to be regarded as an inessential element in, or something external to, the nature of the primary ἀρχή (and, therefore, something which would compromise its simplicity or unity) but was rather that without which there would be no divine knowledge at all; the object becomes a constituent moment of the principle and is compatible with, and, indeed, required by, its unity: the ἀρχή is a pure knowing in which the knower, in knowing the object, knows only himself — the deity is himself only in that return-to-himself, which is 'spirit'.

What the principal consequences of this view of the ἀρχή were can only be tentatively suggested here. The principle is both subject and object without any infringement of its unity. For the Neoplatonists the subject-object relationship did not become a perfect identity in νοῦς and the perfectly unified ἀρχή had to be sought beyond this duality. Such a view of the principle led to the difficulty that the first derivation could not be logically deduced from it: there seemed to be no logical reason why such an abstractly self-identical unity should divide itself into the subject-object relation of νοῦς. The trinitarian ἀρχή sought to avoid this objection: it was not a unity complete in itself prior to its diremption into subject and object, but a unity whose identity consisted in this very act of self-diremption and which was just as much subject as it was object. By insisting on the moment of 'procession' as belonging to the very nature of the ἀρχή the creation of the finite cosmos in space and time assumed a new significance; the sensible world was no cosmic error, incompatible with the divine perfection but was involved in the nature of divine self-consciousness (the Father's consciousness of himself in the Son involves him as the locus of the κόσμος νοητός). Further, and most importantly, the divine knowning (the very essence of the ἀρχή) was an unlimited or infinite one; for it was a knowing in which all otherness or externality which could limit it was overcome.

God's knowledge of the things of the sensible world was not of
them as 'other' but was involved in his own self-knowledge. This
meant that there was no need to look for an intermediary link
between the infinite and the finite world, which would yoke
them uneasily together: they did not need to be brought
together because they had no independent existence apart from
each other. The infinite included the finite within itself as a
moment in its own identity: the infinite was only infinite when
understood as producing a world external to itself, which
nevertheless remained one with itself in its own self-knowledge.
Nor is the infinity of the ἀρχή one of pure indeterminateness,
that is, mere absence of all determinateness. As the ἀρχή
produces the intelligible world out of itself, all the categories of
the intelligible world (i.e. the categories by which the world is
made an object for intelligence) become modes of the divine
self-consciousness: the principle is not in-finite in the sense of
being beyond all limitation but in the sense of being the source
of all determination through which he comprehends only
himself. As a self-determining unity the principle can be *known*;
it is open to intellectual apprehension as never before; this
radical intelligibility of the principle is confined initially to the
religious consciousness, and it lay in the remote future of
philosophy to remove this limitation and attempt to understand
all aspects of nature and spirit in the light of this.

II

It remains to attempt to relate this discussion of the unity
of the principle ot the debate over the nature of the Absolute in
idealism. The position grew out of the Kantian critique of
experience; after Kant it was impossible to accept the ordinary
view of experience as something immediately given for thought
and not constituted by it. The possibility of knowledge was the
unity of the ego and non-ego: how was this unity to be
understood?

The Kantian philosophy left the unity quite inexplicable:
the objects of knowledge were indeed essentially related to the
unity of self-consciousness, but these objects were 'phenomenal'
only − that is, they were not the 'real' objects, which were
regarded as 'things-in-themselves' or things *not* essentially

related to, or knowable by, the subject. Fichte denied the independent existence of things in themselves, external to subjectivity; the non-ego was reduced to a negative condition through which the ego realised its own life of self-determination; but this negative condition was essential to self-consciousness and had to be produced in some inexplicable way out of the ego itself. It appeared as an incomprehensible moment of opposition of the mind to itself. Schelling, however, did not accept this merely negative view of the relation of spirit to nature; the two sides are one in the absolute — that is, the unity of ego and non-ego is a unity of indifference. All objects, whether mind or matter, are simply forms of this identity of subject and object, and, from the point of view of the absolute all these identities are one. Nature is not merely the negative of thought, but has revealed in it the same principle that constitutes the ego in man. Schelling's way of putting it is: there are no qualitative, but only quantitative, differences in things — from the point of view, or within, the absolute.

At first, when Hegel appeared as a colleague of Schelling and they were joint editors of the 'Critical Journal', it seems that he did not object to Schelling's formulation of the identity of the absolute: it was common to both their positions that there is a 'unity' beyond all differences, which realises itself through all distinctions, and in relation to which all differences must be explained: they further agreed on describing this unity as 'spiritual'. Hegel, however, very soon began to distinguish himself from his colleague precisely on the notion of 'spirit' and more particularly about how the absolute was apprehended. Already in the early treatise, "On the Difference between the Fichtean and Schellingian Systems", he is found asserting that the identity of philosophy is not an abstract identity simply opposed to difference but a spiritual unity which differentiates itself in order that, through a process of division and reconciliation, it can achieve a higher unity with itself. Further, the mode of cognition of the absolute, the 'intellectual intuition' of Schelling, is not regarded as exclusive of the process of reflection but as containing it; though at this stage, Hegel still considered thinking within philosophy as quite distinct from that outside it. By the time of the *phenomenology* Hegel's hold upon his own position had strengthened to the point that he had to separate himself clearly from Schelling: hence the critique in the Preface of Schelling's Absolute as the "night in which all cows are black" (Bailey, (trans.) p. 79) and "intellectual intuition" as a "sort of ecstatic enthusiasm which starts straight off with absolute knowledge, as if shot out of a pistol" (ibid. p. 88).

A more adequate view of the absolute is attained only when it is understood as subject: "in my view, everything depends upon grasping and expressing the ultimate truth not as Substance but as Subject as well." (p. 80). He goes on to explain that a being which is truly subject is one which is properly actual (wirklich) only in the process of positing itself, that is, of splitting up what is simple and undifferentiated, of duplicating and setting factors in opposition. "True reality is merely this process of reinstating self-identity, of reflecting into its own self in and from its others, and is not an original and primal unity as such, not an immediate unity as such." The divine life, though no doubt an undisturbed identity, consists in its being objective to itself, conscious of itself on its own account (für sich zu sein).

The echo here of the trinitarian debate, and the many points in the dispute with Schelling that recall the Neoplatonic discussions of the One, are not accidental: it is possible here only to indicate them and to suggest that fuller and more serious study could only confirm the importance to be attributed to the issues with which the intellectual life of the later ancient world was concerned; the obvious increase of interest in these studies, as well as the reviving interest in the Hegelian philosophy, make it a reasonable expectation that this will be so. Hegel saw in the attainment of the trinitatian position the expression in an undeveloped and representational form of distinctively 'Western' culture; the principle needed to be liberated from its theological form and shown to be adequate to the task of comprehending the concrete freedom to which the West aspired. To the end of his life Hegel regarded himself as an orthodox trinitarian — a position which the theologians have not usually been very ready to accord him. But what the trinitarian doctrine in truth is, and what form it takes in later thought, cannot be understood until the content of the ancient disputes is once again comprehended philosophically.

NOTES

1. E. R. Dodds, *Pagan and Christian in an Age of Anxiety,* (Cambridge, 1965), p. 116.
2. J. Trouillard et al, *Histoire de la philosophie,* (Encyclopédie de la plèiade, 1969), p. 896.
3. For a recent discussion of the question, v. Hans Joachim Krämer, Grundfragen der aristotelischen Theologie', *Theologie und Philosophie,* (44 Heft 3, (1969)) p. 363-382.
4. Perhaps most conspicuously Ross in *Aristotle's Metaphysics,* vol. I., Introduction, p. cxlii, (Oxford, 1924)
5. *Enneads,* VI, 9.2, 11. 32 ff.
6. The comment of C. de Vogel in *Greek Philosophy*: Vol. 3, No. 1478, p. 589, (2nd edition, Leiden, 1964).
7. R. T. Wallis, *Neoplatonism,* (London, 1972), p. 158.

The Apprehension of Divinity in the Self and Cosmos in Plotinus

by A. Hilary Armstrong

Dalhousie University

This may seem an odd title for a paper which is intended to commend the philosophy of Plotinus as one which, as I believe, has some contemporary relevance. The words "apprehension of divinity in self and cosmos" are likely to displease irremediably two considerable bodies of contemporary opinion. They will of course displease that very large number of contemporary philosophers to whom a phrase like "apprehension of divinity", or any talk about "God" or "the divine" is meaningless: and those who adhere to some older traditions of Western theistic philosophy will find the language offensively "pantheistic", and, if they can be persuaded to explain this large, vague term of theological abuse further, will say that anyone who talks like this is looking for divinity in the wrong place. He has forgotten that God is the Wholly Other and that there is an unbridgeable gulf between the Creator and his creation. I have some respect for both these groups, and do not think that the arguments which they can bring against the Neoplatonic, or any similar position ought to be neglected. But I do not think that I have either the charismatic or the eristic competence to deal with them. I have not the sort of faith which would enable me, in the proper manner of prophetic theism, to shout religious opponents down with yet another version of what professes to be the Word of God: nor do I think that I am able to argue people out of what is now, especially in the case of the unbelieving philosophers, a settled traditional belief supported by revered authorities. I propose, therefore to address myself to those of our contemporaries, a large and, probably, increasing number, who do not belong to either of these groups and are not likely to find the phrase "apprehension of divinity in self and cosmos" too preposterous to be worth considering further. I have the rather faint hope that by confining myself to positive elucidation for people assumed to be sympathetic I may be able, here and there, to say something which will make the position I am trying to explain seem less ridiculous or shocking to others.

What I propose is that in the thought of Plotinus we do not, to begin with, apprehend divinity in two separate ways, one in our selves and one in the cosmos, but we have a single apprehension or awareness of divinity in self and cosmos taken together, and that we do not in fact leave the cosmos altogether behind until our awareness of divinity becomes so intense that we go "alone to the alone". In explaining this I hope to be able to show that the Neoplatonic way of thinking may still have some life and meaning. We cannot of course expect Plotinus, or anybody else, to do our own thinking for us, and some aspects of his thought which will be discussed in this paper will inevitably seem odd, antiquated and irrelevant to present concerns. But I believe that if we start our own reflections with a study of that thought which is sympathetic as well as critical, Plotinus may give us a lead to a better understanding of the world and may help us to adjust our attitudes and valuations in a way which may help us to deal with some of the most pressing problems of our time, and especially to do something towards closing the gap between man and non-human nature which has been steadily widening through the Christian and rationalist centuries with, as we are now beginning to see, disastrous results.

It is now high time to say something about my use of the words "apprehension" and "divinity". On "apprehension" there is nothing very helpful to be said, because I agree with Plato and many modern religious philosophers in supposing that what it means can only be learnt in practice, and by each in their own way. One can neither explain what is meant by the apprehension of God nor tell anyone else an infallible method for apprehending him. One can only recommend a serious attention to and enjoyment of the world in the hope that those who apply themselves to it, holding in check for a time the desire of power or satisfaction, may become aware of the divine presence. As for my use of "divinity", the Neoplatonic tradition which I am trying to explain, and with which on this point I agree, makes things rather difficult for its interpreters by insisting that the first principle, the One or Good, which corresponds to what most of us who still use the word mean by "God", is absolutely unknowable and ineffable. There is of course nothing scandalous to a modern religious thinker in this insistence. At any meeting of theologians or religious philosophers in the West the unknowability of God is sure to be asserted by a variety of speakers from a variety of different points of view, and it is a commonplace of religious thought in the East. But all too many of those who make this assertion, fail to apply it sufficiently in their practice. They seem to fail to realise that if God is ineffable you can't talk about him: you can only use language which will prepare people's minds to attend to such indications as he may give of his presence. The pagan Neoplatonists, from Plotinus to Damascius, of course knew this very well and stated it with increasing clarity (even if they quite often seem to go rather too far, on their own premises, towards forming concepts or enunciating propositions about the One or making him the premise or conclusion of a discursive argument). The great masters of the Athenian School, Proclus and Damascius, do a good deal at this point to develop what is not always clear in Plotinus (thought I do not myself think that they do more than bring out what is, sometimes at least, implicit in his thought). Both of them emphasise strongly that it is necessary in the end to negate one's negations (which does not mean simply restoring the original positive statements which are negated, with a decorative label, a *huper* – or *eminenter*, attached), otherwise one would be left with a sort of pseudo-definition of One as a something which was not anything, instead of a profoundly fruitful and illuminating silence. And Damascius, following a view of Iamblichus[1] which was not adopted by Proclus, insists that we must go even beyond the One to find the unknowable First. In the first pages of his great critical, and at many points liberatingly destructive, re-thinking of the vast metaphysical system which he had inherited[2], in strong opposition on many points to the too smooth, over-clarified, misleadingly coherent-looking scholastic version of it produced by Proclus, he insists that the One from which all things proceed can not only, in a way, be defined and understood in relation to the all but must in some sense be all things which proceed from it, in however super-simplified a way[3]: and, with an agonized sense of the inadequacy of human thought and language which is impressive and refreshing to those who sometimes feel that Proclus knows much too much about the unknowable, points his readers on to that for which he has no proper name. The most important result of this extreme apophatism for our present purposes is that this unnameable and unknowable divinity is not in a relationship to everything else which can simply be defined as "transcendence"[4]. Its relationship to the world, as we should expect, cannot be defined at all (even by saying that it has no relationship). Once it is clear that God for the Neoplatonists stands in this unknowable relationship to all else, anyone who is religious in a Neoplatonist way is free to see him in mind and world wherever his presence seems to be indicated. And though another side of their thought led the Neoplatonists to think (in one way or another) of his presence as mediated through a hierarchy of lesser divinities, this idea of divine hierarchy is probably incompatible with their ultimate conclusions about divinity (and leads them into many other difficulties) and can, I think, be neglected by a modern who wishes to make Neoplatonism the starting-point for his own religious thinking. The hierarchy of hypostases should, of course, be given its proper place in any historical account of Neoplatonism, and will not be ignored in what follows.

    The first apprehensions which we have of divinity according to Plotinus are on the level of his third hypostasis, Soul. In the great exhortation to return from self-forgetfulness and self-alienation and remember our true selves and our Father which begins the treatise *On the Three Primary Hypostases* every soul is told to remember that it made all living things and the whole world and gave life to everything[5] (in the Plotinian universe everything is alive and is in some sense thought[6]). In the further development of this in the rest of the chapter, and still more in the careful discussion of the relationship of our souls to the Soul of the All which begins the great treatise *On Difficulties About the Soul*[7], Plotinus makes clear that this does not mean that our souls are parts of or simply identical with the cosmic soul which makes the physical universe real, alive and divinely excellent. We are of one kind with it[8] and in that sense just because we are soul can claim its divine creativity as our own. But the living unity of the Plotinian hypostasis, in which every part is the whole in so far as it thinks universally, but each in its own way, admits of considerable differences of character and rank. Plotinus never abandons his conviction, stated in the early treatise *If All Souls are One*[9], of the fundamental unity of soul: but he modifies it in the direction of acknowledging a greater diversity and degree of independence to the individuals within that unity. The World-Soul is our elder sister[10], and our attitude towards her, it seems, should combine a sense of intimate kinship with an affectionate and respectful independence and assertion of fundamental equality. We can aspire to "walk on high"[11] like her, sharing in her formation and vivifying of the whole and enjoying that ideal relationship to body which belongs to her and to the souls of the great parts of the universe, sun, moon, earth and stars. Our awareness of any sort of divinity in ourselves is an awareness of a divinity which, without abolition of differences or loss or personal identity, we share with the living thought which is all the reality of the cosmos, in whose everlasting perfection we can rediscover our own forgotten natures.

This leads Plotinus into some very curious excursions into cosmic psychology in his great treatise on the soul, the second part of which contains extensive discussions about whether the World-Soul, the heavenly bodies, and the earth have memory or perception or need them to perform their functions in the universe.[12] The details of these are not relevant here, but it is important to realise that for Plotinus, as for any ancient Stoic or Platonist, any philosophical psychology which concerned itself exclusively with the nature of the human soul would be hopelessly unsatisfactory and inadequate. (Mediaeval Christians here to some extent follow the ancients; they are interested in angelic psychology, and angels for them at least sometimes have cosmic functions, though these do not seem to occupy a very important place in angelology). Plotinus cannot consider man, as a being who perceives, remembers, thinks and acts intelligently, in isolation from the greater embodied souls which, thought they do not need memory or deliberation (any more than man does at his highest), do act intelligently and have all the awareness of the world whose reality depends on them which is necessary to them. This may seem a mere curiosity of the antique way of thinking, hopelessly out-of-date and incompatible with our vastly extended knowledge of the universe, and particularly of the celestial regions. It would be difficult for us, imaginatively as well as intellectually, to recognise and venerate the goddess Selene in the dreary, dusty receptacle for excessively expensive junk with which we have all become so boringly familiar of late years. But if we study the treatise *On the Soul* and other documents of the ancient faith in the living organic unity of the universe of which we men are not very important parts, and study them sympathetically as well as critically, we may at least begin to feel again the need for some sense of unity with our world and not be content to stand apart from it as isolated, superior thinking beings over against a mass of brute matter in which there is no living thought originatively present, so that we can exploit it as we please in our own supposed interests without worrying about any non-existent cosmic holiness or intelligence, and even imagine that we are necessarily improving it by "humanizing" it. Even if we cannot entirely or uncritically accept Plotinus' way of asserting the unity-in-distinction of reason and nature, we may come to desire to find some satisfactory way of establishing it for and in ourselves.

As our apprehension of divinity, according to Plotinus, progresses we find that we are not only one with other and greater souls in the unity of the Third Hypostasis, but belong, with all Soul, to the greater community of the Second. We are rightful members of the intelligible cosmos which is the Divine Intellect, at once the inner reality and the transcendent exemplar of our perceptible world. A great deal has been written about Plotinus' astonishing accounts of his intelligible world, in which Platonism, Aristotelianism and Stoicism unite with his own immediate experience to give a richly imaginative and philosophically strange picture of a cosmos at once furiously active and timelessly at rest, in which an extreme and delightful variety is held together in the most perfect unity possible below the One. It is an account which brings out very clearly two problems which are implicit in a great deal of ancient and mediaeval thought. One is the paradox involved in the phrase "eternal life". Can we eliminate all ideas of real duration, process and even change from our thought about any eternal reality as completely as the traditional theologies require if we represent that eternal reality as genuinely alive, and living a life of the utmost imaginable fullness and intensity?[13] The other is a question about a complex intuition which is completely non-discursive.[14] Can we at our highest, or even the Divine Intellect, with which we are then one, have an awareness of a reality (even if we are it) which is not only one, but discrete and diversified, with very complex internal relationships, without that awareness being in some way discursive? Is not the clear distinguishing of parts (even Plotinian parts) and the accurate observance of relationships essentially and inescapably discursive? I mention these problems not in order to solve them, which is beyond my capacity, or to suggest that the ideas of eternal life and complex non-discursive thought should be dismissed from further consideration as absurd, which is far from my intention, but to point out that they arise in this context from Plotinus' determination to get everything in the sense-world into his intelligible world. It must for him possess in a far higher degree all the values and beauties of which we are aware here below in all their splendid variety, even if they are values and beauties which seem to us, on careful reflection, to be bound up with transitoriness and passage and dispersion in space and time. This means that the relationship of the two worlds is inevitably a very intimate one, and Plotinus (though his emphasis varies) is sometimes anxious to stress this intimacy and immediacy[15]. And our own relationship with this higher or inner world is so intimate that Plotinus sometimes says that we are it.[16]

When, therefore, we reach the highest apprehension of divinity of which we are capable before the final union and have transcended our limiting particularities, we still find ourselves one with a world or community of living minds, including greater beings than ourselves[17], which is the archetype and inner reality of the world of sense-experience and lower soul-activity. We are by no means alone or isolated and separated from the whole. At this point it will be as well to distinguish two questions which are sometimes confused: First, is the process or ascent, of discovering our true natures and strengthening our apprehension of divinity till we are ready for the final union, best carried out in isolation or co-operatively? The answer to this is not altogether simple. It has often been noticed that the theory of Plotinus differs here very considerably from that of Plato. For Plato[2] progress in philosophy required affectionate co-operation and continual dialogue. A philosophical community like the Academy was absolutely necessary, and the ideal environment for the philosopher would be a larger and more closely integrated community, the philosophical city-state. Plotinus probably did not presume to disagree with Plato on this last point, as the curious episode of Platonopolis shows[18]. But his general conception of the philosophic life is one of withdrawn solitary concentration, as the *Enneads* repeatedly make clear. Contemplation is primary, and is best pursued alone. Communication is secondary, and hinders rather than helps contemplation, though it is the philosopher's duty to impart what he has seen to others and help them to see it for themselves. His position is finely stated in a passage which sums up the teaching of the first six chapters of the treatise on contemplation: "The truly good and wise man therefore has already finished reasoning when he declares what he has in himself to another: but in relation to himself he is vision. For he is already turned to what is one, and to the quiet which is not only of things outside but in relation to himself, and all is within him"[19]. In practice, however, he by no means withdrew from the world or shunned society, till he was compelled to do so in his last illness, and his teaching at Rome was not just a matter of handing down the results of his contemplation to his disciples: there was plenty of vigorous discussion and dialogue[20] (as there must have been earlier in the group around Ammonius) and it is doubtful whether he could have done without it; there is much in the *Enneads* which suggests the stimulus of discussions within his circle. However different his theory was, in practice philosophy seems to have been for him almost as much of a social activity as it was for Plato.

The second, quite different question is: does one discover oneself in the course of the philosophic ascent as an isolated individual, progressing towards a solitary perfection, or as part of a larger whole? The answer to this has already been given. One discovers oneself as part of the largest possible whole, and a part which in a sense is that whole. The boundaries of the self are those of the intelligible cosmos. (This is of course one reason why Plotinus in theory felt less need for a philosophic community; it could add nothing to the All within him). One might almost say that for Plotinus the *corpus mysticum* is the universe and the company of heaven includes the whole inner reality of the world. And no genuine Neoplatonist philosopher can be satisfied to think of himself as a member of any smaller or more exclusive community. Here the thought of Plotinus is in accord with, and the study of his writings may reinforce, some of the best tendencies in the religious thought of our time which are leading more and more to the rejection of the exclusive ways of thinking of the past which separated man from man or man from nature. I am inclined to think that Neoplatonic Paganism and its derivatives have always in our intellectual history been working against the tendencies derived from other sources which have led to the drawing of sharp lines and the making of exclusive divisions between man and non-human life, or Church and world, and so on; in our own time this Neoplatonic pressure against exclusiveness is being powerfully reinforced in various ways, notably by influences coming from India. It is in this inner, intelligible, totality of being that the soul must ascend to its solitary union with the One, and it must make every effort to dwell in it consciously until the moment of union comes. In all the great mystical passages of the *Enneads* it is from the world of Intellect that the ascent is made. We are drawn to enter and unite ourselves with that world by the impulse to union with the Good which comes from the Good, and Intellect only attracts us by the light playing upon it from the Good, without which it is altogether uninteresting[21] (though elsewhere Plotinus seems to think that the beauty of Intellect desired by itself can distract us from the Good[22]). It is for the sake of the Good, and under the impulse of the Good, that the whole enterprise of intellectual ascent and

expansion is undertaken. But it is characteristic of the mysticism of Plotinus that there is no short cut, no way in which the
isolated individual soul can jump straight into the divine
embrace. We must become the All in order to be one with the
One. And it is important to notice how we leave the intelligible
world for the final union and what happens when we do. In the
long passage near the end of his treatise *How the Multitude of
the Forms came into Being and on the Good* in which he makes
his greatest effort to relate his experience[2 3], he explains that
our union is a perfect assimilation to the eternal union which
the Intellect which is the intelligible world enjoys with the
Good in the "loving", "mad", "drunken" state which timelessly
co-exists with its "thinking" state. We are "carried out of
ourselves by the very surge of the wave of Intellect"[2 4]. If we
are to speak of "ecstacy", a term of which Plotinus is not fond,
it is an ecstacy of the whole intelligible cosmos by which we are
carried out of ourselves who have become the cosmos. It is only
when we forget our selves and are no longer aware of our own
existence that we forget the Intelligible All: this is obvious
when we realise that for Plotinus the self which can rise to the
union in which it forgets itself has already become the All. The
over-quoted "flight of the alone to the alone" which ends the
last treatise of the last *Ennead*[2 5] (perhaps over-quoted because
it is so very easy to find) is misleading if it induces us to think
that there is any stage in the ascent of the soul according to
Plotinus when it stands isolated, apart from the whole, aware
only of itself and God. The "Cut away everything"[2 6] which
ends another great mystical passage gives a more accurate
impression: everything must be discarded, including any sort of
self-awareness, all at once at that last moment, but only at that
last moment. It has often been remarked that the mysticism of
Plotinus is totally non-ecclesiastical and non-sacramental, and in
that sense non-communitarian. But it is not the mysticism of a
solitary saint who seeks God in conscious separation from the
worlds of sense and intellect and finds him, apparently, without
any participation in an universal movement of return. According to Plotinus we seek God by enlarging ourselves to unity with
all that he brings into being and find him and leave all else for
him only after and because of that enlargement. We are unlikely

to be able to follow him altogether uncritically at this, any more than at any other, point in his thought. But if we study what he says about the way to the Good which he followed to the end, those of us who are religiously inclined, and perhaps some who are not so, may find that he has a good deal to teach us.

NOTES

1. See Damascius, *Dubitationes et Solutiones* I. 86. 3 ff. Ruelle.
2. *Dubitationes et Solutiones de Primis Principiis, in Platonis Parmenidem* (sometimes cited as *De Principiis*) only available at present in the unsatisfactory edition of Ruelle (Paris 1889 repr. Amsterdam 1966).
3. Cp. Enneads V 2 (11) 1. 1 τὸ ἕν πάντα καὶ οὐδὲ ἕν cp. ch. 2. 24 πάντα δὲ ταῦτα ἐκεῖνος καὶ οὐκ ἐκεῖνος in both places what immediately follows should be taken into account, but neither here nor elsewhere in the *Enneads* does Plotinus really resolve this paradox.
4. *Dubitationes et Solutiones* P. 15, 13-19 Ruelle.
5. V 1 (10) 2.
6. Cp. III 8 (30) 7.
7. IV 3 (27) 1-8.
8. ὁμοειδὴς δὲ καὶ ἡμέτερα V 1, 2, 44.
9. IV 9 (8).
10. IV 3 (27) 6, 13: II 9 (33) 18, 16.
11. IV 8 (6) 2, 21: IV 3 (27) 7, 17: V 8 (31) 7, 34: cp. Plato *Phaedrus* 246c 1-2.
12. IV 4 (28) 6-11 (memory); 22-27 (perceptions): ch. 22, on the psychology of the earth, is particularly remarkable.
13. CP. My *Eternity, Life and Movement in Plotinus' Accounts* of Nous (with the discussion) in *Le Néoplatonisme*, Éditions du Centre Nationale de Recherche Scientifique Paris 1971 pp. 67-76.
14. A good account of what the ancients meant by non-discursive thinking is to be found in A. C. Lloyd's

Non-Discursive Thought - An Enigma of Greek Philosophy in *Proc. of the Aristotelian Society* 1970, pp. 261-274.

15. See especially IV 8 (6) 6, 23-28 and V 8 (31) 7, 12-16.
16. III 4 (15) 3, 22: cp. IV 7 (2) 10, 34-36.
17. cp. VI 4 (22) 14, 16ff. VI 5 (23) 12.
18. Porphyry, *Life of Plotinus* ch. 12.
19. III 8 (30) 6, 37-40: my own translation from *Plotinus* III (Loeb Classical Library) p. 381.
20. *Life* chs. 3, 13.
21. VI 7 (38) 22.
22. V 5 (32) 12.
23. VI 7 (38) 34-36.
24. l.c. 35, 24-27 and 36, 17-18.
25. VI 9 (9) 11. 50-51.
26. Ἄφελε πάντα V 3 (49) 17, 38.

Is Plotinian Mysticism Monistic?

by Plato Mamo

The University of Calgary

Many commentators of Plotinus have been concerned to show that his mysticism is not of the Oriental "monistic" type. The latest is Professor Rist in his book *Plotinus*.[1] Rist adopts the distinction between monistic and theistic mysticism that he found in Zaehner[2] and, one may add, in a number of other writers as well. He then concludes that Plotinian mysticism is of the theistic type and not monistic or pantheistic.

In this paper I wish to defend a monistic interpretation of Plotinus. I shall begin by a very brief attempt to clarify the issue. I shall then offer an interpretation of the mystical passages and a consideration of some of the arguments advanced by opponents of this interpretation, mainly Arnou and Rist. Finally, I shall briefly consider one of the difficulties generated by the monistic interpretation.

Mysticism refers primarily to a kind of experience the chief characteristics of which can be stated, though the experience itself cannot be described adequately. These characteristics are: a) a fusion of cognition and feeling—the subject both knows and is in a state of bliss; b) what he knows is not a determinate entity but rather the "ground", the transcendent source, the formless; c) the mystic knows in no ordinary way but by being united with, assimilated to the object of his vision. He claims that he ceases to be a separate individual and becomes united, "oned", etc. This is the so-called *unio mystica*.

But mysticism may also refer to an attempt at philosophical interpretation of the experience, an attempt to render the strange claims of those who have had it intelligible within a larger metaphysical framework.[3] It is this philosophical mysticism that characterizes Plotinus' work and sets him apart from countless other mystics both eastern and western. It is in this sense that we may ask the question whether his mysticism was monistic or theistic. And clearly the answer to that question will have important implications for the rest of his metaphysics.

Next it might be necessary to say something about the terms monism, theism and pantheism. If the pantheist wishes to claim that the divine is identical with the material world, that "the One and matter are identical and that there is a reconciliation of good and evil",[4] then clearly Plotinus is no pantheist and Rist is right in dismissing that interpretation. Whether it is necessary to understand pantheism in this narrow sense is, of course, another matter. However, let us dismiss pantheism in order to concentrate on monism and theism.

Rist supposes that monism means the absolute identity of the soul with its source, i.e. the One. He supposes that for the monist the separate self is nothing but illusion and that the typical monistic mystic's utterance is "I am God". Following Zaehner, Rist takes the Vedanta as the paradigm of monistic mysticism and then claims that Plotinus, who, as a rule, is very cautious even in the most intensely mystical passages, is no Vedantic mystic and, therefore, he must be a theistic one. There is, presumably, no need to define "theistic mystic". Most Christians and many Christian commentators of Plotinus begin from a premise which is, *prima facie*, opposed to the mystical claims. For them there is always the gap between creator and creature; any talk of the creature becoming the creator is, of necessity, nonsense or heresy. Hence when the mystic claims to be 'oned' with God this must be understood dualistically, i.e. in a way that preserves the integrity of the two spiritual substances: God and the soul. The union then becomes one of contemplation, similarity, love, anything short of absorption. The mystic who, in his interpretation of the experience, follows this Christian metaphysical principle is a theistic mystic. The mystic who talks, seriously, of absorption and loss of the self is a monist. But Plotinus, we are told, is no monist because he does not stress the *absolute* identity of God and soul; *ergo* he is a theist.

It seems to me that placing Plotinus under one or the other of these categories may have some alleged advantages, e.g. it may enable someone to proclaim Plotinus free of the error of monism, but that on the whole it is both pointless and misleading. Indeed, it may be a serious obstacle to the full understanding and appreciation of Plotinus' mystical thought. If, after the latter has been investigated and understood, we need a label then, I submit, monism is more appropriate and less misleading. But to attempt to gain an insight *via* the label seems foolish.

What then is the correct account of Plotinian mysticism? Two basic principles must be recognized. In the first place, everyone who has read Plotinus realizes that his supreme principle is both immanent *and* transcendent. Hence Plotinus cannot be a rigid monist in the sense in which Zaehner speaks of, e.g. Vedantic monism. The transcendent One is the source and origin of all things; it is not identical with them. Nor is there any suggestion that the multiplicity of forms, in all their marvellous diversity, is nothing but illusion.

Secondly, if the supreme is immanent, it cannot be a creator or even a cause in any ordinary sense. This is why Plotinus uses his well-known metaphors: the sun, the root, the spring. Further, the human soul appears to be endowed with extraordinary mobility, as commentators have noted.[5] Indeed, the whole system of the hypostases seems to be a projection of subjective experience and so Plotinus is accused of erecting metaphysics upon psychology.[6] And, as if even this mobility of the soul were not enough to guarantee the essential fluidity and continuity of Plotinian reality, he is the first to distinguish between soul and the *ego* (ἡμεῖς)[7] and the first to be wholly concerned with the conscious individual.[8] And this ego is clearly not tied to the physical entity, the person. It is, as it was recognized long ago,[9] a focus of consciousness. A study of the doctrine of the ego in the *Enneads* will reveal several distinct stages or foci running through the chain of realities up to the transcendent One. It is as if Plotinus, having given an account of the emergence of forms from the "beyond" (ἐπέκεινα) and the emergence of the cosmos from the forms, essentially a Platonic, formalist account, now wishes to supplement it with a postulate that would do justice to his own experience as a mystic. This postulate, the ego, contains all the dynamism, the continuity, the "boiling life" that is so characteristic of Plotinian reality, and enables Plotinus to maintain the ultimate identity of the self with its ground; while his more formal system of hypostases enables him to assert the permanence and reality of individual men.

Thus the proper way to appreciate Plotinus' monism is not to deny the transcendence of the One (indeed no mystic can do that, in spite of Zaehner's unsympathetic comments) but to understand it in a *mystical* sense; in a way that is compatible with its immanence. True, the source is beyond the world and there is, in a sense, "otherness" between it and all other things.[10] But Plotinus often says that nothing is cut off and *we* certainly are not cut off from the One.[11] It is this continuity of the tree with the root which makes possible the mystical "leading up," (ἀνεγωγή) provided one's consciousness becomes wholly purified and simplified and all form, including otherness, is put away.

This ἀναγωγή is, I think, a very important notion which has not received the attention it deserves. It is a thoroughly mystical notion based on the experience of the ascent and the fluid character of the self. It is opposed to a descriptive, formalist metaphysics where "everything", to use Butler's phrase, "is what it is and not another thing". It contains an echo of Heraklitus' unsuccessful search for the limits of the soul. Neglecting this notion, and the mystical continuity it presupposes, has led some people to assert that the higher self reaches only as far as the higher reaches of the Soul and does not extend to the *Nous*;[12] though Plotinus says, "if I and everyone else go back to the intelligible the principle of each will be there." (εἰ ἐγὼ καὶ ἕκαστος τὴν ἀναγωγὴν ἐπὶ τὸ ὀνητὸν ἔχει, καὶ ἑκάστου ἡ ἀρχὴ ἐκεῖ).[13] It may be said that in this passage the "There" (ἐκεῖ) is the *Nous* and, therefore, this ἀναγωγή is irrelevant to our question. But it is not possible that when Plotinus speaks of simplification (ἄπλωσις) and ecstasy (ἔκστασις) and becoming another (ἄλλος γενόμενος) he is not thinking of the same ἀναγωγή which has finally reached beyond the realm of being and where there is coincidence, i.e.

identity of centers. On this level too, neglecting the notion of ἀναγωγή causes a curious distortion analogous to Armstrong's demotion of the ego. It is the conception we find in Arnou and repeated by Rist that the soul and the One are "two spiritual substances" and that the mystical union is a contact between two such substances.[14] If one begins with this view of the matter, natural as this is for a Christian, the mystical oneness will become an insuperable difficulty. How can two substances, each ontologically self-sufficient, possessing its own limits, *unite* without blending or without the annihilation of the self which the theist fears? But in Plotinus' view the One is no "spiritual substance"[15] and the soul of the mystic is hardly that: we are here speaking of the going back to one's origin, we have reached the intelligible archetype, we *are* forms (Αὐτοσωκράτης). It is this noetic self that has the access to the ultimate principle (ἀρχή); not the limited, ordinary substance that is Socrates here.

Indeed the image which most aptly expresses the mystical union is not the sexual contact but the one occurring in the *Tao Te Ching*: "A retreat to one's roots" and the fine Plotinian verse by Yeats "Now I may wither into the Truth."[16] The great monistic image is, of course, the river losing name and shape in the sea.[17] Though Plotinus does not use it, it would be appropriate, as the sea is the source of the river to which the river returns. Better still would be the image of the stream being gathered back into the spring. Clearly this situation could not be described as the union of two substances, and much less as a contact between two substances. It would be a return to our fatherland or to the father.[18]

It is these images of being gathered and being scattered,[19] which are so strangely apt when applied to our conscious life, that best characterize Plotinian reality. And it is the notion of the self operating in this dynamic reality that enables Plotinus to tackle the mystical problem *par excellence:* how the finite, limited self can become the transcendent One. Among the commentators, Trouillard has best appreciated this mobility and "poly-valence" of the ego. "It would be easier to enclose the subject in a situation, a nature or a perspective. But this would be making spirit into a thing. . . Thus the ego oscillates endlessly."[20]

There is then no question of the identity of what seemed
to be two substances so that only the One truly exists. Nor is it
a question of a magical transformation of the finite into the
infinite. The ordinary ego can be surpassed in noetic activity
without the cessation of the lower psychic activities. So too the
noetic ego can be transcended in the mystical ecstasy without
the destruction of its formal counterpart, the Socrates-himself,
(Αὐτοσωκράτης). At the moment of "union" there is no
consciousness of any form, not even the otherness that
normally distinguishes the One from the *Nous*. Qua self the
spiritual reality has become identical with the One. *Qua* a
certain formal personality principle it is eternally emanating
from the One and is, therefore, distinct.

But although the question of Plotinian monism can best be
discussed within these two approaches, the static and the
dynamic, we should not try to press this distinction.[21] For it is
then too tempting to say that Plotinus' monism appears in the
dynamic, "religious" account, while his usual metaphysical
account is dualistic. Indeed there is the opinion that what saves
Plotinian ecstasy from being monistic is just this distinction
between noetic and ontic identity. The soul of the mystic
cannot become identical with the One by "nature"; though
noetically the One fills it and the mystic is no longer conscious
of himself.[22] But I cannot believe that this is a Plotinian view.
Those who accuse him of doing psychology under the guise of
metaphysics are more nearly right. In Plotinus it is very
difficult, as Trouillard remarks[23], to distinguish the noetic from
the ontic and especially so at this level.

The reason for this is that the true background of Plotinus'
mystical idealism is, as is recognized now,[24] the Aristotelian
doctrine that the mind becomes the object of cognition. This
doctrine of "the soul becoming all things" is a typically mystical
conception and leads directly to deification and to a monopsychism of the Plotinan kind.[25] Plotinus adopts it and combines it
with his own psychological notion of attention, turning, looking
at, so that he is able to say, "we are what we desire and
what we look at"[26] and there is no indication that the "being
and becoming" (εἶναι καὶ γί γνεσθαι) is meant only noetically.
The distinction between the nature and the noetic level of the

subject is misapplied here. The soul is not an individual thing having a stable nature. "Soul" is a label for a variety of psychic and intellectual activities characterized by a 'scattering' in time. When consciousness returns to the stage of pure *noesis* it is no longer soul, it has become *Nous*.[27] The nature of the subject is precisely determined by the noetic stage. Having been established in the divine *Nous* we are no longer men.[28]

If there is a distinction between the oscillating, noetic self, and some stable nature, it must be between the ego (ἡμεῖς) and the only permanent *being* corresponding to the individual man, *viz.* his form in the *Nous*. I have argued elsewhere that we must continue to read Plotinus as indeed positing forms of individual men.[29] Moreover, such forms, like all residents of the *Nous*, must be minds themselves[30] and hence potential egos. Yet even here it seems unplotinian to say that by nature Socrates persists though his mind is totally filled with the One. A nature which is not also a phase of consciousness is contrary to the basic premises of Neoplatonism. Perhaps the answer does lie in the way this superhuman mind of Socrates-himself is conceived. Without pressing the distinction between real and mental reality we can speak of this mind *qua* a certain ideal personality type, the form Socrateity; and also *qua* ego, the fluctuating focus which can sink below the level of *Nous* and even become an individual soul without, however, destroying the eternal form, nor this higher ego which is "ours" whenever we choose to recover it. In the same way, *qua* focus of consciousness, the ego can surpass the ideal Socrateity without destroying or obliterating it. But while the form persists, Socrates does not survive. His experience defines the level of his existence and now, when he sees the formless, he becomes another and not himself (ἄλλος γενόμενος καὶ οὐκ αὐτός). The self is obliterated, as all mystics report, though the form is always there to receive it at its first turning away from total unity.

If this is so, then we cannot say, as Zaehner does, that since the soul of the mystic has survived the encounter, the experience of absorption was an illusion, nor that the self survives by nature, nor that some existential otherness remains at the very moment of union. It is not the soul or the ordinary ego that survives. The ego, even the ego established in the *Nous*, is lost; since the idea of an ego remaining in the absence of all multiplicity and differentiation is unintelligible. What remains is the admittedly strange notion of a mind whose formal and intelligible structure is still intact (and still known by all other form-minds) but whose normal self-awareness is lacking because it is now "a mind senseless and in love" (νοῦς ἄφρων καὶ ἐρῶν). In this qualified sense Socrates has ceased to be himself and has become one with his transcendent source. And if this is a possible account then it would not seem inappropriate to call Plotinus a monist while it would be at least misleading to call him a dualist or theist. The latter would imply a radical otherness between the individual substance and the One.

An interesting indication that this kind of qualified monism is not alien to Plotinus' thought is the fact that when Plotinus asks himself: "How is it that I descend again after the vision?"[31] he does not give the answer that would occur immediately to a theist: viz. "God filled my soul but I was the same me all along"; or, "I was there noetically though existentially and really I was still a man." Instead he goes on to talk about the descent of all souls in terms of change of attention, desire to be independent, etc. The psychological question coincides with the metaphysical question of the descent of souls. And what this whole account of the "emancipation" of souls comes to, is just the principle that existential otherness depends on noetic otherness. Ecstasy, far from being an illusion, is a cosmic event. The return is not a temporal event in the history of this person. It is an instance of cosmic emanation, the self-differentiation of the ground. The unfolding history of this person is, as it were, the event of his separation. And the return? "Put away everything" (Ἄφελε πάντα).

It would also seem that the majority of the texts where Plotinus mentions the mystical experience, give the impression, at least prima facie, that the union involves a coincidence and a coalescence. "In his interpretation of the experience Plotinus is nearer to some Indian mystics than he is to the orthodox Christian view."[32] These texts are well known and there is no need to quote them here. Time after time, the Platonic vision (θεωρία, θέα) locutions are corrected by the images of contact, touch, and often enough by term like, "union" (ἕνωσις) "simplification" (ἅπλωσις), "the two become one" (τὰ δύο ἕν γίνεται).

Nevertheless, Arnou, Rist and others have detected a certain dualism in the language used to describe the union. Plotinus, it is said, uses words like "being with" (συνουσία), "presence" (παρουσία) which imply two things and not one, or says clearly that two things become one. For a strict monist, however, the only permissible locution is "I am God." Since Plotinus allows that two beings become united they must persist in their duality. I do not think this is a strong argument. The conclusion clearly does not follow. Even if Plotinus begins by asserting the existence of two things, in view of his own images of being mixed and blended,[34] we cannot conclude that after the union they remain two. The only thing that concepts like "union" and "blending" entail is that there are two things that become blended; not that the blending is, so to speak, ineffective. Similar remakrs would apply to Rist's picking the phrase from V.5.8 "Being one *with that* (ἐκείνῳ) and not two" and claiming that other monistic phrases should be explained in terms of this. Being one with that and not two only means that there are two things that are being oned; not the contradictory view that they are *still two* but not two. As far as the more general claim that one finds in Zaehner, *viz.* that in monistic mysticism there is no love, or its variant that one finds in Rist, *viz.* that because Plotinus says that one surrenders, or that the soul is filled with God he cannot be a monist, this claim seems to be a mistake. Indeed one loves the absolute; indeed one surrenders to it and not to oneself.[35] But this only means that initially, and for reasons Plotinus never tires of giving, there is a distance between the self and its ground. It does not mean that after the surrender he who surrenders is still the same self, or that he whose soul is filled with God is still the same individual being.

Rist further asserts that the sudden character of the vision "hardly fits the notion of the monistic isolation of the soul"[36] though he does not tell us why. And finally, as if to clinch the case against the monist, he cites the metaphor of the converging centers in VI.9.10 "perhaps the most apt description of all" and curiously claims that, in spite of the coincidence of centers, the metaphor preserves the dualism of otherness. But Plotinus' image, though certainly apt, hardly leaves room for such dualistic interpretation. The whole chapter is strongly monistic and, he says, "*even here* when the centers come together they are one" (καὶ γὰρ ἐνταῦθα συνελθόντα ἕν ἐστι). And indeed if the centers are points they *must* be one, if they coincide. Rist chooses to talk of dots drawn on paper at different times and implies that though they *seem* one they would still in some sense be *two*.[37] It is not clear in what sense they could be said to be two. Some strange criteria of individuation must be involved here. At any rate Plotinus is speaking of centers not dots and the coincidence of centers, as well as "his center of centers"[38] are powerful images of the final stage in the expansion and simplification of the self: it has become the One.

There are, however, two other linguistic arguments, used by Arnou, and I now turn to them. Arnou is struck by the frequent occurrence of terms meaning generally "as it were" (ὥσπερ, οἷον) and hesitation-expressing phrases, "if we must say this" (εἰ δεῖ καὶ τοῦτο λέγειν) to be found specifically in VI.9.11 and 10 and concludes that the caution is precisely meant by Plotinus to warn us that the union is no fusion but contact.[39] To this it must be replied that: a) There are many monistic passages not qualified by the οἷον, or any other caution term, notably the center-coincidence image of VI.9.10.[40] b) That the οἷον occurs not only when the threat of monism appears but in many other places; whenever, in fact, we try to speak of the ineffable and of our relation to it. This introduces another large problem for any mystical philosophy, and one which Plotinus has constantly in mind: How shall we speak about the ineffable? At least once Plotinus agrees with Wittgenstein that we must be silent.[41] More often he agrees with Heraklitus that we must *indicate*, must use language for the sake of showing (ἐνδείξεως ἕνεκα). Language is necessary though not exact.[42] Therefore, Plotinus says in the same passage, let us take the "as it were" in each case (λαμβανέτω δὲ καὶ τὸ οἷον ἐφ᾽ ἑκάστου). There are very many passages where he follows this advice[43] and very few of them are meant to be qualifications of the monistic character of the union. c) The audacious saying (τολμηρὸς λόγος) can be justified by the paradoxical nature of the phrases used. To say of the man in ecstasy that he is no longer a self is true. But to say he has become another, is not at all himself, (ἄλλος γενόμενος and οὐδ᾽ ὅλως αὐτός)⁴⁴ is something of an exaggeration for it suggests a magical transformation or a sudden disappearance of the self. And that is not strictly correct. For Socrates is not lost just when he becomes established in the supreme. On the contrary, as many mystics say, he has found the true self. Only the limits of being Socrates are lost. So the "not at all himself" does, still, indicate. But then the "if we must say this" (εἰ δεῖ καὶ τοῦτο λέγειν) becomes understandable. And the "audacious saying" goes with "hard-to-express vision" (δύσφραστον τὸ θέαμα). Who would deny that the mystical claims are strange? But, as a little polemical aside, are the theistic claims less strange?

Arnou's second linguistic argument is the fact that Plotinus uses limiting phrases, like "as far as it can" (καθ ὅσον δύναται). This shows, Arnou claims, that the mystical union does not imply the identity of man and God.⁴⁵ And it must be admitted that such phrases are incompatible with the "coincidence" (rather than "identity") view. But the first five passages quoted by Arnou do not refer to the mystical union as such. Of the ones that do, two contain the vision terms⁴⁶ and the hesitation may be due to Plotinus' belief that the vision language, Platonic and traditional though it may be, cannot fully express the mystical contact. The third is even less conclusive since it concerns the capacity of *soul* to possess the divine.⁴⁷ Moreover, the formula as far as possible (κατὰ τὸ δυνατόν) is another traditional phrase⁴⁸ which may have been a serious qualification for Plato but seems to be a mere echo in the few places where Plotinus uses it. Indeed terms like union, simplification, the coincidence of centers, can hardly be subject to the "as far as possible" qualification. The latter seems most appropriate to the vision image since one can see clearly or dimly; but one cannot *coincide* more or less.⁴⁹

I conclude, therefore, that those who point to the text of Plotinus in support of their view that his mysticism is of the theistic variety are unable to find their proof there. The texts themselves create a strong monistic impression; although it is true, of course that the extreme identity phrases, e.g. "I am God" are lacking. But the reason for this is not that Plotinus was a theist; rather, these phrases would strike him as too crude and inaccurate in view of his own sophisticated notion of the self that can *become* the One only after the most arduous purification and only at the last moment, as it were, of the expansion and simplification of the soul. The phrase "I am God" is apt to be mistaken (and was mistaken, in fact) as the claim that this ordinary man, this pitiful fragment of the cosmos, is the One. But that *is* madness and megalomania and not what the mystic claims.

Moreover, although Plotinus did not easily dismiss personality[50] to the point of elevating its ideal principle to the *Nous*, he often thinks of individuality (probably a lower manifestation of the formal principle of personality) in terms not unlike those of classical Oriental monism. It was no accident that Bréhier began his 'Orientalism' thesis by quoting VI.5.12. "It is through non-being that you have become someone." And, "you no longer say concerning yourself: this is what I am. Leaving behind the limit you become all. Yet you were the all from the beginning. But as you were something besides, this addition reduced you."[51] This passage can be, I think, reconciled with the doctrine of individual forms. Nevertheless, it is in direct opposition to the theistic requirement that the individual soul, as a spiritual substance, persists and survives the encounter with the One. Here the individuality of the soul comes close to being an illusion, an addition of non-being, clearly something to be overcome before a higher stage in the expansion towards totality ($\pi\tilde{\alpha}\varsigma$) can be reached.

It is sometimes said, however, that though Plotinus often speaks as if he were a monist of sorts, he *could not have meant* what he seems to mean because this would create some very serious difficulties within his system. And indeed the position is not free from difficulties even after we make allowances for the fact that it is based on an experience which is beyond our ordinary rational comprehension. If this is to be an argument against the monistic interpretation, one must assume that the theistic interpretation is free from such difficulties. But is there a reason to think that? Let us look at the correct theistic picture as we find it in Rist: "While the soul as a spiritual substance can be enveloped by the One, enraptured, surrendered, wholly characterized so as to become infinite and not finite (5.8.4.33) it is neither obliterated nor revealed as the One itself, nor as the *only* spiritual substance."[52] I confess that I do not understand the picture. If we are willing to say that the soul *becomes infinite* how can its former identity still remain while enveloped by the infinity of the One? Are there two, or any number of, infinite substances? Wouldn't that which distinguishes them be a limit?

The chief difficulty with the monistic interpretation, on the other hand, is that it seems to place a temporal event (suddenly) at the heart of reality emanating in a non-temporal process. Plotinus says that time begins at the level of soul. If the mystical union is an event in the life of some individual then it cannot reach the higher levels of eternal reality. Plotinus does not deal with this difficulty. Perhaps the mystic cannot fully explain this sudden conversion that lifts him out of the body and the ordinary temporal consciousness. Perhaps it may be said that the static system of hypostases is based on the psychological experience and is secondary to it. Hence the experience of liberation from time is not a shortcut to the One but contains the evidence for the metaphysical schema. Secondly, it may be said that the sudden passing away of multiplicity and temporal succession is not a contradiction but a corroboration of the Plotinian view that time is born with the lower stages of psychic activity. The "suddenly" is not itself a temporal event; it marks, rather, the passage from time to the timelessness of true being. Plotinus, following Plato, does not consider the life of the spirit as static. There is activity, boiling life, *energeia*. Time and change, however, are excluded because they involve a scattering, a weakening of this activity. Hence the recovery of the original view-point, though an "activity", is not a temporal process. Indeed it is the opposite: time has been reduced to its root. A similar account can be given (and is given by Plotinus in IV.8) about the descent. That too is not a temporal event. It is a tendency of the active spirit towards separation that generates time. After the wondrous vision we are puzzled. But the explanation, for the mystic, must lie within the experience itself and not with the demands of a dogma or a metaphysical system—even one of one's own making.

NOTES

1. J. Rist, *Plotinus: The Road to Reality* (Cambridge, 1967).
2. R. C. Zaehner, *Mysticism Sacred and Profane* (Oxford, 1961).
3. See W. T. Stace, *Mysticism and Philosophy* (London, 1961) and N. Smart, "Interpretation and Mystical Experience," *Religious Studies*, 1, 1965.
4. Rist, *op. cit.*, p. 216.
5. "The soul is the great wanderer of the metaphysical world." R. W. Inge, *The Philosophy of Plotinus* (London, 1927), Vol. 1, p. 203.
6. E. O'Brien, *The Essential Plotinus*, pp. 30-31.
7. As E. R. Dodds remarked in *Les Sources de Plotin* (Geneva, 1960), p. 385 and later in *Pagan and Christian*, p. 77, note 3.
8. E. Bréhier, *The Philosophy of Plotinus* (Chiacgo, 1958), p. 111. The distinction between soul and ego is mentioned on p. 73.
9. Inge, *op. cit.*, pp. 244-52.
10. τῇ ἑτερότητι μόνον κεχωρίσθαι V.1.6. 52-53.
11. 6.9.9.7., 2.9.16. 12-13, 4.3.9. 6.4.14. 20-23. These passages are referred to by Arnou and again by Rist.
12. A. H. Armstrong, *Christian Faith and Greek Philosophy* (London, 1960), p. 57 and "Salvation, Plotinian and Christian," *Downside Review*, n.s. 75, (1957) p. 132 ff. H. J. Blumenthal in "Did Plotinus Believe in Ideas of Individuals?" *Phronesis*, XI No. 1. 1966, fully accepted Armstrong's "demotion."
13. V.7.
14. "Cette unité n'est pas un mélange . . . ni une fusion, ni une composition, mais le contact de deux substances spirituelles . . . unies comme peuvent l'être de substances spirituelles . . . Arnou, *Le Désir de Dieu dans la Philosophie de Plotin*, (Paris, 1921), p. 246, quoted by Rist, p. 222. Rist's own comments: "While the soul as a spiritual substance can be enveloped by the One . . . it is neither obliterated nor revealed as the One itself, nor as the *only* spiritual substance." Rist, *Plotinus*, p. 227.

15. Many people consider Plotinus' view that the One is beyond Being as a quaint echo of *Republic*, IV 509 and nothing else. In fact it is a cardinal tenet of mysticism. The mystical is "Beyond the world" but it makes itself manifest. cf. Wittgenstein's *Tractatus*, "The World is everything that is the case." "The sense of the world must lie outside the world . . .", "in it no value exists." 6.41, see also 6.522.

16. W. B. Yeats, "The Coming of Wisdom With Time," *Collected Poems.*

17. Mundaka Upanishad, Chandogya Upanishad.

18. VI.9.9.39. Rist, p. 228 comments on the non-sexual eros of the soul for the father. Also I.6.8.

19. οὐ κεχυμένον εἰς αἴσθησιν, ἀλλ᾽ . . . ἐν ἑαυτῷ συνηγμένον. I.4.10. 33-34. Also VI.6.1. 4-5.

20. "Ainsi le moi oscille-t-il sans cesse . . . . Il serait plus façile d'enfermer tout simplement le sujet dans une situation, une nature ou une perspective. On se garderait ainsi, semble-t-il, plus aisement de tout monisme. Mais ce serait faire de l'esprit une chose et manquer le problème en éliminant une de ses données . . ." J. Trouillard, *La Purification Plotinienne* (Paris, 1955), pp. 150.

21. Many writers have noticed the two "pictures" and the need to regard them as at least compatible. H. J. Blumenthal, *Plotinus' Psychology* (The Hague, 1971), pp. 2-3.

22. Zaehner, *op. cit.*, p. 160. Also J. Maréchal, *Etudes sur la Psychologie des Mystiques* (Bruxelles, p. 37-38). "Mais alors, le 'nous' dans ce denuement interieur qui le rend indiscernable de l'Un present, ne devient-il pas Dieu? Par nature, non; par coincidence, 'objective', oui." pp. 69-70. We are also told that P. Agaesse "Distingue deux sens de l'altérité: l'altérité limite ontologique ..,. et l'altérité volonté de rupture ou d'isolement . . . La seconde seulement est annulée . . . La première subsiste . . . pour empêcher l'absorption." quoted by Trouillard, *op. cit.*, p. 150, n.1.

23. "Il nous semble difficile de diviser ainsi l'ontologique et le

noétique dans le neoplatonisme." Trouillard, *op. cit.*, p. 150.

24. A. H. Armstrong, *The Architecture of the Intelligible World in the Philosophy of Plotinus* (Cambridge, 1940) was one of the first to point this out.

25. See P. Merlan, *Monopsychism, Mysticism and Metaconsciousness* (Hague, 1963). Merlan's *Aristoteles Mysticus* has not received the attention it deserves from Plotinian scholars.

26. IV.3.8. 15-16; IV.4.3. cf. I.6.9.7, 24.

27. Γίνεται δὲ ἡ ψυχὴ καθαρθεῖσα εἶδος καὶ λόγος καὶ πάντη ἀσώματος καὶ νοερὰ καὶ ὅλη τοῦ θείου I.6.6.13-15.

28. Παυσάμενος δὲ τοῦ ἄνθρωπος εἶναι μετεωροπορεῖ--- γενόμενος γὰρ τοῦ ὅλου V.8.7. 33-35.

29. In "Forms of Individuals in the *Enneads*," *Phronesis*, XIV, 2, 1969.

30. V.9.8. 1-4, ...ἐσμὲν ἕκαστος κόσμος νοητός. III.4.3.21-24.

31. IV.8.

32. E. R. Dodds, *Pagan and Christian in an Age of Anxiety* (Cambridge, 1965), p. 88.

33. Arnou, *op. cit.*, pp. 248-49. Rist, *op. cit.*, p. 226. Rist does not actually mention the συν words. Rather he follows Zaehner in supposing that any dualistic talk, e.g. οὐδ' ἔτι δύο ἀλλ' ἐν ἄμφω, *ipso facto* excludes monism. W. Eborowicz, *La Contemplation selon Plotin* (Torino, 1958), also singles out dualist terms like συναφή, συνουσία, παρουσία "ainsi que les mots composé de σύν et παρά prouvent clairement qu'il s'agit de l'union de *deux ê tres*" p. 74. From this he moves to an unintelligible conclusion: "il n'ya pas de confusion entre les deux êtres mais il est impossible de trouver dans cette simplicité parfaite . . . une différence quelqonque . . ." p. 75. Rist reaches a similar conclusion on p. 227 of his book.

34. I.6.7.13, VI.7.34, 15.

35. "Does Plotinus mean that one surrenders to oneself?" Rist, *op. cit.*, p. 224.

36. *Ibid.*, p. 224.

37. *Ibid.*, p. 227.

38. VI.9.8. 11-12.

39. "Quelle réserve! Quelle prudence! οἷον...ὥσπερ...εἰ δεῖ καὶ τοῦτο λέγειν ces expressions répetées avec une insistence qui trahit une intention, montrent à l'évidence q'il ne faut pas serrer de trop près ni ces textes, ni d'autres, et que s'il y a unité τά δύο ἕν γίνεται VI.7.35) cette unite n'est pas un mélange (bien que les mots le fassent entendre parfois VI.9.11; 1.6.7 συγκερασθῆναι) ni une fusion, ni une composition, mais le contact de deux substances spirituelles que ne sépare aucune différence." Arnou, op. cit., p. 246.

40. VI.7.35, 23, 35-36; VI.9.9. 52-53, 59; VI.9.11.6; I.6.7.13; VI.8.15.22; VI.7.34. 13-15. And in the most detailed and bold description of the experience in VI.9.11 where ἔκστασις and ἅπλωσις occur there is no οἷον.

41. "What we cannot speak about we must confine to silence." Wittgenstein, op. cit., 6.53, 7. Σιωπήσαντες δεῖ ἀπελθεῖν...VI.8.11. 1-3.

42. VI.8.13. 47-50, VI.8.11. 25-26.

43. The locus classicus of the οἷον is, naturally enough, the whole of VI.8. Especially VI.8.7. 51-53, VI.8.16. 19-21, VI.8.15. 5-7.

44. VI.9.10.15 and VI.9.11. 11-12.

45. "L'expression [καθ' ὅσον δύναται] apporte une preuve que l'union mystique, dans la pensée de Plotin, n'implique, pas l'identité de l'homme et de Dieu." Arnou, op. cit., p. 246. Also p. 248.

46. ...ὡς πέφυκεν ἐκεῖνος θεατὸς εἶναι VI.9.4. 29-30 and ὡς ὁρᾶν θέμις VI.9.9.57.

47. τῶν θείων ὅσα δύναται ψυχὴ ἔχειν VI.9.11. 32-33.

48. Φυγὴ ὁμοίωσις θεῷ κατὰ τὸ δυνατόν. Theaetetus 176B.

49. "It is significant that in later quotations of Plato's phrase, e.g. in Plotinus, the qualifying words κατὰ τὸ δυνατόν are often omitted." E. R. Dodds, Pagan and Christian in an Age of Anxiety, p. 75, note 3.

50. Δεῖ ἕκαστον ἕκαστον εἶναι quoted and rightly emphasized by Inge, op. cit., p. 246.

51. ...Ἀφεὶς δὲ τὸ τοσοῦτον γέγονας πᾶς, καίτοι καὶ πρότερον ἦσθα πᾶς... Γενόμενος δέ τις καὶ ἐκ τοῦ μὴ ὄντος ἐστὶν οὐ πᾶς... VI.5.12. 16-28.

52. Rist, op. cit., p. 227.

Plotinus and Moral Obligation

by John M. Rist

University of Toronto

In contemporary ethical or meta-ethical discussions the concept of moral obligation looms large. People have even come to talk about the ethics of obligation and to contrast this with the older (frequently Aristotelian or sub-Aristotelian) ethics of virtue. Much is now written about the necessity to disassociate statements of fact from statements of value, or about the impropriety of deducing "ought" from "is". "Ought"– statements are often claimed to be ultimately arbitrary, in that it is in the last resort merely a matter of arbitrary choice what kind of moral code an individual may accept. Thus the only test for the superiority of one set of principles to another would be the consistency or lack of consistency each code could exhibit. Attempts are made, of course, to evade this apparently unpopular conclusion by distinguishing hypothetical and categorical imperatives. Thus "If you want to catch the train, you ought to run faster" is separated from "You ought not to kill". But to the objection "Why ought I not to kill?", the only answers seem to be either "You just ought not" – which does not get us very far philosophically – or "You ought not to because killing is a bad thing" – which makes us wonder how we know what bad things are – not to speak of the logical relations between "x is bad" and "I ought not to do x", or the logical grammar of "If you want to do x or be F, you ought not to kill" (If you want to be safe from the police, have a good conscience, be allowed to get on with your work, not spend five years in jail. . .etc.). Though I obviously cannot argue it here, the point I would want to make is that the so-called categorical imperative, if it is to be categorical and not a disguised hypothetical, is arbitrary. It is the realization of this that has made many post-Kantian ethical writers admit that their concern is with the form, not the content of ethical systems. If someone advocates what is commonly regarded as an immoral doctrine, we may hear it said that it is not worth talking to him;

just make sure you don't go near him when you want to buy a second-hand car.

In contrast to philosophers of the type we have mentioned Plotinus is not particularly concerned to tell us directly what we ought to do, still less what it means to use the word "ought". The moral "ought" seems to be rather uncommon in the *Enneads*. Of course, there are examples. If a man is in great pain, he will consider what he ought to do, i.e. whether he ought to commit suicide (I.4.8.8). Suicide is the subject again in another example (I.9.19): a man ought not to take himself out of life so long as there is any possibility of moral improvement.[1] Another example occurs at the end of *Ennead* VI.6.1. Plotinus is concerned first with the question whether one ought not to commit murder, then with whether one ought to know that one ought not to commit murder (VI.8.1.42-44). A final example of a more general kind is for that reason perhaps more generally informative (VI.8.6.16). In this passage the word "ought" does not occur. Instead we have the form of an indirect command: virtue (sometimes) commands a man to lay down his life, and to give up possessions, children and country. Plotinus is saying that according to the dictates of virtue this is the path which should be followed; these are the things which ought to be done. But these examples are not typical material from the *Enneads*. Plotinus has remarkably little to say about what we ought to do.

Of course, it does not follow that he is unconcerned with what ought to be done or thinks it of little importance. Because he has no formal discussion of moral obligation, we should not assume that the concept does not appear in another guise — and even widely — in the *Enneads*. What we must assume is that the whole question is approached in different ways, and we may wonder whether he would judge our use of the term "moral obligation" and our frequent identification of the nature of the moral "ought" misleading. For Plotinus, as for Plato, Aristotle and the Stoics, the good life is a life of virtue and virtue is a state of the soul. Without such a virtuous condition all hope of progress towards God is vain. Objecting strongly to Gnostic antinomianism Plotinus comments that without virtue God is just a name (II.9.15.40); those who use it without virtue are misguided if not hypocritical.

An *Ennead* I.2 makes clear, the Neoplatonic manner of handling the question of the virtues is to see them as a progression. Plotinus is less systematic about this than some of his successors,[2] but he proposes a distinction between the so-called civic virtues — those treated by Plato in the *Republic* (427E-434D) — and the virtues of purification, i.e. those virtues which exist in the soul when it is purified (I.2.7.9). Purification is viewed as a means of freeing the soul from the passions and desires of the body and indeed a separation ($\chi\omega\rho\acute{\iota}\zeta\epsilon\iota\nu$) of the soul from the body as far as possible (I.2.4.5-6). The opening sentences of *Ennead* I.2 draw our attention to the text of the *Theaetetus* (176AB) where Plato speaks of escaping the evil "of this place" and becoming godlike. In practice, this works out to be the process of separating the soul from bodily concerns, and its ultimate identification with *Nous* and conversion to the One.[3] It is, as Plotinus will emphasize again and again throughout the whole of the *Enneads*, a process of freeing the soul, of enabling it to engage in its natural and proper activity. Before looking at the question of how virtue and the free condition of the soul must be related to questions of moral obligation, it will be necessary to pause briefly over some of the material, in *Ennead* VI.8 in particular, on the freedom of the soul itself.

Plotinus begins in VI.8.1 by taking up the traditional question of what is in our power ($\tau\grave{o}\ \grave{\epsilon}\varphi'\ \mathring{\eta}\mu\widetilde{\iota}\nu$). He quickly identifies a voluntary act ($\grave{\epsilon}\kappa o\acute{u}\sigma\iota o\nu$) as an act which we perform under no external compulsion and on an occasion when we know what we are doing. In contrast to this, perhaps, what we are in control of doing ($\kappa\acute{u}\rho\iota o\iota\ \pi\rho\widetilde{\alpha}\xi\epsilon\iota$) need not involve knowledge of what we are doing. A man who kills his father without realizing whom he is killing is in control of the action of killing his father, but his action is not voluntary. But what about a man who does not know that murder is wrong? Can he legitimately claim that his killing someone is not a voluntary action? Ought he to have known about the morality of homicide? At any rate the problem of being able to perform a voluntary act is already associated in Plotinus' mind with a variety of knowledge.

VI.8.2 introduces us to so-called "internal" constraints. How can we be said to be really in control of our acts ($\kappa\acute{u}\rho\iota o\iota$)

when we act under the impulse of fury or lust. It won't do, after all, to say that we are in control of everything we do, and *thus* that all our actions are in our power. If we say that, then not only is there no such thing as *human* action, but even "soulless" substances like fire can be said to be free (If fire burns, it burns freely — a paradoxical conclusion which Plotinus will not toy with). Nor is the mere awareness (αἴσθησις) of an act a test of whether it is an act under our control. To be aware of doing something does not imply to be in control of that action. There must be occasions when reason or knowledge (λόγος, γνῶσις) is in command (κράτει) and independent of desire (ὄρεξις). So there is a knowledge implying action which combats a *desire* to act otherwise; and when we are "in control", such knowledge must be in control. Knowledge is thus distinguished from awareness; it is an élan, a drive to *act* rationally. Plotinus' distinction between awareness and knowledge has some resemblances to Newman's distinction between notional and real assent.[4]

VI.8.3 sums up progress thus far, but there are confusing changes of terminology. If we want to know what is in our power (τὸ ἐφ᾽ ἡμῖν), we must consider our will (βούλησις) — and willing must be understood in terms of reasoning and knowledge. If knowledge is not there, we may be drawn to the right course, to doing what we ought (πρὸς τὸ δέον ἀχθείς) by chance or through a set of reflections deriving entirely from bodily conditions such as hunger, thirst, or too much semen. People who are impelled to act by these motivating factors cannot properly be said to be performing free acts (τὸ αὐτεξούσιον). Free action then is not simply what one does, once again, but what one knows is the proper action. Proposals emanating from *Nous* are free, and action in accordance with them is "in our power" in the strict sense. We come thus close to a definition of free action. It is the action of *Nous* — and therefore the only possible action for the gods. It follows that in so far as our action is in accordance with what is true and known to be true, it is free action. So no one is free when he acts badly. When he is unable to do what is good, we may assume, he is incapable of free action; when he is able to do what is good, he is free.

So far Plotinus has argued that free action cannot be governed by external pressures or by bodily appetites, and that it must be the result of well-grounded reasoning. He now turns to a further question, a question of importance philosophically, but unfortunately rarely discussed by ancient philosophers (VI.8.4). We admit that action uninfluenced by external forces is motivated by desire for the good,[5] but there is still a desire, and, surely, if a desire, then also a need. That would mean, the objection runs, that the resulting action cannot be regarded as free (αὐτεξουσιον). The objection, if it could be sustained, would be serious for Plotinus, for, as he says, it would affect not merely the activity of the soul, but also that of the intellect (Nous). The activity of Nous could not be free if its acts were governed by its nature. Can an act be called free, Plotinus wonders, if it is impossible not to perform it? He then adds a second, less important query: we must distinguish activity, which is the achievement of all beings, from action (πρᾶξις), which seems necessarily to involve lower "substances" than the intellect. Perhaps it is only to the activities of such substances that the word "free" should be applied.

Plotinus meets these objections head on. All compulsion, he argues, must involve a compelling factor from "outside". What he seems to mean is that if someone gives way to his desire for a fourth helping of cassata, he is not simply giving away to an internal constraint; internal constraints are only operative because of the presence of external constraints. The presence of the cassata is necessary to activate the vicious desire. (This may seem unsatisfactory. Perhaps Plotinus is thinking of the presence or the imagined presence of an external agent – but why should it be imagined?) But how does all this affect the question of a desire for the good? The good, Plotinus seems to be saying, is in no sense an external. Desire for the good is not desire for something outside the subject, but the activity of a subject in so far as it exists. Thus any impulse towards the real and fully recognized good has to result in free action. Free action, natural action and good action thus coincide.

Plotinus takes the opportunity now presented to him to offer a further analysis of the concept of "being a slave of one's

own nature" (VI.8.4.22-23). Where we can make a distinction
between potentiality and actuality, he observes, we can distinguish between that which obeys and that which is obeyed. But
where there is no potentiality the distinction is merely verbal.
Thus, apparently, in the case of a being in simple act, (e.g.
Nous), to say that it obeys its own nature is to say that its
nature and the activity it achieves are one. Here again we see the
dynamic Plotinian conception of knowledge, the view of *Nous*
as an élan and as a drive to act rationally, not as a relation
between a mind and a (Platonic?) object of knowledge. As
Plotinus puts it, being and act are identical (VI.8.4.28). Perhaps
reference to what is in one's power ($\tau\grave{o}\ \dot{\epsilon}\varphi'\ \dot{\eta}\mu\tilde{\iota}\nu$) is inappropriate
to this stage, he adds, though he has not rejected the word
"free" ($\dot{\epsilon}\lambda\epsilon\upsilon\vartheta\acute{\epsilon}\rho\alpha$), for to say that something is in one's power
is to speak negatively; it is to refer to being free from
compulsion where compulsion properly indicates an external
pressure. So he concludes the chapter by repeating himself once
again — necessarily, for the point does not seem to be readily
grasped: freedom is the ability to operate for the sake of the
good ($\tau o\tilde{\upsilon}\ \dot{\alpha}\gamma\alpha\vartheta o\tilde{\upsilon}\ \chi\acute{\alpha}\rho\iota\nu$).

It will obviously follow from our argument up to this
point that to ask "Ought *Nous* to act in such and such a way?",
would be misleading. *Nous* will do what it ought to do because
it is able to do what it ought to do. But should we say "*Nous*
will do what it ought to do" rather than "*Nous* will do what is
good?" Perhaps the latter is the more appropriate if we are to
say that an "ought" only arises where there is the possibility of
a subject *not* doing what is good. Thus "ought" would imply
"can but will not necessarily". The term, if that is the usage,
would therefore only be applicable at the level of human
behaviour, not to any activity higher in the scale of reality. To
put it succinctly, though somewhat paradoxically: where there
is freedom, there is no need for a sense of moral obligation. A
sense of moral obligation is necessary and exists where the
possibility of vicious action exists.

Ennead VI.8.5 brings us back to such possibilities. The
chapter opens, as frequently enough, by posing a further
question. We have now defined freedom ($\tau\grave{o}\ \alpha\dot{\upsilon}\tau\epsilon\xi o\acute{\upsilon}\sigma\iota o\nu$) as a
feature of *Nous* qua *Nous*. Does that mean that the term is

inapplicable at any other level? If it has wider application, does it apply to the soul when it acts "in accordance with *Nous*" and when it behaves "in accordance with virtue"? Obviously "virtue" here refers to the best action possible for the soul. Such action is "in accordance with *Nous*" and thus, as we have suggested, will be free action where the notion of moral obligation is inapplicable. If our approach is correct, we should find that the notion of a choice between good and evil will disappear from the virtuous soul. And if moral obligation is supposed to imply an awareness of what we ought to do coupled with the possibility of not being able to do it, such a sense of obligation will disappear from the soul in so far as it becomes more perfectly virtuous.

Clearly in one sense the soul is constrained, and thus "we" are constrained, by external circumstances in a way in which *Nous* is not — and in so far as we are constrained, we are not "free" to act. What we are able to *achieve* does not depend solely on ourselves, for although we may make choices and decisions, and though we may act accordingly, we are not in full control (κύριοι) of events. When we act bravely in battle, the performance of our act depends on the existence of the circumstances which call it forth.[6] All specific moral acts are restricted in this way. So if virtue requires such opportunities (and Aristotle certainly thinks that some — if not all — the moral virtues do), then such virtue is not "free" in the sense with which Plotinus has been concerned in *Ennead* VI.8. And Plotinus will grant that "freedom" must apply to activity, not merely to wanting and reasoning that is designed to lead to activity. Freedom, it seems, cannot be merely a matter of intention and purity of motive. Many actions, even when performed morally and well, can never be free. In fact, all everyday moral behaviour falls into this class; at its best it is "semi-free". All of it exhibits the feature of being constrained by some kind of external pressure. Thus in every case the possibility of the good not being accomplished is real and, it presumably follows, in all such cases it will be appropriate for a man to tell himself, and to tell other people, what he ought to do. When we are in the realm of moral obligation, we are not yet in the realm of virtue. Virtue is "another *Nous*" and, strictly speaking, as the last lines of VI.8.5 indicate, it is outside physical acts and events in time.

The consequences of the arguments we have outlined are drawn in VI.8.6. In so far as a man is living the good life, the life of *Nous* and the life of virtue, his moral acts will be dictated by his virtue, by his *Nous*. Virtue will tell him if he is to sacrifice his goods or his life. A sense of moral obligation may be viewed as a sense of what is right; it is possessed by anyone trying to live in obedience to that element in him or over him which is already living the life of virtue. The claims of a moral obligation, e.g. the need for self sacrifice, will be respected and obeyed in so far as a man has elevated himself to the level of *Nous*. Presumably in the man who has made the most moral progress the sense of obligation will be called upon the least, in that his disposition will be the most free, and he will be the most likely to do what is good as a matter of course, or, in Plotinian language, as a matter of nature. One may suppose, as we have seen, that as virtue becomes more and more identified with a man's character, so his sense of obligation, hitherto necessary, will wither away and be no longer needed.

It is clear then why we hear so little in the *Enneads* about a sense of obligation. The possession of such a state, in the Plotinian scheme, is to be associated with that stage of development at which a man is choosing between right and wrong. It is a stage at which he is still no longer free; his nature, distorted by bodily desires and impulses, cannot follow its natural bent. His "will" to good is thwarted and he still has to struggle to keep himself on the right path. By implication criticising the Stoics and their doctrine of the right act done from pure motives, Plotinus observes in I.2.5.28-6.2 that one stage of the elevation of the soul is attained when the passions are obedient to reason, when *acrasia*, that is, the overcoming of the reason by desires and impulses of a non-rational character, is out of the question. At this stage, says Plotinus, we do not sin, all our action is right action (κατόρθωσις). Nevertheless, *pace* the Stoics, our aim is higher than that: our aim is not merely to be "outside sin"; it is of a positive kind, or, as Plotinus puts it, "to be god" (θεὸν εἶναι). To consider exactly what this means would be to digress, but Plotinus certainly wants to point out that his view of right action involves not the *avoidance* (presumably by a correct and rightly motivated choice among alternatives) of wrong-doing, but a state of soul which will be unchanging and fixed. For if ϑεός means anything precise, it means something unchanging and eternally the same. It is apparently often used to indicate the unchanging *quality* of a subject rather than as the name of a subject itself.

The approach we have adopted runs into certain other problems of vocabulary which should be removed from the path if possible. At I.2.6.14 (I.2 is 19 in Porphyry's chronological list) it is said that virtue does not exist at the level of *Nous*, whereas the opposite view is taken at VI.8.6.5 (chronologically 39). But different uses of the term "virtue" may be seen in different contexts. Aristotle, in the *Nicomachean Ethics*, denies virtuous conduct (acting bravely, liberally, etc.) to the gods,[7] and the moral virtue of the *Nicomachean Ethics* forms one of the bases of *Ennead* I.2. On the other hand, although Aristotle's thought about free will is one of the sources of Plotinus' discussion of the topic in the early chapters of 6.8, the use of terms in VI.8 must not be assumed to be identical with that of I.2 simply because both have an Aristotelian base. Plotinus wrote the two treatises several years apart; it is unhelpful to attempt to identify differences of philosophical position or a development of the theory of virtue on the basis of Plotinus' somewhat slap-happy employment of terms which we vainly wish were technical.

Let us pull some threads together. For Plotinus we may assume that a thing exists insofar as it is good – and I am using "exists" in the strong Platonic sense of existing in an unchanging and imperishable form. In so far as things are not good, i.e. are not characterized by the presence, direct or indirect, of the One or Good, they do not exist in this Plotinian sense. Hence Plotinus will say that unless distracting influences or negative forces are at work, each being will act "for the sake of the good or of its good".[8] Such action for the sake of the good is the free (i.e. unimpeded) action of a substance. "Unfree" action will therefore be action tending to the destruction of the substance, animate or inanimate, which performs it. In fact, as we have

already noticed, Plotinus normally limits the concept of the
unfree to the activities of animate substances.

We have observed already that statments in the form "You
ought not to do x" must often be filled out either as "You
ought not to do x because of y", or, "You ought not to do x if
you want to achieve z". When dealing with statements about
so-called moral obligations Plotinus would undoubtedly wish to
follow a procedure of this sort. How does it work out in
practice? The implication is that "You ought (morally) to do x"
must be rephrased as "If you want to become better, freer,
closer to the good, etc., you should do x". In one sense,
therefore, there is no notion of obligation at all. It is up to each
man to choose what he wants to do. If he wants to act
viciously, let him do so, but it is the job of the moralist (and of
the philosopher) to point out exactly what he is doing. Hence a
so-called moral obligation and perhaps even a sense of moral
obligation, will arise if he chooses to try to act freely in the
Plotinian sense. When he has succeeded in accomplishing such
an action, i.e. when he has raised himself to the level of *Nous*,
moral obligation will no longer present itself to him as
obligation. He will simply act "rightly".

If the Aristotelian commentator Elias does not misrepre-
sent Plotinus' thought, we can check up on an interesting
example of the way Plotinian language about right action
works; we can look at the end of *Ennead* I.9 and compare it
with Elias' quotation of Plotinus' writing on "rational departure", i.e. suicide.[9] *Ennead* I.9 ends as follows: If each man's
soul in the other world depends on its condition when he leaves
this one, we ought not to commit suicide when there is any
chance of improvement. Elias' quotation closes as follows: It is
disordered (ἄτοπον) to take oneself out of life before the right
moment when he who has bound the body to the soul looses
them again. We notice the approach I have already pointed out
in the first passage: if such and such is the case (and if by
implication we are interested in benefitting ourselves in the next
world), then we ought to do x. It is assumed that we want to
benefit ourselves in the next world, and the "ought" is used
with reference to how such benefits can be achieved. The point
is that it is held to be absurd and irrational not to wish for such

a result. This is brought out in the passage from Elias. Here, instead of saying, "We *ought* not to commit suicide and anticipate God in separating soul from body", Plotinus claims that to do so would be disordered or untoward (ἄτοπον). The juxtaposition of the two passages gives us a clear example of the way the implications of the concept of freedom are worked out: what we ought to do (in Plotinus' opinion) is simply what it is rational to do. Thus it follows that the best sort of moral obligation can be understood only as a call to act rationally. If anyone asks why we should do what we ought, he can be told that, since his question implies that good reasons for action should be accepted, he should not cavil at acting in accordance with Plotinus' moral "ought", since it is translatable into a call for rationality.

Plotinus would be gratified to hear that much of the theory we have attributed to him is implicit in Plato's *Republic*. No one would deny that in that dialogue Plato is advocating a particular way of life, a particular tending of the soul, a particular kind of behaviour. The philosopher-king is a pattern we should all strive to resemble. But there are few places in the *Republic* where Plato tells us what we ought to do; he tells us rather what the philosopher-king would do. One example is particularly instructive: the philosopher must return to the Cave (*Republic* 520C1) because it is just for him to do so. Since he is just, he will do what is just. It is Glaucon, who is certainly not a philosopher-king, who imagines that there will be some conflict in the philosopher's mind and that he will, if he returns to the Cave, have to live a worse life instead of a better. According to Socrates, however, the philosopher-king will simply do what is right. His actions and his obligations will always coincide, because he is that sort of man.

But when addressing his readers, Plato does not give them a series of moral commands, nor point to a set of categorical imperatives. Let us consider again the methodology of the *Republic*: to the irritation of those who expect it to take the form of deduction and refutation, it is an exercise in portraiture. Although Socrates goes through a form of refutation of Thrasymachus in Book I, he does not treat the objections of Glaucon and Adeimantus in the same way; instead he offers two portraits, one of the philosopher-king, and the other of the tyrant. He supposes that these pictures represent what we may call the good and the bad life in their starkest form. He invites us to choose which we would prefer for ourselves; he does not bring in the question of rewards and punishments in another life until we have made our choice on the basis of what we would prefer and find expedient in this world alone. He does not tell us we ought not to behave tyrannically, but that if we behave tyrannically we shall be people of particular (in his view unpleasant) dispositions. So we are invited to check empirically whether his characterizations of the virtuous and vicious answer to the facts as we can see them if we look at the world realistically and honestly.

All this is implicitly taken over by Plotinus. As in Plato, so in Plotinus we are not told what is morally good and what we therefore must (or ought to) choose. All kinds of codes of behavior are possible, and there is a sense in which it is a matter for free (even arbitrary) choice which code one selects or which code one lives by. There is no word in Plotinian Greek which exactly translates the English "morality" — though σπουδαῖος or ἐπιεικής are both something like our "morally good" — but there is no reason why Plotinus could not accept that morality is simply a formal term, i.e. that it refers to any (hopefully consistent) code of behaviour freely adopted by an individual man. That is not, of course, to assert that Plotinus would agree that any morality is as good as any other; he thinks that codes of behaviour must be judged in terms of their usefulness and expediency for each of us. We do not fix on a code as intrinsically good and then ask ourselves how it can be expedient, or whether and in what sense it is expedient; we allow a rational judgement of expediency to lead us to the discovery of the Good, and therefore of the good for man.

Plotinus' morality, like that of Plato and Aristotle, is eudaimonistic in the sense that the aim is to secure well being or "happiness". And this well being is best secured by a particular kind of life, aimed at a freedom and rationality of the kind we have discussed. If a man is virtuous (σπουδαῖος), he has all the requirements for happiness and for acquiring what is good (I.4.4.25). These requirements, as we have seen, are basically the ability to perform certain kinds of actions which themselves arise from certain dispositions and states of mind. But a eudaimonistic morality can easily be misunderstood. It might appear as though Plotinus were advocating that, if happiness is the good, we therefore have duties or obligations to ourselves, but none to anyone else. That is not the way it turns out. Although Plotinus certainly believes that we have duties to ourselves – and there is no reason why he should not think so if we have duties to other people – he also believes that a search for happiness – and the consequent duties to ourselves which we shall fulfill in so far as we are successful – entails duties and responsibilities to other people. To explain why this should be so would require a full-scale discussion of Plotinus' metaphysics, for which there is obviously no place here. We must content ourselves with noticing that the world is an interconnected whole, and it is impossible to be concerned with the source of happiness, the Good, without being concerned with, and for, the other items, particularly other souls, which are the products of the Good. The theory is summed up at II.9.16.7ff: "The man who feels affection for something values whatever is akin to the object of his affection; if he loves the father, he loves the children." The theme is necessary and important for Plotinus – and anyone else. Plotinus wants to reject a plea that preoccupation with the divine is inconsistent with a concern for human beings. Concern for human beings implies "virtue" in the normally accepted sense; hence, as we have already observed, Plotinus says elsewhere that virtue (understood here as common decency and ordinary morality) is the first step towards God; without it "God" is a name people mouth (II.9.15.40).

What sort of obligations to others will the philosopher thus wish to carry out? Whatever they are, they will not be carried out grudgingly (φϑόνος ἔξω ϑείου χοροῦ ἵσταται, *Phaedrus* 247A). There is for Plotinus only a limited amount that we can do for other people. Ultimately each man must face reality for himself (μόνος πρὸς μόνον); he cannot find a substitute, anymore than he can find someone to die for him. And what should be done for other people must depend on the possibilities open to them and the choices they have made for themselves about their own lives. Porphyry tells us that Plotinus devoted a good deal of attention to looking after the property of children whose parents had died and for whom he had been made responsible;[10] they needed the money, he held, unless they should turn to a life of philosophy. But necessary as a fulfillment of such obligations is, for Plotinus the real obligation of a philosopher is to teach. In so far as it is possible, the philosopher must announce (ἀγγέλλοντα, VI.9.7.22) the nature of the true relation with the divine.

According to Porphyry Plotinus was a kind man, and there is no reason to reject this testimony. That being so, there are a number of rather harsh sounding passages in the *Enneads* which may be the more informative in so far as they tend to jar liberal sensibilities. Plotinus, like a modern social-worker, is aware that too great an emotional involvement in the misfortunes of those he would like to help will only inhibit his ability to do so. But to say that is not entirely to explain such sections as *Ennead* III.2.8. Let us note a few ideas from this passage: in the gymnasium boys who have kept themselves fit may throw those who have not, and make off with their food and clothes. "Serve them right" is the appropriate reaction — accompanied by a laugh at the expense of the vanquished. The world outside presents a similar scenario: if you don't behave bravely, and in general virtuously, you will be victimized, and deservedly so. "The wicked rule through the cowardice of their subjects; and this is just". It is grotesque to sit around and pray for a good harvest rather than look after the land. The theme is generalized in the next chapter: "It is not right (θεμιτόν) that those who have become wicked should expect others to be their saviours and to sacrifice themselves in answer to their prayers" (III. 2.9.10-12). The message of all this is clear: no one should be expected to look after someone else if that person is able but unwilling to look after himself (and he probably would not be able to look after such a person anyway.) Here we see where the limits of obligation are set: Plotinus seems to be concerned to find a way to balance the concept of obligation to others (which is a part of virtue) with the necessity and possibility of people helping themselves. Those who will not swim should be allowed to sink. And this brings us to the final point I want to make.

Plotinus agrees with Aristotle in holding that there are some things which the good man simply will not do. With reference to such cases to say that A ought to do x is to imply that A can do x. (This of course has nothing to do with the wider question whether Plotinus would hold that in *all* uses of the word "ought", "ought" implies "can" – a dogma of much contemporary ethical theory whose weaknesses and difficulties need not be elaborated here.) But why should Plotinus think that there are any cases in morality in which "ought" implies "can"? On what theory of the psyche does such a view depend? For we must remember the way in which the "ought" is to be understood. Plotinus' view, as we have argued, is that "You ought to do x" (which is a morally good act) must be read as "If you want to be a good man, you ought to do x, and it is expedient to be a good man". So we are saying that he also holds that there are some actions for which it will be true to say "If you want (as you do) to be a good man, you are *able* to do x". But one might object, are we *able* to want to be a good man? Or are all our "wants" in this area fixed, innate, determined by social conditions, etc. Plotinus' view is that not only are we able to want to be a good man, but we do in fact want to be a good man – or at least that there is such a "want" in us, this want being the characteristic "movement" and disposition of the pure and unfallen part of the soul, the so-called "upper" soul.[11] But although this theory explains why "we", as distinct from our upper soul, will want to be good, how does it explain that we are able to be good? The fact is that it does not. Plotinus' problem is as follows: he thinks that it is a matter of observation that some men simply will not do certain acts which may be designated as vicious. He assumes that since all men must have in common that which is the highest element in them – an adaptation of Aristotelian doctrines about *Nous* – they must therefore possess this "higher" faculty. Thus all men possess a higher and purer part of the soul. But surely all this shows is that it is *possible* for all men to avoid certain viciousnesses; it has not explained why in some cases possible behaviour becomes actual behaviour, whereas in others it does not. In the case of the man who thus can do what he ought, but does not do so, we are still faced with the question why Jones does not want to be a good man strongly enough actually to set himself on the way to becoming one. Clearly Plotinus' answer that he is misled by matter, by the body, etc., needs qualification, because we wonder why some people are misled more than others if their "upper souls" are in the same state.

Let us go back to our formulation of the problem in terms of what the good man will not do. For Plotinus no man is good except in so far as he has knowledge and acts in certain ways; and if he knows and acts in these ways, he cannot, by definition, act in a contrary sense. Plotinus' view therefore must be that if a man does not do what he ought to do if he is to be a good man, it can only be because he does not *understand* how beneficial it is to be a good man, and therefore has not chosen to be. In *Freedom and Reason* R. M. Hare put forward the suggestion that people bait bears because they lack the imagination to put themselves in the bear's place. But imagination is not the root of the problem.[1][2] Imagining what it is to be a bear is not being a bear, and a good imagination may only encourage the bear-baiter to persist. But to *understand* the impact of cruelty on the self — and to see that it is not beneficial — may be an adequate motive for leaving the bear in peace. Plotinus would not put an objection to Hare in quite this form, but I should like to argue that what he says about the nature of obligation to others and to the self is sufficient justification for developing his thought along lines of this sort. If this is co-operation with Plotinus, so be it; others would say that it is part of the critical history of philosophy.

NOTES

1. Or "must not", but there is still the suggestion of moral obligation.
2. See L. G. Westerink, *Anonymous Prolegomena to Platonic Philosophy* (Amsterdam, 1962).

3. See J. M. Rist, "Integration and the Undescended Soul in Plotinus", *American Journal of Philology* (1967), Vol 88, pp. 415-422.
4. J. H. Newman, *A Grammar of Assent* (Doubleday edition, New York, 1955), pp. 86-92.
5. Cf. III.8.6.7.
6. See further J. M. Rist, *Plotinus* (Cambridge, 1967), p. 134.
7. *Nicomachean Ethics,* 1178B12ff.
8. III.8.6.7; VI.8.4.36, etc.
9. The immediate origin of the passage of Elias is probably Proclus: either from a commentary on the *Enneads* or a commentary on the *Phaedo*. See L. G. Westerink, "Elias und Plotin", *Byzantinische Zeitschrift* (1964), Volume 57, pp. 26-32.
10. Porphyry, *Vita Porphyry*, ch. 9.
11. II.9.2.9; IV.8.4.31; IV.8.8.2, etc.
12. R. M. Hare, *Freedom and Reason* (Oxford, 1963), pp. 223-224.

Dynamic Structuralism in the Plotinian Theory of the Imaginary

by Evanghelos Moutsopoulos

University of Athens

In 1960, a comtemporary French thinker, Gilbert Durand, published a thesis under the suggestive title *"The Anthropological Structures of the Imaginary: An Introduction to General Archetypology."* I wish to adopt Durand's terminology in order to speak of the *imaginary structures in human reality* in the philosophy of Plotinus.

A certain methodological reversal is possible, I believe, when speaking of the imaginary in the work of Plotinus. One may proceed to an inquiry on the meaning of the imaginary by starting not from imagination considered as a noetical function, but rather from the image, which is the structural reality of imagination in consciousness. In other terms, one may think of the image as the first datum, and not as a product of the imaginative activity.

By operating on such a reversal one may depart from the tradition of Aristotelian and Scholastic views on imagination by considering to what extent, according to Plotinus, it is not the imagination that offers images to the consciousness, but rather the images that fertilize the imaginative activity.

This reversal reveals a whole new perspective in the investigation of Plotinus' thought. However, it should not be considered a revolutionary one. It does not deny the dynamism of consciousness, but simply places emphasis upon the dynamism of the image.

In the fourth volume of his *History of the Psychology of the Greeks*, A. E. Chaignet[1] has perhaps foreseen this aspect of the problem. Although he failed to draw out the full implications of this approach, some of his interpretations show that he has been able to grasp the meaning of certain Plotinian texts, dealing with the problem of the imaginary.

I do not think that Chaignet has discovered any new meanings which were hidden up to his time. What he has done is to point out some extensions of interpretations which had already been accepted, and that he has extended them beyond their traditionally accepted meanings.

In examining two Plotinian texts concerning the relations between being and consciousness, on one hand, and memory and imagination, on the other, Chaignet does not hesitate to refer the activity of recollection, as well as the consciousness of structural forms of existence, to the dynamism of the image, independently from the way it is considered, i.e., either as figurative or not.

The first text is from the *Problems of the Soul*, part one, IV. 3.29: "memory and recollection are functions of the imaginary." The other text is from part two of the same treatise, IV. 4. 3: "the soul is and becomes whatever it recalls." By correlating the two texts we come to the conclusion that the soul changes on the ground of its imaginary activities.

P. V. Pistorius, in his book on *Plotinus and Neoplatonism*, has tried to show that, if the soul really changes (as it is stated in the second of the above texts), according to the object of its recollection, it is due to the fact that recollection carries the soul away from the intelligible world. I quote: "The essential function of the soul when it is freed from the body is intellection or contemplation. Such intellection is timeless. Because there is no past or future in the ideal world, there is no room for memory . . . it is not as if death simply terminated any memory of human life and a new memory era was born. Any memory is annulled, and because there is no time in the ideal world and everything is an eternal moment, there is no possibility of recalling things that happened there."[2] If the soul is capable of recollection, this is due to the fact that it still remains within the limits of time.

In commenting on the same text, Chaignet throws some light on a very different aspect of it. In effect, he states that "to imagine does not mean to possess, but to contemplate, and to become what one contemplates" (*op. cit.*, p. 198). It is not, then, consciousness that grasps an imaginary datum but, on the contrary, it is precisely such a datum that renders the consciousness capable of grasping it in its formal totality.

One should not, of course, attribute to the consciousness a passive structure making of it a completely malleable aspect of the soul. Such a type of consciousness would only have the possibility of formal impressions (IV.3.26), of the kind mentioned by the Stoic tradition which considers the soul as a *tabula rasa*. Against this rather sensualistic stoic empiricism, Plotinus makes clear that, in reality, such impressions take place within the soul, just as in thinking (IV.3.26).

One must take into consideration that the texts of Plotinus mentioned here also refer to the notion of recollection. However, for Plotinus the memory is finally reduced to the imagination (IV. 3. 29). Hence the dynamism of imagination can be established through the memory which is capable of grasping the particular objects of the soul, and through the general capacity of the soul to grasp itself in the reality of its existence; for, as Chaignet writes, "The proper states of the soul are the only objects grasped by imagination" (IV. 3. 29). This assertion is somehow exaggerated, since Plotinus does not deny the reality of the sensible objects, but only the equality of their degree of reality, in comparison with the intelligible objects. In any case, there is no need to make any rapprochement between Plotinus' views, as they are interpreted here, and, for instance, Bergson's own intuitionistic views. One has, however, to point out the similarity of the respective expressions.

Imagination is not confined to represent only sensible objects. Its activity also extends to the reenforcement of formal structures which help make conceivable some states proper to the essence, which are the means through which the soul is aware of itself, without any interference of reason.

Under such conditions, it is possible to say that the soul becomes whatever it represents to itself at an imaginary level, since in reality, what the soul is capable of representing to itself is its own state. Imagination may then be considered as open to images that come from the world of the senses, and also from the depth of existence. Its role consists in structuring the formal data, i.e., the images, in order to enable them to impose themselves upon consciousness.

Yet, the soul does not become "whatever it recalls" in an absolute manner. For, being dependent at this level on the formal data of imagination (which, in turn, is oriented towards the sensible as well as towards the activity of existence) the soul never adopts attitudes which correspond in every respect to its inner reality.

Imagination displays impressive adaptability and dynamism. Imagination, Plotinus says, does not possess its object. However, as it possesses its vision, it makes itself available according to it; as he says at IV. 4. 3:

> In this self-memory a distinction is to be made: the memory dealing with the Intellectual Realm upbears the Soul, not to fall; the memory of things here bears it downwards to this universe; the intermediate memory dealing with the heavenly sphere holds it there too; and, in all its memory, the thing it has in mind it is and grows to; for this bearing-in-mind must be either intuition (i.e. knowledge with identity) or representation by image: and the imaging in the case of the Soul is not a taking in of something (as of an impression) but is vision and condition—so much so, that in its very sense-sight, it is the lower in the degree in which it penetrates the object. Since its possession of the total of things is not primal but secondary, it does not become all things perfectly (in becoming identical with the All in the Intellectual); it is of the boundary order, situated between two regions, and has tendency to both.

In this way, the soul possesses various objects, but possesses them in a secondary way, for it does not entirely become all of them. The soul is something intermediate between the sensible and the intelligible; and, being such, it is oriented towards both of them (IV. 4. 3). It should be understood here that the intermediate character that Plotinus attributes to the soul is analogous to the intermediate character attributed to imagination.

Far from behaving passively, the entire soul is adapted to the image that imposes itself upon the imagination. The soul, then, becomes conscious of that image, since it it aware of itself having already adopted the form of the image in question. This conception will be widened by Proclus in whose work imagination will be considered as having even stronger structuring powers.[3]

Chaignet (*op. cit.*, p. 198) admits that, in this way, an image might be "empty of any real content", and thus become related to error. However, he takes care to add to the above expression the terms "real" and "immediate": "empty of any immediate real content." Thus, this expression completely changes the orientation of an eventual empirical interpretation of his text. The image may, indeed, not be a representation which is completely adequate to the object it represents or to the state of the soul of which it makes consciousness aware. This fact does not, however, render less real the image in question, at least to the extent to which this image impresses itself on the consciousness. Its reality is not an immediate and direct one in relation to the object or the state represented. Yet this same reality becomes immediate and direct in relation to its presence within the consciousness upon which it is imposed. Speaking of the image as well as of the imagination, Chaignet writes that both of them have a magic power that enables them to operate within the whole domain of understanding; and that one of the causes of this magic power resides in the reality of the presence of the image.

According to the above "dynamistic" considerations, Plotinus asserts at III. 7. 8 that the sensitive soul has, through an indefinite image, a sort of premonition of what the being is. Such an indefinite image is not deprived of any form or shape, but simply of the clearness of the data of perception.

Due to its dynamism, imagination permits the passage from one level of the consciousness to another of data corresponding to each one of these levels. It offers to the understanding the contents of the sensible world, as well as offering to the entire soul a certain aspect of its being, even if this aspect is a confused one.

One may understand this coexistence of confusedness and form through a curious and suggestive text of Proclus: "The infinite is left to exist alone in the imagination; for imagination does not conceive the infinite. Indeed, when conceiving something, imagination attributes to it a form and a limit.... But the infinite is not subject to any conception by the imagination which refers to it in an indefinite way ... rather than conceives it. Imagination has a knowledge of the infinite by not conceiving it, just as the sight has a knowledge of the infinite by not conceiving it, just as the sight has a knowledge of the darkness by not seeing it."[4] The meanings of the expression "refers to it in an indefinite way" and of the term "infinite," remind us of the meanings of the above mentioned terms: "indefinite" and infinite image" in Plotinus. The meaning of this text of Proclus, which is really astonishing, may be completed by another text of the *Comment. in Crat.*, 76. 26 (Pasquali): "Imagination is a formative and impure thought."[5]

The only concession of the formative imagination to informative understanding is due to the presence of objects of consciousness deprived of any form, or possessing a form that we discern with difficulty.

The image is the means through which the soul represents to itself whatever exists beyond the senses and beyond understanding. Being more than a simple form, the image exercises its power upon the understanding, of which it shapes, so to speak, the contours in such a way as to subjugate them to the exigencies of existence. In the framework of consciousness, the perceptible image and the intelligible being (called particular concept) coexist within the image. It is in this way that one should understand the role of articulated language in fixing the meaning of concepts. As Th. Whittaker states, "Thought is apprehended by imagination as in a mirror (I.4.10), the notion (*nōema*) at first indivisible and implicit being conveyed to it by an explicit discourse (*logos*)."[6] Only when duplicated through reflection may consciousness grasp itself.

Images of noetic nature are, of course, also present in consciousness. They not only determine, but also fertilize its activity (IV. 4. 11). An image is not only able of representing, but also of provoking a psychical fact with reference to some sensible object. However, it is a psychical fact itself. It is not only a reflection of some higher truth, but also a reality, an activity. It is motion in itself as well as motion of the soul towards what is represented by the image.

The degree of reality of the image does not depend only upon the degree of its similarity to some real model of which it may be an imitation (I. 2. 2; I. 2. 7; VI. 2. 8), but also upon the fact that the image makes consciousness capable of grasping the intelligence, and of representing it to itself, in order to direct itself towards it (in a movement that reminds us of the movement through which the soul is directed towards the Good: V. 6. 5). The image thus becomes the principle as well as the means of the participation of the soul in intelligible realities, although it is not necessarily one of them (III. 6. 14).

The irrational character of the image does not prevent it from having a proper structure, a structure which is due to its coming from inner existence. Furthermore, the image impresses that particular structure of itself on consciousness. However, this very irrational character of the image is illustrated by the fact that the image itself is imposed upon the thought without waiting for the judgment of reason (I. 1. 9). Thought is therefore, for Plotinus, an element of false reasoning and it even leads to false considerations, in spite of the fact that in reality thought and imagination are essentially different from each other (I. 4. 10). However, both thought and imagination are subject to error since the image is connected to opinion, which is thought without reasoning. But rectitude is not necessarily the only truth, and the truth of the image is its reality which is directly related to the reality of existence.

Besides, the image is a reality of the soul, and as such it is opposed to reason conceived as a rational principle, since the image itself is related to the irrational (but not to any unreality) of the soul. Plotinus makes clear the fact that the image is a "stroke of something irrational coming from outside" (I. 8. 15).[7]

It seems that these various expressions referring to a certain shock are due to a common source. However, although Plotinus admits that the image is "a stroke of something irrational coming from outside," he refuses to comment on the nature of this shock which we would then suppose to be something like an impression, But, in that case, the image would not differ from any sensation. The term *"exothen"* (from outside) seems, of course, to suggest such an interpretation and it would be possible to think that the passage in question refers only to images of external provenance, due to sensational operations.

In other words, Plotinus could have given to the various terms denoting the *image (eikon, phantasma, eidolon)*, a more restricted meaning compared to that given to them in other Plotinian texts. Such a fluctuation, however, of which many parallel cases are to be found in Plotinus should not surprise us; for, as Emile Bréhier states in the *Introduction* to his edition of the *Enneades*: "by virtue of the law of the 'genre' he has chosen, Plotinus ignores the art of systematically developing a doctrine".[8] In any case, one should admit that in numerous passages (as in I. 1. 4; III. 7. 8; IV. 3. 30) Plotinus seems to consider the notion of image as denoting something more than a simple sensible impression.

The second part of the sentence, where it is said that the soul "receives the stroke through its compound nature" (I. 8. 15), raises the problem of the relationship between the parts of the soul and the receptivity of the soul concerning external impressions. But, as E. Barbotin remarks in the *Introduction* to his edition of Octave Hamelin's text, in French, on *"The Theory of Intellect according to Aristotle and his Commentators"*,[9] the term *"exothen"* (from outside) seems to have a certain technical significance but without any precise meaning, so that it is not necessary that in this case this same term be taken as denoting any intrusion of the external world into consciousness through the image.

Thus, the image, itself, remains irrational, because it is independent from any control of the reason, and it is present at all the levels of human activity, except the purely physical and physiological one (III. 6. 4). Plotinus even indirectly supposes that the image is radically different from sensation, since he distinguishes two respective functions of the soul to which each of these two kinds of data refer to: the sensitive function and the imaginative function. He even suggests that (at least at a certain level) the activity of the soul is reduced only to these two functions (IV. 3. 23). Plotinus then goes on to state what he has already suggested, i.e., that the irrational character of the image impresses its seal upon the thought, independently of reason, to the judgment of which it is not submitted (I. 4. 10). He now asserts that sensation as well as imagination are subordinated to reason which, through its lower aspects, is akin to the higher aspects of these two functions of the soul (IV. 4. 3).

In the same context, Plotinus thinks that sensation and imagination should also concern the body, namely the part which is most able to receive their activity. Through them, reason, which is completely independent of the body, is indirectly connected to it. What seems to be important in this way of considering the facts is that the various functions of the soul, seen from the viewpoint of the image, seem no longer to be mechanisms consisting of distinct parts. The activity of the soul, therefore, seems to be an organic whole whose particular functions are so closely related that they are confused, in a way, with each other (IV. 4. 1).

The image thus becomes an organized representative structure formed out of initial data which it validates by referring them to the activity of reason (IV. 3. 23). Through a temporary submission of the imagination to reason, the image, which is a form that activates imagination, seems to impose itself in return upon the dynamism of existence in general, from which it comes.

However, no dynamism of the imagination leads to awareness independently of the presence of the image considered as being the image of an object. Such an "objectified image" is all but irrational. Thus, unless one accepts, together with Chaignet,[10] through an excessively analytic and "scholastic" procedure, the fact that the distinctions made between the various forms of imagination may be preserved, and even applied at the level of the image itself (I. 4. 10 and III. 6. 10), it will be necessary to accept the fact that the image is a structure which is originally present at all the levels of the activity of consciousness, and that only later is it submitted to the influence of reason.

The process that such a conception of the image presupposes, in this case, is not at all clear. For the image is considered first as the main vehicle of the tendencies of the inferior soul, and then as imposing on these tendencies a regulative order whose principle must be sought within the region of the logos. Be it as it may, it seems that in Plotinus, this whole theory is based upon the intention that various effects be referred to a unique principle.

This is not incompatible with the synthetic spirit of the philosophy of Plotinus, in spite of certain exceptions which one may easily point out. One has to deal here with the agreement of two different and even opposed facts.[11]

The image has a part to play, according to Plotinus, not only at the level of *theoria*, but also at the level of *praxis*, in other words, at the level of human ethical behavior. Referring to the causes of such a behavior, Plotinus, according to E. Bréhier, makes an allusion to the efforts of Chrysippus to reconciliate destiny (conceived as a connection of causes) with liberty.[12] Within such a general theoretical framework, Plotinus asserts that the provenance of the causes of human behavior is to be found in a principle which is unique; and that they only enable us to proceed towards the direction in which they are pushing us. Representations will then be the effects of former causes, and the tendencies will be in accordance to these representations (III. 1. 7). This is not, however, always the case, for it is possible that images may be opposed to the tendencies of the body, which means that one frequently has to deal with conflicts of images (V. 10. 26).

Representative images are related to irrational manifestations of the soul, and they translate the activity of such manifestations through forms which admit of a certain structural revision. The image thus becomes an epistemological and, at the same time, an existential principle that connects the irrational to the logos. This seems to be due to the fact that, on the one hand, the image is, potentially, a formal structure of behavior as well as a structured form; and that, on the other hand, it is capable of extending its possibilities to the whole existence.

It is possible to admit that, in this context, the connection of the constitutive aspects of man takes place at the level of the image. One may conceive of an ascending and of a descending dialectic of the imaginary in Plotinus, in spite of the fact that their respective articulations are not clearly distinguished. It should only be asserted that, independently of its unconscious antecedents, the image remains a first datum in relation to the imagination considered as a concrete aspect of the consciousness, and that, through the image, the rational consciousness manifests itself as oral speech and as a model of behavior.

In any case, the force of images is equalled by the correspondence of consciousness to them. Being forms either of sensible or of any other provenance, images provoke the apparition of other forms which have previously existed as potential forms in the consciousness. This is why the image and the imagination are not considered separately from each other, but only with reference to the functional relation existing between them. One does not have to consider the imaginative activity, but only the world of the imaginary itself. In effect, the active character of the imaginary seems to be located in the way the dynamism of consciousness is confirmed during its contact with the image.

What is fluid and uncertain does not become an object of consciousness unless it takes a form, provided the form does not have a static character. But as soon as the discursive reason tries to determine this form (and, through it, the object itself by identifying and by consolidating it), the formative image which emerged from former fluidity of the object now vanishes and is replaced by an abstraction.

This does not mean, of course, that the image is reality itself. Plotinus considers the image as a shadow of reality. What renders the image real, at least to a certain extent, is its aptitude to substitute the objective reality by introducing itself into consciousness, and by imposing itself upon it.

This structural aspect of the status of the image and of imagination in relation to the activity of consciousness is such that one may observe in Plotinus the first outline of a dynamic structuralistic consideration of imagination and of the imaginary which is the direct consequence of the reversion of the classical Aristotelian conception of imagination as being a noetic function. By conceiving the image as a first datum, Plotinus becomes the distant forerunner of contemporary psychological structuralism.

NOTES

1. A. E. Chaignet. *Histoire de la Psychologie des Grecs*, Paris 1890, Vol. IV pp. 196 ff.
2. P. V. Pistorius. *Plotinus and Neoplatonism*, p. 95.
3. Cf. *Commentaries to the First book of Euclides' Elements*, 94. 24-25 (ed. E. Diehl): "Imagination suggests forms for objects deprived of any form, and shapes for objects deprived of any shape." One will find similar conceptions in Psellos' work.
4. Proclus. *Eucl.* I. 285. 5-15, ed. Friedlein.
5. Cf. also *Eucl.* I. 94. 24-25 (Diehl).
6. Th. Whittaker. *The Neo-Platonists—A Study in the History of Hellenism* (Cambridge, 1928), p. 51.
7. Damascius [*In Philebum*, 148. 3 (Westerink)] will use a parallel expression: "Imagination proposes the desirable to the irrational desire" in connection with the idea that "whenever there is a recollection of the opinion concerning something sensible, it is as if, on this occasion, a sort of a shake takes place within the whole body". Plato has already used similar expressions in the *Timaeus,* 69 b-c.
8. Emile Bréhier, ed. *Enneades*, vol. I, p. XXX.
9. Paris, Vrin, 1953, pp. 187-190 and 240. "La Théorie de l'Intellect d' après Aristote et ses Commentateurs"
10. Chaignet, pp. 199-201.
11. Th. Whittaker, in p. 52 of his book, has underlined this problem.
12. Bréhier, vol. 3, p. 14, note 4.

Image, Symbol and Analogy: Three Basic Concepts of Neoplatonic Allegorical Exegesis

by John Dillon

University of California

I

The contemporary relevance of this subject is, perhaps, not great. Allegory, as such, is rather out of fashion. But for much of European history allegory has been indulged in freely, in all forms of art, and any discussion of the rules of allegory in any age or culture should be of general interest. Even today, the search for Freudian motifs and Jungian archetypes must have its rules − that is to say, ways of judging when a false analogy has been made.

This paper is simply an attempt to sort out, through an examination of some individual contexts, the possible difference of meaning between two basic terms of Neoplatonic allegory, *eikon* and *symbolon*, and in this connexion the use of the term *analogia/ analogon*. In such company as this, I do not come so mush to instruct as in the hope of learning more. There are, after all, many nooks and crannies of Neoplatonism into which I have not yet penetrated. What chiefly concerns me is the question of the *rules* of Neoplatonic allegory. By what system does one recognise in a given text an image or symbol of metaphysical reality? How can one learn to recognise the correct *'analogia'*? I do not find these rules stated anywhere in the writings of the Neoplatonist commentators. That is not to say that they are not there, however, and I would be glad to have pointed out to me some passage which I have overlooked.

It is possible, on the other hand, that the rules of Allegory cannot be stated precisely, but must simply be derived from experience – sitting at the feet of one's master – and from personal inspiration. I myself, after all, feel that I can now recognise a symbol in a given text and observe the correct analogy, but I would be somewhat at a loss to say on what precise principles I was proceeding, except the simple discernment of points of similarity. This may well seem to be an intolerably vague conclusion, and I would be glad to have the whole question made more definite.

II

That said, let us turn to a few texts. Near the beginning of his *Commentary on the Timaeus*, in connexion with the exegesis of the lemma *Tim.* 17BC (where Socrates declares his intention of giving a recapitulation of his discourse of the previous day on the Ideal State), Proclus makes the following comment (*In Tim.* I 29, 31 ff. Diehl):

"Some (sc. Porphyry), taking the recapitulation of the *Republic* in an ethical sense (ἠϑικώτερον), say that it reveals to us that we must enter upon the contemplation of the Universe in an ethically ordered frame of mind; others (sc. Iamblichus) consider that it has been placed before the whole enquiry into Nature (φυσιολογία) as an image (εἰκών) of the organisation of the Universe; for the Pythagoreans had the habit of placing before their scientific instruction the revelation of the subjects under enquiry through similitudes (ὅμοια) and images (εἰκόνες), and after this of introducing the secret revelation of the same subjects through symbols (σύμβολα), and then in this way, after the reactivation of the soul's ability to comprehend the intelligible realm and the purging of its vision, to bring on the complete knowledge of the subjects laid down for investigation. And here too the relating in summary of the *Republic* before the enquiry into Nature prepares us to understand the orderly creation of the Universe *through the medium of an image* (εἰκονικῶς), while the story of the Atlantids *acts as a symbol* (συμβολικῶς); for indeed myths in general tend to reveal

the principles of reality (τὰ πράγματα) through symbols.
So the discussion of Nature in fact runs through the whole
dialogue, but appears in different forms according to the
different methods of revelation."
This, I think, is a good passage from which to start, as it sets out
– or seems to set out – a clear distinction between an *eikon*
and a *symbolon*, and, further, links the whole theory of allegory
firmly with Pythagoreanism. I believe Iamblichus to be responsible for introducing this theory in its developed form into
Neoplatonism, and he will have derived it from his Neo-
pythagorean sources of inspiration, Numenius, Nicomachus of
Gerasa, or even Apollonius of Tyana. I am not, however,
concerned here with the origins of the theory, but rather with
the nature of it.

We see, then, a three-level system of exegesis set out. The
Pythagoreans, it seems, before revealing directly the truths of
their doctrine, would take the disciple through two preliminary
stages. First, they would present to him *homoia* and *eikones* of
reality. Obviously these were not their famous 'symbols' (of
which Iamblichus gives an extended account at the end of his
Protrepticus); the very word used for them precludes that. An
eikon must be something simpler and more straight-forward.
The only clue we have from this passage is that, in relation to
the doctrine presented in the *Timaeus*, the recapitulation of the
Republic is an *eikon*, while the Atlantis Myth is a *symbolon* (it
is also suggested here that *all* myths are *symbola*). But it is just
here that the difficulties begin. It is not clear, to me at any rate,
nor is it made clear by Proclus, how the recapitulation of the
Republic, or the description of the Ideal State in general, differs
generically, as a representation of cosmic truths, from the
Atlantis myth, or from myths in general. Indeed, a little earlier
in the work (p. 4, 7ff.), Proclus speaks of both the recapitulation of the Republic and the Atlantis myth as representing the
order of the universe δι᾽ εἰκόνων, the Republic being an *eikon*
of its unity (ἕνωσις), the Atlantis myth of its division
(διαίρεσις) and of the opposition of the two basic orders
(συστοιχίαι) within it – or, alternatively, the *Republic* can be
seen as being like to (ὁμοιοῦσθαι) the heavenly realm, the
Atlantis myth to the realm of *genesis* below the Moon. Not only
are both here *eikones*, but they may be seen as images of rather

different things, in one case of unity and diversity extending all through the Universe (a vertical distinction, one might say), or, alternatively, or the superlunary and sublunary realms (a horizontal distinction).

Let us for the moment confine ourselves to *eikones*, and consider in what respect they might reflect reality. For an *eikon*, in fact, 'reflecting' should be the key word. An *eikon* is, after all, properly a mirror-image, or a direct representation, of an original, its *paradeigma*, whereas a *symbolon* merely 'fits together' with some corresponding reality in a higher realm. One might use the comparison of a statue of Winston Churchill, say, on the one hand, with Churchill's cigar – or perhaps, a picture of Cinderella with Cinderella's slipper. The statue and the picture are plainly *eikones*, the cigar and the slipper *symbola* – particularly the slipper. These examples are certainly crude, but perhaps they will do as preliminaries.

If we return for the moment to the statue of Churchill, we can immediately see the difficulties. The statue, if it is a good one, will have a one-to-one correspondence with the various (external) features of its model. But at least the model, the *paradeigma*, is a physical object; we can compare image and archetype with the same faculty. If one takes the most obvious Platonic example, the comparison of the Sun as *eikon* with the Good as *paradeigma*, we have arrived at the point of difficulty. Why is the Sun an *eikon* (*Rep.* 509a9), and not a *symbolon*? Following Plato, we maintain that there is a one-to-one correspondence between Sun and Good. Both are a source of visibility, and even of existence, to the entities subordinate to them, the world of sensible objects and the world of intelligible objects. In the case of the Ideal State of the *Republic*, the three classes therein described must correspond exactly to the triple division of Gods, Daemons and Men in the Universe, and their mutual relations and activities must also correspond. But then, we say, the battle of the Athenians with the Atlantids seems to correspond well enough to the constant struggle in the Universe between the forces of order and disorder, unity and diversity, represented at the highest level by the archetypal opposition of Monad and Indefinite Dyad. What, if anything, makes the one an *eikon* and the other a *symbolon*?

III

For further elucidation of this, I would like to turn from Proclus' *Timaeus Commentary* to his *Commentary on the Republic*, and specifically to the essay in which he discusses the theory behind Homer's mythologising (*In Remp.* I pp. 71-96 Kroll). Here Proclus is seeking both to defend Homer from the charges made against him in the *Republic* and to defend Plato against the charge of inconsistency in his attitude to Homer. This essay makes an important distinction between *eikon* and *symbolon*,[2] and it is a rather unexpected one. How, asks Proclus (72, 9ff), can such stories about the Gods as Homer, Hesiod and even Orpheus tell — rapes, thefts, bindings, castrations and so on — bear any relation at all to divine realities? Must not stories that are to represent (ἀπεικάζεσθαι) things divine imitate the order and unspeakable transcendence of these entities? Here, I think, we have a clue. An Homeric tale, such as, say, the story of Ares and Aphrodite, does not precisely mirror the intellectual calm and unanimity in which the Gods must live. If it in fact resembles that reality in any way, it must do it indirectly. In the course of presenting the common criticism of Homeric myth, Proclus says the following (73, 11ff):

". . for these *symbola* have obviously no resemblance (οὐ ... ἐοικότα) to the essential natures of the Gods. But myths must surely, if they are not to fall short utterly of representing the truth, have *some* resemblance to the nature of things (ἀπεικάζεσθαί πως τοῖς πράγμασιν), the contemplation of which they are attempting to conceal by means of the screens of appearance (τοῖς φαινομένοις παραπετάσμασιν)."

On the other hand, he continues, Plato in many places instructs us mystically about divine matters through *eikones*, bringing in nothing shameful or disorderly or materialistic into his myths, but, while concealing his transcendent intuitions about the Gods, yet presenting by way of concealment visible images (ἀγάλματα) which accurately represent the realities of the secret theory hidden within them.

Now what is the distinction being made here? Surely it is simply that Plato's myths, and indeed the purified myths which

Socrates would propose for the poets, have in them no feature
that is *prima facie* discordant with our conception of divine
nature. That is to say, they bear on their face the signs of being
representations of *some* divine reality — though without
authorised exegesis the layman cannot say precisely what. A
poetic myth, on the other hand, with its rapes and conflicts,
does not mirror the divine nature in this direct way. Nevertheless, it does represent truths about the universe in an indirect
way, as Proclus explains further on (81, 28ff). The binding of
Kronos, for instance, represents the uniting (ἕνωσις) of the
whole creation to the intellectual and paternal transcendence
(ὑπεροχή) of Kronos (82, 14ff). These myths, we learn at 83, 9,
are *symbola*. The Gods, Proclus asserts, actually enjoy hearing
these stories about themselves; that is why such tales are a
feature of mystical rites and ceremonies (83, 18ff).

IV

But let us halt at this example of the binding of Kronos.
Why, one asks, is this a *symbolon* and not an *eikon*? As far as I
can see, the actual distinction centres round the subject matter.
It is not so much a question, I think, of whether or not the
story is discreditable or obscene on the surface — though the
myths in question normally are — as whether or not the story
seems to have a self-contained meaning, not directly pointing to
any truth beyond itself, in the way that a conscious allegory
should. A Platonic myth, or some purified (and thus allegorised)
poetic myth, we would have to maintain, is plainly representative of something else, even as a statue is plainly a statue of
someone or something, whereas an unreformed poetic myth
appears just to be a good story in its own right, as for instance
the Tale of Ares and Aphrodite.

This distinction may or may not seem cogent to us, but it
is at least, I think recognisable. The issue of immorality in the
non-iconic myths seems to me to be secondary, although in fact
both Plato and Proclus dwell on it a good deal, and of course
this 'scandal' of immoral stories had been used ever since the
beginnings of allegory as a compelling reason why these stories
must be allegorised. If we return to our original text in the
Timaeus Commentary, we may now say that the Atlantis Myth,

if it is a *symbolon* and not an *eikon*, must be taken as being a story which does not directly point to any meaning beyond itself—it is a tale of a great war of long ago, and can be regarded as simply history— whereas the recapitulation of the *Republic* has an obvious allegorical signification. We *should* also be able to add that the Atlantis story portrays divine truths in a *prima facie* discordant way. This would imply that the elements of the universe do not fight each other in the same way as the Athenians fought the Atlantids. The problem here is that in fact the elements—or rather the conflicting forces of Form and Matter—*are* fighting each other in very much this way. Why is the portrayal of their mutual relations in the *Republic* iconic, while this is symbolic?

V

But I do not wish to raise difficulties at this stage. If we are to try and confirm the distinction, the *symbolon*, in the Pythagorean system, must be seen as a higher stage of allegory than the *eikon*, first of all, perhaps, because it is more difficult to discern as being allegorical at all, but secondly, I assume, because it tends to represent more ineffable truths, truths which are not susceptible of full representation through *eikones*.

If Proclus himself observed these distinctions in an entirely consistent manner, our task would be much easier, but he does not. In an attempt to shed some further light on the question, I would like to turn now to the consideration of the allegorisation of the characters in the two dialogues *Timaeus* and *Parmenides*, together with the allegorisation of the whole introductory situation in the *Parmenides*, to see if any consistent pattern emerges.

First let us ask ourselves whether we expect the characters (πρόσωπα) of the dialogues to be *eikones* or *symbola*? In the sense that they do not *prima facie* suggest — to the normal reader — that they are representations of any 'higher' truth, one might take them to be *symbola*; on the other hand, they themselves, and their mutual relationships, might be thought to mirror Reality in the same way that the various classes in the Ideal State of the Republic do, and thus qualify as *eikones*. We must now see how the case actually stands. When the identifications of the characters are first made in the *Timaeus* Commentary (I 9, 13ff), the arrangement of the characters – that is, a trio of auditors listening to a single speaker – is described as an *eikon* of the organisation of the Universe:

> "The father of the discourse should correspond (ἀνάλογον ἑστάναι) to the father of Creation (for the creation of the cosmos in discourse is an *eikon* of the creation of the cosmos by the (demiurgic) intellect); while to the demiurgic triad which receives the unitary and generic creation of the Father, there should correspond the triad of those who receive the discourse, of whom the summit is Socrates, joining himself directly to Timaeus by reason of contiguity of life-force, even as in the paradeigmatic realm the first principle is united to that which is prior to the triad."

On the other hand, when the matter is taken up again later (I 198, 25ff, *ad Tim.* 27AB), the arrangement of speeches among the characters is described as a *symbolon* of the creation of the Universe, and the passage ends (200, 2-3) with the sentence: "These things then one may understand in some such symbolic sense as this (οὑτωσὶ συμβόλων) , without, perhaps, reading too much into them."

The sad fact is that, if one checks assiduously through Diehl's index under *eikon* and *symbolon* right through Book I of the commentary one will find the two terms used indiscriminately for characters, events, and even words and phrases. In one passage at least (94, 27f) we find both delightfully combined. The causal principles of creation are said to be represented in the Atlantis Myth 'in images through symbols' (ἐν εἰκόσι διά τινων συμβόλων). Plainly it is only when he is on his very best behaviour that Proclus maintains any strict distinction between the two terms.

In the *Parmenides* Commentary the situation is much the same. At 660, 26ff *Cousin*, the allegorical significance of the places of origin of the various characters is set out:

> "Ionia is a *symbolon* of Nature, Italy of intelligible being; Athens is symbolic of the median position between these, through which an ascent can be made from the realm of

Nature to that of Intellect for souls who are stimulated to such an ascent."

However, after a good deal more of such identifications, during which neither of our key terms is in fact used, we have the phrase 'presents an *eikon* (εἰκόνα φέρει)', employed in two successive sentences of summing up: "The above-mentioned presents an *eikon* of these realities to those not entirely incapable of observing such things." (661, 21), and, a little further down (662, 10), "All these (situations and characters) present an *eikon* of the Gods themselves, and would provide no problems to those who are willing to follow out the *analogia.*"

VI

The third basic term in our investigation has now presented itself forcefully, and we may profitably turn to an examination of it, especially as the allegorisation of the characters in the *Parmenides* Commentary makes use of it more than of either of the other terms. *Analogia* in Neoplatonic terminology always retains something of its mathematical sense of 'geometrical proportion', and is frequently so used in the course of Proclus' commentaries, but in the context of allegorical exegesis proper it signifies the correspondence between the surface meaning of the text (or of the characters, things and actions mentioned in the text) and the metaphysical truths of which it, or they, are the expression. This must have been seen as a sort of fixed mathematical relation, but it is not the sort of relation that could be stated in any kind of formula.

We may at this point suitably reintroduce the Pythagoreans. They are reported by Proclus (*In Tim.* I 33, 4ff), again in connexion with the recapitulation of the *Republic (ad Tim.* 17c), as follows:

> "The account of the Ideal State and the condensed and succinct summary of the classes within it contributed to the general presentation of these descriptions, taken as *eikones,* to (the appreciation of) general truths. And indeed this is precisely how the Pythagoreans used to go about things, tracking down the points of similarity (ὁμοιότητες) in the world on the basis of *analogiai,* and passing from *eikones* to their respective *paradeigmata.*"

The Pythagoreans, then, as we might expect of such mathe-
matically-minded folk, employed *analogiai* to discern what the
surface phenomena they dealt with were *eikones* (and presumably *symbola*) of. Once again, however, there is no clue as to
what precise rules are to be followed in fixing the *analogiai*, and
I would suggest that there were in fact none that could be
formulated. That is not to say that the resulting allegory is
arbitrary, as Fr. Amandus Bielmeier would suggest (*"Die
Wilkür hat hier im einzelnen freies Feld"*, op. cit. p. 76); it is
surely plain that it does in fact follow a fairly strict system. All
I would suggest is that the discerning of the correct 'analogies'
had to be learned by experience.

That there was a distinct sense of correctness and
incorrectness in this area is made plain by a number of passages.
At *In Tim.* I 165, 16ff, for instance, Porphyry is reported as
being criticised by Iamblichus, *à propos Tim.* 24D, for situating
Athena, as described in the passage, in the Moon. Iamblichus'
criticism is that Athena must be ranked higher than the Moon,
which is simply one of her emanations. Porphyry 'has not
correctly preserved the *analogia* (οὐ καλῶς τὴν ἀναλογίαν
διασῴζεσθαι). In the context this seems to mean something
like: 'the correct *analogia* is 1:100; Porphyry has made it
1:10'). At another point, Proclus himself, once again *à propos*
the recapitulation of the *Republic*, makes a remarkable statement. It is possible, it seems, to have various correct *analogiai* to
a given surface phenomenon (*In Tim.* I 57, 22ff):

> "And if we formerly took the πόλις (of the *Republic*) here
> below as representing the realm of generation, and now
> take it as representing the cosmic conflict, that should be
> no cause for astonishment. For it is safe to understand the
> same thing according to various *analogiai* in relation to
> different contexts."

— since, that is, the same thing by virtue of different aspects of
itself can show an *analogia* to different elements of reality. It is
possible, then, to postulate a multiplicity of correct 'analogies',
as well, of course, as a multiplicity of wrong ones.

When we turn to the allegorisation of the *personae* of the
Parmenides (*In Parm.* 628. 1ff), we find in fact that the terms
analogon and *analogia* are those chiefly used (628, 2, 21, 31,

40), though *eikon* is used once (in the phrase εἰκόνα φέρει).
Parmenides is to be taken as *analogon* to the unparticipated and
divine *Nous*, the summit of the noetic world; Zeno is analogous
to that *nous* which is participated by the divine Soul, and
Socrates represents (here ἔοικε is used, which may be taken as a
verbal form of εἰκών) the individual *nous*, capable of receiving
the divine forms. Parallel with this scheme, however, Proclus
declares that these three figures seem to him to 'preserve'
(διασῴζειν) another *analogia*, according to which they represent respectively the three moments Being, Life and Mind
within the hypostasis of *Nous*. Either of these *analogiai* are
acceptable, it seems. They both represent great metaphysical
truths.

   Analogia then, is the principle on which allegorical exegesis
is based, but when one has said that one has still not fathomed
the principles on which it is applied. If one had the rules
according to which one preserved the *analogia*, one would have
the rules of allegorical exegesis set out before one. As I say, I do
not see these rules stated anywhere in the Neoplatonic corpus,
and I do not believe that they can be stated, even though they
can plainly be learned. In the *Anonymous Prolegomena to
Platonic Philosophy*, ch. IX, we find an elaborate set of ten
rules for recognising the subject, or *skopos*, of a dialogue; if
there had been set rules for allegorising, it would be in such a
work as this that one would expect them to be set out.

VII

   This survey has not been particularly comprehensive, I
fear, but I hope that it is at least representative enough to give a
fair picture of the complexities of the situation. It seems to me
to be the case that we have, on the one hand, evidence of a
three-tiered system of Neopythagorean allegorical interpretation, perhaps first connected with the exegesis of Plato's
dialogues by Iamblichus, which Proclus reports but does not
himself follows very strictly − and which, indeed, could not be
followed very strictly in the exegesis of a Platonic dialogue −
and on the other hand, more normal Greek usage, in which the
terms *eikon* and *symbolon*, together with *analogia*, could be
used interchangeably with each other and in combination with a

good many other terms (e.g. ἐκφαίνειν, μιμεῖσθαι, ἀπεικάζειν) to express the relation between the surface meaning of the text and the truths it allegedly represented. I am concerned with trying to distinguish the essence of the Pythagorean system from the looser usage that obscures it.

It seems fairly plain that some authority on Pythago-reanism did describe the school as educating its neophytes first through images, then through symbols, and then by the direct revelation of (mystical) truth. The symbols are plainly the well-known Pythagorean Symbols, of which, as I have men-tioned already, we have a comprehensive survey at the end of Iamblichus' *Protrepticus* (ch. XXI). What might the *eikones* have been? Iamblichus' *Vita Pythagorica* might reasonably be expected to throw some light on this question, especially if, as I have suggested, he is the source of the application of this theory to Platonic exegesis, but in fact this work proves disappointing. There is indeed a good exposition of the Pythagorean theory of *symbola* in cc. 103-105, in which it is explained how the Pythagoreans veiled the truths of their doctrine with the deceptive appearance of the apparently foolish *symbola*, but there is no mention of *eikones* in this connexion, nor any suggestion of a three-tiered system, as opposed to a simple contrast of symbolic and direct instruction. Elsewhere, how-ever, in cc. 64-67, there is a discussion of the use of music in philosophic training, in the course of which music is twice (in c. 66) spoken of as an *eikon* of reality, in this case of the harmony of the universe. This may give us some idea as to what might have been regarded as an *eikon* in a three-tiered system of Pythagorean instruction, but the fact remains that there is no explicit statement of such a system in the *Vita Pythagorica*. The exact provenance of the system, as well as its proper contents, remain, as far as I am concerned, something of a mystery, on which I would welcome enlightenment from this gathering. As regards the application of it to the allegorical exegesis of the Platonic dialogues, this is all that I can find to say at present.

APPENDIX

C. S. Peirce on Icon and Symbol

While not wishing to embark on a full historical survey of the meanings of these terms in Western Literature and philosophy, I think it not unsuitable to make a brief refernce to one modern authority who makes notable use of the terms 'icon' and 'symbol', the American philosopher C. S. Peirce.

In an essay entitled *Logic as Semiotic: The Theory of Signs,*[3] Peirce produces an elaborate set of technical terms for the various possible types of sign. The only aspect of this with which I will concern myself is his definition of Icon, Index and Symbol (I include Index because it is linked closely by him with the other two, and shares in the distribution of characteristics which I find relevant to the understanding of the Neoplatonic distinction):

"A sign either an *icon,* an *index*, or a *symbol.* An *icon* is a sign which would possess the character which renders it significant, even though its object had no existence; such as a lead-pencil streak as representing a geometrical line. An *index* is a sign which would, at once, lose the character which makes it a sign if its object were removed, but would not lose that character if there were no interpretant. Such, for instance, is a piece of mould with a bullet-hole in it as sign of a shot; for without the shot there would have been no hole; but there is a hole there, whether anybody has the sense to attribute it to a shot or not. A *symbol* is a sign which would lose the character which renders it a sign if there were no interpretant. Such is any utterance of speech which signifies what it does only by virtue of its being understood to have that signification." (*op. cit.* p. 104)

Before entering upon a discussion of these definitions, I will append some further basic definitions, for those (like myself) who may be unfamiliar with Peirce's terminology:

"A sign, or *representamen*, is something which stands to somebody for something in some respect or capacity. It addresses somebody, that is, creates in the mind of that person an equivalent sign, or perhaps a more developed sign. That sign which it creates I call the *interpretant* of the first sign. The sign stands for something, its *object*." (p. 99).

First, let me reformulate what I take to be the Neoplatonic, or Neopythagorean, definitions of εἰκών and σύμβολον in terms analogous to those of Peirce. It seems to me that an εἰκών in the three-tiered Pythagorean system is a sign which would lose the character that makes it a sign if its object were removed, *or* if there were no interpretant. It seems to me, in fact, that, rather than answering to Peirce's *icon*, it combines the characteristics of his *index* and *symbol*. An *eikon* clearly points outside itself to some other thing − in Neoplatonic metaphysics, to some noetic reality. Churchill's portrait loses its specific character if *either* there is no such person as Churchill *or* if no one any long recognises Churchill. It is still a painting, but it is not, properly, a portrait of anyone. If we take the Pythagorean use of music as an example, a certain sequence of notes is only a soothing or mind-clearing sound if (as they thought) it accords with the harmony of the spheres and/or there is a mind such as to be soothed or cleared by it. Whether or not the examples from the Platonic dialogues that we have examined fit it uncomfortably, if at all. But perhaps Iamblichus (rather than Proclus) may have seen the ordering of the characters in the *Timaeus*, for instance, as having no significance at all apart from the metaphysical realities they are representing, whereas the Atlantis Myth has a clear and self-contained (historical) meaning, apart from its allegorical use.

What Peirce would call an *icon*, on the other hand, I would want to call a σύμβολον, that is, a sign which would possess the character which renders it significant, even though its object had no existence. A cigar, for instance, which could in certain circumstances stand as a symbol of Churchill, is still a cigar, even if there were no such person as Churchill. I am somewhat bothered by the distinction that Peirce makes here between an icon and an index. The mark of the pencil on the paper is a pencil mark even if there were no such thing as a geometrical straight line. It does, however, imply the previous presence of a pencil. The bullet-hole (*qua* bullet-hole) implies the previous passage of a bullet. If, however, there appears someone (a child, say) who does not understand about bullets, the hole is for him just a hole. But for a person who does not understand about pencils, there is still a mark on the paper.

I do not want to get into an argument with Peirce, however his purposes in definition are somewhat different from mine. What I find useful is his basic distinction between a sign which has no basic meaning apart from its object or interpretant, and one which has. A Pythagorean symbol, it seems to me, has an independent meaning, such a meaning as would conceal from the ordinary public that it is a sign at all. Exhortations to make one's bed when one gets up in the morning, or to avoid main roads, seem perfectly straight-forward. Even pieces of advice which might seem eccentric, such as not to let swallows into the house, or not to stir the fire with a fork, do not point in any particular direction to a meaning beyond their surface one. They have a more devious, or more hidden, relation to reality than does an *eikon*, and are thus properly introduced to the neophyte at a later stage.

In conclusion, I must confess to being by no means convinced myself that there is, normally, any clear distinction between εἰκών and σύμβολον in Proclus' system of allegory, but I hope that this investigation, together with the brief survey of Peirce's terminology, has made some contribution to the elucidation of the problem of those passages where such a distinction *is* being made.

NOTES

1. The only secondary sources which I have been unable to uncover that are of immediate relevance to the subject under discussion (and even these are of limited usefulness) are: A. Bielmeier, *Die Neuplatonische Phaidrosinterpreta-tion*, Paderborn 1930; and A. R. Sodano, 'Porfirio Commentatore di Platone', in Entretiens Hardt XII, *Porphyre*, 1965. Works on allegory in general have not proved helpful in this particular enquiry.

2. There is an interesting discussion of myths in chapters III
    and IV of Sallustius *On the God and the World*, as
    Professor John Whittaker reminds me, but, although
    Sallustius makes a division of myths into various types,
    theological, physical, ethical and so on, he nowhere makes
    a distinction between eikon and symbolon.
3. Printed in *Philosophical Writings of Peirce*, sel. and ed. J.
    Buchler. Dover Publications, 1944.
    Since writing this paper, I have come across an article by
    R. A. Marcus 'St. Augustine on Signs' (*Phronesis* 2:1, 1957),
    which contains much of interest on general questions of
    terminology, and which also, in an appendix (pp. 82-3),
    makes use of Peirce.

PART THREE

The Influence of Neoplatonism

Marius Victorinus Afer, Porphyry, and the History of Philosophy

by Mary T. Clark

Manhattanville College

For a long time and until quite recently Victorinus (4th century African Rhetor who wrote in Latin) was judged to be in the direct line of the descent of Neoplatonism from Plotinus to Augustine. This opinion prevailed not only among those who considered Victorinus' work too obscure to analyze but it was an opinion even held by Paul Henry who in this decade has produced the critical edition of Victorinus' theological treatises. But it is precisely this critical edition[1] which has brought about a growing appreciation of the differences between the metaphysics of Plotinus and that utilized by Marius Victorinus the African.

In the Plotinian triad - the One, the *Nous* and All-Soul - there is subordination of one to the other; true transcendence is present only with the One, said to be utterly incommensurable with the other two Hypostases. Simplicity both characterizes the One and differentiates it from the other two. On the other hand, Victorinus has a perfectly clear metaphysics which supports the "consubstantiality" of the three persons of the Christian Trinity. The Father is *Esse*; the Son is movement or the act which defines this *"Esse."* This movement is a double one: a movement of "life" and a movement of "knowledge". Life is that movement by which *Esse* or "to-be" communicates itself; knowledge is that movement by which it returns to itself. Father, Son and Spirit are consubstantial because as *esse*, life, and knowledge they are mutually implied. In virtue of this mutual implication, life and knowledge are originally confused with *esse* (to-be) or substance; each one of these is the other three; on this position Victorinus bases consubstantiality. The distinction between Father, Son and Spirit proceeds from "predominance." Each one is all three but gets its name from that which predominates. Thus, the Father is more characteristically "to-be" (*esse*); the Son is "to live" (*vivere*); the Spirit is "to know" (*intelligere*). This predominance has to be understood as "dynamic"; in each case it is an action which predominates: the Father exists: the Son reveals the Father: the Spirit returns all to the Father.

This philosophical trinity of Victorinus with its care for equality and consubstantiality is not to be found in the *Enneads* of Plotinus although it is present in the Hymns of Synesius.[2] The Neoplatonic source seems to be Porphyry, for apparently a similar triadism was present in Porphyry's *Philosophy of Oracles*[3] referrred to by Augustine in the City of God as *de regressu animae*; (The Soul's Return). It has been suggested by Professor O'Meara of Dublin that the latter name was given it by Victorinus when he translated it from the Greek into Latin. Furthermore, it may possibly have been among the books of the Platonists read by Augustine in the Latin version of Victorinus just prior to Augustine's intellectual conversion. Theiler thinks so.[4] This work has as its main point the soul's return to the intelligible world. It contains, moreover, an extended exegesis of the Chaldean Oracles.[5] This was probably because Porphyry was stressing that the sacraments prepared by the Chaldean Oracles were not capable of assuring a perfect purification of soul, that only a flight from the body, advocated as it was by Plato and Plotinus, could assure definite salvation to the soul. The deep epistemological reason for this was to be found in the Platonic doctrine of "knowledge by likeness"; a progressive de-materialization was needed for men to be able to approach the Principles which are purely incorporeal - the Triad of Father, Will and Intellect. In the tenth book of the *City of God* (ch. 23) we find this Porphyrian exegesis of the Oracles: the Father and the Begotten of the Father: Paternal Will and Mind. Augustine speaks of this triadism as obscure and incomprehensible. He knows it but does not follow it in his own *De Trinitate*. He is, in addition, quite aware that this is not the triadism of Plotinus. From Augustine we learn that Porphyry

> .....says, too, in the same place that "principles" can purify, lest it should be supposed, from his saying that sacrificing to the sun and moon cannot purify, that sacrificing to some other of the host of gods might not do so. And what he as a Platonist means by "principles" we know. For he speaks of God the Father and God the Son whom he calls the intellect or mind of the Father; but of the Holy Spirit he says either nothing, or nothing plainly, for I do not understand what other he speaks of as holding the middle place between these two. For if like Plotinus in his discussion regarding the three principal substances (*Ennead* V, 1), he wished us to understand by this "third" the soul of nature, he would certainly not have given it the middle place between these two, that is, between the Father and the Son. For Plotinus places the soul of nature after the intellect of the Father, while Porphyry making it the mean, does not place it after, but between the others. No doubt he spoke according to his light, or as he thought expedient; but we assert that the Holy Spirit is the Spirit not of the Father only, nor of the Son only, but of both.

Porphyry's problem, after he decided to accept the authority of the Oracles, was to explain how "life" and "intelligence" could pre-exist in the First God when Plotinus had denied any duality or plurality within the One. He found in the Plotinian *Nous* (influenced by Numenius)[6] the paradigm for a unity of being, life and thought. He then used Stoic physics[7] with its outgo and return to unity by transforming it into a metaphysics of Intelligible Reality. He preserved both Plotinian unity and Stoic expansion in distinguishing two states or rather, moments of Intelligence: repose or interiority and movement or exteriority. This reciprocal interiority of the parts of the intelligible world was able to save Plotinian unity while it would also help Victorinus in his defence of the cause of consubstantiality as defined in the Nicene Creed.

This metaphysics of Porphyry was apparently formed by the confronting of certain expressions of the Platonic *Parmen-*

ides with certain formulas of the Chaldean Oracles.[8] This re-interpretation of Plato through the authority of the Oracles led Porphyry to transform the triadism he received from Plotinus. This was a momentous decision in the history of philosophy. The distinction between "esse" and the existent which Porphyry seems to have been the first to propose in a fairly explicit fashion does indeed depart from the metaphysical past. It makes Porphyry the predecessor of the Pseudo-Dionysius, of Boethius, of John Scotus Erigena, of that emphasis upon the primacy of *esse* which is found in medieval metaphysics. Not only medieval thought, however, but surely modern philosophy shows by a study of Nicholas of Cusa, of Schelling, of Hegel the Neoplatonic influence here analyzed.

The opinion is now strongly advanced that it was under the influence of Porphyry rather than of Plotinus that Victorinus became the author of the first metaphysical treatise in all Latin literature. He (Victorinus) may indeed be the key which assists us to unlock the full metaphysical significance of Porphyry's contribution, but he is far from being the sole channel of Porphyrian thought. Chalcidius in writing his 4th century *Commentary on the Timaeus* used Porphyry's own commentary on that dialogue. Porphyry also survived in the *Isagoge* which Victorinus translated into Latin in 360 A.D. and which was used at first by Boethius. Macrobius in his *Dream of Scipio* shows the influence of Porphyry's *Commentary on the Republic*, on the *Timaeus, On the Return of the Soul, In the Sun*. It certainly seems that it was Porphyry rather than Plotinus who was the point of contact between Latin philosophers and Neoplatonism.[9] Perhaps the proper interpretation of Porphyrian metaphysics was interfered with by being channeled to the Middle Ages largely within the Aristotelian framework operating in the works of Boethius.

If Porphyry was trying, as Pierre Hadot thinks he was, to interpret in Plotinian terms the "revelation" of the Chaldean Oracles which, written in the second century, contained Platonism strongly touched with Stoicism (Middle Platonism), he could not really end up on the side of Plotinus whose First Principle was said to be without life, without thought and whose "One" gave what-it-had-not inasmuch as the Oracles affirmed a First God with life and thought, giving all it had. But perhaps Porphyry provided the metaphysics which allowed room for both the negative and the positive theology of Plotinus in the Fifth and Sixth Enneads. The negative theology is well-known. We may remind ourselves of the affirmative by reviewing those Plotinian passages where Plotinus seems carried away by the truth:

> Our inquiry obliges us to use terms not strictly applicable: we insist, once more, that not even for the purpose of forming the concept of the Supreme may we make it a duality; if now we do, it is merely for the sake of conveying conviction, at the cost of verbal accuracy.

> If, then, we are to allow Activities in the Supreme and make them depend upon will - and certainly Act cannot There be will-less-and those Activities are to be the very essence, then will and essence in the Supreme must be identical. This admitted, as He willed to be so He is; it is no more true to say that He wills and acts as his nature determines than that his essence is as He wills and acts. Thus he is wholly Master of Himself and holds his very being at his will. *Ennead* VI, 8, 13.

And also:

> Lovable, very love, the Supreme is also self-love in that He is lovely no otherwise than from Himself and in Himself. Self-presence can hold only in the identity of associated with associating; since, in the Supreme, associated and associating are one, seeker and sought one — the sought serving as Hypostasis and substrate of the seeker — once more God's being and his seeking are identical; once more, then, the Supreme is the self-producing, sovran of Himself, not coming to be as some extern willed but existing as He wills it. *Ennead* VI, 8, 15.

By a more fundamental metaphysics, a metaphysics of being rather than of unity, Porphyry provided that identification of being with activity which enabled the First Principle to be by its infinity without possibility of predication and yet self-productive by its activity. The fidelity to this deep insight of Neoplatonism that the maximum of universality as indetermination is a maximum of activity and force enabled Porphyry to justify much of what Plotinus says informally of the One in *Ennead* VI, 8, 13 and 15.

Victorinus followed Porphyry in placing act before substance. This was originally accomplished through that union of Stoicism with Platonism referred to above. Stoic substance, endowed with tonic movement, placed itself into motion. "Being" (*esse*) rendered as an infinitive is seen to be self-moving: it lives and it knows. That which differentiates the Neoplatonic Intelligible World from the Platonic or Aristotelian one is this dynamism of mind (found later in Hegel). Action which for the Stoics was the accident of bodies became with Porphyry a Subsistent Principle. The Mind transcends its determinations. Husserl's Transcendental Consciousness is incipient here. Transcendence of mind is seen as a law of being, not merely of thought; this is a metaphysics, not an idealism.

In Porphyrian metaphysics the first moment of the Intelligence coincides with the One;[10] this signifies that in its origin, in its principle, the Intelligence, or Mind is One itself. The second moment is a self-generation, a self-movement, a self-manifestation by which the mind is exteriorized in life and thought, in living thought. The One also has this double aspect; as the Absolute it is alone and incommensurable with the triadic Intelligence, but it is also the Intelligence reduced to its first moment. *Being* in repose and action explains both transcendence or unity and productivity or trinity.

Now, Pierre Hadot has well shown that the doctrinal incoherences in the plan of Victorinus' theological treatises point to the presence of purely philosophic developments placed here and there throughout the books and poorly connected with the whole work.[11] These doctrinal and philosophical "constants" as well as the Greek vocabulary[12] come from Porphyry. This particular set of doctrines found loosely situated in the writings of Victorinus is to be found also within the *anonymous commentary on the Parmenides* discovered in the late 19th century at Turin and recently attributed by Hadot to Porphyry.[13] The structure of the trinity in Victorinus and of the triad in this Commentary is identical: an initial state of immobility which is pure "to-be" (the Father), an Outgoing movement which is life, otherness, infinity; and finally a movement of self-knowledge, of return which is thought. Each of these terms implies the others; the self-generation of Intelligence is triadic; life is triadic. This Porphyrian triad is an ennead. Since they are three times three, they are One. Life was placed between the Father and the Son. When Victorinus takes up this triad, he makes the Spirit a feminine entity between the Father and Intelligence or Son. (*Adv. Ar.* I, 51, 19).

The use of the Porphyrian triad - *esse, vivere, intelligere* - by Victorinus was able to safeguard intellectually the unity of God, i.e. the consubstantiality of Father and Son and Spirit challenged as it was by Arius, but was it really an analogy that could be faithful to the relations within the Trinity?

Apparently Augustine was not satisfied with this first metaphysical treatise on the Trinity in the West. He opened his mind to the thinking on the Trinity done by the Greek Fathers and when in 415 he began his own fifteen books *On the Trinity* he sought within the human soul for analogy after analogy which could better reveal the relations between Father, Son and Holy Spirit as these were revealed in the Sacred Scriptures. Because Porphyry never cited the text of the Chaldean Oracles we cannot be sure whether he was guided by the Oracles in working out his philosophy or whether he interpreted the Oracles as he did in agreement with his own systematic interpretation of the Parmenides dialogue.

Augustine had other major disagreements with Porphyry, to such a degree that Pierre Courcelle can say:

The apologetics of the *De Civitate Dei* were addressed to Porphyry's disciples, who were so numerous in the cultured circles of Africa. Entrenched in his own experience he [Augustine] showed them the harmony that impressed him, at his conversion, between Neoplatonic doctrine and Christian dogma. St. John's prologue and the *Enneads* preached the Word of God. The dogma of the Trinity recalled the doctrine of the three hypostases, which Plotinus and Porphyry supported each in his own way. The dogma of Grace was clearly taught by Porphyry. Is it necessary to go further, like those Christian who were to find in Plato the dogma of the resurrection of the dead? Augustine did not think so (*De Civ. Dei.* XXII, 28;

Eusebius *Praep.* XI, 33), for after long years in the
episcopate he perceived the irreducible oppositions that
distinguished Porphyrian philosophy from Christian
dogma. The incarnation of the Word, the resurrection of
the flesh - these problems were a scandal to the Hellenes,
so profoundly did they scorn the body in pride of spirit.[14]

But while we note the theological contradictions we must
note the metaphysical originality of Porphyry. Even if Augustine's efforts were rewarded to the extent that his *De Trinitate*
has become the standard work on the Trinity in the Christian
West so that Aquinas added little to it, this should not obscure
the greatness of the first step taken by Marius Victorinus the
African when from Porphyry he accepted and worked with the
First Principle as *Esse* and for the first time designated Being as
activity, simple and infinite, a Principle from which substance is
constituted. This Porphyrian analysis, even if it did remain
literally faithful to the Chaldean Oracles and unfaithful to the
declared teaching of Plotinus, yet rendered philosophic justice
to that Plotinian Intelligible World where all is Life! But what
Porphyry explicitly added was the insight into be-ing as
fundamental. In this respect he became the originator of a new
metaphysics. After him Boethius will indeed say that the "to
be" of things is derived from the divine to-be. Because the
philosophical world has only recently become aware of all this,
it can be truly said that many histories will need to be revised.

NOTES

1. Marius Victorinus, *Candidi Arriani ad Marium Victorinum
    Rhetorem de generatione Divina. Adversus Arium. De
    Homoousio Recipiendo. Hymnus* I, II, III. Sources
    Chrétiênnes, Paris, Les Editions du Cerf, 1960.
2. Synesius, *Hymni et opuscula*, ed. N. Terzaghi, I-II, Roma,
    Regia officina polygraphica, 1939-1944.
3. John J. O'Meara, *Porphyry's Philosophy from Oracles in
    Augustine,* Paris, Etudes Augustiniennes, 1959.

4.   Willy Theiler, *Porphyrios und Augustin*, Halle. Schriften der Konigsberger gelehrten Gesellschaft, vol. 10, 1, 1933. Paul Henry, *Plotin et L'Occident*, Louvain, Spicilegium Sacrum Lovaniense, 1934, pp. 46-47.
5.   W. Kroll, *De oraculus Chaldaicis,* Breslau, Breslauer philologische Abhandlungen, vol. 7, 1, 1894. Psellus, *Expos. oraculus Chaldaicis*, P.G. 122, 1136-
6.   Numenius, *Testimonia et fragmenta*, (ed) E. A. Leemans, Bruxelles, Acad. royale de Belgique, Classe de Lettres, Memoires, t. 37, 2, 1937.
7.   Pierre Hadot, *Porphyre et Victorinus,* Vol. I, Paris, Etudes Augustiniennes, 1968, p. 489.
8.   *Ibid.*, pp. 102-146.
9.   Pierre Courcelle, *Late Latin Writers and their Greek Sources*, Cambridge, Mass. Harvard University Press, 1969, pp. 415-418: "The dissemination of Porphyry's principal works throughout the entire civilized West, from the end of the fourth century to the beginning of the sixth, is significant."
10.   Porphyry, *On the Parmenides*, 143a. cf. Marius Victorinus, *Adv. Ar.* IV, 241, *Adv. Ar.* I, 57, 7.
11.   Pierre Hadot, *Porphyre et Victorinus*, II, *Textes*, Paris, Etudes Augustiniennes 1968.
12.   *Ibid.* In this volume P. Hadot provides an Index of the Greek philosophic words used by Victorinus and an Index of the vocabulary of the Fragments of the *Commentary on the Parmenides* of Porphyry.
13.   W. Kroll, *Ein neuplatonischer Parmenidescommentar in einem Turiner Palimpsest*, in Rheinisches Museum, t. XLVII, 1892, pp. 599-627.
14.   Pierre Courcelle, *op. cit.* p. 419.

Schelling's Neoplatonic System-Notion: *'Ineinsbildung'* and Temporal Unfolding

by Michael G. Vater

Marquette University

I

It is difficult to document the full influence of Neoplatonism upon the development of Schelling's thought, for he is a philosopher at once original and eclectic, situated in his own time and yet able to think within the inherited traditions. His 'Neoplatonism' is more a matter or affinities holding between his thought and the themes and preoccupations of the Neoplatonists than one of bookish or directly textual inheritance.[1] Early in his speculative career his contact with Neoplatonism comes through Spinoza and Leibniz, particularly the former. He is in contact with the 'tradition' from the start, but it hardly need be said that the 'tradition' has very little of the text and spirit of Neoplatonism about it after it has passed from Proclus to the Areopagite, from Dionysius into all of scholastic thought and finally come to light again in Spinoza. Schelling did not read Plotinus, not seriously at any rate, until 1804[2] and he did not begin to make contact with the text of Proclus until 1820.[3] Even then his acquaintance with Neoplatonism is fragmentary, more speculative than scholarly. This indeed is Schelling's typical style of thought. Most of his positions and the dynamic of their growth spring from the contemporary philosophical arena. In his younger days, prior to 1801, his wrestling with Kant and then Fichte about the limitations of a "*Reflexions-philosophie*" shapes his thought. Later in life, after 1820, the conflict with Hegel (and with his younger self that authored the System of Identity) over the limitations of reason itself is determinative. Typically Schelling will range historical precedents and justifications around these contemporary conflicts, and treat them with quite a free hand. Usually the Platonic traditions are assimilated to Schelling's own positions, and not just in one period but throughout the whole course of development of his central and all-determinative problematic— the confrontation of reason as philosophical system with intractable individuality, with facticity.[4] Platonism alone seems to have a philosophical language, a way of getting beyond the fragmentary and expressing the eternal, or rather, it is a model of thought guided by intellectual intuition bending the "patchwork of our language" to philosophical employment.[5] Platonism alone stands outside of the snarl of discordant but equally erring positions which makes up modern philosophy; it alone escapes 'Reflexion' and stands inside the truth.[6]

Schelling's respect for the Platonic and Neoplatonic traditions is not abstract; he sees himself living within the tradition, thinking its thought. It is no accident, then, that at the most crucial stage of his philosophical formation, the point where he feels he has achieved a satisfactory grasp upon 'system' and elevated philosophy above Fichtean subjectivity and reflexion, he announces the claim in Neoplatonic guise. The dialogue *Bruno* of 1802 represents historical Neoplatonism in the person of Anselm as the philosophical synthesis of all the conflicting traditions of ancient thought, the radical pluralism of materialism and the radical monism of Eleatic thought; Neoplatonism alone is conceptually inside the mystery which beauty shows and demonstrates, the unity of the divine and the natural, the intertwining of the eternal and the insubstantial individual through the mediation of ideas in their productive or 'psychic' function.[7] In the same way, the dialogue represents in the person of Bruno the philosophical synthesis of the modern world, the reconciliation of idealism (Fichte's *Wissenschaftslehre*) and ralism (Schelling's philosophy of nature). Schelling repeatedly stresses the cognate nature, even the continuity, of the two syntheses; just as Neoplatonism bound the disparate worlds of sense and spirit together through the notion of ideas and the illusory or autolimited character of the finite, so the System of Identity combines realism and idealism, at one and the same time saves the concreteness of philosophy and guarantees the comprehensiveness of its systematic grasp.[8] Schelling perceives himself as taking up and continuing *in pertinent terms*, the questions namely of philosophical *Wissenschaft*, the Neoplatonic problematic of system and structure—the question of the reconciliation of opposites, of the ingathering of the fragmentary and (on its own terms) inexplicable into a world, of the restoration of psyche to its appropriate level of functioning.

Schelling puts on the person of Giordano Bruno, then, and represents himself as the modern Neoplatonist, even though his knowledge of Bruno was scant and entirely second-hand.[9] Neoplatonism means for him above all *systematic* thought, speculation which reconciles, integrates, harmonizes and achieves a point of view transcending conflict and opposition. In this sense all systematic philosophy is 'Neoplatonism,' the conceptual ascent to the vision of the eternal or the Absolute within the dialectic of the finite and the infinite, the isolated thing and the conceptual order.[10] The sole object of all philosophy is "the Idea of ideas"—the union of the universal and the particular, of species and individual, the Idea which is in itself "the undividedness of the already differentiated from the One."[11]

The *Bruno* is not an isolated instance. Since his earliest speculative days as a disciple of Kant and Fichte, Schelling had thought along the lines of the Neoplatonic problematic of the unity of being. The task was to bring Criticism to the status of system, to make it science or the mutual interpenetration and reciprocal determination of form and content.[12] In 1801, with the first announcement of the 'System of Identity,' Schelling lays claim to a comprehensive structural grasp of the totality of phenomena, to a system grounded in the ultimate non-difference or togetherness of a substantial unity like the Neoplatonic One and the structures of subjectivity-objectivity which scientific analysis of phenomena reveals.[13] The *Presentation of My System* is deeply stamped with both the methodological and structural rigor of Spinoza,[14] and the notion of

togetherness of being through structure, of identical articulation
in the real and in the ideal working a total congruence of
philosophical knowledge and reality, continues the tradition of
Neoplatonism as transmitted from Proclus to Pseudo-Dionysius
to Aquinas and come to flower again in Spinoza and Leibniz
among the moderns.

Schelling is not a 'modern Neoplatonist' in that he adopts
a classic notion of system. Rather he attempts to think the
notion of system, and to be guided by reason's *demand* for
system. It is not any achieved system that draws his speculative
attention, but its *possibility* in a unified and intelligible world
and its *necessity* for the shaping of such a world in concepts.[15]
Thus in the System of Identity we identify the Neoplatonic
influence not so much with any imitation of a type-ektype
metaphysics or any mirroring of orders of procession and
reversion as with the concern for apprehending being as
structured, thus ultimately graspable as a whole. It is because
his guiding problematic is the Neoplatonic search for the inner
order and coherence of being that Schelling's system takes on
typically Neoplatonic forms in its unfolding. For it is the
demand of systematizing reason that isolated particularity give
way to integral totality which raises the Platonic question of the
legitimacy of the finite, which suggests that the only individuals
containable within the system are purely formal or structural
instances of the system-principle (identity)—these are the
"Potencies" or groupings of beings akin to Neoplatonic hypostases, later the "ideas" or universal individuals—and which
finally sees individuation or the multiplication of the finite as
an ultimate surd, a "fall" from the rationality of system.[16] And
it is the system-demand which pushes Schelling beyond the
formal System of Identity, its confrontation with the ultimacy
and permanence of individuation that forces his turn to the
philosophy of spirit developed 1809 and thereafter.

II

It would generally be more useful in establishing the
Neoplatonic trend in his thought to contrast Schelling's precise
system-notion with its historical Neoplatonic counterparts

rather than merely indicate affinities.[17] The Neoplatonic system grew out of a definite world and in response to definite problems and it is obvious that any use of Neoplatonism, even any attempt to rethink its fundamental problematic along with it, must leave this determining context behind. We shall understand more of Schelling's Neoplatonism, especially his concern for system, if we make quite clear how it differs from the historical models Plotinus and Proclus provide.

The basic impulse to system is a will to wholeness, to totality of grasp, to a conceptual outworking of a unity of being. For the historical Neoplatonists the possibility of this unified grasp of being lies in being itself, on the side of the objective. A basic sense of the term τὸ εἶναι for Plotinus, for instance, is that kind of order, coherence and organic unity necessary for there to be a world. Being is the possibility of cosmos.[18] For something to be, in a pertinent sense, is for it to be capable of taking its place in a world (or system), to be "in the intelligible" or to be in that which is a cosmos in virtue of its dependence upon the intelligible. Being also signifies, or is at least synonymous with, organism or living totality; at the appropriate level of being, as Plotinus sees it, intellection and life and existence all coincide, viz. in nous.[19] Being is a living whole, and the task of system is to apprehend it as such, through the discovery of the lines of outpouring unity and epistemic-psychic reunification, through the discovery of structure.

Proclus, though insisting upon linearity of structure more than Plotinus, is no less intent upon thinking the Whole as organically united. With his emphasis on casuality and participation he brings to light more forcefully than Plotinus the ancient world's demand for unity and finitude as the defining parameters of system.[20] For Proclus system is or reflects the work of casuality; all that exits is gathered into a Whole through structures of asymmetrical relation or subordination. Sequence is subordination, and all our logic, consequently all our knowledge, is grounded in that differentiation-in-continuity which sequence bring about, namely casuality.[21] Causality unifies; sequence leads back to an origin, a first. The system, a reflection of the work of casuality, leads the totality back to unity.

For the Neoplatonists, then, the chief category behind the system-notion is unity. Now Schelling indeed shares this taste for the organic integrity of being, but thinks it not through unity alone, but through a dialectic of *unity and totality* in which ultimately abstract original unity proves to be a vanishing moment.

The category of totality is the key to Schelling's system-notion. He is a philosopher in the transcendental tradition and conducts his metaphysical inquiries from the vantage-point of the question: How is a world possible for me? For him system is not merely a unified accounting of a pre-articulated whole of being, not a total enumeration of the given, but the totalization of being as it is articulated inside *Wissenschaft*. It must be imagined as in some sense active and processive, through not in any discursive way, since it is not a matter of dividing off item from item but of moving within the whole. "One cannot describe reason; it must describe itself in everything and through everything."[22] Only for systematic reason is there a universe. The totality is unified only in being brought to the unity of the Absolute in reason, and yet that unity or Absolute Identity *is* and *is real* only as totality. "Absolute Identity is not cause of the universe, but the universe itself."[23]

Schelling's system-notion is generally distinguished from that of the Neoplatonists in three ways: (1) Schelling's system is committed to unity *and totality*, and he will in no way allow the Whole to be thought away for the sake of the One; (2) he refuses to think the unity-totality relation through any thing-oriented or thing-modelled schema such as part-and-whole; (3) he denigrates causality to a merely phenomenal linkage, a bridge between appearances and itself an expression of an unbridgeable gulf between actuality and possibility.[24] Structure, the backbone of system, is not unidirectional asymmetrical relation (like subordination and causality) but is reciprocity, coordination, the commutation of opposites. The stamp of Fichte's influence upon Schelling is evident here: Causality links appearances, but reciprocity links, or strives to link, the opposed metaphysical orders of subjectivity and objectivity.

Schelling's system-notion is further distinguished from the Neoplatonic sources in its fundamental direction. For Schelling, unlike the historical Neoplatonists, theory overtakes and comprehends praxis. There is no goal or purpose for system extrinsic to itself, no life-goal for whose sake system is pursued. The will to system is first and foremost an affair of knowledge, or to put it somewhat differently, *knowing* is the decisive act of spirit, the act in which spirit is most 'about itself,' and it is not in any way for the sake of any finite thing, act, or even self. Schelling insists, therefore, that systematizing knowledge, philosophy constructed in "intellectual intuition," as he calls it, is not characterized by subjectivity or centration upon a 'self,' but rather by an abstraction from subjectivity, an 'ecstacy' or abandonment of self.[25] "That I say, 'I know, I am the knower,' this is the πρῶτον ψεῦδος."[26]

The knowing which Schelling considers constitutive of system is indeed act; it is the work of will—but not of will centered and particularized (*Eigenwille*); rather it is general will, *Verstand*.[27] It is this type of comprehending activity of man as spirit, at once both a knowing and a founding, which Schelling termed *intellectual intuition*. It is the organ of *Wissenschaft* or systematic philosophy and it defines system's stance as primarily theoretical. Later in the Philosophy of Freedom Schelling redefines intellectual intuition and maintains that the activity constitutive of system (the temporal division and reconciliation of the opposed principles, Ground and Existence) delivers man back to his primal status as the Word, the expression of the Absolute, at once the medium of and the witness to Creation. Since he is at the center of being and like to that center, man as spirit carries a con-science (*Mitwissenschaft*) of the Creation; all things are contained in that knowledge and man does not so much know them in it as he is *himself that science.*[28]

In Schelling's eyes, then, system is a self-enclosed, self-founding theoretical whole. System is self-bearing, self-containing, and even of the static System of Identity it is not inaccurate to suggest that in some sense system is subject, the self-enactor.[29]

In the System of Identity Schelling sees system, or the Absolute which system in a sense creates and in a sense reflects, as a theoretical or conceptual enterprise which consists in the equilibration or indifferencing of the subjective and objective aspects in all real beings. The primal or substantial being is Identity. Its formal or cognitive character is subjectivity-objectivity. And the work of system is to identify or balance out knower and known in things, to reduce them to a structure of subject-objectivity and incorporate them within identity. System takes its origin in intellectual intuition, the indifference of knower and known, and *proves* out that indifference in the totality of phenomena. It is the establishment of intellectual intuition, its concretion, the revelation that the structure it represents at first abstractly as the 'identity of the differentiated' actually structures the world and brings it to 'system' or togetherness in the conceptual.[30]

In the course of Schelling's development there is a crucial change in the way he conceives system, a change coincident with the shift of his intense interest from philosophy of nature to philosophy of spirit between 1806 and 1809. While in the perspective of the Identity-System spirit and subjectivity were seen to *dwell within* system's comprehension and to be innate in system's self-movement, with the *Essay on Human Freedom* the perspective is reversed and system becomes the decisive act of spirit, the product of freedom's conquering over the facticity of the Ground, the effect and the instrument of Ego's ultimate conquering of Non-Ego in the historical and world-creating division and reconciliation of being.[31] Spirit's life is now seen to be the production of system and structure, the subjugation of nature to history, the rescuing of intelligibility or "world" from facticity. As different as this notion of spirit's activity is from the stasis of intellectual intuition in the System of Identity, the fundamental system-notion has not altered. 'Spirit' which decides the structure of being in its activity is not subjective, centered upon a self, but is the original subject, the locus of $\theta\epsilon\omega\rho\iota\alpha$ or the conscience of Creation, the agent active in intellectual intuition.

The basic impulse and direction of the Neoplatonic system-notion, in contrast, is toward praxis, toward the definitive establishment of the subjective as the core of being. In both its Plotinian and Procline forms it bears the stamp of Socratic-Platonic interiority; system is not for disinterested contemplation, but for actuation of the self. While the conceptual or theoretical burden of Neoplatonic system is the founding of the togetherness of μέθεξις and ἔρως, the equilibration of the ontological and the psychic order or the orders of procession and reversion, ultimate philosophical interest is centered upon psyche and its reintegration into the true order of being.

For the Neoplatonists being has already unfolded itself into a structured Whole, a Whole, however, which is less than its origin. In some sense the process of production is falsity, the establishment of being upon the basis of non-being, and the only *use* of the articulated structure into which being has unfolded in its going-forth is to undo the complexity, to reascend to simplicity and unity. In Plotinus, for instance, the chief interest is psychic rather than metaphysical; his concern is for elevation, transcendence, conversion, union with a substantial Absolute, and *not* the further discernment and expression of structure in the world which is Schelling's concern. Even for Proclus, seemingly obsessed with the outworking of a mechanical causality in the cosmos, the whole point of structure is the possibility of psychic return. The meaning and importance of procession is reversion, and it is only this possibility of inwardness and self-concentration at every level of being which rescues any multipliticy from utter dispersal.[32] For both Plotinus and Proclus the goal of philosophy is practical and religious, the actuation of self—or rather the de-activation of that dependent and outward self which moves among imperfectly unified multiplicities.

For Schelling system is creative of world; for the Neoplatonists it holds out the possibility of transcending the world. As Schelling's thought evolves from 1794 to 1821 (the beginning of the Late Philosophy) the notions of expression, bringing into the light, the issuance of godhead into creative divinity more and more dominate his system-notion. Intellectual intuition becomes more outgoing, manifestive, productive. It recovers its original Kantian sense of a creative or constitutive act of knowing.[33] System becomes ex-pression, the mirror of divine Creation. In Plotinus, by way of contrast, knowledge is always introverted, secretive and restorative, a struggle back through externality to unity—ultimately to the One, to the Unmanifest.

III

An examination of the exact meaning of 'structure' within the system-notions of Schelling and the Neoplatonists and an analysis of their respective models of structure (*Ineinsbildung* and hypostasis) strengthens the impression that Schelling pursues the Neoplatonic system-problematic in a way markedly different from his historical predecessors.

For Schelling structure is the work of intellectual intuition, a knowing in which the subjective and objective are balanced-out, brought into equipollence, but not abolished as opposite.[34] Structure originates in reason's activity, then, or grows out of the root presupposition of any knowing that there must be a convergence of knower and known,[35] and it proves itself out or legitimates its function of articulating being by making system possible, by facilitating the philosophical 'construction' of the world. Through the indifference of subjectivity and objectivity in intellectual intuition a *world* is first made possible, a grasp of the differentiated finite particulars in all the orders both of nature and spirit such that their *community, interdependence* and radical *ontological* sameness are made to appear. Each particular is revealed to be, at bottom, not an independent substance but an *instance* of substantial Identity (which as expressed or manifest in 'form' is subject-objectivity). The opposition of nature and spirit is shown to be only relative, as is that of object and subject; they are indifferential structures differently indexed or overbalanced, only directionally opposed then, equally grounded in the indifferential relationality which is at once the standpoint, agent, and presupposition of intellectual intuition.[36]

System is all a matter of like knowing the like, i.e. of spirit moving in intellectual intution, or abstraction from subjectivity, recognizing the same structural equipollenence of opposites which is its life in knowledge as the founding structure of all things transparent to knowledge and able to be brought to system. This indifference in knowledge—the non-ultimacy of the subject-object distinction—coincides with and mirrors the substantial Identity at the basis of things. Indifference means the non-difference of knower and known, that, without any abrogation of their opposition, what the one is, the other is also.[37]

As Schelling conceives it, indifference characterizes not only the differentiated unity of subject and object *inside* knowledge, it determines the convergence of knowing and being as such. The 'form' of the Absolute—that is, its infinite position as differentiated subjects and objects in a world—is indifferent with its substantial or in-itself aspect, absolute Identity, and thus it is that system is possible.[38] Structure is discoverable *in the world* because, on one side, knowing is articulation or the imposition of structure, and because, on the other, being is already articulated, because at its most substantial level, it is a knot of identity and difference open to the glance of reason. Thus every being is an instance of indifference, fundamentally alike, or comparable with, every other being; structure recurs throughout the whole and makes possible groupings, totalities; every being recapitulates all others.[39] This way in which the articulation of thought and the articulability of being as structure dovetail into one another makes it apparent why Schelling's dominant image of the work of system-building reason is speaking, expression. *System is language*; spirit speaks in the world; reason discovers the intelligibility of the given and makes it into a world. In its active aspect as expression, as spirit, it is self-affirmation, the expressed bond between all things, a stamp which imprints its own character on all it comes into contact with, the "All-Copula." In its objective aspect, it is system.

Whereas Schelling's notion of system-structure derives from the subject-object polarity discoverable in knowing, for the Neoplatonists structure is basically a matter of the interrelation or derivation of beings, objective entites not wholly dependent upon structural relationships for their being, in some sense substantial in their own right. Structure, the possibility of system, is conceived ontologically. It is not an affair of the psyche and its realms of experience, but of the relations which obtain between beings on account of *production* and *derivation*. There is a general and comprehensive order of relations which beings have as beings or as hypostases come-to-stand in virtue of transcendent Unity, and this objective order of relations determines and circumscribes the place of subjectivity, even of that intellective act above psyche which is like what Schelling called subjectless intellection or intellectual intuition.

Determinative of the Neoplatonic cosmos, then, are not the ways of thought but certain abstract and objective principles—we might call them principles of integrity, sufficiency and power. Every integral being is productive, and every kind is linked to lesser kinds through production, maintains Plotinus, and this kind of linkage through production is virtually the only generalized and non-metaphorical attempt at explaining the process of hypostasis he makes.[40] Proclus takes over the same explanation as the chief principle of procession, holding that a being which has power necessarily acts to the utmost of its power and *produces*, or else it is sterile and imperfect.[41]

Production is not simply the communication of being and unity, though. The responsibility for there being further hypostasis beyond any given level of production involves a possibility of return, a possibility of re-centration. The full system-notion is production *and* return, procession and reversion, i.e. there is a gatheredness of being because all beings have a common origin and derive from one another in sequence *and* can return to that unity and in fact do strive toward that unity as their end.

As the Neoplatonists conceive it, there must be something of a lack in production, at least on the side of the produced or derivative hypostasis. For it is only such a lack, such a dependence on the prior whence a being derives its (relative) independence, which can compel an eventual turning about, a turning inward. Reversion is in some sense an undoing of production, a reflection on the Neoplatonists' part of the primitive Platonic feeling that spirit is somehow lost in the world, even a world gathered into an ordered and graded totality of perfection. We might say that there is at least one aspect of production which is a lessening of perfection and integrity, so that, at best, it is neutral or accidental that being has gone forth from unity, that differentiation has occurred.[42]

When contrasted with Schelling's notion of system as expression, as world-creating, there appears to be a kind of introversion in the Neoplatonic system-idea of production. The actualization of the further possibility for being which production represents is in fact a perfection only inasmuch as it is a perfection of the origin and producer. The Whole is perfected not by some further addition, some further expression and stabilization of the primal power, but by that power's self-containment as superior when being goes forth to further hypostasis. The concept of hypostasis means mutual externality in the outflow of productive power; it means that beings produce beings without the prior being touched, altered or in any way affected. There is a communication of being and integrity, and yet at the same time a distancing.[43] There is gatheredness of dispersed being or κοινωνία only through causal ranking and hierarchy.[44]

IV

We can proceed from this point to isolate the system-logic and determine the model of structure at work in Schelling's philosophy as contrasted with that of the historical Neoplatonists. The whole difference in their respective approaches to system will be formulable through a contrast between reason as commutation of opposites (*Ineinsbildung*) and the Plotinian idea of hypostasis as double-act.

We might analyze the differing system-logics in terms of a fundamental relation and the rule or operation of its application. For Schelling the relation is identity in intellectual intuition, the organic indifference of subjectivity and objectivity. The operation whereby it is applied is equilibration, commutation of opposites, the mutual in-and uni-forming of subjectivity and objectivity into one another. In reason's intuition the isolated particular is reduced to a formula, to an instance of differently indexed indifference. The overbalanced indifference of the isolated individual is balanced-out in relative totalities (the potencies) in both nature and spirit, and the cycles of recurring structure converge into an organic unity. Behind this whole activity of intellectual intuition is *Ineinsbildung*, commutation of opposites; it is only because of reason's ability to see one objective phenomenon, e.g. electrochemical reactions, as more subjective than another, say magnetic attraction, that the whole structural viewpoint which is the basis of system can be introduced.

This *Ineinsbildung* is an intermediation of strict identity and the instanced identity of the universe, totality. Through this commutation the absolute Identity which is reason's postulate and fundamental law, hence the one *substantial* moment which must be conceived to underlie system, is reflected into and revealed in the totalized relative identities or points of indifferential structure which are the world.[45] As Schelling sees it, the One and the Totality not only coexist, but are of equal rank and priority, built into one another, ultimately differentiable not as substances but only as aspects.[46]

In the Neoplatonic system-logic the basic relation is the identity of self-relation or self-centration, which when instanced in pure form is sufficiency. This relation is imposed upon a kind of quantified, or better, geographical grid which combines the gradations from inner to outer, from one to many, and from more down to less one upon the other. The result is hierarchy, asymmetrical interdependence of beings—*cosmos* as a simple function of series and subordination. As Proclus especially makes clear, the structure of being is wholly vertical, simply transcendence-and-subordination. Hierarchy is established not organically and through replicative structure, but in terms of a single scale whose defining terms are either simplicity or dispersal of ideally self-centrating activity.[47]

The Neoplatonic system-notion has built into it an irrevocable commitment to particulars and to substantiality, however much its basic impulse, working toward a community of being, demands the sublimation of the externality of objective being into that inwardness in which psyche at its fullest powers moves. Schelling's notion of the systematizing power of reason involves, on the other hand, a commitment to overcoming particularity, to abolishing the substantiality of the individual and to the redefinition of 'the substantial' in systematic terms, i.e. as a function of totality and structure.

The two system-notions are indeed similar, for system is, after all, a thorough-going interconnection and interrelation of particulars, no matter how accomplished. They are similar, but do not coincide. And a final comparison of the ideas of *Ineinsbildung* and hypostasis will show that for Schelling, *system is dependent upon overcoming individuality* as such, while for the Neoplatonists it is dependent upon the maintenance of differentiation through order and hierarchy.

Both Plotinus and Proclus, when they speak technically of hypostasis, talk not only of production or περίλαμψις or participation but of a certain double-functioning or double-power constitutive of each being on each level of being which guarantees both production and differentiation of levels. Proclus states the idea rather baldly at first: "Every productive cause produces the next and all subsequent principles while remaining steadfast within itself,"[48] glossing over the question of power, act, and communication of actuality with his as yet uninterpreted notion of causality. Later he remarks that causality is possible only because the nature of power (δύναμις) is twofold. There is an active and a passive sort of power, and the two are interlocked so that all coming to be is an interfunctioning of the two, the one power active and so 'causative,' the other an imperfect power and so merely potential or dependent upon the former for perfection.[49]

This double-power schema is a translation of Plotinus more unwieldy (and infrequently employed) notion of hypostasis as a double- ἐνέργεια into Proclus' typical language of causality. The clearest instance of the Plotinian notion occurs in *Ennead* V. 4. 2: 26-37:

> ...But how can an act of intellection come to be if this primary intelligible remains in itself? We must distinguish two kinds of act, one of which is *of* each substance itself, the other of which is *out of* that same being. The first activity of the being is identical with the being itself; the one from it and out of it, necessarily following upon it, is something different from it ... From the one act remaining in its native place and element and reaching its fulfillment there, comes a begotten activity, intellection, which takes hypostasis. Since it comes from the greatest of all powers it attains to full being and substantiality.[50]

This notion of double-functioning is Plotinus' device for translating the ὄντα-εἴδωλα structure of Platonic ontology into metaphysical categories incorporating the dynamism and stress on organic coherence of Aristotle's ontology. The quality of life, which Plotinus so characteristically associates with substance or being, expresses the basic capacity of anything real to produce an image that is living, an offshoot that attains to hypostasis in its own right.

And yet hypostasis remains a process of individuation more than one of communication; it is centration, concretion of activity to hard particularity. Hypostasis is defined from the point of view of production, a category of objectivity, and so can have that life and intermediation which Schelling suggests in the idea of commutation or *Ineinsbildung* only derivatively. All the relations which define hypostasis are vertical, whereas the dominant idea in Schelling's distinguishing a 'substantial' and 'formal' aspect of the Absolute, in his making its life their inbuilding, is that of *reciprocity* or a *play* inside systematic knowledge (and inside it point of origin, intellectual intuition), a movement at once vertical and horizontal, a movement that defines a structure for the phenomenal world, but does not abolish its concreteness in doing so. The activity of systematic reason in its inbuilding, in its play, encompasses and comprehends all isolated factors, brings them together for the first time into a cosmos.[51]

This play of inbuilding opposite aspects into one another is what Schelling calls the 'formal' aspect of the Absolute, that element responsible, as it were, for its self-knowledge. This 'form,' already a process of inbuilding subjective and objective tural basis for all, builds itself into the Absolute's substance— pure Identity—and in turn reflects that identity in its processes of integration.[52] Form or *Ineinsbildung* conquers over substantial identity inside systematic knowledge, over the unmanifest and unarticulated Neoplatonic One. *Ineinsbildung* thus is in one sense the destruction of what is ontologically prior, pure unity, and in another sense the reconstruction or 'saving' of that unity on the level of spirit's own identity—its own bridging life of knowledge which bring isolated particulars into a world, which is not content with externality and sequence, but demands organic unification.[53] It is a movement from being to being's construction in thought, and in that respect it is similar to historical Neoplatonism's turn away from objective externality toward the inwardness of psyche. And yet, if it is a turn toward the inner it is *also* a redirection outward, an expression, a reconstruction of the universe as given as a universe adequate to spirit's way of being. It is not an ascent to a higher cosmos, a τόπος νοητός, but the first formation of cosmos.

More and more as Schelling moves toward the Philosophy of Freedom and *Ineinsbildung* becomes not the already-accomplished work of the Absolute standing behind and constitutive of system but the timely task of the human spirit living in history, thus an active process, does he approach endorsing a fully dualistic notion of system. The ontological polarity of Ground and Existence, the philosophical polarity of factical individuality and conceptual systematic grasp, and the temporal process of division and revelation in spirit's life which these polarities occasion all indicate a definitive turn away from Greek ways of thought on Schelling's part, an abandonment of the Neoplatonic system-problematic with its demand for unity, hierarchy, integrity as oneness and completeness as *stasis*. Indeed in following out the problem of individuality which developed in the System of Identity and in the recognition of facticity in the Philosophy of Freedom, Schelling comes close to endorsing an eternal matter[54]—or a permanent Non-Ego—over and against which the spiritual (God and man, together in the Creation) must progressively define itself, not only inwardly in knowledge, but outwardly in time and in history.

NOTES

1. Werner Beierwaltes has carefully enumerated most of the pertinent affinities in *Platonismus und Idealismus* (Frankfurt a.M., 1972) pp. 100-144. More to our interest and more central to the concerns of this paper is his suggestion that these affinities grow from one central point, from a shared problematic—a concern for 'the One as the principle of philosophy, a principle discoverable only in and through spirit's work of freedom (p. 144).

2. 1804 was a year of critical Platonic and Neoplatonic influence upon Schelling. In February he thanks Windisch-

mann for his German translation of the *Timaeus*, remarking that he is tempted to read it as a late or Christian document, not a product of antiquity. *Aus Schellings Leben in Briefen*, ed. G. L. Plitt (Leipzig, 1869) vol. II, pp. 8-9. Later the same month he thanks Windischmann for the edition of Jacob Boehme he has sent. Plitt, II, p. 10. In April he requests the works of Bruno and the Ficini edition of Plotinus. Plitt, II, p. 16.
In September of 1805 he requests Windischmann to send other Plotinian texts on the nature of matter, time, space, death and finitude. Curiously enough, in the same letter he admits that the Platonic-sounding term *Abfall* whereby he had been trying to indicate the adventitious character of the finite considered in itself was only metaphorical and unsuited for conducting exact analysis. Plitt, II, pp. 72-73.

3.   Beierwaltes, *op. cit.*, p. 104n.
4.   There is a kind of achieved consensus in recent Schelling scholarship that the variegated sixty-year career of speculation, for all of its apparent changes, pursues one central problematic and has one metaphysical preoccupation alone, viz, the testing of systematic speculation against 'the real.' Schelling's ultimate contribution is seen to be the limitation of the notion of system, the discovery of intractable individuality and the facticity of even spirit. Cf. W. Schulz, *Die Vollendung des deutschen Idealismus in der Spätphilosophie Schellings* (Stuttgart & Cologne, 1954), J. Habermas, *Das Absolute und die Geschichte* (Bonn, 1954), Martin Heidegger's 1936 lectures *Schellings Abhandlung uber das Wesen der menschlichen Freiheit* (Tübingen, 1971), and F. W. Schmidt, *Zum Begriff der Negativität bei Schelling und Hegel* (Stuttgart, 1971). For the limited purpose of this discussion we find it useful to make these relative distinctions in Schelling's development. The young Schelling's work is diverse but most original in its concern with nature, so we shall call the years 1794-1800 the 'Philosophy of Nature.' The years 1801-1806 are the System of Identity. The works of 1809 - 1815 are appropriately called the System of Freedom, and the writings of 1821-1854 the Late Philosophy or the Positive Philosophy.

5. Vom Ich. *Schellings Werke* (nach der Original-ausgabe in neuer Anordnung, ed. M. Schröter) Munich, variously 1959-1968, 1:216.
6. Würzburg Introduction to Philosophy, *Werke* 6:79.
7. Bruno, *Werke*, 4:231 and 4:229.
8. *Ibid.*, 4:235-236 and 4:320-321.
9. X. Tilliette, *Schelling: une philosophie en devenir*, Vol. I, (Paris, 1970), p. 337.
10. Bruno, *Werke*, 4:301.
11. *Ibid.*, 4:243.
12. The Possibility of a General Form for Philosophy, *Werke*, 1:91 and 1:93.
13. The earliest expression of the system-idea is this:
    The absolute Identity exists in the individual under the same form in which it exists in the Whole, and conversely, it is in the Whole in no other form than in that under which it is in the individual (*Werke*, 4:132).
    The following text from the *Lectures on Academic Studies* provides the clearest and most representative statement of the whole system-notion:
    The Absolute simply for itself is necessarily pure Identity, yet the absolute form of this identity is to be in an eternal manner sujbect and object... Neither the subjective nor objective element in this eternal act of cognition is the Absolute, but that which is equally the substantial core of both, which accordingly is disturbed by no difference. The same identical essentiality is in the objective side of this absolute production a forming of ideality into reality and in the subjective side a shaping of reality into ideality. The same subject-objectivity is in both of these and [thus] the whole substantial core of the Absolute is posited in the absolute form. (*Werke*, 5:281)
14. In a letter of 25 May, 1801 Schelling apologizes to Goethe for retaining his edition of Spinoza while he works upon the expansion of his *Presentation. Schriften der Goethe-Gesellschaft*, Vol. 13, (Weimar, 1898), pp. 217-218.
15. Kant's mention of a systematic use of pure reason—or reason operating under a principle of thorough-going determination and providing a total field of all possible

predicates or determinations as a background for the specification of the possibility of any one particular—may have attracted Schelling's attention in this direction. Cf. *Critique of Pure Reason*, A571-73, B599-601.

16. The development of the problem of individuality and individuation in Schelling's thought can be briefly indicated here. The System of Identity basically reduces particularity to differently indexed or articulated universal structures, structures of indifference or subject-objectivity. Individuality for the system is a function of structure and each individual is able to recapitulate all others. The "Bruno" of 1802 indicates Schelling's awareness of a new problem: Individuality on systematic terms in no way accounts for phenomenal plurality "*or*" for the spatial, temporal and causal textures of the interconnection or disconnection of phenomenal individuals. Individuation is seen to be explicable only as a sort of self-exclusion from the organic particularity of systematic individuality ("ideas").

Philosophy and Religion, 1804, proposes an account of particularity reminiscent of Erigena's Christianized and historicized Neoplatonism—the "fall" of the ideas away from the Absolute (pure ideality) and their return, enriched by reality.

Aphorisms Introductory to the Philosophy of Nature, 1805, explains finite particularity as the perfect particularity of ideas (or systematic individuals) intuited through distorting complexes of external relations. This is the most sophisticated explanation of individuality the System of Identity offers, and the most rigorously Neoplatonic.

In the *Essay on Freedom* of 1809 Schelling gives up the attempt to think finitude as an aberration of the organic particularity congenial with system and finds himself forced to adopt a primitive ontological principle of individuation, the *Grund*. Henceforth he thematizes the confrontation of system and intractable individuality as the overriding philosophical question.

17. It is easy to locate texts which state the Identity-System in a strikingly Neoplatonic guise, i.e. as a three-levelled

hierarchy of being. Though they do indicate the influence of Plotinus after 1804, they somewhat conceal Schelling's precise systematic interest, which we maintain, is Neoplatonic and which antedates any casting of the system into a three-orders-of-being form. For example,

From eternity and in eternal ways this *unity* creates images of itself in the infinite. From this eternal in-forming of unity into infinity, however, sensible nature wrenches itself free and is the mere *appearance* thereof—or the eternal inbuilding subsisting under mere relations.

Aphorisms Introductory to the Philosophy of Nature, *Werke*, 7:176.

18. Cf. *Ennead* IV.7.8⁵ :46-9:2 and *Ennead* V.9.9:3-8. Both texts derive from Plotinus' meditation upon the *Timaeus*. Cp. also IV.8.6:18-28.

19. *Ennead* I.6.7:8-12; *Ennead* V.6.6: 20-21.

20. Proclus insists that thought must come to rest in one principle or lose itself in the infinite. It must come to a stand, fall into an order, proceed by determinate method, and accomplish its work in a finite set of operations. Cf. *Elements of Theology*, 2nd ed., tr. E. R. Dodds (Oxford, 1963), Props. 4, 11.

21. *Element of Theology*, Props. 6, 7, 11. Note the argument for Proposition 11:

. . . But if all things were uncaused, there would be no sequence of primary and secondary, perfecting and perfected, regulative and regulated, generative and generated, active and passive; and all things would be unknowable. For the task of science is the recognition of causes. (Dodds, *op. cit.*, p. 13.)

22. Aphorisms Introductory to the Phil. of Nature, *Werke*, 7:146.

23. Presentation of My System, *Werke*, 4:129-130.

24. Bruno, *Werke*, 4:250-251.

25. Presentation of My System, *Werke* 4:114-115. Compare the Erlangen Lectures of 1820-1821, published under the title *Initia Philosophiae Universae*, ed. H. Fuhrmans (Bonn, 1969), pp. 38-41.

26. Würzburg System of 1804, *Werke* 6:140.

27. The Private-Course at Stuttgart of 1810, Werke 7:467.
28. Ages of the World, draft of 1811, *Werke Nachlassband*, (Munich, 1946), p. 5.
29. Cf. the early Schelling's definition of system, Commentary on the Idealism of the *Wissenschaftslehre, Werke,* 1:400.
30. It is this self-concretizing and self-establishing character of intellectual intuition which moves Schelling to speak of systematic philosophy as "revelation" or "self-affirmation of the Absolute" – or more generally as "expression"– long before any theistic or indeed substantial connotations are attached to the term *Absolute.* Cf. *Werke,* 7:53, 7:59, 2:362.
31. Consult M. Heidegger, *Schellings Abhandlung über das Wesen der menschlichen Freiheit* (Tübingen, 1971). For the interesting suggestion that the *Grund/Existenz* dichotomy relfects the Fichtean polarity of Ego and Non-ego see M. Vetö, "Le fondement selon Schelling," *Revue Philosophique de Louvain,* 70 (Aug., 1972), pp. 393-403.
32. *Element of Theology,* Props. 15, 16, and especially 17.
33. Consult *De mundi sensibilis atque intelligibilis forma et principiis* (1770), section 10, for Kant's first definition of intellectual intuition as a divine or 'principiating knowing' or perhaps a *'cognitio symbolica.'*
34. *Werke,* 4:322-23, 6:143.
35. Würzburg System of 1804, *Werke* 6:137.
36. Deduction of Dynamic Processes (1801), *Werke* 4:77-78 and Presentation of My System, 4:123.
37. This definition of indifference seems to have been relatively enduring and of final validity for Schelling. Cf. *Werke,* 5:216, 7:205, and 'Ages of the World,' *Nachlassband,* p. 50. In "Philosophy and Religion," a work influenced by Schelling's actual reading of Plotinus, Schelling dismisses all other ways of defining indifference and makes the Absolute pure identity. Cf. *Werke,* 6:24-25.
38. For the first statement of this position, see Presentation of My System, Props. 19, 21, 22, 23, *Werke,* 4:122-123.
39. On the recapitulative nature of the recurring relative totalities or 'potencies' see 4:290-291, 4:419, 4:426, and

5:367. On the recapitulative nature of the perfect individuals or 'ideas,' whose function in the system is the same as
that of the potencies, see 5:389-390, 7:163, and 7:203.

40. *Ennead* IV.8.6:7-11 is typical of this line of thought
which receives more technical formulation elsewhere as a
principle of double-power or double-functioning.

41. *Elements of Theology*, Prop. 25.

42. Schelling clearly mirrors the hesitation of the Neoplatonic
tradition, mediated as it is to him through Spinoza, when
he declares that no system can solve the problem posed by
the first synthesis or derivation, the passage from the
infinite to the finite. *Werke* 1:34.

The centrality of the Neoplatonic system-problematic to
the process of his thought is attested by the reappearance
of the same quandary in the latest formulation of the
system-question:

It is as if the whole world lies within the nets of the
understanding or of reason, but the question is
precisely this: How has it come into these nets?
Manifestly there is something other and something
more in the world than mere reason, and what is
more, something which struggles to transcend these
boundaries.

Munich Lectures on the History of Philosophy, *Werke*,
10:143-144.

43. Proclus expresses all the contradictory nuances well:

. . . In so far, then, as it has an element of identity
with the producer, the product remains in it; in so far
as it differs, it proceeds from it. But being like it, it is
at once identical with it in some respect and different
from it: accordingly it both remains and proceeds,
and the two relations are inseparable.

Element of Theology, Dodds translation, Prop. 30 argument, p. 35.

44. *Ibid.*, Prop. 28 argument.

45. Typical of Schelling's expression of this intricate notion is
this passage, heavy with Spinozistic connotations:

This eternal—eternal by the very concept—reflexion
into one another of form and substance is the realm

of nature or the eternal birth of God in things and the equally eternal reassimilation of these things into God, in such fashion that . . . nature itself is the full divine existence, God seen in the actuality of his life and self-revelation. *Werke*, 7:59.

46. Proclus himself entertains the notion of a coordinate unity and manifold as principles of being, but finds himself forced to reject the suggestion as leading to an infinite regress in search for an actual one. *Elements of Theology*, Prop. 5, argument.

The closest that Neoplatonism actually comes to Schelling's systematizing operation of *Ineinsbildung* is suggested by Proclus' assertion of the equivalence of immanence, procession, and reversion: "Every effect remains in its cause, proceeds from it, and reverts upon it." *Elements*, Prop. 35. Note that Proclus asserts this equivalence to obtain only within the overarching relation of causality, within its implied demand for subordination.

47. Cf. *Elements*, Prop. 20. Proclus indeed mentions a replicative function of systematic ordering– "All things are in all things"–but fails to integrate this into the predominant scheme of causal ordering. *Elements*, Prop. 103.

48. *Elements,* Prop. 26.

49. *Ibid.,* Props. 78 and 79.

50. Other significant instances of the double-act explanation of hypostasis are: *Enn.* V.1.6:28-34; *Enn.* V.2.1:12-18; *Enn.* IV.8.6:7-10. In *Enn.* II.6 the double-function schema is generalized into a solution to the problem of the nature of qualities in *nous* and in the sensible.

51. Aphorisms Introductory to the Philosophy of Nature: "The spirit of true philosophy is the inbuilding and uni-forming of the general and the particular in infinite ways", *Werke*, 7:142. Cf. Further Expositions of My System, *Werke*, 4:394, 4:415.

52. Bruno, *Werke*, 4:327, Further Expositions, *Werke* 4:380.

53. Thus Schelling's insistence, throughout the System of Identity, that the appropriate method of systematic philosophy is not dialectic, which is just a dynamic form of exclusion, and thus confined within the sphere of

'Reflexion,' but an *Eins-und ineinandersetzen. Werke*, 4:399.

54. Cf. Essay on Human Freedom, *Werke*, 7:357-359. Compare Plotinus' definition of matter as the "darkness of the individual thing," *Ennead* II.4.5:6-8.

The Problem of Ordered Chaos in Whitehead and Plotinus

David F. T. Rodier

The American University

In this paper I shall attempt to show how the study of neoplatonism might help elucidate certain problems in process philosophy. I shall do this by directing attention to Whitehead's puzzling accounts of creativity and of non-statistical judgments of probability in *Process and Reality* and show how certain difficulties in his accounts might be clarified by considering them as reflecting certain central and familiar problems in the philosophy of Plotinus. I shall begin by analyzing the problems of Whitehead's account and attempt to state what I feel are his important underlying presuppositions. I shall then turn to a discussion of "sympathy" *(sympatheia)* and matter in Plotinus' philosophy. Finally I shall attempt to show that Whitehead's category of creativity and his non-statistical probability are expressions of the same philosophic concerns as Plotinus' account of matter and *sympatheia,* and perhaps they may be only the reinterpretation of a neoplatonic theme in terms of process metaphysics.

I

Even as sympathetic an interpreter as Donald W. Sherburne has characterized Whitehead's account of the category of creativity in *Process and Reality* as "elusive"[1] and "terse to the point of obscurity."[2] Certainly, Whitehead's formal definitions are formidably technical:

'Creativity' is the universal of universals characterizing ultimate matter of fact. It is that ultimate principle by which the many, which are the universe disjunctively, become the one actual occasion, which is the universe conjunctively.[3]

'Creativity' is the principle of *novelty*. An actual occasion is a novel entity diverse from any entity in the 'many' which it unifies. Thus 'creativity' introduces novelty into the content of the many, which are the universe disjunctively.[4]

However, Whitehead's explicit analogy between his category and Aristotle's matter helps to clarify these definitions:

'Creativity' is another rendering of the Aristotelian 'matter,' and of the modern 'neutral stuff.' But it is divested of the notion of passive receptivity, either of 'form,' or of external relations; it is the pure notion of the activity conditioned by the objective immortality of the actual world – a world which is never the same twice, though always with the stable element of divine ordering. Creativity is without a character of its own in exactly the same sense in which the Aristotelian 'matter' is without a character of its own. It is that ultimate notion of the highest generality at the base of actuality. It cannot be characterized, because all characters are more special than itself. But creativity is always found under conditions, and described as conditioned. The non-temporal act of all-inclusive unfettered valuation is at once a creature of creativity and a condition for creativity.[5]

From these passages two things become clear: (1) creativity is the dynamic element in Whitehead's process philosophy; (2) creativity is not to be understood as change merely in the sense of a universal flux, but as a principle of novelty. The first point, *i.e.* the dynamic nature of creativity, underscores Whitehead's overt divergence from Aristotle. This divergence is clear even in Whitehead's analogy between creativity and Aristotelian matter, since in the Aristotelian system matter is the potentiality for change while in Whiteheadian metaphysics creativity is the necessity for change. The universe of the process philosopher not only is ever changing but it must of necessity ever be changing. For Whitehead, at least, "The elucidation of meaning involved in the phrase 'all things flow,' is one chief task of metaphysics."[6] Nevertheless, this change which characterizes the universe is not a mere Cratylean flux. It is an ordered, directed change: the change of a universe which is always "a creative advance into novelty."[7] That the flux of the universe is always in the direction of novelty is not the result of constraint placed on unsystematic and random change by some divine Demiurge. Rather in Whitehead's scheme God, who is the "creature of creativity,"[8] acts to direct and guide the operation of creativity by the valuation of possibilities in his primordial nature.[9] Nevertheless, God's activity is one of heightening the novelty of the creative advance. It does not as such bring novelty into being. In and of itself creativity is, as we have seen, always a movement towards novelty, apart from any specific divine intervention.[10] At this point one wonders whether Whitehead's category of creativity might not have more in common with Aristotle's matter than he noticed. Not, it is true, with matter characterized as passive but with matter characterized as "yearning for form as the female yearns for the male."[11] Certainly, Whitehead seems almost to say that in and of itself creativity requires not only the creation of another entity but of an entity which is novel in a non-trivial sense, *i.e.* has more than a numerical difference between itself and all other entities. Precisely this same conceptual tension between change in the sense of something different and change in the sense of something interesting occurs in Whitehead's discussion of probability and the justification of induction. And so it is to his account of "non-statistical judgments of probability" that we must turn.

II

Whitehead's account of "non-statistical judgments of probability" occurs in section eight of part two of *Process and Reality*. In contrast to his category of creativity, his account of these non-statistical judgments has been little noticed.

Whitehead begins by summarizing the four lines of argument by which he defends induction on the basis of his metaphysical system. These are:

> ...(i) that each actual occasion has at the base of its own constitution the environment from which it springs; (ii) that in this function of the environment abstraction has been made from its indefinite multiplicity of forms of definiteness, so as to obtain a concordant experience of the elements retained; (iii) that any actual occasion belonging to an assigned species requires an environment adapted to that species so that the presupposition of a species involves a presupposition concerning the environment; (iv) that in every inductive judgment, and in every judgment of probability, there is a presupposition, implicit or explicit, of one, or more, species of actual occasions implicated in the situation considered, so that [by (iii)] there is a presupposition of some general type of environment.[12]

To understand this account we must remember that for Whitehead each actual occasion (and these actual occasions are, among other things, the ultimate thing in the physical world) creates itself. However, this self-creation is not *creatio ex nihilo,* rather each actual occasion uses as the material for its self-creation both the world as available to it and its subjective aim, which is, as it were, the directionality given by God for its self-creative process. The first two of Whitehead's propositions state the limitation which the given world imposes on the freedom of each actual occasion to make itself. Any new actual occasion can come into being only in relation to the world as it is when the actual occasion arises. However great the novelty of a new actual occasion, it arises on the basis of its past which provides the initial data for its self-constitution. Whitehead insists that he can avoid strict determinism here, however, since, although the past is always given, there always are many different ways in which the past may be apprehended (this is Whitehead's abstraction "...from its indefinite multiplicity of forms of definiteness").[13] But just as the necessity of an actual occasion's arising from a definite, given past means that any actual occasion must in some sense of the words reflect and embody its past so this same necessity entails that, given an actual occasion, its past must have been of a certain kind ("any actual occasion belonging to an assigned species requires an environment adapted to that species").[14] Whitehead summarizes both these lines of argument in a single sentence: "Thus the basis of all probability and induction is the fact of analogy between an environment presupposed and an environment directly experience."[15]

Before further developing Whitehead's account, it might be well to emphasize just how radical is his break with his British Empiricist tradition. For Hume, and for many contemporary writers, matters of fact are atomic and have no relationships or infinitely many relationships. For Whitehead not only are there real internal relationships among things, but any given thing presupposes a determinate set of possible environments out of which it could have arisen. The relationship between an actual occasion and its environment is not so strong as to allow the environment completely to determine the actual occasion but neither is it so loose as to allow just anything to arise from anything. In this reasserting of the principle of "like gives rise to like," Whitehead remains closer to the classical tradition than many modern philosophers.

Whitehead continues his discussion by noting that there is another principle which is relevant to the discussion of induction. This principle is "The principle of the graduated 'intensive relevance' of eternal objects to the primary physical data of experience" which "expresses a real fact as to the preferential adaptation of selected external objects to novel occasions originating from an assigned environment."[16] This principle is the statement in the context of the theory of induction of Whitehead's doctrine of "subjective aim." As was stated above the absolute freedom of the self-creation of any actual entity is limited both by its past which provides it with the data from which it is to work and by its subjective aim. This subjective aim is defined, somewhat obscurely, by Whitehead as the "endowment which the subject inherits from the inevitable ordering of things conceptually realized in the nature of God."[17] Whitehead goes on to explain that God:

. . .is that actual entity from which each temporal concrescence receives that initial aim from which its self-causation starts. That aim determines the initial gradations of relevance of eternal objects for conceptual feeling; and constitutes the autonomous subject in its primary phase of feelings with its initial conceptual valuations, and with its initial physical purposes. Thus the transition of the creativity from an actual world to the correlate novel is conditioned by the relevance of God's all-embracing conceptual valuations to the particular possibilities of transmission from the actual world, and by its relevance to the various possibilities of initial subjective form available for the initial feelings.[18]

Since, then each actual occasion has this intuition (or in Whitehead's terminology "prehension") of "the graduated order of appetitions constituting the primordial nature of God,"[19] and since this vision, present as the subjective aim, is the most intense vision of what the actual occasion could become, there is the overwhelming tendency for most actual occasions to tend to fulfil this divinely given vision. But if the self-creation of every actual entity tends usually to conform to the order given in the primordial nature of God then the future will tend always to produce novelty, since, in the Whiteheadian metaphysics, "God is the organ of novelty, aiming at intensification."[20] Thus, Whitehead arrives at "an intuition of probability respecting the origination of some novelty."[21] This is "an intuition of an intrinsic suitability of some definite outcome from a presupposed situation," which "depends upon the fundamental graduation of appetitions which lies at the base of things, and which solves all indeterminations of transition."[22] These judgments neither are statistical in nature nor are they justified by appeal to any statistical theory of the nature of physical reality. But equally they are not religious in nature although any judgment of non-statistical probability is ultimately based upon a vision of the way the primordial nature of God is grasped by the particular actual occasions. But such non-statistical judgments "lie at a far lower level of experience than do the religious emotions,"[23] for "the concept of religious feeling is not an essential element in the concept of God's function in the universe."[24]

In Whitehead's account of creativity and of non-statistical judgments of probability we see a common, underlying theme: that of a dynamic tendency in the universe which is in some sense limited so that the dynamism of things does not become a dissolution into chaos but remains ordered. However, this ordered nature of change must never be thought of as imposed on the dynamism from without. The nature of creativity itself is directed towards novelty and the direction-ality of each actual occasion towards novelty of the highest intensity, although derived from the primordial nature of God, is part of the internal concrescing nature of each actual occasion. It is precisely this peculiar structure of dynamic, but self-ordered, principles of change which I think might be illuminating and illuminated by comparison with Plotinus. I am not intending to assert that there is any direct influence of Plotinus on Whitehead. Indeed Plotinus' name is never men-tioned in *Process and Reality*. What I do intend to show is that the same set of problems occurs in Plotinus' philosophy and that perhaps a juxtaposition of the two philosophers' accounts may illuminate each. The Plotinian equivalent of Whitehead's creativity seems to be matter; that of non-statistical judgments of probability seems to be *sympatheia*. I shall discuss these two in reverse order.

III

In Plotinus' philosophy *sympatheia* is not only a principle of causal explanation but also a quasi-dynamic aspect of nature. The early history of the doctrine of *sympatheia* is obscure. The idea may have derived from primitive ideas of sympathetic magic.[25] It is still unclear just when the idea moved from the sphere of magic to that of philosophy.[26] The proximate source of Plotinus, use of the term seems to be stoic.[27] For the Stoics the term *sympatheia* was not quite free from magical connota-tions since it was frequently used to explain the validity of the various types of divination commonly used.[28] For Plotinus also *sympatheia* is used to explain why the predictions of astrologers were occasionally correct and why charms might be effective.[29] In an early passage[30] Plotinus lists a number of effects of *sympatheia* which do not seem to be too far removed from the realm of homeopathic magic: the growth of animals and plants is affected by their *sympatheia* with sidereal configurations;[31] the kinds of things which are characteristic of various countries are determined by *sympatheia;* and human differences both physical and mental are affected by *sympatheia.* However, it is not clear whether this passage gives Plotinus' own theory or is rather a polemical statement of an opponent's position. The most extensive discussion of *sympatheia* by Plotinus occurs in the group of treatises devoted to "The Aporia concerning Soul"[32] which seem to come from near the middle of his writing. In this discussion Plotinus implicitly distinguishes between two kinds of *sympatheia* by sharply distinguishing between states of affairs which are signs of other states of affairs (the *sympatheia* presupposed by divination) and states of affairs operative upon other states of affairs (the *sympatheia* presupposed by magic). For convenience a terminological distinction not used by Plotinus will here be introduced: the *sympatheia* presupposed by divination will be termed predictive *sympatheia* while that presupposed by magic will be called operative *sympatheia.* Predictive *sympatheia* is a universal condition which exists because the universe is an organic whole and thus each part of the universe in some way mirrors the action of every other part. Since predictive *sympatheia* is grounded in the nature of the cosmos, Plotinus discusses it in terms of the relations holding between Soul and the phenomenal world. Operative *sympatheia* on the other hand is a local rather than a universal condition. Magic is effective because one part of the universe is in a condition of *sympatheia* with certain other specified parts of the universe. Operative *sympatheia* is also discussed by Plotinus in terms of perception, which is one of the most accessible phenomena involving interaction between two limited regions of the universe. A discussion of each kind of *sympatheia* will allow us to see their common dynamic aspect.

Predictive *Sympatheia*

As has been said, predictive *sympatheia* exists because the universe is an organic whole. The fact that Plotinus chooses to interpret the phenomenal universe in terms of an organic model means that causality in terms of external relations will not be a sufficient explanation of phenomenal change. Instead the ultimate explanation of the physical world will be in terms of internal relations. The distinction between internal and external relations is made by Plotinus in the following way:

> For just as the directing of a single animal is either from without and from the parts or from within, from the ruling principle; so medicine starts without and goes various ways from part to part and plans each act, but nature works from within, not needing to plan. The directing of the universe ... is not according to the model of medicine but of nature.[33]

Plotinus' position here must be distinguished from a model of reality in terms of coherence. He is not saying here that the nature of each event is determined by the total context of all the events with which it is connected, although he might wish to assert a variant of the coherence position also, as will be seen in discussing operative *sympatheia*. But such a coherence theory would still be in terms of part influencing part and so be in terms of the model of medicine, that is, in terms of external relations. Here, however, Plotinus is asserting that each part of the universe is related to each other part in terms of its own internal structure. Each thing in the Plotinian universe contains the seminal reasons of all[34] and so could develop in different ways. This is rather like the empiricist assertion that any state of affairs can logically follow any other. And as with the empiricist account, Plotinus' "seminal reasons" are not sufficient to account for physical objects and the general tendency of things to develop in an orderly manner. But predictive *sympatheia* implies that each thing in the physical world presupposes Soul existentially as a principle of the unity of the phenomenal world in its development. The souls of individual things in the physical world are united in their grounding in Soul.[35] This unity is more than a union of souls derived from the prior identification of each with a common object of knowledge. Although the unity of individual souls does not imply an identity of passions and desires, since these result from the interaction of soul and material complexes, it is the kind of unity which various parts of an organism possess by virtue of being members of a single living being.[36] This unity is an ontological unity both of origin (since the souls are all derived from Soul) and of activity (since the souls are acts of Soul). United in this manner the souls will be modified by any changes in Soul and will be altered by Soul as its activity in the souls is affected by the changing conditions of physical existence. This modification of the souls affects physical objects and so inhibits the activities of the seminal reasons constituting the various objects. Since the modification of physical objects is conditioned by the total state of all souls, the alteration in any one object will be a sign of the total state of affairs in the universe. This kind of modification may then be used predictively. Predictive *sympatheia,* then, expresses the universal tendency to change and randomness. It is the activity of the non-rational aspects of physical existence upon the rational structures of the seminal reasons.

Operative *Sympatheia*

Although a firm opponent of Ptolemy and other hellenistic astrologers,[37] Plotinus admits a form of sidereal efficacy, and thus a form of operative *sympatheia,* which seems superficially quite similar.[38] However he insists that any sidereal influence is neither the result of the elemental nature of the stars[39] nor of their volitions.[40] Operative *sympatheia* as Plotinus develops the concept is quite different from external constraint, for the magician, "operates from no outside standground."[41] And, of course, operative *sympatheia* exists apart from human employment and desire.[42] The basic model which he uses to interpret operative *sympatheia* is that of resonance:

> The prayer is answered by the mere fact that part and other part are wrought to one tone like a musical string which, plucked at one end, vibrates at the other also. Often, too, the sounding of one string awakens what might pass for a perception in another, the result of their being in harmony, and tuned to one musical scale; now, if the vibration in a lyre affects another by virtue of the sympathy existing between them, then certainly in the All—even though it is constituted in contraries—there must be one melodic system; for it contains its unisons as well,

and its entire content, even to those contraries, is a
kinship.[4 3]
This passage clearly shows that operative *sympatheia* is
grounded in Logos, *i.e.* that harmonizing effect of Soul present
in the physical world, since operative *sympatheia* exists as a
result of the universe's being "a single harmony."[4 4] But
operative *sympatheia* is not Logos. It is a result of Logos. Since
the phenomenal world forms a single system it is possible for
one part to affect another. This would be impossible in a world
of discontinuous atoms. However, since the phenomenal world
is not only a single system but a single system resultant from a
logically prior unifying structure, there exists not only physical
impacts between things, mechanical causality, but there is also
action at a distance between similar things which does not
affect intervening objects,[4 5] *sympatheia.*

Although unlike mechanical causation in that it acts at a
distance, the action of operative *sympatheia* is similar to that of
mechanical causation in that it is capable of precise formulation. The seminal reason of any particular thing in the
phenomenal world comprises a carefully balanced harmony of
attributes. However, the action of the seminal reason is affected
by the state of affairs in the universe at the moment in which it
acts. If there is simultaneous with a particular thing other things
having structures similar to that thing but differing from it in
that certain attributes of the first are more pronounced in the
others, then those attributes in the first will also tend to
become predominant in it. Thus operative *sympatheia* is a
modification of the activity of seminal reasons[4 6] but its action
is not random since it is both the result of the underlying
pattern of the cosmos and is capable of being described in terms
of probabilities. Operative *sympatheia* is also properly termed
sympatheia (although it is quite different from non-causative,
predictive *sympatheia*) since operative *sympatheia,* like predictive *sympatheia,* is grounded in the organic nature of the
universe.

IV

Plotinus' discussion of matter is, as is well-known, noto-
rious for its supposed confusion of moral and ontological

categories. However, I feel that that charge is merely the result of a verbal confusion, and that Plotinus simply uses the term "evil" in a very odd sense, one which is divergent from the earlier Platonic tradition. Plotinian evil is a state or mode of things rather than a class of events and so it is not the same as physical evils. It is not that Plotinus denies the existence of physical evils. He recognizes their existence and even that they are in a proper sense evil. But when he speaks of evil he means the quality of existence which is prior to the evil events and in which they participate. Plotinus' theory thus is the reverse of the Christian neoplatonist, Augustine. In Augustine while there are morally evil acts the emphasis is upon the mode of existence which is the ground of moral evil, i.e., sin. While physical evils become, for Augustine, almost accidents of physical things, in Plotinus moral evils are acts of the souls and do not pertain to the proper nature of Soul. But for Plotinus evil is a fundamental condition of physical things. It should also be noted that for Plotinus evil as a condition of existence contains no moral disapprobation. That a thing participates in evil does not mean that the thing in question is (morally) bad. It is the case that evil provides the occasion for morally wrong acts on the part of individuals, but evil, as such, is not, in the Plotinian system, wicked. Evil is quite clearly limited by Plotinus to the principle of instability in the physical world.[47] Given this definition of evil, Plotinus believes that he can demonstrate that its existence is necessary. Wickedness could only be necessary if that which gave rise to it were also morally evil, but that the Divine Triad, which is the cause of beings, is morally evil Plotinus denies. Moral evil remains, for Plotinus, a fact of experience, but for him, unlike both the middle-platonists and the gnostics, the fact of moral evil is relevant to a description of the *psychical* but not the *physical* world.

It may be questioned whether the choice of the term "evil" is a particularly fortunate one and it may be argued that this special usage is at least partially responsible for his meaning being misinterpreted as a gnostic theory of Matter.[48] It certainly can not be denied that the differences between the Plotinian and the gnostic theories of Matter would have been much more evident if Plotinus had used some term such as "creativity" or "pure potentiality" instead of the term "evil" to describe Matter. However, in defense of Plotinus' usage it must be admitted that he had already extended the use of "potential" to include both the Aristotelian "potency" and the Plotinian "possibility" and any further extension of terms related to potentiality would only have increased the possibility of misinterpretation. Further, in the Platonic tradition "The Good" and "The One" were used interchangeably. When applied to The One the term "good" was understood to be used without any particular moral connotations. Therefore, Plotinus had at least a precedent for terming that which was completely contrary to The One, "evil" and for expecting his interpreters to realize that "evil" was, like "good", being used without any moral implications. Once we see that Plotinus does not confuse axiological and ontological matters and that he uses the term "evil" to mean unlimitedness or complete instability rather than moral wickedness, the metaphysical function of Plotinian Matter is seen strikingly to resemble that of Whiteheadian creativity. Since Matter is pure limitlessness, pure lack, it receives Form. Unlike Aristotelian Matter, Plotinian Matter has no inherent tendency towards Form. Rather it is complete randomness or pure indeterminacy.

> "Matter becomes mistress of what is manifested through it: it corrupts and destroys the incomer, it substitutes its own opposite character and kind, not in the sense of opposing, for example, concrete cold to concrete warmth, but by setting its own formlessness against the Form of heat, shapelessness to shape, excess and defect to the duly ordered."[49]

As a condition of the manifestation of Form, Matter is unstable. Matter is able to assume any Form and there is no more reason for its assuming one Form than another. Therefore, the manifestation of any Form in Matter has the unstability of Matter and will not possess even momentary stability. A partial exception to this universal instability exists in the heavenly bodies, but their stability is due to the fact that the fire which composes them cannot mutate into another element because of its spatial position, not to any inherent stability of Matter. Apart from the heavenly bodies there is only generic endurance

in the physical world. Matter, for Plotinus, does not individu-
ate[50] but its instability is such that Forms in it are not
perfect.[51] In this there is no actual assigning of a positive
activity to Matter. The inhibition of the Forms is a negative act.
It takes place not by a positive opposition of some other Form
but by a simple tendency to any other Form.[52]

V

By now certain obvious parallels between Whitehead's
non-statistical judgments of probability and category of creativity on the one hand and Plotinus' use of *sympatheia* and
category of Matter on the other will have become evident. It
only remains to state, in conclusion, these similarities more
sharply.

Both the Whiteheadian non-statistical judgments of probability and the Plotinian *sympatheia* were attempts to introduce
a special factor into the causal analysis of physical phenomena.
Both were attempts to see the occurrence of changes in the
physical world as determined by more than the simple
operation of past events. Both were attempts to add as it were a
verticle causal dimension to the horizontal determination of the
past. Although Plotinian *sympatheia* viewed as a kind of
synchronic causation may seem more familiar to us than
Whitehead's vision of novelty as always the more probable
event, there appears to be no reason why Whitehead's account
of non-statistical probabilities might not also be interpreted as a
kind of synchronic causative factor. If this possibility is
allowed, then although the judgments of probability would
remain non-statistical, they might well be capable of being
analyzed mathematically.

The analogies between Plotinian Matter and Whiteheadian
creativity seem, at first glance, to be more remote than those
between *sympatheia* and non-statistical judgments of probability. Yet, if my argument that Plotinus' use of the term "evil" is
not primarily axiological, then more similarities emerge. Both
Matter and creativity are the fundamental dynamic principles
responsible for the ongoingness of the universe. Both are
attempts to take randomness and chaos seriously in construct-

ing a metaphysical system. Both are attempts to give a consistent philosophic account of Plato's myth of The Receptacle. The feeling may remain that nevertheless the connotation of the two terms is radically different – that somehow creativity is a more "positive" concept than Matter. It should be remembered, however, that even for Whitehead the processes of change in the cosmos may assume the apparent evil aspect of "the remorseless working of things," and that, ". . .if the best be bad, then the ruthlessness of God can be personified as *Atè*, the goddess of mischief. The chaff is burnt."[5][3] I think that the real difference between Matter and creativity is not one of positive as opposed to negative connotations. It rather depends upon the relation of each term to the other basic categories of the metaphysical system. For Plotinus when all is said and done, and despite the extreme qualifications necessary to state it correctly, Matter is in some sense ontologically dependent on The One. In Whitehead, however, God and creativity are, at best, interdependent. Thus the real contrast is between two dynamic accounts of the physical world, one of which sees all things as all unified in terms of an ultimate transcendent principle; the other of which sees everything as involving at least two ultimate principles, not engaged in a gnostic battle of good and evil, but still irreducibly distinct. Perhaps the real contrast is Whitehead's Platonism versus Plotinus' neoplatonism. If this is the case, then surely the juxtaposition of the two is mutually illuminating.

NOTES

1. Sherburne, Donald W., *A Key to Whitehead's Process and Reality* (New York: 1966) p. 32.
2. Sherburne, *op. cit.* p. 33.
3. Whitehead, A. N., *Process and Reality* (New York: 1929) p. 31.
4. Whitehead, *op. cit.* pp. 31-32.
5. Whitehead, *op. cit.* pp. 46-47.
6. Whitehead, *op. cit.* p. 317.

7. Whitehead, *op. cit.* p. 340.
8. Whitehead, *op. cit.* p. 47.
9. *ibid.*
10. Whitehead, *op. cit.* p. 31.
11. Aristotle, *Physics* 192a 20-24.
12. Whitehead, *op. cit.* p. 314.
13. *loc. cit.*
14. *loc. cit.*
15. Whitehead, *op. cit.* p. 314.
16. Whitehead, *op. cit.* p. 315.
17. Whitehead, *op. cit.* p. 373.
18. Whitehead, *op. cit.* p. 374.
19. Whitehead, *op. cit.* p. 315.
20. Whitehead, *op. cit.* p. 104.
21. Whitehead, *op. cit.* p. 315.
22. *ibid.*
23. *ibid.*
24. Whitehead, *op. cit.* pp. 315-316.
25. *cf.* Thorndike, Lynn, *A History of Magic and Experimental Science* (New York: 1923), Vol. I, p. 84-86.
26. Thorndike is almost certainly incorrect when he states, without documentation, that, "Heracleitus was perhaps the first philosopher to insist upon [the principle of sympathy] *(op. cit.* p. 84)." He appears to have in mind Heracleitus fragments 51 and 54 (Diels); however, in those fragments Heracleitus is asserting the existence of universal harmony, a concept related to, but quite different from, universal sympathy.
27. Sambursky, S., *Physics of the Stoics* (New York: 1959), p. 42.
28. Lebreton, J., *Histoire du Dogme de la Trinité* 8th ed. (Paris: 1927) Vol. I. p. 93. However, not all stoic defenses of divination appeal to *sympatheia*. Cicero (*De Div.* I. 56) gives a stoic defense based upon the closed causal structure of the world.
29. IV. 4.39, 40.
30. III.1. [3]. 5.
31. I find I must disagree with Bréhier, MacKenna-Page, and Armstrong in interpreting the Antecedents of "ἀπὸ τῆς

τούτων συμπαϑείας" in III.1.5.8 as referring to the various motions enumerated in lines 2 to 4 rather than the stars of line 2, although Plotinus does not elsewhere seem clearly to distinguish συμπάϑεια between living things and sidereal bodies from συμπάϑεια between living things and sidereal configurations.

32. IV.3 [27]; IV.4 [28]; IV.5 [29].
33. IV.5.11.1-7.
34. V.7.2.
35. IV.9.1.
36. IV.9.2.
37. II.3 and Bréhier's *notice ad loc. cit.*
38. IV.4.30.
39. Plotinus went so far as to attack Ptolemy's inconsistency in attributing more than the heating-cooling nature that his stated Aristotelianism would entail.
40. IV.4.32.1-2.
41. IV.4.40.
42. IV.4.41.
43. *ibid* (MacKenna-Page translation).
44. IV.4.41.7.
45. IV.4.32. It should also be noted that Plotinus' account of vision in IV.5.1-3 depends upon operative *sympatheia.*
46. contra Gelpi, Donald, "The Plotinian Logos Doctrine," *The Modern Schoolman* (1960) p. 304 footnote 23.
47. *cf.*, I.8.5, where evil is explicitly distinguished from any particular bad things—including injustice.
48. I.8.3; II.4.16.
49. I.8.8.
50. V.7.
51. I.8.8.
52. *loc. cit.*
53. Whitehead, *op. cit.,* p. 373.

Plotinus and Sartre, An Ontological Investigation of Being-Other-Than

by John N. Deck

University of Windsor

This morning, then, having freed our minds from all cares and being assured of untroubled liesure in a peaceful exurban retreat, we will undertake nothing less than a meditation on otherness.

This Meditation will be philosophic rather than what is usually called historical. I am talking about otherness, and I am concerned with Plotinus and Sartre only insofar as they can furnish hints, leads, corroborations. I am not attempting to display the influence, if any, of Plotinus upon Sartre (or of Sartre upon Plotinus) or to trace their common source in Parmenides and Plato. I am not, except when and insofar as it furthers the development of the theme, comparing and/or contrasting Plotinus and Sartre.

In the course of this account of otherness we will observe that we are saying things that are strikingly similar on the one hand to the words of Plotinus in the third century and on the other to those of Sartre sixteen hundred years later. The suggestion I wish to make is that a significant, I should say *the* significant, account of otherness is bound to reproduce what we shall honour Plotinus by calling Plotinian themes, since Plotinus came first.

So I mean this to be historical in another sense. That contemporary philosophic enterprises, whether wittingly or unwittingly, find themselves in living contact with Plotinian

notions is the most proper testimony to the continuing vitality
of Plotinus. The best commentary on a philosopher is to
philosophize.

For reasons which will emerge soon, it is appropriate to
approach otherness *via* the otherness revealed in an analysis of
knowledge, mind, the knower. I am using these terms *in propria
persona;* I will indicate, when opportune, certain similarities
among mind, Plotinus's Nous, and Sartre's For-Itself.

Knowledge is knowledge *of*. It is knowledge of (about)
tree, horse, table, etc. More generally it is knowledge of being.
Here at once appears *otherness.* Being is other than knowledge.

At first this otherness shows itself as an externality of
being to knowledge. Knowledge is being represented as one
"thing", the object of knowledge as another. But this cannot
stand. The object of knowledge is the *known*. The known *qua*
known is related to knowledge. There is no known without a
knowing. And conversely, there is no knowing without a
known. The otherness can no longer be represented as thing
barging against thing, but as relative opposition. And the
otherness is internal to both the knower and the known. The
knower needs the known; this need is internal to the knower
(this need *is* the knower) and so the known is "in" the knower.
The known needs the knower to be a known; this need is
internal to the known and so the knower is "in" the known. So
the knower and known are one, but are not *the* One. The
knower-known is not only a dyad, but is through-and-through
dyadic – dyadic on both sides.

Thus knowledge is what it is not, and is not what it is.[1]
Knowledge is the object, is lost in the object, has as its content
the object, is "identical" with the object – except that it is not
the object, it is other than the object, it is the negation of the
object.

As Sartre has it:

The first procedure of a philosophy ought to be to expel
things from consciousness and to reestablish its true
connection with the world, to know that consciousness is a
positional consciousness *of* the world. All consciousness is
positional in that it transcends itself in order to reach an
object, and it exhausts itself in this same positioning. All

that there is of *intention* in my actual consciousness is directed toward the outside, toward the table . . . all knowing consciousness can be knowledge only of its object. (BN lxi)

The dialectic through which we have been passing began, apparently, with the mind's having a transcendent object – "knowledge is *knowledge* of." All too soon, the transcendent object became "the known," which emerged as strictly coordinate with "the knower." At the same time knowledge was seen as dyadic, indeed it seemed to have no other discernible "feature" than to be a dyad. But then the transcendent object could not be kept out of play. Knowledge is seen ultimately *as other than itself because it is other than the transcendent object.*

(Self-knowledge (a) depends on a transcendent object on pain of being contentless and (b) is still dyadic, still a "relative opposition" of knower and known.)

Plotinus's Nous, in being other than the One (the transcendent object) is other than itself: a through-and-through knower-known, a through-and-through one-many, a through-and-through dyad. (Cf. V, 6, 1; VI, 4, 11, 15-20 etc.)

Similarly Sartre's For-Itself (roughly, consciousness), in being other than the In-Itself (the transcendent object) is other than itself. It is not "self-identical" (in *his* terms: in Plotinus's language *it is not the One.*) It is "its own nothingness" (BN 28) – or in Plotinus's language, it is primitively an 'intelligible' matter; in short, it is otherness.

Is the self-othering of Mind the paradigm of otherness; And is it the source of all otherness?

To philosophize a bit: To the extent that there are things which are utterly separate from, and out-of-relation to, one-another they are not properly *other* from one another. (It is significant that they cannot be spoken of without these manifest contradictions "not other from one another"! – their lack-of-relation can be 'meant' but cannot be said.) If one looks at an ascending scale of being, it is only as things enter into causal reciprocities which are more and more intimate that otherness ceases to have a merely abstract logical nature and becomes concrete opposition. Thus the otherness of a living thing from itself, the opposition of its present state (in the course of its development) to its essence, which otherness is the principle of its growth, is a more concrete and therefore a more intense otherness than the relatively external otherness of one living thing from another. The otherness within life (Plotinians read: soul) is a weak adumbration of the otherness within knowledge. The Other achieves its truest nature only in dynamic tension with the Same.

Plotinus's matter (matter-matter, not intelligible matter) represents the level of absolute dispersion of which we have just been speaking, just as do the out-of-relation "in-itselfs" of which Sartre sometimes speaks. For both, the otherness that deploys itself in order, in potency-act progression, in movement which is not mere dispersion, is basically the otherness of mind.

A subsidiary point: Sartre, perhaps because of a Cartesian bias, has little to say about conscious beings below man (brute animals) or about living beings below consciousness (trees). Now if one forgets about these, one can present a plausible case for the For-Itself (in plain language, man or the human mind) as the origin of all negation, and so of all otherness, of all potency, and, we might add, of all movement that can count as movement and of all life that can count as life – indeed, not only the origin of these, but even their sole locus. Whatever is not human mind can be made to seem an in-itself beyond the same and the other.

This, of course, cannot be the truth even with respect to the sub-organic, because the sub-organic is not in point of fact a region of absolute dispersion and externality. The obvious external relations in this region exist only as coordinate with internal relations. Thus Plotinus is much more sound in taking nature to extend to the earth as well and in recognizing nature as logos and life.

Still less can Sartre be considered correct when plants and animals are once taken account of. Here much more one must recognize internal self-otherness and self-othering which Plotinus represents, with suitable qualifications, as life, logos, even contemplation.

To return to the main theme: There is something fundamentally sound in Sartre's intuition. To put it in Plotinian terms: life, logos, contemplation, attain their essential reality, their highest truth, in mind, in Nous. Nous is, in an Hegelian sense, "the truth of" what is below Nous. Nous is the real reality of what is below it.

By taking "knowledge is knowledge *of*" as our starting-point we were able to display the otherness from itself lying at the heart of knowledge, an otherness, it will be recalled, which does not disappear in the case of "self-knowledge." It has been seen also that the self-othering of knowledge is the highest level of othering, it is "the truth" of the other otherings.

As the highest othering, the highest level of being-involved-with-non-being, is mind causeless, independent?

The notion of the causeless must be distinguished carefully from that of the self-caused, although often this is not done. Causeless means what it says – it refers to that which has no cause, either itself or anything else. The original logical division appropriate here is not between self-caused and caused-by-another, but between *caused* and *causeless*. Self-caused and caused-by-another are species, so to speak, of *caused*. (Hume was well aware of this point.) Plato's Good is causeless, Aristotle's unmoved movents are probably meant to be causeless, although this is compromised by the καθ᾽ αὐτήν of *Metaphysics* Λ , 7 (often translated "self-dependent") and the ambiguity (at least) of "self-knowing knower". St. Thomas's God is causeless. Plotinus's One is causeless (according to the "incorrect" mode of speaking, however, it "makes itself": VI, 8, 13; *cf*. VI, 8, 7). Descartes, on the other hand, as is well known, refers to God as the *causa sui*.

Is mind causeless? As the causeless, the independent, mind would spin all reality out of itself. But this is not the case. The internal relation which is the self-othering is here the internalization of an external relation. Mind – to be mind – needs, as we have seen, an object transcending mind.

We know very well that Plotinus sees this. The Nous needs the One. The relation to the One is the basis of the Nous's self-relation – this Plotinus expresses by saying that the Nous turns to the One to become a knower (V, 2, 1). Its "intuitive reception", its "looking at" the One is the continuing condition for its dyadic knowing on its own level (VI, 7, 35). Also we must give weight to the passages in which he refers to the One as the intelligible (e.g. V, 4, 2; V, 6, 2) – the One is the "external" "intelligible" by reference to which alone the Nous becomes intelligible to itself.

For Plotinus, then, the Nous is not causeless. It is caused by the transcendent object, the One. The One is causeless.

Sartre, too understands the need for the transcendent object. He toys with the notion of consciousness as self-cause, "the existence of consciousness comes from consciousness" (BN lxvi). But what consciousness causes is its own nothingness, in his expressive phrase it "nihilates" – in an active sense of 'making nothing' – its own nothingness. Its nothingness, however, must be the nothingness *of something,* that is, its nothingness must depend after all on the transcendent object, which he calls the *In-Itself.* So it is not, ultimately, self-cause.

Is Sartre's transcendent object, the In-Itself, causeless?

When Sartre describes the In-Itself, his language is close to Plotinus's "descriptions" of the One. What does *this* remind you of?

> Being is uncreated. But we need not conclude that being created itself, which would suppose that it is prior to itself . . . Being is *itself.* This means that it is neither passivity nor activity. There is activity when a conscious being uses means with an end in view . . . the self-consistency of being is beyond the active as it is beyond the passive, . . . [it is] inherence in itself without the least distance. From this point of view we should not call it "immanence", for immanence in spite of all *connection* with self is still that very slight withdrawal which can be realized – away from the self. But being is not a connection with itself. It is *itself.* It is an immanence which cannot realize itself . . . an activity which cannot act (*cp.* Plotinus V, 6, 6, 3-5) because it is glued to itself.

> But if being is in itself, this means that it does not refer to itself as self-consciousness does . . . It is itself so completely that the perpetual reflection which constitutes the self is dissolved in an identity. That is why being is at bottom beyond the *self,* and our first formula can be only an approximation due to the requirements of lan-

guage . . . Being in itself has no *within* which is opposed to a *without* and which is analogous to a consciousness of itself.

. . . being is isolated in its being and . . . does not enter into any connection with what is not itself.[2] Transition, becoming . . . – all that is forbidden on principle. [It] can encompass no negation. It is full positivity. (BN lxxvii ff.)

Is this "uncreated" causeless? Sartre, I suppose, has said that it is. "Uncreated."

But at this point Sartre labours under a twofold difficulty. One side of this appears to be merely logical and easily dealt with, the other is more profound. Ultimately, however, they can be seen to fit together.

On the "logical" side. Sartre is haunted by the phrase *"causa sui"*. He sees more-or-less that *causa sui* is "an impossibility" – either because there is something basically wrong with the notion itself or because neither of the "candidates," the For-Itself or the In-Itself, qualifies as *causa sui* and their "merger" is impossible. (BN lxvi; lxxvii; 758-9; 762) But, paradoxically, the impossible *"causa sui"* would be the only phrase which could represent for him what we have called the independent. And thus, for all his calling the In-Itself the uncreased, he does not see it as *above* the impossible self-caused, but below it:

Being is without reason, without cause, and without necessity; the very definition of being releases to us its original contingency. (BN 758; *cp.* BN lxxix)

It is only by making itself for-itself that being can *aspire to be* cause of itself. (BN 758, italics mine.)

Although the use Sartre makes of the word "contingent" here is common enough, it is perhaps well to point out that he does not mean that the In-Itself is contingent on, or dependent on, anything, but rather that it is simply "not necessary," that it is a pure happening (if that word can be purged of all connotation of activity and/or passivity), as he says, a "venture" (BN 760). The notion would be conveyed better by the Greek conception "by chance."

Sartre has not "happened upon" the Plotinian notion of "above chance and necessity." (*Cf.* VI, 8, 9) Along the lines we have been developing, we could regard this as a simple logical failure. For him the necessary would be the impossible *ens causa sui.* He has available to oppose it only the "by chance." (And so the For-Itself is similarly "by chance", the "absolute event")

But other motives are in play here. One I may mention briefly; it does little credit to Sartre. Would any one have suspected from the description of the In-Itself which I just quoted that Sartre tries to make this notion do duty for individual existents? But this is the case. The "above chance and necessity" of what he *seems* to be describing cannot be let to emerge when the "In-Itself" is confused with "individual" beings which are (rather primitively) conceived as coming and going "contingently", i.e., by chance.

The *For-Itself* is not the independent either — as we have seen. But in the place of saying that it leans on the independent or strives for the independent, Sartre will say (characteristically) that it is a continuous and unsuccessful attempt to found itself, to be an *ens causa sui.* It is unfounded, but it tries to found itself. It tries to become a For-Itself In-Itself, but of course it cannot succeed. And yet its whole dynamism, (at least as this is portrayed at the very end of *Being and Nothingness)* is derived from its efforts to achieve in-itselfness.

And so the Nous strives towards the One, but can never be the One. It is "founded" only in and through its striving for the One.

But why does Sartre not follow this through and say similarly and without qualification that the For-Itself does not found itself, but is founded on the In-Itself? Because the For-Itself is striving not simply to be an In-Itself, but to be an In-Itself without relinquishing its for-itselfness.

Why "without relinquishing its for-itselfness"? At first glance, the answer is simple, and indeed Sartre gives it: because only as a For-Itself could it be an *ens causa sui.* The "ideal being" would be "the In-Itself founded by the For-Itself and identical with the For-Itself that founds it." (BN 762)

But if the *ens causa sui* is, as he reiterates, impossible, why does he not seek beyond it for the causeless, the independent, or rather, why when he half-discovers the causeless does it appear as a by-chance that itself "would" need the completion of self-causing? Why does *"everything take place as if* the In-Itself in a project to found itself gave itself the modification of the For-Itself"? (BN 759-760)

To be in-itself for-itself. To be in-itself without being monolithic, dead, "just there." To be the One, but the One which *knows*. What Sartre does not clearly see here, but what is really operative, is that the knowledge, consciousness, aspect of what has been called the For-Itself is struggling to get free of the for-itselfness, the duality, while retaining the advantages it had with the duality – the advantage of being conscious. "Consciousness does not surpass itself toward its annihilation: it does not want to lose itself in the In-Itself of identity." (BN 110) "It would be its own foundation not as nothingness but as being and would preserve within it the necessary *translucency* of consciousness" (ibid., italics mine).

Consciousness is consciousness *of*. Knowledge is knowledge *of*. These were the uncriticized propositions with which we began. They brought us far in our meditation upon knowledge, but they did not, after all, present the innermost nature of knowledge. There is something about knowledge which is not expressed by "the one-many", "the dialectic of the same and the different," "that which is itself and not itself", "that which is what it is not, and is not what it is" and similar expressions, no matter how adequately transformed.

Here I shall use a Plotinian term, but I must caution you at the outset that I am not using it, at least immediately or obviously, as Plotinus most significantly used it. When I say ἐγρήγορσις, wakefulness or awakeness, you think naturally of the place in VI, 8, 16 where he speaks of the super-knowledge of the One as an eternal awakeness. To make matters more complicated, I shall bring this doctrine into the discussion a bit further on. But as I use *awakeness* now I am thinking of a "feature," admittedly sufficiently obscure or rather philosophically obscurable, in human knowledge, in our own knowledge.

Awakeness. An indirect approach to it can be made by
"sensing" the unsatisfactoriness of accounts of knowledge as
dual. "To know is to become the other." Even when this is
transformed to "to know is to become the known" or "to know
is to become the known, not in representation but in entity and
truth," we get the sense that knowledge is, strangely, being left
out. "The knower is, and is not, the known." Even when the
initial contradiction (for common sense) has been surmounted,
when the full internality of the knower-known interrelation has
been grasped, have we as yet expressed knowledge? Or have we
grasped only a duality, which, however much it may be a dynamic
internal tension, however much it may exceed the sensible, however much it may exceed the "material", still seems after all from
a higher point of view wooden, unalive, unawake? With respect to
Plotinus: Does not his ready identification of being
with knowledge, of order with knowledge – at the Nous
level – indicate that here he is not really expressing knowledge?
The term "awakeness" seems best, but it is not without its
dangers. The effort must be made to catch a glimpse, in
"awakeness", of something which is beyond or underlying
being-awake-to (for even here the duality may creep in), and
beyond or underlying awakeness as the negation of that to
which it is awake.

Other possible terms are even more quickly and immediately involved in duality. Even if "consciousness" had not
been spoiled for us by the iteration of "consciousness is
consciousness *of*", the word "consciousness" is in itself already
dual. "Awareness" summons the "*of*." "Intellectually alive" –
"Intellectually alive *to*." And life, we have been saying, is
through-and-through dual.

"Subjectivity" can convey a strong intimation of awakeness (I have heard it said, with becoming carelessness, that
modern philosophy – Descartes – "discovered subjectivity"),
but "subjectivity" can submerge itself in the *dyad* subjectivity-
objectivity. Nevertheless, Descartes' *cogito* carries something of
the notion. Sartre seems to approach it most closely in his
notion of the "pre-reflective *cogito*."

Sartre recognizes that there is not, for every act of
consciousness, a full-blown self-reflection. But neither can there

be an *"unconscious consciousness"*. So he develops the notion consciousness (of) — with the "of" in parentheses — and says that every consciousness of an object is consciousness (of) consciousness. Consciousness (of) consciousness is the pre-reflective *cogito*, it is "what can properly be called subjectivity" (BN lxxiii).

His reasoning here is open to serious preliminary objections. There cannot be an unconscious consciousness, but this means only that there cannot be a consciousness which is not conscious of an object — not that there cannot be a consciousness which is not conscious of — or (of) itself. If consciousness is thought of after the model of a mirror, it is obvious that a mirror can mirror objects without in any way mirroring itself. Or if consciousness is thought of as an affector or as an affected, there can, seemingly, be an affector which does not affect itself, and an affected which is not affected by itself.

These objections can be answered by engaging once more in the dialectic of the dual, which is, at bottom, what Sartre himself does. The "of" in parentheses becomes a weakened — and for that reason a more intense — version of the "of" without the parentheses. It comes to express the original through-and-through duality of consciousness, its non-identity, its lack of coincidence with itself, its failure to be an In-Itself, its failure to be a "thing."

(I would suggest, in this restricted vein, that Sartre is reversing matters here — that the non-thingishness of human consciousness is not present from the outset, but is something to be achieved. Human consciousness emerges *eventually* as reflectively self-knowing, and from this vantage-point it can be seen that it is in germ or potency originally self-knowing. But to be in germ or in potency self-knowing is to be below self-knowing. And even Plotinus's pseudo-history of the Nous is better in that it speaks of phases in which the Nous is not yet Nous i.e., in Sartre's language, more like a *thing*. The pre-reflective *cogito* would, on this showing, be rather more than less thingy — it would not yet have undergone actual self-othering.)

But by this time it is plain that Sartre's critic and Sartre himself have left behind whatever hint of *awakeness* may have been conveyed by the expressions "pre-reflective *cogito*" and "no unconscious consciousness." We are back with the dyad, and it is amusing that Sartre, who is acute enough to see the duality of reflection, indeed the duality of "knowledge" (as he distinguishes knowledge from "consciousness") and call this duality by its proper name, the dyad, does not formally recognize that he has made the pre-reflective *cogito* itself nothing else but a dyad. An unpleasant critic might say that the modern has allowed himself to drift down Greek bypaths.

Now let us explore if and how the "awakeness" which I am proposing as the innermost essence of human knowledge can be tied to Plotinus's specific use of *awakeness.*

I need not do more than remind this audience of Plotinus's thoroughgoing treatment of the duality-within-unity, the unity-within-duality of knowledge, nor how this consideration leads him in numerous places, preeminently in *Ennead* V, 6, to state that the One has no knowledge. Nor that he is not satisfied with this doctrine, so that he returns to the question in V, 4 and VI, 8 to find ways of saying that the One knows. He is plagued with dualistic expressions, he must speak "improperly", but he labours to purge the dualistic expressions of their dualism and to say:

If, now, the One's act does not become but is always, and is a kind of wakefulness which is not other than the one who is awake, being a wakefulness and an eternal super-knowledge, it will *be* in the way it is awake. The wakefulness is beyond being and Nous and intelligent life; the wakefulness is itself. (VI, 8, 16, 31-36)

Here is an eternal super-knowledge which is not dual.[3] According to VI, 8, 18 it is the source of the dyadic knowledge that is the Nous. There is in the One a sort of intelligence which is not the Nous. The One is the centre; from it radiate being and Nous. Being and Nous are poured forth from the One and depend on its "intellectual" nature.

A modest development of Plotinus's philosophy here would start from seeing explicitly the trace of the awakeness of the One in the knowledge of the Nous, just as the unity of the Nous is the trace of the One. Thus it would emerge that not only is there a knowledge which is above duality, above othering and self-othering, but that even in human knowledge, which is shot through with duality, the essence of the knowledge is not the duality but rather its imitation and intimation of the knowledge which is above duality. In short, the wakefulness which is human knowledge would be displayed as an imitation of the wakefulness which is the One.

Let us go way back. We had asked whether the self-otherer could be independent and had suggested that the self-otherer needs the external other. Now we have traced intimations of our own, corroborated by notions found in Sartre and Plotinus, that the highest concrete self-otherer, the knower, is not at base a self-otherer so much as a wakefulness. A wakefulness which imitates the external wakefulness. The latter is not a For-Itself In-Itself within the limits of that vocabularly. But it is what For-Itself In-Itself was trying to express: A knowing, independent reality above chance and necessity.

NOTES

1. This phrase is adapted from Sartre's description of the For-Itself (BN lxxviii). (Sartre's *L'Être et le Néant* (1943) is referred to in the English translation of Hazel E. Barnes, *Being and Nothingness,* New York, Washington Square Press, 1966).

2. Here, as also on BN 763, Sartre shows that he appreciates *the one-way relation.* The For-Itself is related to the In-Itself; the converse is not true. Similarly the Nous (and all things) are related on the One (VI, 9, 3, 49-51; *cf.* VI, 8, 7, 44-46), but the One is not related to them.

3. How tenuous this may be in Plotinus himself, however, is indicated by the fact that only a few lines before he could say "The One, as it were, made itself by an act of looking at itself. The act of looking at itself is, in a way, its to-be." The qualifications are there, but the formula greatly resembles that of the conscious self-cause that Sartre toys with and criticizes.

Paul Elmer More and Neoplatonism

by K. W. Harrington

Emory University

I *Introduction*

In the last decades of the nineteenth century and the first decades of the present one, the theological-idealistic orientation of American university education and philosophy gradually found itself unable to withstand the onslaughts of the rising philosophies or pragmatism and naturalism. These new movements wrought fundamental transformations in social and educational theories and practices as well as in philosophy. In education, pragmatism and naturalism succeeded by 1910 in replacing the old prescribed curriculum, with its emphasis upon the classics and mathematics, with a variety of elective courses of study which took the inclinations and abilities of the individual student into consideration and offered him the alternative of concentrating upon more "practical" studies such as the physical sciences and modern languages. Methodologically, both movements were characterized by a strong commitment to science, with science being understood as a method of inquiry rather than a definite body of knowledge. In the investigation of its subject-matter—nature, which the naturalists treated as an all-inclusive and non-defined category—science as a method excludes radical dualisms of any kind. Man's mind is not separate from nature, and his values, instead of existing in some separate realm find both their origin and their fulfillment in nature.

The multifarious influences of pragmatism and naturalism were opposed by a group of intellectuals loosely united under the name Humanists. Two of the early Humanists, Paul Elmer More (1864-1937) and Paul Shorey (1857-1934), were also leading American Platonic scholars of the first part of the twentieth century. As professors of the classics, these scholars were distressed at the replacement of the prescribed curriculumn with the elective system, as this meant that students were no longer required to take Latin and Greek. More and Shorey were among the first to challenge the assumption that attention to the present and practical is more essential to education than an emphasis on the Great Tradition of the past.

In the 1920's and 30's, the older Humanists merged with a group known as the New Humanists. This group began as a literary movement designed to combat the influence of naturalistic tendencies in the writings of such men as Dreiser, Sinclair, Anderson, Dos Passos, and Hemingway. Originally, the New Humanists were interested primarily in restoring interest in the classics and in denying the natural and spontaneous. The movement gradually broadened its interests to include those of the older Humanists, namely the opposition to all forms of naturalism and an attempt to return American college education to the old prescribed curriculum with its emphasis on the classics. The leaders of the New Humanists were Irving Babbitt of Harvard, Paul Elmer More of Princeton, and Norman Foerster of the University of Iowa.

The most fundamental belief of the New Humanists and the older Humanists was an absolute dualism between man's "lower" nature, which he shared with other animals, and his "higher" nature, which was not a part of physical nature and was characterized by will, conscience, morality, and religion. This conception of human nature the New Humanists believed to be a fundamental postulate of the philosophy of Plato and to have found additional support in early Christian and medieval thought, an, indeed, to be the central conviction of all genuinely "humanistic" thought. Other beliefs which the New Humanists thought they had derived from Plato and others in the Great Tradition were an ethic of restraint and denial of bodily pleasures; a strong social conservatism and a belief in the unchanging nature of truth, values, and human nature.

Of the leaders of the New Humanists, Paul Elmer More was especially influenced by the Platonic tradition, and indeed considered himself to be a Platonist. This paper explores certain features of More's interpretations of Plato and Plotinus. I will argue that although More considered himself to be a Platonist, he ascribed to Plato certain ethical and psychological doctrines which are in fact much closer to the philosophy of Plotinus than to that of Plato. Indeed, More considered the ethics of the two philosophers to be in essential agreement. However, More was sharply critical of some aspects of the metaphysics and mysticism of Plotinus, which he regarded as running counter to genuine Platonism. The respective sections of this paper attempt to do the following: 1) place More's treatment of the Platonic tradition in the context of the major strands in his intellectual make-up, so that one may understand his approach to Plato and Plotinus; 2) consider his treatment of that aspect of Plotinus' philosophy which he considers to differ markedly from that of Plato—viz. what More terms Plotinus' metaphysical "monism" and its attendant mysticism—and his criticism of its influence upon Christianity; and 3) finally, argue that More's fundamental belief in dualism and his desire to make Plato compatible with Christianity led him to regard the ethics of Plato and Plotinus as being quite similar to one another, whereas there are in fact important differences between the two. The significance of this for More's thought is that his own ethical beliefs are seen to be in much closer agreement with Plotinus than with Plato, so that his philosophy is in some respects more Neoplatonic than Platonic in character.

II. *More's intellectual background*

The understanding of Paul Elmer More's interpretation of the Platonic tradition is enhanced considerably by viewing it within the framework of the major stages of his philosophical development and the predominant strands in his intellectual make-up. More abandoned an early Presbyterian religious affiliation while still in his teens, and was not to return formally to Christianity until 1925. But despite his early rejection of Christianity, he acknowledged that he was always obsessed by an awareness "of a mystery beyond the sense, out of which my dualist philosophy was to spring, those intimations of a whole ghostly world corresponding to something latent in the soul itself,"[1] and he retained throughout his life a certain evangelistic fervor. In his biography of More, Arthur Hazard Dakin remarks of More's teaching at Princeton: "He did not analyze ideas for their own sake . . . . In the end he saw only a right direction or a wrong direction, truth or falsehood, order or chaos, health or disease, life or death."[2]

An early enthusiasm for the literature of German romanticism was gradually superseded by a deep devotion to the Greek and Latin classics. Probably the single most decisive turning-point in More's intellectual life was occasioned by his discovery of an exposition of the thought of the Manicheans. In a letter to Robert Shafer, dated October 22, 1931, he describes this event and its significance as follows:

> Then, in 1891, I chanced upon Baur's *Das Manichäische Religionssystem* . . . . Such mental excitement as that book gave me I had never known before and have never felt since. It was as if the religious sense, like a drowning man, had laid hold of something to which it could cling . . . . This was the principle of dualism,—a crude mechanical sort of philosophy as taught by the Manicheans, but through the really magnificent allegory in which their mythology flowered hinting at a deeper and subtler truth.[3]

The principle of dualism first discovered in Manicheanism was to become fixed firmly in More as his single most important intellectual conviction, one which he was to retain until the end of his life and which was to appear and reappear as the most persistent theme in virtually all of his writings. Introduced to Oriental philosophy by his study of the Manicheans, More turned to the religion and philosophy of India and went to Harvard in 1892 to study Sanskrit and Pali. In 1894 he published a fictionalized account of his embracing of Eastern philosophy, *The Great Refusal,* which preaches the detachment of Hindu philosophy and the illusoriness of earthly romantic love.

There was a gradual transition in More from Hindiusm to Platonism to which it is impossible to assign a precise date. His essays "Plato" (1909) and "Definitions of Dualism" (1913) show the increasing hold of Platonism on his thought. It is in the essay "Plato", published in the sixth series of the *Shelburne Essays,* that More outlined for the first time the conviction which he was to maintain throughout his life as the basic teaching of Plato's writings. Here he defined the "religious instinct" which he finds basic to all religions and religious philosophies, among which he includes Plato's, as:

the bare consciousness of a dual tendency in human nature . . . . As the goal of this tendency we speak of an eternal changelessness, of a self-sufficient joy, and of infinite life—in the other direction lies the sense of our personality as concerned with variety and change and that world of phenomena, which is a reflection, it may be . . . of a dissipation within ourselves. In this way we come to distractions and restlessness, to self-seeking, competition, envy, jealously, and strifes; to misery, devouring egotism, lust, and violence. Its end is despair and the irreparable decomposition of death.[4]

Although More shifted his attention more and more exclusively to Greek philosophy, particularly Plato, the Eastern influence was still strong enough in 1917 for him to anticipate the accusation that his Vendantic dualism had acted as a kind of Procrustean bed upon which he had forced his book *Platonism,* published in that year. An examination of *Platonism* does indeed reveal the influence of his early absorption in the world-renouncing Eastern religions with their emphasis upon the detachment of the individual from social concerns in favor of a solitary quest for spiritual fulfillment. This influence encouraged him to read into Plato's ethics and psychology certain features which are in fact much more characteristic of the fundamentally Oriental and religious philosophy of Plotinus, with its intense desire for flight from the world of physical nature, than of the philosophy of Plato with its devotion to the social life of the *polis* and its emphasis upon the inseparability of personal excellence and social cooperation.

More's own personal predilections and convictions led him to read into Plato's philosophy an extreme moral, psychological, and metaphysical dualism, and to say of the ethics of Plato and Plotinus that they are almost identical.[5] He also came to regard Christianity as the fulfillment of the philosophy of Plato. The development of the Greek tradition and its culmination in Christianity is set forth in his major philosophical work, *The Greek Tradition,* a six-volume series into which he incorporated *Platonism* as the introduction. The central thesis of this work, which traces Greek thought from the death of Socrates in 399 B.C. to the Council of Chalcedon in 451 A.D., is that Greek literature, pagan and Christian, from Plato to St. John Chrysostom and beyond that to the Council of Chalcedon, is essentially a unity. "The initial impulse to the movement was given by a peculiar form of dualism developed by Plato from the teaching of his master Socrates."[6] Christianity was the true heir and developer of Platonism. "It is this tradition, Platonic and Christian at the center, this realization of an immaterial life, ... that lies behind all our western philosophy and religion."[7] The volumes in the series are: *Platonism* (1917); *The Religion of Plato* (1921); *Hellenistic Philosophy* (1923); *The Christ of the New Testament* (1924); *Christ the Word* (1927); and *The Catholic Faith* (1931). During the writing of *The Christ of the New Testament* More became convinced of the need for a connecting link between the two worlds of permanence and change and was converted to Anglo-Catholic Christianity. The purpose of *The Christ of the New Testament* is to show that "Christ was a person who embraced within himself the full nature of divinity and the full nature of humanity."[8] Of the Incarnation More says that it is "the one essential dogma of Christianity, ... that it is the mythological expression ... of the Platonic dualism, and thus forms a proper consummation of the Greek Tradition."[9] His decision to reembrace Christianity resulted from the conviction that: "The Ideal philosophy of Plato waits for its verification upon no belief in anything outside of what we can test and know in our immediate experience .... But the full scope of religion requires a theology and a mythology as well as a philosophy, and if the crowning element of religion is to be more than a reasonable conjecture, ... then I see not whither we are to turn save to Christianity."[10]

The significance of this brief intellectual biography is that More's attitude toward the Platonic tradition was strongly influenced by his fundamental belief in dualism and after his conversion to Anglo-Catholic Christianity by his religious beliefs as well. He interpreted Plato in the light of these beliefs, and approved of just those features in the philosophy of Plotinus that agreed with his sifted Platonism. His basic criticisms of Plotinus, to which I will now turn, were based upon his conviction that certain parts of Plotinus' philosophy are unacceptable to the Christian.

III. *More's criticism of Plotinian metaphysics and mysticism*

We have seen that More considered the ethics of Plato and Plotinus to be in essential agreement. He did, however, distinguish sharply between the metaphysics of the two philosophers.

> There are, as I see it, two modes of thought running through the *Enneads* . . . . One of these is a simple but profound philosophy, expressing a genuine psychological experience and closely related to Platonism; the other is a metaphysic, of Aristotelian and Stoic stamp.[11]

Plotinus' `most significant metaphysical departures from authentic Platonism are, according to More, his placing of the Ideas in the Divine Mind rather than granting them an independent status as did Plato, and the Plotinian conception of the One with its attendant mystical "monism" (by which More simply means that the various levels of being emanate from the Being of God), which contrasts sharply with Plato's conception of the Demiurge and his account of creation. This substitution of a metaphysical monism for the dualism of Plato More believes to be due primarily to the influence of Aristotle. Against Plato's dualism of forms and changing world Aristotle sets a dualism between an inseparable union of form and matter in individual objects, and a God Who stands in complete isolation from conscious and voluntary contact with the world.[12]

> Hence in place of the living concrete dualism of Plato's divine energy working upon the slowly yielding potentiality of the world, we have in his successor a

metaphysical dualism which partitions the universe into two incommunicable realms: on the one side a congeries of individual things and persons, each with its own energy and potentiality and its own end, and on the other side, set in absolute goodness utterly unattainable by any individual of this world; as absolute widsom which yet has no knowledge of or concern with the concrete sum of existences; as absolute energy exercized in contemplation, not even of itself for that would imply a distinction between knower and known, but in pure eternal contemplation of contemplation; and as an absolute cause which yet of itself effects nothing.[13]

More claims this Aristotelian concept of a transcendent God to have merged at an early date with Neopythagoreanism and various Oriental streams of thought, which commonly regarded themselves as being Platonic rather than Aristotelian and which culminated in the metaphysics of Plotinus.[14] Plotinus reduces the Aristotelian dualism to a monism, thus disavowing the isolation of the world from God, and completes their reconciliation by viewing God as the efficient cause from which the world evolves as well as the final cause towards which man's ethical nature strives.

Plotinus' metaphysical monism and its concomitant mysticism come under attack in More's chapter on "Christian Mysticism" in *The Catholic Faith*. Here More distinguishes among several kinds of mysticism: 1) The conviction of supernatural realities accompanied by a sense of the illusory nature of the phenomenal world. To this type of mysticism, which More associates with Plato, and, in the Christian tradition, with Gregory of Nazianzen, he attaches the rather clumsy appelation "mystihood". 2) An immediate contact with supernatural reality, whether given a) through sensuous sights and sounds or b) by spiritual communication. More's chief exemplar of this "quasi-mysticism" in St. Augustine. 3) Absorption of the soul in this reality, whether conceived as a pancosmic or a transcendental Absolute. Such an absolute mysticism is best represented by Plotinus. Finally, in Christianity such figures as pseudo-Dionysius and St. John of the Cross fall into a category of "mixed mysticism" which falls between 2) and 3).[15] Although closely approaching the position of Plotinus, this kind of mysticism necessarily guards itself against the heresy of teaching a complete union of the soul and God.

The only kind of mysticism to which More gives his approval and which he considers to be compatible with Christianity is the first. Gregory of Nazianzen is praised for his humility in asserting that God, Who is infinite and incomprehensible to the intellect of man, can be known to mortals only as He is revealed through His works. It is impossible for man to know or to see God Himself.[16] Any claim beyond this More considers to be presumptuous and inimical to Christianity. Even St. Augustine, whose relatively mild descriptions of contact with the Deity hover between actual and desired vision, comes under criticism by More for laying claim "to a kind of intimacy with the divine nature which would have repelled the spiritual humility of a Gregory Nazianzen and the earlier Christians."[17] But it took a Greek Christian to assimilate the "full virus"[18] of Plotinian mysticism into Christianity. This was accomplished by the pseudo-Dionysius, "who carried the thought of Plotinus and Proclus to its logical conclusion in the *via negativa* and at the same time gave it a thin veneer of Christian respectability."[19] The treatises of the pseudo-Dionysius were a major influence in the wave of mysticism which invaled theology in the course of the twelfth century.

More's major objections to mysticism are clearly revealed in his discussion of St. John of the Cross, where the charges of arrogance and presumption on the part of the mystic recur.[20] More's second major criticism is that the extreme asceticism advocated by many mystics is incompatible with the doctrine of the Incarnation. If the flesh were as contemptible as St. John of the Cross believes it to be, then God would not have assumed the human form. The Incarnation is also rejected in that the direct contact of the soul with God eliminates the necessity of Christ as the Mediator. And as the asceticism of St. John involves not only the purgation of the pleasures and faculties of the body, but extends itself to all revelations and manifestations of supernatural things that come to the soul in sensuous form, it destroys, in effect, the sacramental use of natural things.[21]

More in no way impugns the integrity or the sincerity of the mystic. But he denies that the experience which the mystic has is in fact a direct contact with God. His final objections to mysticism are: "1) that an actual experience connected with a common trait of human nature is accepted naively as having a spiritual value which does not belong to it; 2) that this experience is variously interpreted in accordance with the particular religious belief of the time and place, and 3) that this arbitrary interpretation reacts to colour the naive experience."[22]

The actual experience which, according to More, the mystic confuses with contact or union with God can be accounted for rather easily. The mind experiences a diversity of sensations and other kinds of awarenesses. When it makes a judgment that a thing is of such and such a kind or unifies diverse experiences in some kind of way, it also exercises the ability to experience or have knowledge of unity as well as diversity. Either of these two modes of experiencing—diversifying and unifying—can be carried to extremes. An extreme awareness of diversity is a form of insanity, a condition in which there is no continuity or unity in experience. At the other extreme there is a definite and probably not uncommon experience of having all variety and diversity swallowed up in a feeling of absolute unity. And it is this feeling which More claims the mystic mistakes for union or contact with God.

More is unquestionably correct in supposing Plotinus' metaphysics and mysticism to be incompatible with genuine Platonism. Let us consider the following passage in which Plotinus describes the experience of union with the One:

> Sometimes I wake from the slumber of the body to return to myself; and turning my attention from external things to what is within me, I behold the most marvelous beauty. I then fully believe that I have a superior destiny. I live the highest life and am at one with the divinity. Established there, my activity raises me above all the other intelligible beings. But if, after this rest in the divine, I descend from Intelligence to discursive reasoning, I do not understand the manner of and reason for my descent, how my soul ever could have entered into a body, being what I

have seen her to be herself, even when she still is associated with a body.[24]

Compare this Plotinian passage with that in Plato's *Symposium* at 209d-210a, where Diotima tells Socrates the following:

> Well, now, my dear Socrates, I have no doubt that even you might be initiated into these, more elementary mysteries of Love. But I don't know whether you could apprehend the final revelation, for so far, you know, we are only at the bottom of the true scale of perfection.[25]

And after Diotima has ended her instruction and initiation of Socrates, we find Socrates, adding to his recollection of the fictional event which he made the core of his praise to love, the following:

> This Phaedrus—this, gentlemen—was the doctrine of Diotima I was convinced, and in that conviction I try to bring others to the same creed, and to convince them that, if we are to make this gift our own, Love will help our mortal nature more than all the world. And this is why I say that every man of us should worship the god of love, and this is why I cultivate and worship all the elements of Love myself, and bid others do the same. And all my life I shall pay the power and the might of Love such homage as I can. So you may call this my eulogy of Love, Phaedrus, if you choose; if not, well, call it what you like.[26]

Plato's Socrates could never claim to have acquired identity with the divine. The claim would be hubristic. Plotinus attained the union with the Divine Mind and appeals to his personal experience to confirm the authenticity of the vision and the union. Socrates does nothing of the sort.

However, although More did correctly identify certain significant differences in Plato and Plotinus, he overlooked others that are equally important. In the final section of this paper I will argue that More's religious faith and fundamental belief in dualism led him to read into Plato's philosophy several positions which are in fact much more characteristic of the thought of Plotinus, and that More's conviction that the ethical doctrines of the two philosophers are quite similar is mistaken.

IV. *Criticism of the essential agreement More sees
between Plato and Plotinus*

We have already seen that in spite of his criticisms of
Plotinus' metaphysics and mysticism, More spoke with favor of
what he conceived to be most essential features of Plotinus'
ethics because he regarded Plotinus as espousing the same kind
of ethical dualism which More ascribed to Plato. He goes so far
as to say of Plotinus' account of the various stages of the soul's
ethical ascent that: "It is almost pure Platonism, with however
two important exceptions. Plato nowhere gives a hint of that
mystical vision wherein at last the seer and the seen merge
together in one indistinguishable act of objectless contemplation."[27] The second difference in the ethics of Plato and
Plotinus More considers to be the value and importance which
the latter attached to art.

A complete critical evaluation of the areas of agreement
which More finds in the philosophies of Plato and Plotinus is of
course far beyond the scope of this paper. I will confine myself
to a brief discussion of More's treatment of the following
subjects in the two philosophers: 1) the basic dualism of their
ethics and psychologies; 2) physical pleasure, and sex as an
illustration of it; and 3) the importance of the social life in
ethics, including the nature and significance of *eros* and
dialectic.

1. Dualism in ethics and psychology—In *Platonism* and
The Religion of Plato, More develops the thesis that a moral
dualism is at the heart of Plato's philosophy, and that upon this
foundation other dualisms—psychological, metaphysical, and
epistemological—arise. A particularly intimate relationship
exists between Plato's moral and psychological dualisms. More
goes to some lengths to establish that Plato's apparently
tri-partite soul is in fact a dualism of higher and lower parts, the
higher part being composed of that part of *nous* which concerns
itself with knowledge of the forms, and the lower part of the
soul comprising the part of *nous* which concerns itself with
doxa as well as *to thymoeides* and *to epithymetikon,* which
More translates as "concupiscence."[28] And so: "Philosophy
then may be defined to be the [higher] soul's discovery of

itself, as an entity having a law and interests of its own apart from and above all this mixed and incomprehensible life of the body. That I take it . . . is the beginning of the Platonic religion and, if not the beginning, certainly the consummation of Christianity."[29] Morality involves, for More, a complete suppression of the demands of the lower part of the soul. The only command which the higher part of the soul issues to the lower part is "Thou shalt not." "Men are loath to accept this purely negative view of what is highest of their being; every instinct of the concupiscent soul cries out against this complete severance between the law of the spirit and the law of nature."[30]

In this respect More regards Plato and Plotinus to be in complete agreement. He even goes so far as to say of Plotinus' mood of "dismay at the subservience of the soul to its own mean and impure desires, and at the unceasing change and instability of its mundane interests" that "such a feeling . . . lies close to the origin of all philosophy."[31]

That such a position is to be found in Plotinus can hardly be challenged. Although Plotinus speaks of the soul both as a unity and a plurality, he also frequently refers to it in terms of a dualism of the higher part which belongs to the sphere of Nous, and the lower part which is directly connected with the body.

> Everyone is double, one part the composite, one the Man Himself; and the whole universe is likewise double, one part being that compounded of body and a soul bound to body, and the other the Soul of the All which is not in body, but enlightens the traces of itself which is its body.[32]

The higher part of the soul is uncontaminated by matter and remains grounded in the intelligible world, but the lower part is contaminated by its association with matter and must be purified by means of an ethical ascent. In numerous passages Plotinus makes it quite explicit that the first stage of the ascent of the soul, which culminates in the acquisition of the civic virtues, begins with a complete renunciation of the flesh and its desires.

> One certain way to this knowledge [of God] is to separate first the man from the body—yourself, that is, from your body—next, to put aside that soul which moulded the

body, and very earnestly, the system of sense with desires and impulses and every such futility, all setting definitely towards the mortal: what is left is the phase of the soul which we have declared to be an image of the Divine Intellect.[33]

But contrary to More's interpretation, Plato's most frequently expressed position is to see a harmony and cooperation among the three parts of the soul, with man's reasoning faculty guiding and controlling rather than suppressing and denying the other two parts. This is clear from the psychology in Book Four of the *Republic* and the myth of the charioteer in the *Phaedrus.* The charioteer is concerned to guide and control his two horses, not to beat either of them to death. And while Plato assigns physical pleasures to the bottom of his scale of goods to be sought, he seldom rejects them entirely. In the *Phaedo,* the dialogue in which Plato most clearly seems to renounce the body, it is not all clear that Socrates himself believes in the immortality of the soul or the futility of the body's concerns.[34] And one must not lose sight of the dramatic context of this dialogue—an old man facing imminent death can hardly be expected to be excessively preoccupied with reflections on the pleasures of the flesh.

2. *Sex as an illustration of physical pleasure*—A good case can be made for the claim that in the case of sex, which because of its complex emotional and intellectual overtones, is never merely a physical pleasure, Plato only disapproves of those relationships which are exploitive and unproductive, although Plotinus clearly regards sex as inimical to the ethical quest.

It is quite easy to distort a writer's meaning by removing his thought from the cultural climate in which he lived, particularly if he is addressing himself to ethical issues. Plato's so-called renunciation of the body and its pleasures, including sex, is a case in point. Like his criticisms of art, his criticisms of sex must not be taken out of the context in which they were written. Since Plato's fellow Athenians of the fifth and fourth centuries placed a high value upon artistic expression and were frank sensualists, Plato can afford to set very high standards for both art and sexual relationships without totally rejecting either. Good art is that which copies the forms instead of imitations of the forms in the changing world;[35] a good erotic relationship is one which leads to procreation in the beautiful. The ascent of the ladder of love in the *Symposium* does not necessarily involve the rejection of physical love as one reaches the higher rungs. True philosophical *eros,* which culminates in the vision of beauty, begins with the love of bodies, and Socrates says at the conclusion of his speech: "I cultivate and worship all the elements of love myself, and bid others to do the same."[36] The *Phaedrus* distinguishes between exploitive sexual relationships, which are bad, and good sexual relationships, in which the two parties are concerned for the growth and development of their partners. Plato's only explicit renunciations of homosexual love are in the *Laws,*[37] a work of his old age which is quite difficult to reconcile with many of his other dialogues, and the *Republic,*[38] which seems to exclude all forms of *eros* and is probably not to be taken literally as Plato's conception of an ideal society.

More himself is rather embarrassed by the extreme sensuousness of Plato's language:

There are passages of the *Symposium,* and more particularly of the *Phaedrus,* in which the passionate colour of his language so envelops the allurement of particular objects that some effort of the mind is required to remember the ideal beauty of which they are supposed to be manifestations. The danger is heightened when he speaks with curious lack of indignation of pleasures which the world has agreed to hold unnatural and to reject the instinctive abomination. Yet in these few isolated passages where the attraction of sensuous beauty seems for the moment to have veiled the purer ethical vision, we do him a great wrong if we fail to remember that it is a passing cloud before the sun of the soul, not an eclipse. We need then to turn to the strange confession of Alcibiades at the close of the *Symposium,* and to learn again how rigidly beauty and all the seductions of pleasure were held in subjection to the refraining will. The Socrates of Plato may have portrayed himself playfully as a slave to any beautiful body and as wise only in erotic lore; when it came to the test of action he could master the lawless impulses of the flesh unflinchingly and, as it seems, without a pang of regret.[40]

It is true that Plato constantly urges moderation in erotic conduct and self-control in the case of erotic relationships which would not be productive. Socrates refuses to submit to the advances of Alcibiades because Alcibiades is corrupt: although the better elements in his nature desire to possess Socrates' wisdom, his motive for wanting a physical relationship is that he wishes to make a conquest of this extraordinary man, to exercise power over him. Alcibiades admits extreme frustration over his inability to find a way to bend Socrates to his will.[39] For Socrates to succumb to his desire for Alcibiades would destroy any effectiveness that he might have as a teacher, and would only serve to nourish Alcibiades' vanity and conceit. But moderation and self-control are one thing; total denial is another.

3. *The importance of the social life in ethics*—One of the fundamental differences between Plato and Plotinus which More overlooks completely is Plato's strong emphasis upon the *social* nature of the quest for the good life. Plotinus constantly urges self-sufficiency; Plato denies that self-sufficiency is within the range of human possibilities. For Plotinus the ascent of the soul is a solitary affair, repeatedly spoken of as "the flight of the Alone to the Alone;"[41] for Plato, one reaches knowledge of the forms through *procreation* in the beautiful. Regardless of whether one is producing physical offspring or beautiful discourses, procreation inevitably involves more than one person. Although More consistently speaks of Plato's philosophy as being "otherworldly,"[42] the picture of life that Plato presents in the dialogues is the public life with all of its hustle and clamor, hurrying businessmen, rough jests, and noisy laughter. And the protagonist of most of Plato's philosophical dramas, Socrates, withdraws only at rare intervals from his constant involvement with his fellow men to the solitude of contemplation.

For Plotinus, the attainment of the four civic virtues, Justice, Courage, Temperance, and Wisdom, belongs to the lowest stage of the ethical ascent. These virtues do not belong to God.

> But, at the beginning, we are met by the doubt
> whether even in this Divine-Being all the virtues find
> place—Moral-Balance (Sophrosyny), for example; or
> Fortitude where there can be nothing alluring whose lack
> could induce the desire of possession . . . .

> We cannot expect to find There what are called the
> Civic Virtues, the Prudence which belongs to the reasoning
> faculty; the Fortitude which conducts the emotional and
> passionate nature; the Sophrosyny which consists in a
> certain pact, in a concord between the passionate faculty
> and the reason; or Rectitude which is the due application
> of all the other virtues as each in turn should command or
> obey.[43]

Since the ultimate quest is to first to become God-like and
finally to be united with the One, these virtues which are not
possessed by the One are of limited usefulness. But there is no
suggestion in Plato that there are any higher excellences that the
Civic Virtues which govern the living of men together as well as
the operations of the individual soul.

It is quite significant that More refers to Plato's dialectic as
"the philosophy of the soul discoursing with herself, . . . and so
passing ever upwards to larger and more comprehensive
truth."[44] Although Plato does refer to dialectic as an inter-
nalized dialogue with oneself at *Sophist* 440 and *Theaetetus*
178, his many other references to it insist that dialectic is a kind
of discourse of two or more persons with each other. Dialectic
is spoken of as "the power of conversation";[45] "the art
concerning discussion;"[46] or "the art of asking and answering
questions."[47] The necessity for the social nature of dialectic is
closely related to Plato's view of *eros* as procreation in the
beautiful. As dialectic is the only method for gaining knowledge
of the forms, and as dialectic necessarily involves a conversation
or discussion, Plato quite clearly means to say that the
attainment of wisdom and excellence are not solitary guests. To
attempt self-sufficiency is hubristic.

In conclusion, this paper has explored certain features of
Paul Elmer More's interpretations of Plato and Plotinus.
Although More correctly identified some of the major differ-
ences in the two philosophers, he found a fundamental

agreement between their ethics which does not in fact pertain. He was motivated in this regard by his desire to regard the philosophy of Plato as being compatible with Christianity and with the belief in dualism which More shared with the other New Humanists. Although More considered himself to be a Platonist, his ethics was in fact closer to that of the Neoplatonists than to that of Plato.

NOTES

1. Paul Elmer More, "Marginalia, Part I," *American Review* VIII (November 1936), pp. 25-26.
2. Arthur Hazard Dakin, *Paul Elmer More* (Princeton U. Press, 1960), p. 212.
3. P. E. M. to Robert Shafer, October 22, 1931. Quoted in Francis X. Duggan, *Paul Elmer More* (Twayne Publishers, Inc., 1966), p. 20.
4. P. E. M. "Plato," *Shelburne Essays,* vol. VI (Houghton Miflin Co., 1909), pp. 321-322.
5. P. E. M., *Hellenistic Philosophies* (Greenwood Press, 1923), p. 184.
6. P. E. M., *The Religion of Plato* (Princeton U. Press, 1921), p. vi.
7. *Ibid.,* p. vii.
8. P. E. M., *The Christ of the New Testament* (Princeton U. Press, 1924), p. 1.
9. *Ibid.,* p. 2.
10. *Ibid.,* pp. 291-292.
11. *Hellenistic Philosophers,* p. 178.
12. An assessment of the correctness of More's interpretation of Aristotle is beyond the scope of this paper. However, it seems to me that More, like many other thinkers of a religious temper, has exaggerated the importance of Aristotle's Unmoved Mover. This hypostatization of a perfect knower who acts as a final cause for creatures motivated by a desire to know does not occupy a position in Aristotle's philosophy significant enough to consider it

as the sole occupant of one side of a metaphysical dualism. Nor is the Unmoved Mover an essentially religious concept.

13. P. E. M., *The Catholic Faith*, p. 226.

14. *Hellenistic Philosophers*, p. 215.

15. *The Catholic Faith*, pp. 207-209.

16. *Ibid.*, pp. 231-232. In this connection More also regards Plato to have taught that "our knowledge of Ideas in this life is not to be immediate vision or contact, but by inference." (p. 216). This is a curious claim in the light of the *Symposium*.

17. *Ibid.*, p. 238. In this same passage More criticizes St. Augustine for surrendering to the "monistic seductions" of Plotinus by placing the Ideas in the Divine Mind. Since More apparently retained the independent existence of the Ideas, one can question whether he was in fact a Christian.

18. *Ibid.*, p. 242.

19. *Idem.*

20. More points out that there is a very fine line dividing the complete union of the soul with God in Plotinus, which is rejected by the Christian, from the kind of experience described in such passages as the following from the pen of St. John of the Cross, quoted in *The Catholic Faith*, p. 255:

> The thread of love binds so closely God and the soul, and so unites them, that it transforms them and makes them one by love; so that, though in essence different, yet in glory and appearance the soul seems God and God the soul. Such is this marvellous union. God Himself is here the suitor who . . . absorbs the soul with greater violence and efficacy than a torrent of fire a single drop of the morning dew.

21. *Ibid.*, p. 283.

22. *Ibid.*, p. 287. More fails to indicate that objections 2) and 3) would not apply to Plotinus.

23. *Ibid.*, pp. 287-290.

24. *Ennead* IV. 8. 1. Translated by J. Katz, in *The Philosophy of Plotinus, Representative Books from the Enneads.*

25. *Symposium* 209d-210a, translated by Michael Joyce, in *Plato: The Collected Dialogues*, edited by E. Hamilton and

H. Cairns (Pantheon Books, 1966). All quotes from Plato are from this edition of the dialogues.

26. *Symposium* 212b-c.
27. *Hellenistic Philosophies,* p. 184.
28. P. E. M., *Platonism* (Princeton U. Press, 1917), chp. 5, "Psychology," *passim,* and *The Religion of Plato,* pp. 220-222.
29. *The Religion of Plato,* p. 48.
30. *Platonism,* p. 146.
31. *Hellenistic Philosophies,* p. 179.
32. *Ennead* II. 3. 9. See also II. 1. 5; III. 4. 3; IV. 8. 7; V. 2. 1. This and all following quotes from the *Enneads* are from the McKenna translation.
33. *Enn.,* V. 3. 9. See also I. 1. 5; I. 2. 3; II. 3. 9. It is interesting that More occasionally remarks that Plotinus is a thorough-going ascetic (e.g., *The Religion of Plato,* p. 266; p. 228) but that Plato is not *(The Catholic Faith,* p. 221; *Platonism,* p. 82). One wonders in what sense More regarded Plato's asceticism to be mitigated, since he is supposed to have advocated "a complete severance between the law of the spirit and the law of nature." *(Platonism,* p. 146).
34. "It is not sufficiently recognized that Plato does not, in the strict sense of the word, 'teach' anything at all about the fate of the human soul. Socrates speaks about it in myths, which are part of the dramatic structure in Plato's works. Plato's references to the authority of the priests and theologians of the mystery religions are undoubtedly an indication of the origin of these mythological symbols, but are in no way an indication of what they meant to Plato himself. For him they contained a profound symbolic relaity; they were venerable allegories, images, and phrases for something that he preferred not to express in his own language. It is a mistake to use them as evidence for a Platonic theory or history of the soul." Paul Friedlander, *Plato* (Pantheon Books, 1958), vol. I, p. 29.
35. *Republic* 500e.
36. *Symposium* 212b. The famous passage at 211d at which Socrates says that one who has attained the vision of

Beauty will "never be seduced again by the charm of gold, of dress, of comely boys . . ." can easily be interpreted to mean that once one has reached the ultimate goal of *eros,* mere beauty and superficial display will no longer be enough to hold one.

37. *Laws* 836b-842a.
38. *Republic* 403b.
39. *Symposium* 219d.
40. *Platonism,* pp. 194-195.
41. *Enn.,* I. 6. 7; V. 1. 6; VI. 7. 3.
42. "In Platonism the emphasis lies heavily on the union of other-worldliness and morality in the philosophy of Ideas." *The Christ of the New Testament* (Princeton U. Press, 1934), p. 23. See also p. 5, p. 14, and p. 17. One may also challenge in this connection More's references to Plato as a "religious" philosopher.
43. *Enn.,* I. 2. 1.
44. *Platonism,* pp. 195-196.
45. *Republic* 511b.
46. *Sophist* 237a.
47. *Republic* 534d.

Contributors

A. Hilary Armstrong M.A. (Cantab.) F.B.A. is currently Professor of Classics and Philosophy at Dalhousie University in Halifax, Nova Scotia, Canada. He has served as a contributor to numerous journals, collections of papers and proceedings of conferences on Neoplatonism and on early Christian thought, including articles on Neoplatonism in the *Encyclopedia Britannica* and in the *Dictionary of Ideas.* His books include: *The Architecture of the Intelligible Universe in the Philosophy of Plotinus, An Introduction to Ancient Philosophy, Plotinus, Plotinus Enneads* I-III, in Loeb Classical Library, and *The Cambridge History of Later Greek and Early Mediaeval Philosophy* (general editor and author of Part III).

John P. Anton is Fuller E. Callaway Professor of Philosophy at Emory University. He is co-editor of *Diotima* and author of *Aristotle's Theory of Contrariety, Naturalism and Historical Understanding, Philosophical Essays*; and has published numerous articles on classical, Hellenistic philosophy, and modern and contemporary themes. He is presently completing a book on the Alexandrian poet C. P. Cavfy.

J. P. Atherton is Associate Professor of Classics in Dalhousie University in Halifax, Nova Scotia.

H. J. Blumenthal is Lecturer in Greek at the University of Liverpool. His publications on Neoplatonism include: *Plotinus' Psychology* and various articles. He was a participant in the 1969 Paris and 1970 Rome Congresses on Neoplatonism.

Mary T. Clark is Chairman of the Department of Philosophy of Manhattanville College in Purchase, New York. She is the author of *Augustine, Philosopher of Freedom, Augustinian*

Personalism, An Aquinas Reader and *Problem of Freedom* and the translator of Marius Victorinus' *Theological Treatises*. Her articles include studies of the thought of Marius Victorinus. She is currently president of the American Catholic Philosophical Association.

J. N. Deck is Professor of Philosophy in the University of Windsor. His writings include *Nature, Contemplation and the One* and various articles on St. Thomas.

J. M. Dillon is Associate Professor of Classics in the University of California at Berkeley. His primary field of interest is the history of Platonism, particularly Neoplatonism. His publications include *Iamblichi Chalcidensis In Platonis Dialogos Commentariorum Fragmenta* (1973) and *The Middle Platonists* (1976).

Michael Dunn is an Instructor in the Department of Classics of the University of Texas.

John Fielder is Assistant Professor of Philosophy in Villanova University in Villanova, Pennsylvania. His doctoral dissertation was on *The Concepts of Matter and Emanation in the Philosophy of Plotinus*.

J. N. Findlay is presently University Professor in Boston University. Included among his publications are *Hegel: A Re-Examination, The Discipline of the Cave, The Transcendence of the Cave, Ascent to the Absolute* and *Plato: An Interpretation of the Written and Unwritten Doctrines*, and more than forty articles.

R. Baine Harris is Professor of Philosophy and Chairman of the Department of Philosophy at Old Dominion University in Norfolk, Virginia. Included among his writings are *Authority: A Philosophical Analysis* (ed.) and a dissertation on the Neoplatonism of Dean Inge. He is presently serving as Executive-Director of the International Society for Neoplatonic Studies.

K. W. Harrington is Assistant Professor of Philosophy at Emory University. Her writings include articles on "John Dewy's Ethics and the Classical Conception of Man," and "Irving Babbit and Hellenism," in *Diotima.* She is currently writing a book on Plotinus.

Plato Mamo is Associate Professor of Philosophy in the University of Calgary, Calgary, Canada. His writings include various articles on Neoplatonism.

Evanghelos Moutsopoulos is Professor of Philosophy and Rector of the University of Athens, Greece. He is the author of twenty volumes including: *La musique dans l' oeuvre de Platon, The Critique of Platonism by Bergson, An Introduction to an Axiology of Aesthetical Object,* and *Philosophical Apprehensions* and over two-hundred articles.

J. M. Rist is Professor of Classics the University of Toronto. His publications include: *Eros and Psyche; Plotinus: The Road to Reality; Stoic Philosophy; Epicurus: An Introduction;* and some forty articles, mostly on Ancient Philosophy.

David F. T. Rodier is Associate Professor of Philosophy at American University in Washington, D.C. Among his writings are a dissertation on Plotinus and articles on Whitehead.

R. T. Wallis is Associate Professor of Classics at the University of Oklahoma. His publications include a book, *Neoplatonism*, and other articles on Neoplatonism.

Michael Vater is Assistant Professor of Philosophy at Marquette University. His writings include a dissertation on Schelling and Neoplatonism.

John Whittaker is Professor of Classics and Head of the Department of Classics at Memorial University of Newfoundland. His writings include numerous articles on the Middle Platonic and Neoplatonic tradition. He is currently preparing a critical edition of the Greek text of the Middle Platonic *Didaskalikos* of Alcinous (Albinus).

ACKNOWLEDGMENTS

Appreciation for assistance in reading and preparing this manuscript is expressed to J. Winifred Alston of Brock University, John P. Anton of Emory University, Henry J. Blumenthal of the University of Liverpool and David F. T. Rodier of The American University. The editor also expresses thanks to VaLeta and David Rodier for preparing the Index of Proper Names.

INDEX OF PROPER NAMES